EXPERIMENTS WITH MARXISM-LENINISM IN COLD WAR SOUTHEAST ASIA

EXPERIMENTS WITH MARXISM-LENINISM IN COLD WAR SOUTHEAST ASIA

EDITED BY MATTHEW GALWAY AND MARC H. OPPER

ANU PRESS

ASIAN STUDIES SERIES MONOGRAPH 16

For Charlotte

ANU PRESS

Published by ANU Press
The Australian National University
Canberra ACT 2600, Australia
Email: anupress@anu.edu.au

Available to download for free at press.anu.edu.au

ISBN (print): 9781760465292
ISBN (online): 9781760465308

WorldCat (print): 1336522667
WorldCat (online): 1336522659

DOI: 10.22459/EMLCWSA.2022

This title is published under a Creative Commons Attribution-NonCommercial-NoDerivatives 4.0 International (CC BY-NC-ND 4.0) licence.

The full licence terms are available at
creativecommons.org/licenses/by-nc-nd/4.0/legalcode

Cover design and layout by ANU Press

Cover photograph: 'At an anti-aircraft emplacement in a Laotian liberated area. The fighters and commanders of an air defence unit of the Laotian People's Liberation Army are studying Chairman Mao's theories on people's war. They praise as a great, unassailable truth Chairman Mao's wise assertion that "imperialism and all reactionaries are paper tigers".' *China Pictorial* 7, 1968, page 35. Public domain.

This book is published under the aegis of the Asian Studies Editorial Board of ANU Press.

This edition © 2022 ANU Press

Contents

Abbreviations ... ix

Maps and plates ... xiii

Foreword ... xv
Brantly Womack

Introduction ... 1
Marc H. Opper and Matthew Galway

Part One

1. 'One eye in the chain of the Asian movement': Muslims adapting Marx in the Dutch East Indies, 1927–42 ... 33
   Lin Hongxuan

2. 'The most dissolute and dishonest' Khmer to aid China: Hu Nim and indigenising the Maoist ideological system, 1955–77 ... 69
   Matthew Galway

3. Buddhist socialism and national identity in colonial and postwar Burma: An analysis of U Nu's political thought ... 107
   Khine Thant Su

4. Heavier than Mount Banahaw: 'Five Golden Rays' and the 'Filipinisation' of Maoism ... 137
   Ramon Guillermo, Teo Marasigan, Amado Anthony G. Mendoza III and Dominic Sy

5. Partai Republik Indonesia: Communist exiles and their noncommunist approaches to anticolonialism ... 165
   Kankan Xie

Part Two

6. Forging the masses in Malaya: Mass mobilisation, the united front and revolutionary violence in Malaya, 1939–51 ... 199
   Marc H. Opper

7.	Recycling violence: The theory and practice of reeducation camps in postwar Vietnam Hoang Minh Vu	219
8.	Return to armed revolution: The Pathet Lao and the Chinese Communist Party on paths to national liberation Nicholas R. Zeller	239
9.	'Victory of the aggregate strength of the era': Lê Duẩn, Vietnam and the three revolutionary tidal waves Khuê Diệu Đỗ	271
10.	Becoming Marxist: Ethnic Hmong in the Communist Party of Thailand Ian G. Baird	299
Index		333

Abbreviations

AAKC	Association d'Amitié Khmero–Chinoise (Khmer–Chinese Friendship Association)
AEK	Association des Étudiants Khmers (Khmer Students Association)
AFPFL	Anti-Fascist People's Freedom League (Burma)
ARVN	Army of the Republic of Vietnam
BPP	Border Patrol Police (Thailand)
CCP	Chinese Communist Party
CID	Criminal Investigation Department
Comintern	Communist International
COSVN	Central Office for South Vietnam
CPK	Communist Party of Kampuchea
CPP	Communist Party of the Philippines
CPT	Communist Party of Thailand
DBA	Dobama Asiayone (We Burmans Association)
DEI	Dutch East Indies
DK	Democratic Kampuchea
DRV	Democratic Republic of Vietnam
FGR	*Five Golden Rays*
FUNK	Front uni national du Kampuchéa (National United Front of Kampuchea)
GMD	Guomindang
GRUNK	Gouvernement royal d'union nationale du Kampuchéa (Royal Government of the National Union of Kampuchea)

ICP	Indochinese Communist Party
ICSC	International Commission for Supervision and Control
LPP	Lao People's Party
MCP	Malayan Communist Party
MNLA	Malayan National Liberation Army
MPAJA	Malayan People's Anti-Japanese Army
NAM	Non-Aligned Movement
NIS	Nederlandsch-Indische Spoorweg Maatschappij (Dutch East Indies Railway Company)
NKPM	Nederlandsch Koloniale Petroleum Maatschappij (Dutch Colonial Petroleum Corporation)
NLHX	Neo Lao Hak Xat (Lao Patriotic Front)
PARI	Partai Republik Indonesia (Indonesian Republican Party)
Partindo	Partai Indonesia (Indonesia Party)
Pathet Lao	Lao People's Liberation Army
PCF	Parti Communiste Français (French Communist Party)
Permi	Persatuan Muslim Indonesia (Indonesian Muslim Union)
PKI	Partai Komunis Indonesia (Communist Party of Indonesia)
PLA	People's Liberation Army (China)
PLAT	People's Liberation Army of Thailand
PNI	Partai Nasional Indonesia (Indonesian National Party)
PRC	People's Republic of China
PSII	Partai Sarekat Islam Indonesia (Islamic Association Party of Indonesia)
RKU	Royal Khmer University
RLG	Royal Lao Government
RVN	Republic of Vietnam
Saṅgam	Saṅgam Rāstr Niyam (Popular Socialist Community)
SRV	Socialist Republic of Vietnam
UEK	Union des Etudiants Khmers (Khmer Students Union)

US	United States
USSR	Union of Soviet Socialist Republics
VCP	Vietnamese Communist Party
VSTP	Vereniging van Spoor-en Tramwegpersoneel (Association of Railway and Tram Workers)
VWP	Vietnamese Workers' Party
WWII	World War II
YMBA	Young Men's Buddhist Association

Maps and plates

Plate 2.1 Head of state Norodom Sihanouk (second from right) with Communist Party of Kampuchea members, including ministers Hu Nim (far right) and Khieu Samphan (centre left), during his 1973 inspection tour of the liberated zone. 73

Plate 2.2 Front cover of the second issue of the *Revue Association d'Amitié Khmero-Chinoise*, September 1965. 82

Plate 2.3 Norodom Sihanouk, Cambodia's head of state, and other distinguished Cambodian guests arrive in Beijing on 11 April 1973 after an inspection tour of the Liberated Zone of Cambodia and a friendly visit to the Democratic Republic of Vietnam. 97

Plate 2.4 Hu Nim (centre) warmly greets head of state Norodom Sihanouk during his 1973 inspection tour of the liberated zone. 102

Map 10.1 CPT strongholds from the late 1960s to the early 1980s. 313

Foreword

Brantly Womack

The basic revolutionary question 'What is to be done?' excites an intellectual dialectic of virtually infinite dimensions. Most immediately, there is the tension between the desired revolutionary direction—what should be done—and the circumstances of the moment: what can be done. Each of these poles is a nest of further contradictions. What should be done is a commitment to transformation, sometimes at mortal risk to oneself, and usually shaping the activist's future. One's conviction of both the necessity of transformation and its possibility must be absolute. The critique of the present is founded on the absolute and universal validity of ideology. But an ideology is not a simple moment of enlightenment. There are various texts, various teachers and various revolutionary experiences elsewhere. What to believe absolutely? Whose teaching or example should be followed? But these questions do not address the current practical problem the activist faces of what can be done now. Do we wait for the proper moment? Do we join with other critics even though their ideas are different? Do we compromise with incumbent forces? How should we organise? To some extent the theories, teachers and examples suggest answers, but they are often conflicting, and never dealing with this place, this point in time. Compared with Mao Zedong or Hồ Chí Minh, Hamlet had it easy.

Trying to understand the thinking and actions of revolutionaries is important because they stand at the forward edge of what was imagined to be possible in their societies in their times. Regardless of whether they succeeded, they marked a limit of imagined possibilities. As the editors point out in the Introduction, at the time most of the close interest of outsiders (other than fellow revolutionaries) was in defending the existing order—to know their enemy to defeat it. But from a greater historical distance it is important to get inside the minds and organisations of the revolutionaries to grasp a vital part of the vivid present of their societies. How urgent did its problems seem? Which thinkers were attractive, and why? How did they view their interactions with other groups, and with international revolutionaries? In what respects were they original in their adaptations of general theories? Could they make the claim Mao made, that their thoughts were the creative application of Marxism-Leninism to the circumstances of their societies? Did they make that claim?

It is especially important to understand the revolutionary thinkers and currents of Southeast Asia because the region is so diverse and its politics moved so far in the twentieth century. Indeed, before the foundation of the Association of Southeast Asian Nations (ASEAN) in 1967, Southeast Asia was not a region but rather a collective location. Colonialism had splintered the existing order and, during the nineteenth and twentieth centuries, had forced their societies and economies to serve their various Western masters. Vietnam, Laos and Cambodia became French Indochina; Burma became part of British India; and the maritime world of Southeast Asia was split between the Dutch, the British, the Spanish and, later, the Americans.

Siam (since 1939, Thailand) survived by adroit diplomacy with the encroaching British and French empires. What Southeast Asia had in common was an orientation towards Europe. It is hardly surprising that the most avant-garde Western criticism of imperialism, Marxism-Leninism, with the Soviet Union as its success story and willing teacher, became the common ideological resource of Southeast Asian revolutionaries. But each colonial and postcolonial situation was radically different from that of its neighbours and, except for Indochina, there was little connection between them. Hence the very different manifestations of revolutionary hopes and practices described in this book.

The purpose of this book is not to present a coherent picture of Marxist-Leninist thinking and movements in Southeast Asia, but rather the opposite. It is the diversity of the movements and their approaches that sheds light on vastly different intellectual, cultural and political situations. Some individual movements succeeded, others failed. I thank the editors and authors for bringing to life the spectrum of ideas and actions that contributed to the diverse political fabric of Southeast Asia today.

Introduction

Marc H. Opper and Matthew Galway

The Cold War was anything but 'cold' in Asia, let alone Southeast Asia. US President Richard Nixon once remarked: 'The Cold War isn't thawing; it is burning with a deadly heat.'[1] Whether it was the decades-long conflict in the former French Indochina or insurgencies in the Coral Triangle, Southeast Asia was a theatre for some of the twentieth century's most defining conflicts. As is too common, the superpowers of the United States, the Soviet Union and China tend to receive the most scholarly attention. Big-power politics, détente, rapprochement and triangulation are all Cold War buzzwords that invoke memories of the period and enforce the primacy of superpower dictation of era-defining events. But aside from extant vertical analyses of the Cold War in the region, scholars have taken great strides in understanding the aetiology, processes and outcomes of conflicts in Southeast Asia during the Cold War. Scholars of Cold War Southeast Asia have shifted the paradigm towards focusing on the agency of Southeast Asian actors themselves rather than foregrounding them only insofar as they responded to the dictates of Moscow, Washington, DC, or Beijing.

Initial efforts straddled the line of Cold War history *from above* and *from below* by examining how decolonisation movements across Southeast Asia and the ongoing superpower rivalry worked hand-in-glove.[2] Some

---

1   Richard Nixon, quoted by Sarah Slobin, 'A Nation Challenged: Hearts and Minds', *The New York Times*, 11 November 2001.
2   Odd Arne Westad, *The Global Cold War: Third World Interventions and the Making of Our Times* (Cambridge, UK: Cambridge University Press, 2007), 5; Christopher Goscha and Christian Ostermann, 'Introduction: Connecting Decolonization and the Cold War in Southeast Asia', in *Connecting Histories: Decolonization and the Cold War in Southeast Asia, 1945–1962*, Christopher Goscha and Christian Ostermann, eds (Washington, DC, and Stanford, CA: Woodrow Wilson Center Press and Stanford University Press, 2009), 1–12.

highlight the multiple dimensions of specific conflicts during Southeast Asia's Cold War.[3] Hack and Wade have flipped the script, so to speak, to shine the spotlight on local forces that 'drew in' outside actors 'for their own ideological and material purposes'.[4] Day and Liem instead foreground social and cultural phenomena of the Cold War in the region, either by examining cultural dimensions of the Cold War in Southeast Asia or by highlighting oral histories.[5] Tuong Vu and Wasana Wongsurawat stress that 'Asian actors' visions and political loyalties during the Cold War spanned a much wider range—not limited to the nation-state as the ideal political community'.[6] Ang provides a methodical history of Cold War Southeast Asia by exploring the 'mindsets' of major political actors and how their world views were moulded by the 'cultural ideals that reflect their own traditions and their response to universalist and international aspirations'.[7]

This volume complements this new wave of recent and forthcoming scholarship of the Cold War in Southeast Asia and stresses the agency of Southeast Asian actors over the intellectual and political forces that entered their worlds.[8] Our focus in the pages that follow is on such forces and

---

3   Odd Arne Westad and Sophie Quinn-Judge, eds, *The Third Indochina War: Conflict between China, Vietnam, and Cambodia, 1972–79* (New York: Routledge, 2006).
4   Karl Hack and Geoff Wade, 'The Origins of the Southeast Asian Cold War', *Journal of Southeast Asian Studies* 40(3) (2009): 443, doi.org/10.1017/S0022463409990014; and Goscha and Ostermann, 'Introduction', 9. See also Goscha and Ostermann, *Connecting Histories*, 335–402.
5   Tony Day and Maya H.T. Liem, *Cultures at War: The Cold War and Cultural Expression in Southeast Asia* (Ithaca, NY: Cornell University Press, 2010); Sangjoon Lee and Darlene Machell Espena, 'Asian Cinema and the Cultural Cold War', *Asian Cinema and the Cultural Cold War Virtual Conference 2021*, jointly organised by Wee Kim Wee School of Communication and Information, Nanyang Technological University, and School of Social Sciences, Singapore Management University, 20–22 May 2021, available from: www.acccw2021.com/; and the forthcoming study by Hajime Masuda in the Re-conceptualizing the Cold War: On-the-Ground Experiences in Asia project, National University of Singapore and NUS Museum, 29–30 June 2021, available from: networks.h-net.org/node/22055/discussions/5181889/call-papers-%E2%80%9Creconceptualizing-cold-war-ground-experiences-asia%E2%80%9D.
6   Tuong Vu and Wasana Wongsurawat, eds, *Dynamics of the Cold War in Asia: Ideology, Identity, and Culture* (New York: Palgrave Macmillan, 2009), 3.
7   Ang Cheng Guan, *Southeast Asia's Cold War: An Interpretive History* (Honolulu: University of Hawai'i Press, 2018), 3.
8   See Anna Belogurova, *The Nanyang Revolution: The Comintern and Chinese Networks in Southeast Asia, 1890–1957* (Cambridge, UK: Cambridge University Press, 2019), doi.org/10.1017/9781108635059; John Sidel, *Republicanism, Communism, Islam: Cosmopolitan Origins of Revolution in Southeast Asia* (Ithaca, NY: Cornell University Press, 2021); Christopher Goscha, *The Road to Dien Bien Phu: A History of the First War for Vietnam* (Princeton, NJ: Princeton University Press, 2022); Joseph Scalice, 'Crisis of revolutionary leadership: Martial law and the communist parties of the Philippines 1959–1974' (PhD diss., University of California, Berkeley, 2017); Dominique Caouette, 'Persevering revolutionaries: Armed struggle in the 21st century, exploring the revolution of the Communist Party of the Philippines' (PhD diss., Cornell University, Ithaca, NY, 2004); and Kasian Tejapira, *Commodifying Marxism: The Formation of Modern Thai Radical Culture, 1927–1958* (Kyoto: Kyoto University Press, 2001).

actors' responses to them, whether in intellectual engagement, praxis or ongoing adaptations thereof, across peninsular and archipelagic Southeast Asia. Our volume brings together several left-wing Southeast Asian political actors who engaged with revolutionary ideology and indigenised it in theory and praxis in their respective polities. Extant scholarship has accomplished this separately, but neither across as expansive a geographic/temporal range nor with the actors under examination as the primary focus of their respective analyses. Contributors to this volume focus on individuals and political parties as they wrestled with revolutionary ideologies in different times, different ways and different contexts. Each chapter explores the adaptations and examines how the various indigenisations took on distinct forms because of temporal, geographic and sociocultural factors. Not all the actors under analysis became avowed Marxist-Leninists or Maoists; rather, they took these ideological discourses seriously and, in varied ways, the lasting imprint of such intellectual and practical engagements was evident. In this way, our volume's overarching theme of individual agents' dialogic engagement with revolutionary ideologies from without, which they approached as useful tools to reverse the historical trends that exploited and oppressed them, adds to the extant historiography of and debate about Cold War narratives in its focus on a diversity of engagements with such ideologies and the resulting adaptations. The gap this volume seeks to fill is that relating to individual agency and the diversity of engagements in the process of indigenisation, as each chapter supplements and/or revises our understanding of Cold War narratives through placing primacy on Southeast Asian–language primary sources—often by the figures and parties themselves—to track such engagements. The goal, then, is to provide a fuller perspective of what these ideological discourses meant to individuals and organisations in theory and praxis across an expansive temporal scope.

The second part of the Nixon quote above states: 'Communism isn't sleeping; it is, as always, plotting, scheming, working, fighting.' Previous studies of left-wing ideologies in the region have tended to cast communism in the same light: as an insidious, activating agent that turns ordinary people into extraordinary (and extraordinarily violent) zealots. Such studies elide complexities regarding what drove people to engage with radical ideas or cast those who did as passive recipients who were easily duped or 'intoxicated' because of foreign pressures.[9] The results are

---
9 See Julia Lovell, *Maoism: A Global History* (London: Bodley Head, 2019).

studies that conceive of left-wing ideologies as readily available blueprints for 'organisational weapons'. Cold War warriors have variously described these ideologies as: 1) part of an international communist conspiracy, 2) the rantings of madmen, and/or 3) nonexistent and merely a *post hoc* justification for violence. In the context of the Cold War, these characterisations (made by incumbent governments and even scholars) of insurgent ideologies usually stress their foreign origins and role in facilitating Soviet or Chinese control over a region. This partisan predisposition is in many ways what Guha calls the 'prose of counterinsurgency': the tendency of conflict narratives, based as they are on incumbent documentation, to reflect the imperatives of counterinsurgents.[10]

This is most evident in discussions of the ideology of the Communist Party of Kampuchea (CPK, Paks Kummuynīst Kampuchea)—an especially extreme case—and studies of the ideology of the Partai Komunis Indonesia (PKI, Communist Party of Indonesia). Although there is no question the CPK committed heinous acts of violence against the civilians of Democratic Kampuchea (1975–79), its ideology is nevertheless still worthy of analysis in a way that avoids constant normative condemnation or an exclusive focus on the violence of its rule. As for the PKI, although it was once the largest and oldest Asian communist party, there has been no meaningful analysis of its ideology for nearly a half century.[11]

The analytical purpose of this book, importantly, is to neither condemn nor justify, but understand how ideologies arose in intellectual thought streams, to track their transformation when they reached Southeast Asian milieus and explore the way they were implemented in praxis. Indeed, the paucity and distortion of our knowledge of these ideologies provide fecund ground for scholarly exploration. Our aim is to build on studies like Tuong Vu's essay on Vietnamese communist ideology. Vu draws on newly available materials and previously overlooked Vietnamese Communist Party (VCP) internal documents and reports to argue the VCP 'never wavered in [its] ideological loyalty during the period when key decisions about the civil war were made (1953–1960)'. It bent, but never broke from its 'binary world view' (arguably Manichean, of good socialism versus evil

---

10   Ranajit Guha and Gayatri Chakravorty Spivak, eds, 'The Prose of Counter-Insurgency', in *Selected Subaltern Studies*, Ranajit Guha and Gayatri Chakravorty Spivak, eds (Oxford, UK: Oxford University Press, 1988).
11   Rex Mortimer, *Indonesian Communism under Sukarno: Ideology and Politics, 1959–1965* (Ithaca, NY: Cornell University Press, 1974); and Donald Hindley, *The Communist Party of Indonesia, 1951–1963* (Berkeley, CA: University of California Press, 1966).

capitalism) despite major disputes within the Soviet Bloc leading up to, and in the aftermath of, the Sino-Soviet Split. The VCP, Vu concludes, 'did not downplay socialism but in fact boldly promoted it with the new formulation "To be patriotic is to build socialism"'.[12] The bulk of this edited volume, accordingly, will consist of the presentation of the contents of these revolutionary ideologies on their own terms and their transformations in praxis by using primary source materials that are free of the preconceptions and distortions of counterinsurgent narratives. A unifying strength of our work is its focus on using primary sources in the original languages of the insurgents themselves.

Studies of ideology in Southeast Asia

The imperative of colonial powers, local elites and the US Government to prevent the spread of communism fuelled a boom in research (both academic and non-academic) on communism in Southeast Asia after World War II. Studies from this period have provided some of the most thorough analyses of the origins, processes and outcomes of communist movements in the region. Yet the overwhelming focus of research during the Cold War was on practice rather than theory. Research examined the leaders and organisations of left-wing movements, their interactions with other left-wing movements and with the Soviet Union and the People's Republic of China, and how they deployed violence, *inter alia*. Largely absent from these studies was a thorough discussion of revolutionary ideology.

Charles B. McLane's *Soviet Strategies in Southeast Asia* is an important work on the region.[13] McLane's proficiency in Russian gave him important insights into Soviet policy. His personal and professional connections, too, granted him access to material that was otherwise classified and to

---

12　Tuong Vu, '"To Be Patriotic is to Build Socialism": Communist Ideology in Vietnam's Cold War', in *Dynamics of the Cold War in Asia: Ideology, Identity, and Culture*, Tuong Vu and Wasana Wongsurawat, eds (New York: Palgrave Macmillan, 2009), 34.
13　Charles B. McLane (1920–2008) specialised in the international relations of the Soviet Union. He served in the US Army during World War II in the Psychological Warfare Division. He served as a cultural attaché at the US Embassy in Moscow for several years in the early 1950s, earned a doctorate at Columbia University in 1955 and taught at Dartmouth University from 1957 until he retired in the 1980s. 'McLane, Charles', in *A Maine Writer* [online] (Augusta: Maine State Library, 2020), available from: www.maine.gov/msl/maine/writdisplay.shtml?id=97836.

prominent political leaders of the time (including Ngo Dinh Nhu of South Vietnam and Phoumi Nosavan of Laos). He opens his book with a discussion of theory, albeit in a dismissive manner:

> Whatever one may think of the relationship between theory and practice in Soviet foreign policy, the deference Moscow pays to theory compels us to know what it is, or what it is said to be. It is possible to discover this without succumbing to the Marxian notion that theory, or ideology, is derived from certain immutable laws. In reality, as the following discussion will show, much of Soviet theory, and indeed much of Soviet practice itself, is contrived, answerable to no fixed logic and as fluid as theory and practice are in less pretentious systems.[14]

McLane then proceeds to analyse the debates around the approach of the Soviets and the Communist International (Comintern, or Third International) to revolution in East and Southeast Asia, and in colonial countries more generally. He devotes special time and attention to debates over defining the stage of history in which colonial countries existed and the related question of whether communist movements there should ally with bourgeois-democratic national liberation movements.

Each subsequent section of McLane's book opens with a discussion of the Soviet Union's approach to revolution at the time and examines how communist parties in Southeast Asia implemented Soviet policy. He concludes the chapter with the following observation:

> [W]ith regard to the importance of theory … it is not sufficient to argue either that theory *determined* Soviet policies in the East or that it merely *graced* them. No formula has ever been devised to explain when a given Soviet action relies on doctrine and when doctrine is appealed to subsequently to rationalize the action. The versatility of theory in Soviet behavior, or perhaps the versatility of its practitioners, is such that few have satisfactorily explained its function.[15]

McLane was chiefly interested in ascertaining the extent to which theory determined practice and vice versa, but largely depicted Southeast Asian communist parties as passively receiving doctrine from Moscow and implementing it with varying degrees of success. Completely absent is

---

14 Charles B. McLane, *Soviet Strategies in Southeast Asia: An Exploration of Eastern Policy under Lenin and Stalin* (Princeton, NJ: Princeton University Press, 1966), 3.
15 ibid., 78–79. Emphasis in original.

recognition that Southeast Asian communist parties had an active role in the reception, analysis and adaptation to a new context of Marxist-Leninist theory.

Another impressive history is Justus van der Kroef's *Communism in South-East Asia*. He presents a broad history of the origins of Southeast Asian communist parties and an examination of their policies and organisations in the 1970s and early 1980s. His study also highlights these parties' diplomatic relations with Beijing and Moscow and what he calls the communist parties' 'programs and tactics', where he comes closest to considering ideology as he identifies their common theoretical characteristics. He lists these as: 1) a belief that countries exist in a democratic phase of historical development (national bourgeois and new democratic, among others); 2) the challenges to the development of class consciousness posed by the existence of multiple ethnic groups and religions; and 3) recognition that increasing socioeconomic inequality will stimulate the further development of class consciousness.[16]

But van der Kroef's analysis—detailed as it is—does not consider the role of ideology beyond these common characteristics and fails to indicate whether any communist party in Southeast Asia developed a novel revolutionary ideology except for the extreme case of the CPK. He states that the CPK's class analysis of Democratic Kampuchea under its rule held that 90 per cent of people were revolutionary, 8 per cent were a 'middle force' who were sympathetic to the revolution and 2 per cent were 'hesitant and undecided'.[17] Other than stating that this classification was 'innovative in emphasis', van der Kroef holds that this was in agreement with Leninist and Maoist class concepts, but otherwise does not elaborate on possible theoretical development by the CPK.

More recent attempts by Robert Alexander, William Heaton and Thomas Marks explain the rise of Maoism in intellectual thought streams either through the scope of international relations, as a nationalist response to the limitations of the Bolshevik model of organisation, or through the perspective of strategy and operational art vis-a-vis Mao Zedong's military tactic of 'People's War'.[18] Other scholars such as Kenneth Fuller,

---

16 Justus Maria van der Kroef, *Communism in South-East Asia* (London: Macmillan, 1981), 134.
17 ibid., 133–34.
18 Robert J. Alexander, *International Maoism in the Developing World* (Westport, CT: Praeger, 1999); William R. Heaton, 'China and Southeast Asian Communist Movements: The Decline of Dual Track Diplomacy', *Asian Survey* 22(8) (August 1982): 779–800; and Thomas A. Marks, *Maoist People's War in Post-Vietnam Asia* (Chiang Mai, Thailand: White Lotus, 2007), xv.

Huynh Kim Khanh, Bertil Lintner, Cheah Boon Kheng and Donald Hindley, among others, explore the emergence of radical ideological discourses such as Marxism-Leninism and Maoism on a micro-scale. Their studies focus on specific national communist parties and their ideological formulations, engagements, successes, defeats and continuing struggles to survive.[19] Although each of these is a pathbreaking study, the problem with their analyses is an oversimplification of a complicated dialogue between external ideological discourse and its recipient. Radical ideological discourses like Maoism appear as *events* rather than a *complex program*, *vocabulary*, *syntax* or *critical interpretative paradigm* with which Southeast Asian radicals interpreted their own global positionality.[20] Such radicals then engaged with ideas *in praxis*, and always with agency, in pursuance of ways to practically reverse negative historical trends in their respective homelands.

Another important work is Clive Christie's *Ideology and Revolution in Southeast Asia, 1900–1980*. As with McLane's earlier study, Christie's scope is broad and examines communist parties and their ideologies in Burma, Cambodia, East Timor, Indonesia, Laos, Malaya/Singapore, the Philippines, Thailand and Vietnam. Christie's book:

> represents an attempt to analyse the ideological background to the endeavours of Southeast Asian intellectuals, writers and political leaders to respond to Western dominance; to come to terms with what was seen as the 'malaise' of traditional Asian societies; to formulate effective strategies of resistance to the West; to create a political and ideological base for the newly emergent independent

---

19 Kenneth Fuller, *A Movement Divided: Philippine Communism, 1957–1986* (Quezon City: University of the Philippines Press, 2011); Huynh Kim Khanh, *Vietnamese Communism, 1925–1945* (Ithaca, NY: Cornell University Press, 1986); Bertil Lintner, *The Rise and Fall of the Communist Party of Burma* (Ithaca, NY: Cornell University Southeast Asia Program Publications, 1990); Cheah Boon Kheng, *Red Star Over Malaya: Resistance and Social Conflict during and after the Japanese Occupation, 1941–1946* (Singapore: NUS Press, 2003); Donald Hindley, *The Communist Party of Indonesia, 1951–1963* (Berkeley, CA: University of California Press, 1966). See also Part III in Arif Dirlik, Paul Healy and Nick Knight, eds, *Critical Perspectives on Mao Zedong's Thought* (Atlantic Heights, NJ: Humanities Press, 1997), 267–385.
20 Matthew Galway, 'Specters of Dependency: Hou Yuon and the Origins of Cambodia's Marxist Vision (1955–1975)', *Cross-Currents: East Asian History and Culture Review* 31 (2019): 126–61, doi.org/10.1353/ach.2019.0021; Matthew Galway, 'Red Service-Intellectual: Phouk Chhay, Maoist China, and the Cultural Revolution in Cambodia, 1964–1967', *Journal of Southeast Asian Studies* 52(2) (June 2021): 275–308, doi.org/10.1017/S0022463421000436; and Fabio Lanza, 'Global Maoism', in *Afterlives of Chinese Communism: Political Concepts from Mao to Xi*, Christian Sorace, Ivan Franceschini and Nicholas Loubere, eds (London and Canberra: Verso and ANU Press, 2019), 85.

states; and—in broader terms—to reflect on and understand the long-term historical significance of the relationship between the West and Asia.[21]

Although ambitious, *Ideology and Revolution* is not without its faults. The most glaring of its shortcomings is its uneven coverage. Indonesia and Vietnam receive extensive coverage whereas the author devotes a mere three pages to the Malayan Communist Party (MCP). Christie does examine the ideology of the Vietnamese and Cambodian communists in detail, with a particularly welcome emphasis on CPK ideology. However, the source material for the book consists of works in English, French and Bahasa Indonesia at the expense of swathes of important source material in the original languages of the varied parties under examination. Christie's focus is also not exclusively on communist parties, but also on nationalists more generally. This is doubtless a strength of his book, but it also limits the volume's ability to examine thoroughly anti-imperialist, mostly *left-wing* revolutionary movements.

In addition to the understandable linguistic limitations of previous studies, an important conceptual shortcoming of the extant work on revolutionary ideology in Southeast Asia is that very little attention has been paid to how Southeast Asian revolutionaries wrestled with the development of new theories of revolution. Most revolutionaries in the region engaged in dialectics with Marxism-Leninism, which represented for them a radical ideological discourse and critical interpretative paradigm with purportedly universal applicability. In seeking to apply its general principles to their respective revolutions, Southeast Asian revolutionaries also adapted it, as with any idea or ideology travelling between cultures. The goal was to render it congruent with contemporary norms so that it could address more faithfully the specific challenges a revolutionary party faced in its country and historical situation. A fuller analysis of the indigenisation of revolutionary ideology thus requires an examination of the international milieu in which theorists devised such ideologies, the intellectual development of the men and women who formulated new theories of revolution and an assessment of their efforts in light of the Marxist-Leninist-Maoist canon.

---

21 Clive J. Christie, *Ideology and Revolution in Southeast Asia, 1900–1980* (Richmond, UK: Curzon Press, 2015), 2.

Theory and approach

To understand the development of distinctly Southeast Asian variants of Marxism-Leninism-Maoism requires a fuller appreciation of what Karl Mannheim termed the 'social milieu' of the intellectuals who engaged with left-wing ideology. This will allow an understanding of the origins of 'radicalisation' among intellectuals or political elites.[22] A social milieu includes the prevailing ideological forces, the dimensions of these intellectuals' upbringing and the nature of the texts that they produced. It also includes the physical and intellectual sojourns that they undertook that brought them into contact with radical ideas and people who shaped their world views.

One useful approach is by Sinologist Philip Kuhn, whose analysis of the origins of the Taiping vision uncovers the processes whereby ideas were shaped by social experiences. Kuhn explores the transformation and indigenisation of Christian doctrine into a characteristically Chinese millenarian ideology. He identifies three salient aspects of an external idea's indigenisation and implementation in practice that are relevant to our exploration of ideology in the pages that follow: 1) the original language of composition of the material(s); 2) the historical circumstances from which these materials emerge; and 3) the process by which such 'foreign' or 'external' materials became important to, and were made normative by, sectors of society outside the group that initially appreciated and received them.[23] These features provide us with a useful guide to tracking how ideas intertwine with the historical situations and sociocultural milieus in which they emerge and take on certain features that tie them inextricably to the interpreters who first engaged with them.

The development of communist ideology in Southeast Asia represents an important and underappreciated instance of what Edward Said called 'travelling theory'. Said identified the three critical conditions, or processes, for the movement of ideas across cultures as production,

---

22 Karl Mannheim, *Ideology and Utopia: An Introduction to the Sociology of Knowledge*, Louis Wirth and Edward Shils, trans (London: Routledge & Kegan Paul, 1936), 265.
23   Philip A. Kuhn, 'Origins of the Taiping Vision: Cross-Cultural Dimensions of a Chinese Rebellion', *Comparative Studies in Society and History* 19(3) (July 1977): 350.

transmission and reception.²⁴ This volume seeks to illustrate the utility of Said's triad by exploring the reception of theory in Southeast Asia—that is, the nature and form of adaptation and the processes by which ideas move from abstract theory to adapted theory to implemented practice. Southeast Asia's ethnogeographic diversity, along with the range of experiences of the intellectuals under analysis with lived cultures, makes it all the more important to track their complex encounters and dialectical engagements with radical thought. This includes the fraught (and often multiple) failings of adapting ideas intellectually from without to suit socioeconomic situations within strata and social topographies with which the leftists under analysis had little prior exposure.²⁵

Defining ideology

Any focused analysis of ideology requires unpacking the term 'ideology'. As a concept, ideology's meaning has evolved many times since its 1796 coining by French aristocrat and philosopher Antoine Louis Claude Destutt, comte de Tracy (1754–1836), who termed his science of ideas an '*idéologie*' during the French Reign of Terror (1793–94). More recently, Louis Althusser defined ideology as 'the imagined existence (or idea) of things as it relates to the real conditions of existence'.²⁶ Hannah Arendt regards it as something distinct from mere opinion. For Arendt, ideology 'claims to possess either the key to history, or the solution for all the "riddles of the universe," or the intimate knowledge of the hidden universal laws which are supposed to rule nature and man'.²⁷ Common to these definitions of ideology as a concept is that they do not address the centrality of practice, or how ideology moves from thought or world view into the realm of direct action—a key feature that differentiates ideology from abstraction.

---

24   Edward W. Said, *The World, the Text, and the Critic* (Cambridge, MA: Harvard University Press, 1983), 226–47. Also quoted in Timothy Cheek, 'Chinese Socialism as Vernacular Cosmopolitanism', *Frontiers of History in China* 9(1) (1 January 2014): 106. Cheek has referred to these three aspects elsewhere as the social conditions of a theory's origination, institutionalisation and constraint in a new context, and the 'possibilities for revivification of the radical resources of theory once again'.
25   Matthew Galway, 'Boundless revolution: Global Maoism and communist movements in Southeast Asia, 1949–1979' (PhD diss., University of British Columbia, Vancouver, 2017). See also Matthew Galway, *The Emergence of Global Maoism: China's Red Evangelism and the Cambodian Communist Movement, 1949–1979* (Ithaca, NY: Cornell University Press, 2022), 1–19.
26   Louis Althusser, *Lenin and Philosophy, and Other Essays* (New York, NY: Monthly Review, 1971), 162.
27   Hannah Arendt, *The Origins of Totalitarianism* (San Diego, CA: Harcourt, 1968), 159.

Although the definitions above are useful, ideology exists as a set of intangible ideas that exercise force in the tangible world. Stewart Hall holds that ideology is an important tool of hegemony that 'stabilize[s] a particular form of power and domination; or which reconcile[s] and accommodate[s] the mass of the people to their subordinate place in the social formation'.[28] This understanding takes as its object ideology as promulgated by a governing party or elite in defence of an established political authority. However, the formulation and promulgation of ideas are hardly the preserve of incumbent governments and are often deployed by oppositions (armed and nonviolent) with pretensions to reform the state or capture power.

For the purposes of this book, it is useful to consider two separate but related definitions of ideology. The first is a more narrowly empirical definition advanced by Francisco Gutiérrez-Sanín and Elisabeth Wood, which describes ideology as:

> [A] more or less systematic set of ideas that includes the identification of a referent group (a class, ethnic, or other social group), an enunciation of the grievances or challenges that the group confronts, the identification of objectives on behalf of that group (political change—or defense against its threat), and a (perhaps vaguely defined) program of action. Ideologies also prescribe—to widely varying extent, from no particular blueprint to very specific instructions—distinct institutions and strategies as the means to attain group goals.[29]

The second, more sociological definition comes from Clifford Geertz, who understands ideology as a system for understanding and action when 'institutionalized guides for behavior, thought, or feeling are weak or absent'. Ideologies, then, serve as 'maps of problematic social reality and matrices for the creation of collective conscience'.[30] To understand how ideology functions, one must grasp the 'relationship between the socio-psychological stresses that incite ideological attitudes and the elaborate symbolic structures through which those attitudes are given a public

---

28   Stewart Hall, 'The Problem of Ideology: Marxism without Guarantees', in *Stuart Hall: Critical Dialogues in Cultural Studies*, David Morley and Kuan-Hsing Chen, eds, 2nd edn (New York: Routledge, 1996), 24–25.
29   Francisco Gutiérrez-Sanín and Elisabeth Jean Wood, 'Ideology in Civil War: Instrumental Adoption and Beyond', *Journal of Peace Research* 51(2) (2014): 215, doi.org/10.1177/0022343313514073.
30   Clifford Geertz, *The Interpretation of Cultures* (New York: Basic Books, 1973), 218, 220.

existence'.³¹ Ideology acts as a meeting ground for some kind of novel challenge posed by external factors (not necessarily foreign, but external to the status quo) and existing cultural systems. Thus, Gutiérrez-Sanín and Wood's definition places primacy on ideology as a set of political paradigms whereas Geertz's characterisation illustrates the broader sociological origins of ideology in general and, for the purposes of this volume, revolutionary ideology in particular.

Both definitions of ideology draw attention to an important aspect of understanding the development of left-wing revolutionary ideologies in Southeast Asia. The indigenisation of Marxism-Leninism and Maoism was a sociological process that occurred in areas where revolutionary elites engaged with concepts that provided plans for mobilising against prevailing domestic and international power structures and founding a more egalitarian system. Chen Kuan-Hsing's notion of 'critical syncretism' is especially helpful in this regard, as it endeavours to 'move beyond the limits of colonial identification on the one hand, and the postcolonial politics of resentment on the other hand'.³² Although rooted in cultural studies, his concern is to 'avoid reproducing colonialism and to go beyond the politics of resentment that bind colonizer and colonized together'.³³ As Chen details further:

> The key issue here is the object of identification. The formation of the colonized subjectivity has always been passive, reactive, and imposed, and the colonizer has been its only object of identification. In the decolonization movement, nativism and identity politics shift the object of identification toward the self. This self, however, is still conditioned by an active dis-identification with the colonizer ... The direction of identification put forward by a critical syncretism is outward; the intent is to become others, to actively interiorize elements of others into the subjectivity of the self so as to move beyond the boundaries and divisive positions historically constructed by colonial power relations in the form of patriarchy, capitalism, racism, chauvinism, heterosexism, or nationalistic xenophobia.³⁴

---

31   ibid., 207.
32   Chen Kuan-Hsing, *Asia as Method: Toward Deimperialization* (Durham, NC: Duke University Press, 2010), xiii.
33   ibid., 72.
34   ibid., 97.

For our purposes, the utility of critical syncretism lies in Chen's goal to turn attention to those local practices of anti-imperial or leftist activism that have been hitherto airbrushed out of public consciousness. 'Critical syncretism takes an alternative understanding of subjectivity as its starting point', he continues, and:

> [t]he aim is not simply to rediscover the suppressed voices of the multiple subjects within the social formation, but to generate a system of multiple reference points that can break away from the self-reproducing neocolonial framework that structures the trajectories and flow of desire.[35]

Our goal is thus to restore focus on and, arguably, primacy to those local norms, modes, resources and ways of seeing the world in dialogic engagement with thoughts and practices that entered Southeast Asian leftists' life trajectories.

The role of revolutionary metropoles

Contributions to this volume focus on the indigenisation of revolutionary ideologies and their praxis in Southeast Asia. But importantly, none of these ideologies formed in a geopolitical vacuum. The revolutionary metropoles of Moscow and Beijing, principally, served as beacons of revolution for colonised peoples in Southeast Asia. Although neither Moscow nor Beijing led a revolution in Southeast Asia directly, they nevertheless provided inspiration and support to revolutionaries from, and in, the region. Such metropoles were also rich wellsprings for the theoretical and empirical writings that underpinned Southeast Asian radical intellectuals' own approaches to revolution. Beyond the written word, some of the men and women who led and/or participated in leftist movements in Southeast Asia often visited the Soviet Union and/or China, further informing their views of socialism, capitalism and revolution.

The 1919 founding of the Comintern and subsequent flow of revolutionaries and radical ideas to and from Moscow set Southeast Asia on a path to independence, revolution and social transformation. Anna Belogurova's study of the MCP shows that Moscow and Beijing provided important intellectual resources to Malayan communists that led them to develop their concept of a multiethnic Malayan nation. For example, the

---

35 ibid., 101.

conflicting interpretations of the term *minzu* (民族) by the Comintern and the Chinese Communist Party (CCP) led to the Comintern's sponsorship of a 'Malayan' national party and a revolution by 'Malayans'. This ultimately 'conformed to the nascent idea of a national Malayan identity among Chinese immigrant communists and their jurisdiction over both the Nanyang and Malaya'. The MCP case highlights the centrality of revolutionary international organisations that were operational in Southeast Asia. As Belogurova avers, 'local developments—whether in Singapore or Shanghai or Manila—cannot be understood without a basic understanding of global interactions'.[36]

The importance of revolutionary metropoles as sites of theoretical innovation and cosmopolitan experience is also evident in the sojourns of many Asian radicals who formed clandestine global networks in cosmopolitan Asian 'core' cities such as Tokyo, Shanghai, Hong Kong, Singapore and Hanoi. As Tim Harper notes, radical intellectuals such as Indonesian national hero Tan Malaka (born Ibrahim Gelar Datuk Sutan Malaka, 1897–1949; 'Tan' is a Minangkabau courtesy name) and Vietnam's Nguyễn Ái Quốc (Hồ Chí Minh) travelled not as men of luxury or comforts, but often as itinerant workers, students and, frequently, exiles en route to becoming communists. Their sojourns from colonised spaces to cosmopolitan capitals and major epicentres of radical or avant-garde thought led them to forge lasting global networks. As Harper explains, would-be radicals like Tan Malaka, Manabendra Nath Roy and Hồ Chí Minh:

> were the first to travel in large numbers far beyond their own countries, to meet each other across Asia, Europe, and the Americas, and to begin to explore what they had in common. Their itineraries might begin in Saigon, Sumatra, or Calcutta, but they then dispersed across three oceans to Tokyo, Paris, Amsterdam, San Francisco, New York, Berlin, and Moscow, before converging again in Asia, in Canton, Shanghai, or Singapore … They experienced a world of connections but also a world upside down: the underbelly of the great port cities of empire where they found they were able more freely to organize and act. The sites of their struggles were the waterfront, the lodging house, the coffee shop, the clandestine printing press in the back alley. They made these places centres of global awareness, and their experience of

---

36 Belogurova, *The Nanyang Revolution*, 56, 233.

> a secret underworld of empire helped shape a spectrum of radical ideas—about class and national identity, the position of women, the function of art and literature, the history of the future.[37]

John Sidel's book on the cosmopolitan origins of Southeast Asian revolutions builds on Harper's study with its focus on major Southeast Asian cores, ranging from Hanoi to Jakarta and Manila. Such sites served as important spaces for transcontinental encounters and networks. Sidel contends:

> With the deepening integration of these areas of Southeast Asia into the world capitalist economy in the latter half of the nineteenth century full-blown market societies began to crystallize, giving rise to new social classes, modern public spheres, and diverse new social imaginaries and modes of consciousness, expression, association, and action, most notably in the urban port entrepôts of the region, but also radiating out into their rural hinterlands through the market's expanding circuitries.[38]

Such cosmopolitan spaces provided fecund ground for intellectuals to forge new connections, undertake ambitious sojourns and encounter as well as wrestle with new ideas that would one day underpin their respective *Weltanschauungen*.

Shanghai served as such a space for Tan Malaka. His correspondences with Henk Sneevliet (1883–1942), Dutch labour leader, Indies Social Democratic Association (ISDV) founder and Comintern functionary, led him to visit the Comintern's Far Eastern Bureau in Shanghai in January 1923. Alongside the Pan-Pacific Trade Union Secretariat, the Far Eastern Bureau played a fundamental role in supporting communist activities in Asia.[39] In line with the Comintern's overarching mission, Tan Malaka was sent to Rangoon (Yangon) as an operative to establish a liaison nexus between India and the Dutch East Indies.[40] Before Tan's departure, however, Shanghai arose in his thinking as a symbol of many past injustices and a signal of a future yet to be realised. He began to interpret the dark side of the international concessions and Japanese colonialism

---

37 Tim Harper, *Underground Asia: Global Revolutionaries and the Assault on Empire* (London: Allen Lane, 2020), 19.
38 Sidel, *Republicanism, Communism, Islam*, 14.
39 Onimaru Takeshi, 'Shanghai Connection: The Construction and Collapse of the Comintern Network in East and Southeast Asia', *Southeast Asian Studies* 5(1) (2016): 116–17, doi.org/10.20495/seas.5.1_115.
40 Ruth T. McVey, *The Rise of Indonesian Communism* (Singapore: Equinox Publishing, 2006), 127.

a decade later in Indonesia as signals of Dutch colonialism's impending downfall.[41] Shanghai thus served a dual function: as the headquarters of Asian communist activity and as a specific space in which the very forces that communists sought to overcome were laid bare. Foreign visitors' awareness of what Rebecca Karl describes as a 'shared world stage' of colonialist/imperialist subjugation ultimately came to light.[42]

Likewise, interwar Paris served as an important locus where intellectuals from the broader Global South convened, experienced and, through comradeship during study, found their radical 'voices' that fuelled their respective revolutions. Interwar Paris, Michael Goebel notes, was host to 'roughly 100,000 non-Europeans by 1930' and 'more people from the Global South than any other contemporary city worldwide, except perhaps New York'.[43] Activists and leftists from across the Global South flocked to Paris to study and expand their horizons, and many emerged from their social experiences there as radical figures who would lead anti-imperial movements in their homelands. Not unlike Tan Malaka's experience in Shanghai, 'colonial subjects' in Paris 'witnessed at first hand the discrepancy between universalist republican ideals and discriminatory practices, kindling skepticism about France's "civilizing mission"'.[44] As time passed, the same intellectuals came to recognise their plight was not in isolation, as a 'heightened awareness, often through comparisons and extrapolations from one case to another, helped enable new forms of thinking because interstices cracked open room for experimentation and alternative ideas, as well as practical leverages'.[45]

Importantly, the influence of revolutionary metropoles was highly variable between different parties and over time. The CCP's experience was somewhat typical in this regard. The Comintern provided direct support for the CCP's establishment and oversaw some of its early activities. However, Comintern influence diminished considerably after the

---

41 Abidin Kusno, 'From City to City: Tan Malaka, Shanghai and the Politics of Geographical Imagining', *Singapore Journal of Tropical Geography* 24(3) (2003): 327–39, doi.org/10.1111/1467-9493.00162. On Tan Malaka's important writings, see Tan Malaka, *From Jail to Jail*, Helen Jarvis, trans. (Athens, OH: Ohio University Press, 2017).
42 Karl's focus is on this revelation in prewar China of a 'shared world stage with other peoples and countries' that were dealing with a 'temporal/spatial problem inherent in a modern global history'. Rebecca Karl, *Staging the World: Chinese Nationalism at the Turn of the Twentieth Century* (Durham, NC: Duke University Press, 2002), 198.
43 Michael Goebel, *Anti-Imperial Metropolis* (Cambridge, UK: Cambridge University Press, 2015), 10.
44 ibid., 4.
45 ibid., 9.

mid-1930s, after which local communists like Mao Zedong took on most of the ideological work. Indeed, one of the ways Mao established himself as CCP leader was by taking on a role as a theoretician and formulating a novel form of Marxism-Leninism. In Southeast Asia, both the MCP and the CPK initially drew ideological inspiration from Moscow and Beijing, respectively, before striking out on their own and engaging in their own formulation of Marxist-Leninist ideology.

A sociology of intellectuals

This book is a study of ideology and praxis in revolutionary movements in Cold War–era Southeast Asia. Those who spearheaded the various political organisations under analysis were intellectuals. This makes it even more important to adopt an approach that examines how intellectuals positioned themselves as visionaries and radical reformers. Here, we use a 'sociology of intellectuals' approach to track the politicisation of intellectuals-turned-worker/peasant visionaries to reveal the connection between ideological journeys and political actions. But this sociological approach does not treat these intellectuals merely as idealistic patriots or social reformers who sought foreign ideologies only insofar as they were useful for national liberation and social transformation; rather, this approach reveals the dynamic between ideological explorations, social experiences and the pursuit of political power.

Three distinct approaches to the sociology of intellectuals—at once transforming and transformed—have evolved across decades of scholarship in the twentieth century. Charles Kurzman and Lynn Owens identify such approaches as: 1) intellectuals form a class in themselves, whose proponents include, among others, Julien Benda (the foundational sociologist of intellectuals) and, more recently, Pierre Bourdieu; 2) intellectuals as class-bound representatives of their group of origin, which is a position Antonio Gramsci and Michel Foucault have notably held in their scholarship; and 3) intellectuals as amorphous, classless and unbound to their group/class of origin (proponents of this approach include Karl Mannheim and Edward Shils).[46]

---

46 Charles Kurzman and Lynn Owens, 'The Sociology of Intellectuals', *Annual Review of Sociology* 28(1) (2002): 63–90, doi.org/10.1146/annurev.soc.28.110601.140745.

This book treats intellectuals as simultaneously class-bound and free to transcend class. In the predominantly agrarian societies of Southeast Asia, intellectuals were networked individuals engaging in situated thinking and responding to the 'cyclical phenomenon' of colonial/post-independence exploitation, stark rural–urban divisions and underdevelopment.[47] As Mannheim once intimated (albeit not about literati from the region): intellectuals' education introduced them to 'opposing tendencies in social realities'—notably, languages, syntaxes and critical interpretative paradigms—'to attach themselves to classes to which they originally did not belong … to choose their affiliation'.[48] Yet the intellectuals' role was, as Foucault and Gilles Deleuze hold, as a revolutionary force. As grounded in their class, too, intellectuals are 'to struggle against the forms of power in relation to which [they are] both object and instrument: within the domain of "knowledge", "truth", "consciousness", and "discourse"'.[49] By dint of their training and situated thinking, they are 'cogs in the power/knowledge machine and thus may explore and disable it'.[50]

For our purposes in the pages that follow, however, the best working approach to intellectuals is from Edward Said. He regards the intellectual as:

> a representative figure that matters—someone who visibly represents a standpoint of some kind, and someone who makes articulate representations to [their] public despite all sorts of barriers … intellectuals are individuals with a vocation for the art of representing, whether that is talking, writing, teaching, appearing on television. And that vocation is important to the extent that it is publicly recognizable and involves both commitment and risk, boldness, and vulnerability.[51]

The intellectuals under analysis were indeed in the business of representing and balancing commitments, risk and vulnerability to considerable degrees throughout their careers. An idea or ideological discourse did not arise in our intellectual founders' thinking solely for its utility in interpreting their exploited situation, but because it was the most effective strategy

---

47 Samir Amin, *Les effets structurels de l'intégration internationale des économies précapitalistes: une étude théorique du mécanisme qui a engendré les économies dites sous-développées* [*The Structural Effects of the International Integration of Precapitalist Economies: A Technical Study of the Mechanism that Generated the Underdeveloped Economies*] (Paris: Université de Paris, 1957), 1–9, 139–41, 484–85.
48 Mannheim, *Ideology and Utopia*, 156–58.
49 Michel Foucault and Gilles Deleuze, 'The Intellectuals and Power', *Telos* 16 (1973): 104.
50 Kurzman and Owens, 'The Sociology of Intellectuals', 70.
51 Edward W. Said, *Representations of the Intellectual: The 1993 Reith Lectures* (New York: Vintage Books, 1994), 12–13.

in helping them to reform society and/or seize state power. A 'sociology of intellectuals' approach is therefore most useful in explaining why young intellectual patriots and social reformers (not mutually exclusive) in Southeast Asia turned into radical nationalists, hardened communists and, in the most excessive cases, brutal killers of not only their nation, but also their comrades once they had state power in hand.

A key challenge and opportunity for the intellectuals and movements under examination is translation. The works of Marx, Lenin, Stalin, Mao and others were translated into the local vernacular, to be sure, but there quickly emerged a problem: the works written by foreign socialists were, of necessity, written in service to revolution in other social contexts and could not be easily applied to local circumstances.[52] This realisation left revolutionaries staring into what Alasdair MacIntyre called in his analysis of Aristotelian and Confucian treatment of the virtues 'the void': the space between the prescriptions of established theory and local reality.[53] Geertz provides an equally helpful explanation of this void and how it gives rise to ideologies. In his view:

> It is a confluence of socio-psychological strain and an absence of cultural resources by means of which to make sense of the strain, each exacerbating the other, that sets the stage for the rise of systematic (political, moral, or economic) ideologies.[54]

In this light, one may regard linguistic translation as but the first step in a broader process of using foreign concepts to understand local realities and then using local realities to expand on established ideology. The process of translation thus gives way to indigenisation.

Theoretical indigenisation refers to the method of formulating, applying and reformulating ideology over time. One may conceive of the indigenisation of revolutionary ideology in Southeast Asia as occurring because of both exogenous and endogenous influences. Said's 'travelling theory' provides an important framework to this effect. As he articulated in his 'Traveling Theory' essay:

---

52 See Oliver Crawford, 'Translating and Transliterating Marxism in Indonesia', *Modern Asian Studies* 55(3) (May 2021): 697–733, doi.org/10.1017/S0026749X20000104.
53 Alasdair Macintyre, 'Incommensurability, Truth, and the Conversation between Confucians and Aristotelians about the Virtues', in *Culture and Modernity: East–West Philosophic Perspectives*, Eliot Deutsch, ed. (Honolulu: University of Hawai'i Press, 1991), 117–18.
54 Geertz, *The Interpretation of Cultures*, 220.

> Like people and schools of criticism, ideas and theories travel—from person to person, from situation to situation, from one period to another. Cultural and intellectual life are usually nourished and often sustained by this circulation of ideas, and whether it takes the form of acknowledged or unconscious influence, creative borrowing, or wholesale appropriation, the movement of ideas and theories from one place to another is both a fact of life and a usefully enabling condition of intellectual activity.[55]

For Said, a 'recurrent pattern' forms for the movement of ideas across cultures: a point of origin; the passage of an idea from one place and time to another and its introduction, acceptance and toleration; and its rebirth through 'new uses [and] a new position in a new time and place'.[56] This last pattern may constitute the process of indigenisation (termed elsewhere normativisation, normalisation and localisation).

In Southeast Asia, indigenisation entailed combining the universal principles of Marxism-Leninism with the circumstances of a country. In practice, it meant ascertaining the period of historical development into which a country fell, the structure of society, the distribution of power and the means by which existing political and economic arrangements could be challenged to bring about greater political, economic and social equality. For example, in China, Mao was the most important figure in the 'Sinification of Marxism'—an intellectual movement that gave birth to several distinctly Chinese approaches to revolution. These included (but were not limited to) the mass line and the united front and, more broadly, the reconciliation of the place of the peasantry within the larger process of proletarian revolution. Likewise, in Southeast Asia, the indigenisation of ideology spawned several distinct ideological innovations that constituted components and even the basis of revolutionary movements in the region.

The cynical reader may ask: 'Does any self-professed Southeast Asian communist party constitute a legitimate subject for study?' The answer must be in the affirmative so long as the party and its leadership sought to do anything more than act as a printing press for works by Marx, Lenin, Mao and other prominent left-wing theorists. Our approach regards the process of reception, analysis and adaptation as constituting the indigenisation of ideology, *independent of its successful implementation and the attendant overthrow of the existing order.*

---

55 Said, *The World, the Text, and the Critic*, 226.
56 ibid., 226–28.

This book's chapters illustrate the various stages and processes of the indigenisation of Marxism-Leninism and Maoism across Southeast Asia. The first chapter, on Indonesia, is illustrative of the early stages of indigenisation: there, communists confronted a social reality in which Islam was central to social life. Marxism could not be relevant in Indonesia unless it coexisted with Islam. To reconcile and intertwine Marxism and Islam was the first step in creating a body of theory rooted in the social reality of Indonesia. Chapter Six examines a later stage of indigenisation by showing how Malayan communists applied revolutionary theory to Malaya, only to confront a deeply problematic 'void': spontaneous support for the MCP did not materialise as its leaders had planned.

In response, the MCP drew on the Marxist-Leninist and Maoist canon to formulate a new theory of revolution that they held would bridge the 'void' between leftist theory and local practice. Chapter Two, on Kampuchea (Cambodia), highlights the process whereby Maoism arose for one CPK leading figure to fill this void. As an ideological system with a built-in critical interpretative paradigm, ideological discourse and radical vocabulary for interpreting global cyclical inequality, Mao's analyses of China's rural plight and diagnoses of China as semifeudal and semicolonial resonated with Cambodian intellectuals who recognised a shared experience of global market-capitalist exploitation with Maoist China. As Cambodia's political scene became inhospitable for progressives like Hu Nim, who engaged with Maoism as discourse in writing, Maoism as radical praxis became an attractive alternative to fill this void with concrete, radical action.

Indigenising communism across Southeast Asia

The leaders of communist movements across Southeast Asia faced similar questions and challenges as they sought to attain independence, political power and social transformation. The ways in which Southeast Asian revolutionaries responded to these challenges constitute three of the main themes of the chapters that follow.

The first of these challenges was that, although Marxism-Leninism-Maoism provided a theoretical framework for understanding political and economic underdevelopment, local conditions throughout Southeast Asia precluded mechanical application of the Soviet or Chinese experience. The cultural, economic, ethnic, geographic, political, religious and social diversity of Southeast Asia necessitated revolutionary intellectuals to acknowledge what Brantly Womack calls 'the reality of the embedded situation' to 'fill' the space between the prescriptions of established theory and local reality.[57] Just as Mao had to find a way to reconcile the local with the universal, the domestic with the international, so, too, did Southeast Asian revolutionaries. Chapters Two, Four, Six and Eight all explore this theme in action in Southeast Asia, with each examining certain key processes of 'Kampucheanisation', 'Filipinisation', 'Malayanisation' and 'Laoisation', respectively. Chapter Two examines the Kampucheanisation of Maoism through close textual exegesis and an intellectual biography of a CPK minister. Chapter Six highlights the primacy of violent struggle in 'Malayanised' Marxism-Leninism and its role in transforming ordinary civilians into MCP supporters. The focus in Chapter Four is the transformative power of translation and interpretation of Maoist texts, as well as the practical dimension of 'Filipinised' Maoism. Chapter Eight explores how 'the national question' that was already a constituent part of global revolutionary theory became an integral component of 'Laoised' Marxism-Leninism and played a role in shaping the practice of the Pathet Lao's movement to capture state power. All four chapters shine overdue light on how radical figures in Southeast Asian communist movements applied Marxism-Leninism creatively to their respective historical situations and, in so doing, produced an indigenised variant that purportedly maintained the universality of the original theory.[58]

A second, related challenge was drawing on local cultural and historical resources to articulate ideology in a way that made it relevant to local conditions. In some cases, this meant finding ways to integrate religious

---

57   Brantly Womack, *The dialectic of domestic and international in the history of the Communist Party of China*, Working Paper Series (Charlottesville, VA: University of Virginia, 2020).
58   On this phenomenon in Mao's adaptation of Marxism-Leninism, see Nick Knight, *Rethinking Mao: Explorations in Mao Zedong's Thought* (Lanham, MD: Lexington Books, 2007), 199. Arif Dirlik argued likewise:

> Mao did not reduce Marxism to a Chinese version or view China merely as another illustration of universal Marxist principles. His exposition of the relationship is at once metonymic (Chinese Revolution reduced to aspect or function of Marxism in general) and synecdochic (intrinsic relationship of shared qualities). The result was a conception of the relationship that insisted on China's *difference* and yet represented Chinese Marxism as an embodiment of Marxism.

Arif Dirlik, *Marxism in the Chinese Revolution* (Lanham, MD: Rowman & Littlefield, 2005), 97–100. Emphasis added.

systems into an atheist and materialist ideological system. In others, it meant drawing on local history and experience to articulate new revolutionary paradigms. The results of these efforts were strands of communism that, like Maoism, retained the essence of Marxism-Leninism, but were simultaneously embedded in local conditions. In Chapter One, Lin Hongxuan places Islamic identity in the spotlight in his discursive analysis of the interplay of religion and Marxism during the Indonesian nationalist movement. Chapter 10 examines how the Hmong developed a genuine commitment to Marxism via engagement with Marxist and Maoist materials through the Communist Party of Thailand (CPT), with many drawn to radical thought because of hardship and a desire to ameliorate their standards of living. Chapter Three explores U Nu's early engagements with Marxism to frame his brand of socialism around Buddhist moralism, which in turn guided political and economic reforms. Whether it was faith or historical conditions that hastened one's receptivity to radical, or at least anti-imperialist, thought, each case here highlights how local frames of knowledge and awareness of local conditions go hand-in-glove with ideological adaptation and practice.

Third, the application of ideology and the evolution of the political environment birthed a dialectical process of theorisation and application as old theoretical paradigms reached the limits of their practical applicability. In its examination of the Partai Republik Indonesia (PARI, Indonesian Republican Party), Chapter Five explores how Indonesian communist exiles adapted their strategies, broke from the Comintern and played important roles in influencing the Indonesian nationalist movement in the Dutch East Indies. Chapter Nine explores VCP General Secretary Lê Duẩn's concept of *ba dòng thác cách mạng* ('three revolutionary tidal waves') of world revolution, as the Vietnamese communists—now in power and without an occupying enemy to defeat—set their collective sights on 'exporting' this concept to the world. Chapter Seven analyses the theory and practice of *cải tạo* ('reeducation') in South Vietnam and how the now-governing Vietnamese communists drew on foreign and domestic resources, not to mention their past experiences, for the theory and practice of their prisons. These three chapters emphasise the importance of creative adaptation once an ideology—in theory and/or in practice—has either failed or outlived its utility. In each case, the framers needed to uncover new resources from within and/or without to revivify the guiding ideology and legitimate the continuance of the revolutionary course.

Crafting theory, making revolution

This book is divided into two thematic sections that examine left-wing ideologies in theory and praxis across Cambodia, Indonesia, Laos, Malaya, Burma (Myanmar), the Philippines, Thailand and Vietnam. The first section contains chapters that place primacy on intellectual engagements with Marxism-Leninism and Maoism in Southeast Asia. The second section examines those intellectual engagements and indigenisations in praxis, whether in communist party–state contexts or in revolutionary base areas.

Part One: Intellectual engagements with Marxism-Leninism and Maoism

In Chapter One, on the Dutch East Indies (Indonesia), Lin Hongxuan (National University of Singapore) shows how Islamic identity and Marxism coexisted and were sometimes even deeply intertwined in the political imagination of the Indonesian nationalist movement from 1927 to 1941. Through a discursive analysis of socialist and Islamist newspapers, female authors and novels of the first half of the twentieth century, Lin shows that putative Indonesians were engaged in a complex and diffuse project of 'translating' the world to Indonesia, selecting what they saw as the most valuable intellectual fruits of Europe and Asia and adapting them to the Indonesian context. This process was multivalent: it could take the form of learning from the Islamic heartlands, building on an older dynamic of Islamic reformism/modernism emanating from Cairo since the nineteenth century, or it could take the form of applying Marxist critiques of capitalism and imperialism to the Dutch East Indies. It could also take the form of women's rights activism—clearly influenced by the European suffragette and socialist movements but refracted through the lens of Islamic identity and culture. This project of translation and adaptation ultimately undergirded the Indonesian nationalist movement's intellectual dynamism and adaptability, which positioned it well to make connections between Islam and Marxism that we often consider counterintuitive today.

In Chapter Two, Matthew Galway (The Australian National University) explores how future CPK Central Committee member and Minister for Information Hu Nim (aka Bhoās) encountered radical texts, including Maoist materials in French translation. In Cambodia's global 1960s, he engaged with them creatively with a view to implementing major structural changes in Cambodia, against the backdrop of Phnom Penh's radical urban culture. The chapter tracks Nim's involvement in radical student circles in Paris in the 1950s and his eventual membership in the China-curious, progressive Samāgam Mittphāp Khmer–Chin (Khmer–Chinese Friendship Association). Galway argues that Nim was a networked individual responding to crises, for he experienced globalisation and capitalism as ever-present alien hegemonies. But he did not merely graft foreign radical ideological discourse on to the Cambodian situation; rather, as a close textual exegesis of Nim's writings and political career reveal, his reception of radical ideas was at once *dialectical* and *dialogic*. Nim *spoke back* to, and with, these discourses by indigenising them to suit Cambodian realities, and ultimately proposed novel solutions that he framed through serious engagement with radical foreign thought. Thus, contrary to claims that he and other Paris-educated Cambodian leftists were mere figureheads, Nim's reception of and engagement with radical thought as critical interpretative paradigms and radical vocabularies and syntaxes were central to the production of what became *Cambodian Maoism*.

In Chapter Three, Khine Thant Su (University of Wisconsin, Madison) turns attention to U Nu, who partially reconciled Marxism with Buddhism and authored short stories in which he explored the question of whether Marxism was compatible with Buddhist values. One such story, entitled 'I Am a Supporter of Bon Wada', was published through the Nagani Book Club in the late 1930s. Nu made himself into a character in this story, called Ko Nu, debating with a character named Ko Sein whether communism actions were incompatible with Buddhist values. But despite these engagements with Marxism, he held that it could only bring about material liberation from colonial rule and was ultimately incapable of providing spiritual liberation. In the post-independence period when he embarked on creating a socialist welfare economy, U Nu similarly argued that socialism was merely a step towards restoring Burmese society to its original prosperity as symbolised by the Buddhist notion of the *Padaythabin*, the 'Tree of Fulfilment'. As prime minister (1948–1962), U Nu emphasised moral reform as the starting point for political and economic reform. Why did he believe that the reversal of the social problems brought on by colonial rule must begin not with further engagement with Marxism, but with moral reform of society via revival of Buddhist ethics? Su argues that U Nu established an alternative form of modernity in Burma by pairing his political and economic reforms with moral education of the people—a modernity that actively resisted Euro-American cultural hegemony. In examining U Nu's speeches and writings from the 1930s to the 1950s, Su illustrates that U Nu's understanding of what constituted moral action in political and economic matters changed in response to the different political contexts of the colonial and post-independence periods.

Chapter Four, by Ramon Guillermo, Amado Mendoza, Dominic Sy (University of the Philippines, Diliman) and Teo Marasigan (independent activist and critic), presents a study of the Philippine translation, dissemination and multigenerational reception of the *Lao wupian* 老五篇 ('*Five Old Articles*') or *Five Constantly Read Articles* of Mao Zedong. Although less well-known internationally than the *Little Red Book*, these articles were some of Mao's most popular works in China, and were used during the Cultural Revolution as an educational tool for the formation of socialist consciousness. After the reestablishment of the Communist Party of the Philippines in 1968, the *Five Old Articles* went on to play a significant role in the nationwide dissemination of Maoist ideas in the archipelago. Repackaged as a basic text for activists and translated into Tagalog as *Limang Gintong Silahis* ('*Five Golden Rays*'), these essays have become the most durable, memorable and popular of Mao's works in the country. By looking into the translation and interpretation of these texts across 50 years of Philippine activism, this study shows how the *Five Old Articles* were not simply read as guides to the development of a proper socialist consciousness. Rather, they were also transformed into a distinct kind of 'ethical technology' for mass activists within the practical and ideological development of Philippine Maoism, which both broke away from and established continuity with existing moral discourses in the country.

In Chapter Five, the volume's second chapter on Indonesia, Kankan Xie (Peking University) explores the PARI, formed by Tan Malaka, and its clandestine activities outside the Dutch East Indies in the aftermath of the 1926–27 uprisings. Kankan argues that although PARI members played a limited role in shaking the foundations of Dutch colonial rule, their operations outside the colony exerted an important and lasting influence on Indonesian politics. Importantly, as Kankan shows, PARI broke from the Comintern and espoused a nationalistic approach to anticolonial struggle that did not abandon wholesale its ideological commitments. Although communist movements largely went dormant inside the Dutch East Indies because of the colonial government's full-scale suppression, PARI activists adapted accordingly, and even managed to influence the country's nationalist movement through noncommunist networks. Once communism regained its prominence during Indonesia's national revolution of the post–World War II period, however, ideological debates between different leftist groups, which dated back to the PKI's split after 1926, remained central to the power struggles over the legitimacy and leadership of the new communist movement. Kankan's chapter sheds long overdue light on the importance of PARI as the closest reincarnation of the PKI during the interwar years, irrespective of the fact that it never succeeded in establishing a significant presence in Indonesian nationalist politics.

Part Two: Indigenisation in praxis

Chapter Six, by Marc H. Opper (American University), explores the ideological origins of the MCP's strategy of violence against civilians during the early years of the Malayan Emergency (1948–60). Drawing on previously unavailable and overlooked source material, Opper shows that when confronted with the imperative of leading a revolution in a relatively developed capitalist colony, the MCP developed a novel Marxist-Leninist social ontology that held that violent struggle could forge often reluctant civilians into resolute supporters of the party. This ideological development had important implications for the behaviour of the MCP and its prospects during the emergency and ultimately represented an important attempt at the Malayanisation of Marxism-Leninism.

In Chapter Seven, Hoang Minh Vu (Fulbright University Vietnam) examines the theory and practice of 'reeducation' after the Government of the Republic of Vietnam collapsed in 1975. Vu argues that the VCP's reeducation system had Soviet and Chinese elements, but was also shaped by Vietnam's socialist and colonial-era penal institutions. VCP leaders accused roughly 200,000 people of serving the fallen Republic of Vietnam (RVN), and subsequently incarcerated them for their alleged crimes. These prisoners became 'students' in secluded camps in which the VCP subjected them to political reeducation classes and reform through manual labour during sentences that ranged from one week to more than two decades. The VCP's goal was to rehabilitate them in the socialist mould, which could only be done through hard lessons, strenuous labour and a total overturning of their world views. Low rations, poor health care, difficult terrain and the harshness of the work and punishments meant that many died in the process. The VCP ultimately denied graduates certain vocational and educational opportunities in the new socialist society, and many emigrated from the country. Vu's chapter thus sheds light on certain obstacles to applying foreign theories to practice and the complex interplay between radical thought and the negative, often violent legacy left by the long shadow of European colonialism.

Chapter Eight, by Nicholas Zeller (University of Wisconsin, Madison), argues that CCP and communist Pathet Lao thinking on the question of national liberation and its role in socialist revolution was mutually constitutive and informed by the onset of the Lao civil war (1959–75). From the short-lived neutralist coup d'état of Captain Kong Le in August 1960 to the conclusion of the Geneva conference on Lao neutrality in July 1962, both parties developed commitments to armed struggle as the only viable path to national self-determination and the role of a specifically revolutionary nationalism in achieving that goal. The chapter begins by clarifying the deep Marxist roots of socialist internationalism and writing on the national question. It then turns to People's Republic of China (PRC) intelligence reporting on the Kong Le coup and its mutual efforts with the Pathet Lao before and during the Geneva conference to create the right international and domestic political conditions for revolution. This history reveals that Marxist-Leninist ideology, as it applied to CCP–Pathet Lao relations, was not driven by nationalism as though it was some outside force. Rather, nationalism, or 'the national question', was already part of the political theory of international revolution that was given practical life in Laos in the early 1960s.

Chapter Nine, by Khuê Diệu Đỗ (Harvard University), explores the origin and evolution of the concept of the 'three revolutionary tidal waves' in post-unification Vietnam. Advocated by VCP General Secretary Lê Duẩn during the early years of the Vietnam War until his death in 1986, the 'three revolutionary tidal waves' became the cause, direction, legitimacy and ambition of the Vietnamese communists for more than two decades. They believed that the global socialist revolution, the workers' movement in capitalist countries and the national liberation movement in the colonised territories (with Vietnam as its vanguard) composed the three 'tidal waves' of world revolution. Thanks to the force of history, the party asserted, these high tides rose to create the 'collective strength' of the era to attack imperialism on all sides. Its original goal was to seek international support for Hanoi's war efforts; reunification in 1975 significantly boosted the position and, ultimately, arrogance of Vietnam. This culminated in the VCP's decision to 'export' this concept to countries in the Non-Aligned Movement, as leaders stressed the importance of the third 'wave'. International events such as the US–China diplomatic normalisation, Vietnam's invasion and occupation of Democratic Kampuchea in 1979, the 1978–80 Sino-Vietnamese border war and the collapse of the Eastern Bloc ultimately weakened the role of the first 'wave' and highlighted the magnitude of the third wave. Although scholars now consider the 'three revolutionary tidal waves' one of the most prominent legacies of Lê Duẩn, this chapter sheds overdue light on the VCP's designs to export its revolution globally on completing its initial revolution for independence and reunification.

In Chapter 10, Ian G. Baird (University of Wisconsin, Madison) examines the process whereby ethnic Hmong in northern Thailand began studying with the CPT, both in their mountain villages and in secret schools located in northern Laos along the border with China. By the late 1960s, many CPT-aligned Hmong were engaged in armed conflict against the Thai military, although most only joined after their villages were burned. Soon, much of the Hmong population in northern Thailand was living in mountainous CPT base areas, which were effectively territories under the full control of an aspiring *amnat lat* ('Maoist state') within the geographical body of Thailand. Most lived in these expansive base areas until they fell apart in the early 1980s. It is true that the Hmong knew little about Marxism when they first joined the CPT. Most joined in response to harsh discrimination and because of Thai military attacks on their communities. Many also wanted to obtain formal education, and they generally desired equal rights in Thai society. It is incorrect, however, to assume that all the Hmong who joined the CPT had little interest in or knowledge of Marxism. Although no Hmong ever joined the Central Committee of the CPT, by the time the party disintegrated, several Hmong leaders had gained provincial political leadership positions and had become committed Marxists. In this chapter, Baird takes a first look at Hmong Thai engagement with Marxism and Maoism during the CPT period.

Part One

1
'One eye in the chain of the Asian movement': Muslims adapting Marx in the Dutch East Indies, 1927–42

Lin Hongxuan

Contrary to both Indonesian nationalist historiography and popular historical imagination, Marxist analytical tools and frames of reference played an important role in the Indonesian anticolonial struggle. Scholarship on Indonesia continues to evince a strong tendency to typologise anticolonial activism into different *aliran* (lit., 'streams') such as 'nationalist', 'communist' or 'Islamic'. As a way of glossing the broad outlines of political allegiance, these labels are useful, but they obscure as much as they illuminate. Using the concept of distinct streams reinforces the impression that these were largely separate and competing visions of how independent Indonesia ought to be constituted. This is deeply misleading; there is no lack of evidence to suggest these streams overlapped significantly and that activists who identified as 'Islamic' or 'Marxist' often crossed the porous border between organisations.[1] This chapter will show how Marxist ideas were central to the political thought of the most prominent anticolonial activists, many of whom were Muslim. Adapting

---

1   Lin Hongxuan, 'Ummah yet proletariat: Islam and Marxism in the Netherlands East Indies and Indonesia, 1915–59' (PhD diss., University of Washington, Seattle, 2020), 294–306.

Marxist analytical tools to suit Indonesian realities, they creatively synthesised visions of a just and equitable Indonesian future that drew on a wide variety of inspirations.

Where Marxism is given any credit at all by Indonesian nationalist historiography, it is in relation to the Partai Komunis Indonesia (PKI, Indonesian Communist Party). The PKI, in association with the Islamic organisation Sarekat Islam, is highlighted as the locus of resistance to the colonial state in the 1920s, which culminated in a series of unsuccessful uprisings in 1926–27. This fits comfortably into a nationalistic narrative of protonationalist antecedents populating the political landscape as history unfolds teleologically; such a vision leads inexorably towards independence. Other agents and their motives are obscured—subsumed by the impulse to focus on larger-than-life figures like Sukarno or the romance of the agentive *pemuda* (lit., 'youth').[2] In reality, a diverse political landscape with many political actors coexisted in both tension and collaboration with Sukarno's Perserikatan Nasional Indonesia (Indonesian Nationalist Association), later the Partai Nasional Indonesia (PNI, Indonesian National Party), and Marxist ideas informed their anticolonial activism to a significant degree.

The PKI was remarkably successful in the 1920s and the 1950s, which explains the scholarly tendency to focus on it as the nexus of Marxist discourse and practice in Indonesia. However, there were many other political actors who also actively drew on Marxist frames of reference. In the 1950s, the Tan Malaka–inspired Murba Party and Acoma Party brought competing visions of how communism would be achieved in Indonesia to bear against the PKI. Even intellectuals from Masyumi (the main Islamic political party of the 1950s) incorporated aspects of Marx's ideas into their political philosophies.[3] More famously, President Sukarno himself selectively incorporated Marx's ideas into his political vision—expressed as early as 1926 in *Nationalism, Islam and Marxism*. He did so again during the 1950s and 1960s in the political slogan 'Nasakom'—a portmanteau of nationalism, religion and communism ('*nasionalisme*', '*agama*' and '*kommunisme*').

---

2   Benedict R.O.G. Anderson, *Java in a Time of Revolution* (Ithaca, NY: Cornell University Press, 1972), 125–65.
3   Kevin W. Fogg, 'Indonesian Socialism of the 1950s: From Ideology to Rhetoric', *Third World Quarterly* 42(3) (August 2020): 465–82, doi.org/10.1080/01436597.2020.1794805; and Lin, 'Ummah yet proletariat', 327–59.

In the 1930s, important anticolonial organisations such as Mohammad Hatta and Sutan Sjahrir's Pendidikan Nasional Indonesia movement (Indonesian National Education; hereinafter Pendidikan) embraced the relevance of Marxist analytical tools. Even Islamic anticolonial organisations such as Persatuan Muslim Indonesia (Permi, Indonesian Muslim Union) evinced a willingness to engage with socialist ideas. This chapter will show how Marxist ideas were very much at the heart of the anticolonial movement, suffusing the intellectual field in which activists operated and influencing the most prominent anticolonial activists. In their attempts to articulate an Indonesian future *sans* imperial parochial tutelage, these anticolonial activists drew freely from the intellectual heritage of Europe as well as the hard-won experiences of other revolutionary movements, from the Union of Soviet Socialist Republics (USSR) and China to Turkey and the Philippines. As part of this broader synthetic project, many were able to reconcile Marxist ideas with their Islamic identity. This chapter seeks to complement Kankan Xie's Chapter Five on individuals and debates directly associated with the PKI and the Communist International (Comintern) by showcasing a different cultivar of Indonesian Marxism—one whose roots were also indigenous and with an equally strong claim to the allegiance of many Indonesians.

1930s *pergerakan* print culture

The suppression of the PKI after the 1926–27 uprisings signalled a turn towards stricter press and censorship laws, with freedom of assembly for political purposes severely curtailed. In the discursive realm, this took the form of the *persbreidel* ('press-bridling ordinance') of 1931, which empowered the governor-general to prohibit publication of any periodical for an unspecified period, as opposed to extant charges of *persdelict*, which were 'press offences' under the Dutch East Indies (DEI) penal code.[4] These new restrictions curtailed the vitality and capacity of the *pergerakan* (lit., 'movement'), whose members could no longer voice their frustrations in inflammatory words on the printed page or on the stage

---

4   Nobuto Yamamoto, 'The Dynamics of Contentious Politics in the Indies: Inlandsche Journalisten Bond and Persatoean Djoernalis Indonesia', *Keio Communication Review* 36(2014): 5, www.mediacom. keio.ac.jp/wp/wp-content/uploads/2014/04/01YAMAMOTO.pdf.

at mass public rallies, as they had done in the 1920s.[5] The restrictions on political activity resulted in an intensification of effort in vernacular print culture, which flourished during the early 1930s despite the *persbreidel*.[6] This chapter is bookended by the suppression of the 1926–27 uprisings and the Japanese occupation (1942–45), during which political activity of any sort was heavily suppressed and largely driven underground. Though comparatively repressive, this period—which could be glossed as the DEI's long 1930s—produced a surprisingly large and sophisticated corpus of radical print culture.

Print culture constitutes a particularly rich vein of source material because of the plethora of newspapers being published from the 1910s. Many had short print runs due to financial troubles and censorship, but they were legion, and the sheer diversity ensures they remain understudied. One 1971 index lists more than 1,000 Indonesian newspapers published across 55 cities throughout the archipelago, most of which began publication during the colonial period.[7] Moreover, despite limited circulation and low literacy rates, many such newspapers had a surprisingly wide reach, as literate subscribers would often read aloud to friends and family, before passing on the newspaper to another literate person.[8] This prolonged the lives of newspapers, with their contents reverberating through communities weeks after the initial publication, and helped circulate *pergerakan* ideas in a largely illiterate agricultural society.

Despite these obstacles, *pergerakan* activity did not disappear during the 1930s; rather, the energies of anticolonial activists were channelled by the repressive political climate into new realms of activity. In the Pendidikan's case, this entailed the cultivation of a national awakening through education. Print culture constitutes a particularly important corpus of source material in this period because it was one of the principal ways in which the *pergerakan* could continue to express itself despite the omnipresent spectre of *persbreidel*. With the *pergerakan* denied the

---

5   The *pergerakan* comprised a wide range of anticolonial activists of diverse ideological backgrounds, whose political activism ranged from agitating for independence to fostering the 'national awakening' of an Indonesian nation. What united them was their conviction of both the possibility and the necessity of shaping a distinctly Indonesian future free from Dutch control.
6   Nobuto Yamamoto, 'Print power and censorship in colonial Indonesia, 1914–1942' (PhD diss., Cornell University, Ithaca, NY, 2011).
7   G. Raymond Nunn, *Indonesian Newspapers: An International Union List*, Occasional Series 14 (Chinese Materials and Research Aids Service Center Inc., 1971).
8   Rianne Subijanto, 'Enlightenment and the Revolutionary Press in Colonial Indonesia', *International Journal of Communication* 11(2017): 1370–71, doi.org/10.5117/TVGESCH2017.3.SUBI.

platform of broadcasting their ideas at public rallies and propagandising within labour unions, newspapers, educational materials and novels became the repositories and vehicles of anticolonial discourse.

This post-1927 *pergerakan* generation was mindful of the costs of premature revolt. Instead, they channelled their efforts into the creation of study circles (the Pendidikan), social clubs (alumni clubs), student organisations (the Diniyyah student union and scouting organisations like El Hilaal), 'cooperative' political parties that sat on the semi-elected colonial advisory council known as the Volksraad—such as Sarekat Islam's successor, the Partai Sarekat Islam Indonesia (PSII, Islamic Association Party of Indonesia)—and ostensibly apolitical associations (like Permi) that would serve the pedagogic function of preparing Indonesians for eventual independence. Moreover, because the Dutch *ethici*[9] had not yet fully abandoned the civilising mission they had embraced earlier in the century, *pergerakan* print culture remained relatively prolific despite censorship. The newspapers most closely associated with the PKI bore the brunt of censorship under the new press laws restricting publications in vernacular languages, but even identifiably socialist Pendidikan newspapers like *Kedaulatan Ra'jat* ('*The Sovereignty of the People*') continued to publish through most of the 1930s; it ran from 1931 to 1938, though with many gaps between issues.[10]

The strongly pedagogical character of 1930s *pergerakan* activism requires some contextualisation. In *The Rope of God*, James Siegel argued that an Islamic society was understood by the Acehnese to mean a commonwealth of Muslims in free association with one another, rendering them more than the sum of their cultural attachments and local allegiances.[11] The signifier 'Islam' represented the triumph of *akal* ('reason') over *nafsu* ('desire'), and an Islamic society was one capable of competing with the model offered by the Dutch because a society peopled by pious Muslims was one constituted by rational and compassionate actors. Such rational actors—a concept perfectly compatible with being Muslim—were what the *pergerakan* of the

---

9   *Ethici* were the proponents of the Dutch *Ethische Politiek* ('Ethical Policy'), which was introduced in 1901 and aimed to improve material conditions for DEI subjects through investments in education and infrastructure, as opposed to the pre-1901 emphasis on profit extraction.
10   Rudolf Mrázek, *Sjahrir: Politics and Exile in Indonesia*, Studies on Southeast Asia (Ithaca, NY: Southeast Asia Program, Cornell University, 1994), 157. *Daulat Ra'jat* only ran from 1931 to 1934, ending with the 1934 crackdown in which Sjahrir and Hatta were imprisoned. The Pendidikan, however, was not proscribed and continued to exist with limited popular influence and intellectual output.
11   James T. Siegel, *The Rope of God* (Ann Arbor, MI: University of Michigan Press, 2000), 115–27.

1930s sought to cultivate through education. Whether it was urban study clubs that gave rise to the Pendidikan and PNI, or the networks of reformist Islamic schools run by Sumatra Thawalib, Diniyyah, Muhammadiyah and Taman Siswa, these educational endeavours expressly aimed to develop 'Indonesian' subjects. Their purpose was nothing less than the transmutation of colonial subjects with localised political allegiances and affective ties into Indonesian subjects. These individuals would constitute the atomic units of the putative polity of Indonesia—a replacement for the incumbent colonial polity of the Dutch East Indies. Print culture was central to this pedagogical effort, and it is in print culture that its traces are most visible.

The Pendidikan in three periodicals

One organisation whose ideas epitomised the confluence of Islam and socialism was the Pendidikan Nasional Indonesia. It was also known as the PNI-Baru or New PNI—a deliberate allusion to Sukarno's nationalist party, the PNI. The Pendidikan had grown out of similar intelligentsia circles to the PNI in 1927 and was proscribed in 1934.[12] Unlike the PNI's focus on building a mass party and popular mobilisation, the Pendidikan was more cerebral, focusing on cadre training. It also found significant success in organising trade unions, particularly in Surabaya and Semarang. At its peak, in February 1933, the Pendidikan had 32 branches (26 of them on Java) and controlled several trade unions.[13] This section examines three newspapers published by or closely associated with the Pendidikan: *Daulat Ra'jat* ('*Hail the People!*'), *Banteng Ra'jat* ('*The People's Bull*') and *Api Ra'jat* ('*The People's Fire*'). The Pendidikan was founded by Sutan Sjahrir and Mohammad Hatta, two Dutch university–educated ethnic Minangkabau *pergerakan* activists of post-1926 vintage. They had come of age participating in Sukarno's Pemuda Indonesia (Indonesian Youth) organisation in the late 1920s, and had cut their teeth in the Netherlands as part of the left-leaning Perhimpunan Indonesia (Indonesian Association).[14] The Pendidikan was founded in August 1931

---

12   John Ingleson, *Workers, Unions and Politics: Indonesia in the 1920s and 1930s*, Brill's Southeast Asian Library (Leiden: Brill, 2014), 4.
13   Takashi Shiraishi, *The Phantom World of Digul: Policing as Politics in Colonial Indonesia, 1926–1941*, Kyoto CSEAS Series on Asian Studies 23 (Singapore and Kyoto: NUS Press and Kyoto University Press, 2021), 209–13.
14   Klaas Stutje, *Campaigning in Europe for a Free Indonesia: Indonesian Nationalists and the Worldwide Anticolonial Movement, 1917–1931* (Copenhagen: NIAS Press, 2019), 156–61.

as part of a reorganisation of the *golongan merdeka* ('free groups'), which were described by the Dutch colonial police in December 1931 as 'less developed radical elements including some old communists … merely individual clusters not tied in any coherent network'.[15]

These *golongan merdeka* had roots in the study clubs and student societies of the late 1920s—groups that self-consciously cloaked themselves in the legacy of resistance to the colonial state as enacted by the PKI and Sukarno's PNI. Many *golongan merdeka* in Batavia, Surabaya and Bandung had been formed by disgruntled PNI members following Sukarno's imprisonment and the PNI's dissolution in 1931.[16] At the behest of Hatta and Sjahrir, who were still in the Netherlands at the time, these *golongan merdeka* met in August 1931 to federate as a national movement, resulting in the Pendidikan. Naming the organisation 'Indonesian National Education' helped it avoid the status of either a 'party' or an 'association', thereby avoiding the necessity of registration and approval.[17] Its members remained free to affiliate themselves with other organisations and political parties. The choice of name was deliberate in other ways: the Pendidikan's acronym, PNI, was the same as that of Sukarno's recently suppressed nationalist party. This self-conscious positioning of the movement within a tradition of radical resistance to the colonial state was mirrored in popular discourse: the Indonesian press of the 1930s often referred to the Pendidikan as the 'New PNI' to distinguish it from Sukarno's PNI. Continuities in rhetoric and arguments—both of which evinced a strong socialist flavour—were perceptible between the 'old' and the 'new' PNI.[18]

The Pendidikan was deeply conscious of the need to distinguish itself from the other claimant to the mantle of Sukarno's PNI, the 'cooperationist' Partai Indonesia (Partindo, Indonesia Party). The Pendidikan attracted many former PNI members who wanted no part in Partindo's focus on piecemeal economic reform and Volksraad participation.[19] After some

---

15 Mrázek, *Sjahrir*, 77.
16 John Ingleson, *Road to Exile: The Indonesian Nationalist Movement, 1927–1934*, ASAA Southeast Asia Publications Series 1 (Singapore: Heinemann Educational Books, 1979), 145.
17 Mrázek, *Sjahrir*, 79.
18 J.D. Legge, 'Daulat Ra'jat and the Ideas of the Pendidikan Nasional Indonesia', *Indonesia* 32(1981): 161.
19 Ingleson, *Road to Exile*, 154. The Volksraad was the closest thing the DEI population had to parliamentary representation, other than the lone Indonesian in the Dutch lower house of parliament, Rustam Effendi (who served from 1933 to 1946). It was a semi-elected advisory council to the governor-general, and the electorate was severely restricted to male DEI residents with substantial wealth. The European planter class and the native aristocracy were, unsurprisingly, well represented in and dominated the Volksraad.

prevarication, it was Partindo that Sukarno ultimately joined after his release from prison in December 1931. While celebrating Sukarno's release, Pendidikan publications were conscientious in highlighting Partindo's allegedly *ningrat* ('aristocratic') character, arguing that its leaders came from the elite stratum of Javanese society.[20] By contrast, the Pendidikan attracted members whose families had been sufficiently wealthy to enable them to access a degree of education but who did not have particularly good prospects within the Dutch civil service. Commensurately, the Pendidikan struggled to attract the same level of support as Partindo under Sukarno's charismatic leadership, especially on Java, which was the political centre of gravity. By August 1933, Partindo could claim some 20,000 registered members on Java and Permi some 10,000 in Sumatra, while the Pendidikan could claim approximately 1,000 members spread across 12 branches on Java and 250 in West Sumatra.[21] Besides the urban intelligentsia, the Pendidikan also tried to focus its outreach on Java on the agrarian labouring classes. It was most active in Cirebon and Indramayu—areas outside the Javanese heartland whose economies were dominated by large sugar plantations.[22]

Sjahrir and Hatta returned to Indonesia in January 1932, and Sjahrir promptly reorganised the *golongan merdeka* of Batavia to form a Pendidikan branch. He installed himself as the chairman of the editorial board of *Daulat Ra'jat*, the Pendidikan's theory-centric newspaper.[23] By the early 1930s, the Pendidikan was publishing several newspapers in the key cities of Batavia, Bandung, Surakarta (Solo) and Yogyakarta.[24] At a public meeting in Batavia in March 1932, Sjahrir told his audience the Pendidikan 'wants to educate, and thus to map the path which leads to freedom', emphasising the Pendidikan was not a political party and its aim was to 'bring clarity', not to 'make agitation'.[25] This reserved stance reflected the climate of surveillance and censorship that followed the 1926 uprisings and the investment of the ultraconservative Bonifacius Cornelis de Jonge as governor-general of the DEI in 1931. However, it also reflected a reorientation of strategic emphasis in the *pergerakan*: under

---

20 Mrázek, *Sjahrir*, 91.
21 ibid., 89; *Kedaulatan Ra'jat*, [*The Sovereignty of the People*], 10 October 1932; Taufik Abdullah, *Schools and Politics: The Kaum Muda Movement in West Sumatra (1927–1933)* (Ithaca, NY: Cornell Modern Indonesia Project, 1971), 185.
22 Mrázek, *Sjahrir*, 88.
23 ibid., 84.
24 ibid., 96.
25 ibid., 84–85.

the charismatic but rather bookish Hatta and Sjahrir, the Pendidikan was to pursue a course of developing the base—the grassroots that would nurture a new *pergerakan* generation. This generation would find more effective ways of resisting Dutch rule, as outright revolt and appeals for Soviet aid had failed.[26] This emphasis on education and cultivation was evident in the newspapers associated with the Pendidikan: their writing was often cerebral and pedagogical, including expositions of Marx's ideas, rendered in plain language.[27] At the same time, Pendidikan newspapers also embraced an identifiably Islamic identity, which was evident in the rhetoric and metaphors they employed.

There are several reasons I describe the Pendidikan as a socialist rather than a communist organisation, although the Dutch security apparatus tended to think of it as the latter.[28] The Pendidikan was not eager to embrace the label 'communist', presumably because its leaders were wary of being associated with the recently proscribed PKI. Hatta himself had even described communism as the enemy of the nationalists on at least one occasion, although George Kahin readily recognised Hatta's facility with Marxist theory.[29] However, Sjahrir had published articles in Amsterdam's socialist newspaper *De Nieuwe Weg* ('*The New Way*') in the 1930s advocating the eventual formation of a mass revolutionary party.[30] This might seem contradictory, but it is unsurprising once one abandons the assumption that all Marxists were necessarily communists or beholden to Moscow. The word 'communism' was occasionally used in articles published by Pendidikan newspapers, but only in the context of explaining communism or gleaning insights from the teachings of Marx. This was evident in articles entitled 'Komunistis' ('Communism') and 'Peladjaran Karl Marx' ('The Teachings of Karl Marx'). These articles explained the differences between communism, socialism, Bolshevism

---

26   Legge, 'Daulat Ra'jat and the Ideas of the Pendidikan Nasional Indonesia', 159. Legge has an excellent anecdote about Hatta's 'school-masterly performance'.
27   Soewardi, 'Peladjaran Karl Marx [The Teachings of Karl Marx]', *Banteng Ra'jat*, [*The People's Bull*], 25 April 1932. *Das Kapital* was translated and serialised in *Daulat Ra'jat* from the 20 April 1933 issue.
28   Mrázek, *Sjahrir*, 91.
29   M. Hatta, 'Partai Indonesia and I', *Bintang Timoer*, [*Star of the East*], 3 August 1931; George McTurnan Kahin, *Nationalism and Revolution in Indonesia* (Ithaca, NY: Cornell Modern Indonesia Project, 1952), 281. As Ingleson points out, this was likely the result of bitterness engendered by the expulsion of Sjahrir and Hatta from the Perhimpunan Indonesia in November 1931 because of their willingness to cooperate with noncommunist nationalists in defiance of Comintern dogma. Marxism was central to Sjahrir and Hatta's politics, but so was an openness to other beliefs, motivations and ideologies. This set the stage for productive conciliations with Islam. See Ingleson, *Road to Exile*, 148.
30   Ingleson, *Road to Exile*, 147.

and social democracy.³¹ Both articles were clear that Bolshevism was not synonymous with communism and its defining features were a willingness to use violence in seizing power, as well as the establishment of a party dictatorship—a position the Pendidikan clearly did not endorse.³²

Despite its obvious attraction to Marx's ideas—even focusing its activities on former PKI strongholds—the Pendidikan was careful to avoid identifying itself as a communist organisation.³³ It remained a pedagogical rather than agitative organisation. The ideas Pendidikan members sought to disseminate were part of the same corpus of scholarship and ideology that animated communists; however, they did not see themselves as a branch of a global communist network and did not seek to organise a vanguard of the proletariat as the Bolsheviks had done. Neither did they cultivate cells within the military as the PKI had done before 1926, choosing instead the European study club model of reading and discussion of texts, including Marxist ones.³⁴ Influenced by Marx as well as Austrian socialists like Otto Bauer and Max Adler, the Pendidikan most often described itself as 'proletarian' in its newspapers, which suggests it is best understood as a Marx-influenced socialist organisation.³⁵

'Komunistis', published in the 10 November 1932 issue of *Daulat Ra'jat*, showed remarkable sophistication in parsing the differences between the Bolshevik articulation of communism and the social-democratic interpretation of communism. It identified '*kaoem sosialis kiri*' (the 'socialists of the left') as distinct from the '*kaoem komoenis opisieel*' ('official communists') on the basis the latter were committed to violent revolution and taking instructions from Moscow.³⁶ It managed to strike a relatively impartial tone, explaining the relative positions of these different articulations of communism, and even attempted to explain why the social democrats, socialists and communists would mutually recriminate one another as reactionary. It characterised socialists as advocating the interests of the working class in opposition to their

---

31 Soewardi, 'The Teachings of Karl Marx'; Anonymous, 'Komunistis [Communism]', *Daulat Ra'jat*, [*Hail the People!*], 10 November 1932.
32 Soewardi, 'The Teachings of Karl Marx'; and Anonymous, 'Communism'.
33 Pradipto Niwandhono, 'The making of modern Indonesian intellectuals: The Indonesian Socialist Party (PSI) and democratic socialist ideas, 1930s to mid-1970s' (PhD diss., University of Sydney, 2021), 45–46.
34 Ruth T. McVey, *The Rise of Indonesian Communism* (Ithaca, NY: Cornell University Press, 1965), 29; Pradipto Niwandhono, 'The making of modern Indonesian intellectuals', 45.
35 Anonymous, 'Communism'; Mrázek, *Sjahrir*, 93.
36 Anonymous, 'Communism'.

employers, but argued that socialists stopped short of toppling the existing government, although they theoretically agreed with the dictatorship of the proletariat and the use of violence if necessary.[37] Although the article did not explicitly endorse either side, the Pendidikan's organisational structure and activities clearly positioned it within its own definition of socialism.

That said, 'Komunistis' also argued there were ultimately few ideological differences between socialists and communists because both were based on the teachings of Marx; they differed only in their practical application.[38] The fact *Daulat Ra'jat* saw the need to publish this article suggests the Pendidikan saw itself as connected to, but still distinct from, communist resistance to the colonial state—a prudent position to take given the climate of surveillance and repression. The article's description of socialism was clearly aligned with the relatively unconfrontational stance adopted by the Pendidikan. It positioned socialism as drawing on the same corpus of ideas (*Das Kapital* was specifically invoked), sharing the same aspirations (an eventual dictatorship of the proletariat) and role models (the USSR) and using the same language—the importance of seizing *alat penghasilan* ('the means of production') is mentioned—as the communists.[39] After all, this was an organisation with close ties to Tan Malaka's PARI and alumni of Sumatra Thawalib, a modernist Islamic school whose students and teachers were influenced by Marxism and that produced many avowed Islamic communists.[40] More succinctly, this was an organisation that sought to clarify and disseminate Marx-inspired critiques of capitalism and imperialism, without taking instructions from Moscow. That suffices for the label 'Marxist', but not communist in the sense of Comintern affiliation. It would be fair to say the Pendidikan sympathised with communism and never denied its shared lineage with Soviet Bolshevism or indigenous Indonesian articulations of communism. Ultimately, however, it represented a different approach to achieving similar goals.

---

37   ibid.
38   ibid.
39   ibid.
40   Shiraishi, *The Phantom World of Digul*, 141–42. Tan Malaka's Partai Republik Indonesia (PARI, Indonesian Republican Party) was a clandestine communist organisation formed after the 1927 suppression of the PKI, and was primarily active from 1927 to 1932. It embraced communism but rejected subordination to Moscow's imperatives.

Interestingly, the Pendidikan was as identifiably Islamic as it was socialist. Key Pendidikan leaders such as Hatta moved in a distinctly Muslim social milieu, and Rudolf Mrázek's description of him is revealing:

> Hatta clearly moved in the same orbit as the students from Cairo and Mecca, and as the Permi activists. Hatta himself had made plans to stop by Mecca to perform the *haj* on his way back to Indonesia from Holland upon the completion of his *doctorandus* degree: although this plan did not work out, it was widely publicized in the Indonesian press, and lent his return a 'specifically Islamic accent'.[41]

Moreover, Pendidikan leaders in Sumatra, such as Darwis Thaib, were sometimes drawn from the ranks of Permi itself.[42] Others were students and alumni of modernist Islamic schools and maintained their membership in Islamic organisations such as the Persatoean Moerid Diniyah School (Union of Diniyyah School Students) even after they became Pendidikan members. The extent of the Pendidikan's immersion in an Islamic milieu was evident in an article Darwis Thaib published in *Daulat Ra'jat*, in which he wrote:

> A member of the Pendidikan Nasional Indonesia who dies while fighting for national freedom, is he judged by Allah as a *kafir* ['infidel']? To be a nationalist such as the Pendidikan wants one to be, does this make a Pendidikan member a *moertad* ['apostate'] to Islam?[43]

The Pendidikan's hybrid Islamic and socialist character is corroborated by Hatta's memoirs. Hatta described the Pendidikan curriculum as aiming to provide cadres with a robust understanding of 'the broad outlines of Indonesian history, the history of the *pergerakan* itself, the distinction between cooperation and non-cooperation, the growth of Imperialism, the creeping reach of Capitalism, colonialism, and the sovereignty of the people'.[44] According to Hatta, cadres' core readings were articles from *Daulat Ra'jat*, Sukarno's *Menggugat Indonesia* ('*Indonesia Accuses*',

---

41 Mrázek, *Sjahrir*, 97.
42 Anonymous, 'Berita PBPMI [PBPMI News]', *Medan Ra'jat* [*The People's Field*], 10 September 1932. Darwis Thaib was one of the three members of Permi's leadership training committee, which also included Permi's foremost leader, Iljas Jacoub. Moreover, Darwis Thaib regularly contributed articles to Permi's newspaper, *Medan Ra'jat* ('*The People's Field*').
43 Darwis Thaib, 'Ke ... Persamaan! Socialis, Kommunis, dan Kedaulatan Ra'jat [To ... Equality! Socialism, Communism, and People's Sovereignty]', *Daulat Ra'jat*, 10 January 1933.
44 Mohammad Hatta, *Untuk Negeriku* 2 [*For My Country*] (Jakarta: Kompas, 2011), 30–31.

a collection of speeches he gave at his trial in 1930), as well as Hatta's own *Indonesia Vrij* ('*Free Indonesia*') and *Tujuan dan Politik Pergerakan Nasional di Indonesia* ('*Purpose and Politics of the Indonesian National Movement*').[45] Although Sjahrir and Hatta often criticised Partindo and resisted merging with it, they had enough in common with Sukarno's synthetic tendencies to justify assigning his work as part of the Pendidikan corpus. Among their commonalities were a deep commitment to critiquing colonial capitalism and an attachment to Islam. Hatta's own commitment to Islam was also evident in his autobiography: he mentioned an invitation from the PSII activist (and later Masyumi Party chairman) Soekiman Wirjosandjojo to edit a PSII-linked newspaper, *Utusan Indonesia* ('*Indonesian Envoy*').[46] Hatta was too busy with *Daulat Ra'jat* to take up the offer, but he was explicit that *Utusan Indonesia* mirrored the positions of the Pendidikan, and that the PSII and Pendidikan had very good relations.[47]

The confluence of Islam and socialism was perceptible in a variety of Pendidikan newspaper articles, but especially in the Pendidikan's main theoretical organ, *Daulat Ra'jat*. *Daulat Ra'jat* embodied an articulation of socialism influenced by the Dutch Marxist Sociaal-Democratische Arbeiderspartij (Social Democratic Workers' Party). It was the theoretical companion publication to the Pendidikan's main press organ, *Kedaulatan Ra'jat* ('*The Sovereignty of the People*'), and ran from 1931 to 1934.[48] It was more explicitly pedagogical than *Kedaulatan Ra'jat* in the sense that it focused on explaining socialist ideas rather than reporting on contemporary events. Highly didactic in tone, it rarely ran articles on current events, and the promotional section was dominated by advertisements for textbooks, evening classes and correspondence courses.[49] In his study of *Daulat Ra'jat*, J.D. Legge admitted its radical and nationalist aspects but characterised it as secular.[50] Contrary to Legge's analysis, Islamic imagery and language were imbricated in *Daulat Ra'jat*'s articles alongside explications of Marxist theory.

---

45 ibid., 30.
46 ibid., 31.
47 ibid., 31.
48 Mrázek, *Sjahrir*, 87.
49 ibid., 85.
50 Legge, 'Daulat Ra'jat and the Ideas of the Pendidikan Nasional Indonesia', 156.

On 10 November 1932, *Daulat Ra'jat* ran the article 'Komunistis'[51]—an attempt to situate communism within an Indonesian context. It argued that both the people whom the colonial state identified as communists and those who called themselves communists were just violent men using violent means to achieve their goals for Indonesia. Their primary goal was a society characterised by *sama rata, sama rasa* ('same level, same feeling')—a distinctly Indonesian articulation of social egalitarianism previously evoked by both Sukarno and Tan Malaka.[52] The article went on to argue that the agentive *orang berkerdja* ('workingmen') were often willing to work with *reaksioner* ('reactionaries') like the insurgents waging holy war against the Dutch—as had happened in Banten in 1926—out of sheer necessity.[53] While dismissive of this confluence, the article nevertheless admitted a basis (anticolonial resistance) on which self-declared communists and Muslims had cooperated in the past.

Despite the article's dismissive attitude towards the allegedly inchoate communism of the 1920s, it was published alongside a cartoon that drew on both socialist and Islamic imagery. It depicted a man in a business suit, with a halo labelled '*oewang*' ('money') around his head and wings on his back, smiling and smoking a cigar while carrying a book labelled 'BIBLE' in both arms. The cartoon was mockingly captioned: 'The angel of capitalism spreads civility!' *Daulat Ra'jat* invoked religious imagery that drew on a perceived link between Christianity and exploitative colonialism, depicting the smirking and winged Christian capitalist—presumably, soaring above the labouring masses. In this cartoon, colonial economic exploitation was deliberately conflated with the Christian identity of the Dutch planter, conjuring up the image of a capitalist angel inhabiting the lofty realm of the sky, abstracted from the quotidian suffering endured by wage labourers in a commodity-oriented plantation economy. In this image, the smirking angel blithely preaches the virtues of both capitalism and Christianity while remaining indifferent to the suffering that makes possible the lofty status of the *colon*.

This cartoon caricatures and rejects the status quo of colonial society by identifying capitalism and Christianity as the enemies of the Indonesian people, who are both unhappy participants in an unequal colonial economic relationship and Muslims living under the rule of a nominally

---

51 Anonymous, 'Communism'.
52 ibid.
53 ibid.

Christian polity.[54] One of the central anxieties driving *kaum muda* (lit., 'young faction', referring to modernist Muslims) through the nineteenth and twentieth centuries was discomfort with the success of Christian missionaries in the outer islands, as well as the undeniable political dominance of nations associated with 'Christendom'. For many *kaum muda* organisations, their emphasis on modernist education was aimed specifically at making Islam a competitive alternative to Christianity, thus reducing the effectiveness of proselytisation. Anxieties about the capitalist–Christian axis would thus have resonated particularly with Indies Muslims, who felt Islam was under siege both at home and abroad. This provided for an important but understudied strain of *pergerakan* ideas: the articulation of socialist ideas informed by, and articulated within, an Islamic social context. Significant numbers of Indies Muslims, including Pendidikan members, envisioned an egalitarian future for Indonesia, and critiqued the colonial state in a hybrid idiom that mixed Islamic and socialist discourses.

This admixture was evident in other articles as well. The author of 'Indonesia Dalam Lingkoengan-Keadaan Doenia' ('Indonesia in the Current World') mocked the Dutch tendency to blame social unrest in the DEI on foreign instigation from Moscow.[55] The author sardonically raised the spectre of the *momok Bolsjewik* ('Bolshevik devil') and pointed out the longstanding claim of the *chotbah pemerintah* (lit., 'government sermon') that social unrest in the DEI was due to foreign instigation. The use of '*chotbah*' here is interesting, because the author was drawing on a specifically Islamic lexicon. The *chotbah*, an indigenised transliteration of *khutbah*, refers to the customary sermon preached by the imam of a mosque to his congregation during the communal Friday prayers. The *khutbah* has a particular political resonance because the imam would customarily invoke a blessing at the end of the sermon for the community's political leadership, and it was implied that the political leader thus named was owed the political (or at least symbolic) allegiance

---

54   While the Netherlands has had no establishment church since 1796, Indonesian popular perceptions of the Netherlands as a Christian polity remained dominant.
55   Anonymous, 'Indonesia Dalam Lingkoengan-Keadaaan Doenia [Indonesia in the Current World]', *Daulat Ra'jat*, 10 August 1932.

of the congregation. Various imams leading the Friday prayers had included mentions of the Dutch Queen Wilhelmina on various occasions, at the behest of the colonial authorities.[56]

The use of '*chotbah permerintah*' indicated a grudging acknowledgement of the reality of Dutch power even in religious matters, but it also utilised the *khutbah* as a critical metaphor against the Dutch colonial state's carefully cultivated image of *rust en orde* ('tranquillity and order'). The Dutch colonial state positioned itself as a secular political authority that respected Islam; in using the phrase *chotbah pemerintah*, *Daulat Ra'jat* subverted that formulation by insinuating the Dutch consolidated political power through manipulating religion. 'Propaganda' was certainly part of the Pendidikan's lexicon, but *khutbah* seems to have been the preferred term for rebutting Dutch claims that communist agitation was driven by Bolshevik agents. The insinuation was this: much like the hollow *khutbah* preached by compliant imams in the pay of the colonial state, the *chotbah pemerintah* on Bolshevik subversion was an empty claim that was meant to anesthetise Indonesians. This vocabulary might have been adopted simply because it resonated with *Daulat Ra'jat*'s intended audience—that is, readers would have been more familiar with the concept of *khutbah* than the concept of propaganda. Whether or not that was the case, it is undeniable the term *khutbah* would have had special cultural resonance, evoking a transgressive image of Dutch interference in Islam. It therefore constituted a useful rhetorical strategy to undermine the claims of the Dutch colonial state.

The article proceeded to reference the famed Orientalist and former Dutch adviser for native affairs Christiaan Snouck Hurgronje, citing his rebuttal of the idea that social unrest in the DEI was the result of foreign agitation.[57] Interestingly, Snouck was quoted at length in the original Dutch, alongside an Indonesian translation. This provides a sense of the mixed audience *Daulat Ra'jat* attracted: a spectrum with Indonesians who had access to Dutch-language education at one end and those who had access to vernacular education but not to Dutch institutions like the European Primary School (*Europeesche Lagere School*, ELS) and More Advanced Primary Education (*Meer Uitgebreid Lager Onderwijs*, MULO), at the other. Indonesian was still evolving as a language and not everyone

---

56   Nico J.G. Kaptein, *Islam, Colonialism and the Modern Age in the Netherlands East Indies* (Leiden: Brill, 2014), 145.
57   Anonymous, 'Indonesia in the Current World'.

spoke it fluently; indeed, many of Sjahrir and Hatta's well-educated peers were likely to be most comfortable with Dutch. The article's author endorsed Snouck's argument that the pre-1927 *pergerakan* was a mix of aristocrats, holy warriors (Muslims waging *jihad*) and protocommunists, which the author collectively labelled *extremisten* ('extremists') and *kaum yang terkiri* ('partisans of the left'), rather than Soviet puppets.[58] The author also endorsed Snouck's view that these groups were not mutually exclusive, but were motivated by a shared goal: resistance to Dutch colonial authority. The use of Snouck's characterisation of the uprising's participants indicated the Pendidikan embraced its eclectic *pergerakan* lineage, including both Islamic and communist resistance to colonial rule.

The author went on to argue that the social conditions of the 1930s had given rise to *pergerakan* groups that were even more inclusive than those of the previous generation. He argued they possessed an improved level of sophistication and consciousness that made them wary of '*Jihad atau langkah Jayabaya dan Heru Cakra*' ('paths of Holy War chosen by Jayabaya and Heru Cakra'—Javanese kings of antiquity').[59] Therefore, the *pergerakan* of the 1930s could be differentiated from the social movements that gave rise to the Cilegon peasants' revolt of 1888 and the PKI uprisings of 1926–27.[60]

Here, the author was suggesting that the Pendidikan, while rejecting the inchoate rebellion of the past, located itself within the same tradition of resistance to Dutch rule. Moreover, by endorsing Snouck's assessment of the uprising's participants, the author indicated the Pendidikan was comfortable with a genealogy that included distinctly Islamic roots. At the same time, it signalled its openness to the intellectual fruits of Europe, including Orientalist scholarship. The article went on to proudly state that the *pergerakan kemerdekaan Indonesia* ('Indonesian independence movement') was—happily—taking on radical undertones:

> The Indonesian independence movement has evinced signs towards radicalism, such that the Indonesian people easily embrace the radical principles of communism—we remember the extensive influence of the PKI and the Sarekat Rakyat in the

---

58   ibid.
59   ibid. The implication here is the *pergerakan* understood violent *jihad* and the recurring pattern of mystically inspired rebellion to be ineffective means of resisting Dutch colonial authority.
60   Anonymous, 'Indonesia in the Current World'. For more on the Cilegon peasant rebellion, see Sartono Kartodirdjo, *Protest Movements in Rural Java: A Study of Agrarian Unrest in the Nineteenth and Early Twentieth Centuries* (Singapore: Oxford University Press, 1973).

past—which lives on in the courageous opposition to the effects of the colonialism [of the present generation of *pergerakan*], and which desires to steer the destiny of the Indonesian people.[61]

Revolutionary and socialist in political philosophy, the Pendidikan comfortably wore the mantle of anticolonial resistance handed down from the 'aristocrats, Holy Warriors and proto-communists'—an eclectic band glossed as 'partisans of the left'.[62] Rather than reject preceding attempts to undermine colonial rule as misguided or primitive, the Pendidikan embraced the complex pedigree of the *pergerakan*, conscious that it mixed Islam and communism.

This embrace of the pre-1927 *pergerakan* was visible in the Islamic overtones of the arguments and language deployed in other *Daulat Ra'jat* articles. In an article from 10 January 1933, Darwis Thaib presented a particularly nuanced argument: anyone who died while serving the nationalist cause was a *kafir* ('infidel') because he idolised the motherland. However, if a partisan died fighting for freedom while keeping himself *bertauchid* ('believing in the oneness of God'), he would reach Heaven.[63] This perspective embraced the Islamic language of martyrdom and monotheism (in the sense of avoiding idolatry), which suggests its appeal to the newspaper's target audience. At the same time, it framed religious martyrdom within secular goals such as independence for the DEI. This was perfectly in keeping with Sjahrir's insistence the Pendidikan needed to speak the language of the masses, though not necessarily court mass membership.[64]

Other Pendidikan newspapers struck a similar tone. *Banteng Ra'jat* ('*The People's Bull*') began publication in Yogyakarta in 1932 and sometimes mirrored *Daulat Ra'jat*'s didacticism while remaining a daily broadsheet. An article entitled 'Pergerakan Ra'jat' ('The People's Movement') was typical. It argued the Indonesian *pergerakan* was part of a global 'people's movement'—an oeuvre that included the Dutch Republic's struggle against Spain during the Eighty Years' War, Turkey's resurgence under Mustafa Kemal Atatürk, Sun Yat-sen's Chinese republic, Egypt's struggles

---

61 Anonymous, 'Indonesia in the Current World'. The Sarekat Rakyat (SR), or People's Associations, were the grassroots appendages of the PKI and were closely affiliated with the Sekolah Rakyat (People's Schools), which aimed to mobilise the population by cultivating nationalist awareness through education. The PKI and the SR were both suppressed after the 1926–27 uprisings.
62 ibid.
63 Darwis Thaib, 'To … Equality!'.
64 Ingleson, *Road to Exile*, 150.

for substantive independence under Arabi Pasha (Ahmad 'Urabi) and Zaghlul Pasha (Saad Zaghloul), as well as the Indian independence movement under Mahatma Gandhi.[65] Interestingly, Turkey and Egypt were singled out for having effectively resisted foreign imperialism.

These examples are telling, because the Pendidikan was positioning the struggle for Indonesian independence within a broader movement of anti-imperialism from the sixteenth century. This was an attempt to highlight the *pergerakan*'s place in a broader trajectory of historical development that resonated with Marx's dialectical materialism. This article implied the *pergerakan* was like any of these successful nationalist movements, and thus deserving of the consideration given to such celebrated causes. These movements deserved one's regard because they were part of the inexorable march of history—the principle of national self-determination overrunning the last bastions of empire. It was an attempt to situate the *pergerakan* historically, to show it possessed coherence and meaning, that it could not be dismissed as inchoate natives running amok or a communist conspiracy masterminded from afar—as the colonial security apparatus and the Dutch planter community were wont to claim. Like the Indian movement for *swaraj* ('self-rule'), it had yet to achieve success, but success was but an eventuality—a sentiment derived from the Hegelian and Marxist conceptions of history. As this article succinctly put it:

> In order for us to understand the emergence of the *pergerakan*, we must first look to Asia, to the other movements of this age; in the grand scheme of things, we are but one [of many] *pergerakan* … the Indonesian *pergerakan* is but one eye ['link'] in the chain of the Asian *pergerakan*.[66]

This internationalist outlook coexisted alongside a highly particularistic conception of the Pendidikan's genesis. The same article posited the Indonesian *pergerakan* originated in 1908 with the formation of Budi Utomo (Noble Endeavour), a politically quiescent organisation for Javanese aristocrats aimed at promoting Javanese culture in the face of perceived encroachment by Dutch-language education. It connected Budi Utomo to a long list of much more radical organisations, such as the Eurasian-dominated Indische Partij (Indies Party), which openly agitated

---

65   Anonymous, 'Pergerakan Ra'jat [People's Movement]', *Banteng Ra'jat*, 25 November 1932.
66   ibid.

for Indonesian independence under elite Eurasian leadership, Sarekat Islam, the PKI and, finally, the PNI.[67] The article waxed lyrical about the importance of Sarekat Islam in particular:

> [A]lthough freedom of association at the time [1910s] had been restricted by regulation III R.R., especially the existence of political groups, nevertheless uncountable numbers of Indonesian people, the *zachtste volk van de aarde* ['the gentlest people on the Earth'], were able to quash the regulation with the accumulated strength of spirit in the Sarekat Islam movement, even though it had only arisen in 1912.[68]

The *pergerakan* of the 1930s, including the Pendidikan, was positioned as a continuation of the tradition of resistance to the colonial state spearheaded by the overtly religious Sarekat Islam in the 1910s and 1920s. As with other anti-imperialist movements across the world, the *pergerakan* was portrayed as arising spontaneously in righteous opposition to imperial rule. However, rather than dismiss earlier iterations of resistance as primitive, this article embraced Pendidikan's predecessors, choosing to celebrate a specifically Islamic antecedent alongside communist and nationalist movements of various political persuasions. The Pendidikan's identity and political vision were sufficiently ambitious that it saw itself as simultaneously part of the hallowed tradition of Islamic resistance to infidel rule, as well as part of a wave of anti-imperialist solidarity sweeping the globe. These Pendidikan newspapers propounded Marx-inspired solutions to the injustices of colonial rule, but they also articulated their arguments against empire within the idioms of both Islam and international anticolonial solidarity.

The combination of an Islamic world view with socialist ideas, methods of mobilisation and the language of revolution was also evident in *Api Ra'jat* ('*The People's Fire*'), published in Solo (Surakarta) from 1932 to 1933. *Api Ra'jat* was closely associated with the Pendidikan, but in tone and language, it differed greatly from the theory-centric *Daulat Ra'jat*, which was edited by Sjahrir himself and published in Batavia.[69] The location

---

67 ibid. Sarekat Islam was a movement founded in 1912 to advance the economic interests of Muslim textile traders, which quickly evolved into the first Islamic political party of the DEI and attracted (from 1917 to 1923) many radicals who would go on to become prominent PKI leaders after Sarekat Islam split into noncommunist and procommunist factions in 1923. See McVey, *The Rise of Indonesian Communism*, 1–47.
68 Anonymous, 'People's Movement'.
69 Mrázek, *Sjahrir*, 96.

of its publication is significant, and goes some way to explaining the differences in tone and language. Solo lay in the *voorstenlanden*, the princely states where two of the four extant Javanese royal courts still held nominal sway (under the oversight of Dutch advisers). Before 1927, the city had also been a known stronghold of Islamic communists such as Haji Misbach.[70] Unlike the Dutch-educated Sjahrir and Hatta, self-declared Islamic communists like Misbach and Haji Datuk Batuah did not come from the upper-middle-class background that nurtured so many *pergerakan* leaders. Nor did they come from the proletarian milieu of the Semarang trade unions, as had the prominent PKI leaders Semaun and Darsono. Instead, they were educated in Islamic institutions and drew their support from both pious Muslims and the labourers who worked the sugar plantations of the Javanese interior.[71] Despite his lack of union connections or personal ties to the PKI leadership, Haji Misbach was effectively an autonomous leader and labour organiser in the Solo region. The PKI could do little but accept his de facto authority as representative of the Solo PKI committee, though it did not always agree with his often-abrasive approach to anticolonial politics.[72]

This milieu of strident Islamic communism enabled repeated and successful mobilisations against perceived injustices on the sugar estates and gave rise to radical newspapers in Solo that tended to be more fiercely critical of the Dutch colonial state than their more cosmopolitan counterparts in Batavia. They were also more self-consciously Islamic in their posture. *Api Ra'jat* was published in low Javanese rather than the nationalist *lingua franca* of Bahasa Indonesia, which had long since become the favoured language of *pergerakan* publications. Moreover, *Api Ra'jat* possessed a markedly informal tone, reminiscent of spoken rhetoric, which stood in clear contrast to the formal prose of other Pendidikan publications like *Daulat Ra'jat*. Examples of this include the use of non-standard spelling for dramatic effect: '*federasinya nanti hanya bisa direpotkan perkara kontribusiiiiiii saja*! [the codification of regulations can only be disrupted by (financial) contributions!]'[73]

---

70 Syamsul Bakri, *Gerakan Komunisme Islam Surakarta 1914–1942* [*Surakarta's Islamic Communist Movement 1914–1942*] (Yogyakarta: LKiS Pelangi Askara, 2015).
71 Takashi Shiraishi, *An Age in Motion: Popular Radicalism in Java, 1912–1926* (Ithaca, NY: Cornell University Press, 1990), 112.
72 ibid.
73 Anonymous, 'Merobohkan Peraturan Pemerintah tentang Sekolah Buas [Tearing Down the Government Regulations on the Wild Schools]', *Api Ra'jat*, 1 October 1932.

Api Ra'jat was also notable for its lack of advertisements. Even radical *pergerakan* publications from 1920s Solo, such as Misbach's *Medan Moeslimin*, could count on a few regular advertisers such as sympathetic restaurants and hotels, scant as these were. The Congres Journalisten Indonesia (Congress of Indonesian Journalists) highlighted the importance of advertising for the financial stability of *pergerakan* publications at its August 1931 conference, but *Api Ra'jat* seemed uninterested in, or incapable of, tapping this source of revenue.[74] *Api Ra'jat*'s intended audience likely had very limited disposable incomes, as it carried no advertisements at all. Its combination of informal language (low Javanese) and lack of advertising suggests it catered to a mass audience that had received a basic vernacular education and who underwrote publication costs through subscriptions. This was a recipe for financial precarity, which explains its short print run. It is likely that *Api Ra'jat*'s intended audience were urban wage labourers, sharecroppers, plantation labourers, agricultural tenants and even smallholders, collectively known as *marhaen*.[75] *Marhaen* as a conceptual category had been popularised by Sukarno, but the term was widely used by a range of Marxist movements, including Tan Malaka's followers and the Pendidikan.[76] The term *marhaen* was regularly used by *Api Ra'jat* itself when addressing its readers, and this underscores the paper's position as a direct descendent of the *bacaan liar* ('wild literature') publications that dominated the *pergerakan* publishing ecosystem before the 1926 uprisings.[77] *Bacaan liar* were similarly subscription-funded and short-lived, and tended to revel in the same kind of incendiary and colloquial language as *Api Ra'jat*.

In an article entitled 'Merobohkan Peraturan Pemerintah tentang Sekolah Buas' ('Tearing Down the Government Regulations on the Wild Schools'), *Api Ra'jat*'s simultaneously Islamic and socialist orientations were clearly discernible. The article was a strident, emotive defence of the *sekolah buas* or *sekolah liar* ('wild schools')—schools that were unlicensed and unsupported by the Dutch colonial state, and which the Dutch sought to rein in by imposing regulations on the hiring of teachers and

---

74   Yamamoto, 'The Dynamics of Contentious Politics in the Indies', 14.
75   *Marhaen* also included shopkeepers, petty traders and cottage industry workers, among other professions, as well as the indigent poor like sharecroppers and seasonal labourers, incorporating social elements whom Marx and Engels would have classed as the *lumpenproletariat* or *mittelstand*.
76   Sukarno, *Marhaen and Proletarian*, Claire Holt, trans., Translation Series (Ithaca, NY: Modern Indonesia Project, Cornell University, 1960).
77   Hilmar Farid and Razif, '*Batjaan Liar* in the Dutch East Indies: A Colonial Antipode', *Postcolonial Studies* 11(3) (2008): 277–92, doi.org/10.1080/13688790802226694.

the structure of the curriculum.[78] The article lambasted the Dutch for denigrating these wild schools as *sekolah hutan* ('jungle schools'), accusing the government of disrespectfully implying that such schools were good only for producing *orang hutan* ('jungle folk'), like the *orang mirip-mirip* (a common pejorative for aboriginal Austronesian peoples like Papuans, who were at the bottom of the racialised colonial hierarchy of civilisational status).[79] Instead, it blamed the supposedly inadequate state of these schools on the government's withholding of its support:

Original	Translation
Membayar gurunya … tidak!	[Does the government] pay teachers? No!
Ikut medirikan … tidak!	Does it collaborate in founding schools? No!
Menyewakan rumahnya … tidak!	Does it lease lands for schools? No!
Meminjamkan bukunya … tidak!	Does it loan books to schools? No!
Tetapi tiba-tiba hendak ikut-ikut keliling dan memeriksa.	But the government suddenly wishes to hover on the margins and check schools [euphemism for surveillance].[80]

This excerpt provides a sense of the exhortative and rebellious tone of *Api Ra'jat*, as well as the centrality of education to its political agenda, just like the Pendidikan. The socialist overtones were undeniable: '[T]he Indonesian people who possessed conviction [of the *pergerakan* cause] would "storm the gate of freedom", which was impossible to do merely by opposing regulations on jungle schools.'[81] This was followed by a plan for popular mobilisation: 'the people need to educate themselves' by reading newspapers published by other *pergerakan* organisations such as Budi Utomo, Perserikatan Buruh Indonesia (Indonesian Workers' League), the Perikatan Perkoempoelan Isteri Indonesia (League of Indonesian Women)

---

78 Abdullah, *Schools and Politics*, 111–22. This ordinance provoked almost unanimous *pergerakan* resistance throughout 1932 and 1933, spearheaded by Ki Hadjar Dewantara of the Taman Siswa schools, with thousands of anti-ordinance rallies held. Many Sumatran *pergerakan* institutions like the Sumatra Thawalib and Diniyyah schools were deeply opposed to the ordinance and agitated robustly against it, organising rallies and publishing numerous critiques.
79 Anonymous, 'Tearing Down the Government Regulations on the Wild Schools'.
80 ibid.
81 ibid.

and Istri Insaf (Aware Women).[82] In a plan reminiscent of socialist and anarchist strategies of resistance, readers were exhorted to form committees to coordinate antiregulation agitation wherever there were wild schools, calling on these committees to 'discipline' school inspectors so they never returned. Readers were asked to prepare themselves for unemployment or to become freelancers or contract labourers in service of the wild schools, such that the schools might grow from strength to strength and increase in number. Finally, readers were asked to be prepared to go to jail for their actions and convictions.[83]

This militant call to organised defiance of the implementation of Dutch state policy was mirrored by the article's positioning of itself within a long tradition of resistance to Dutch rule:

> A 100 [sic] years ago, the Indonesian people were aggravated, but it was only [the Javanese prince] Diponegoro who suffered the punishment. In the era of the PKI and SR [People's Associations], Indonesia was aggravated again, but it was the PKI and SR that were punished. In the era of the PNI, Indonesia was aggravated yet again, but it was only Soekarno who suffered punishment. On 1 October 1932, the Indonesian people are in upheaval again, but they are spineless. They are in upheaval because they are buffeted by regulations such as those imposed on the jungle schools.[84]

The article couched its opposition to the wild school ordinance as part of a sustained, century-long effort to resist encroaching Dutch authority. It drew on the legacy of the PKI's resistance to the Dutch colonial state in the same breath in which it laid claim to descent from Diponegoro, the Indonesian example *sans pareil* of a Muslim prince waging a righteous but doomed *perang sabil* ('holy war') against the infidel.[85] Immediately after connecting its arguments to a history of oppression and (failed) resistance, including a communist uprising, it went on to lament: '*Ya Allah, Allah, kok berkepanjangan ceritanya?* [Oh God, Oh God, why do you prolong this tale?]' Here, we see the imbrication of socialist methods of

---

82 ibid.
83 ibid.
84 ibid. Diponegoro was a Javanese prince who led a successful long-running insurgency against the expansion of Dutch rule from 1825 to 1830, known as the Java War.
85 Diponegoro himself invoked *jihad* against the Dutch, though he also drew on Javanese mystical precepts to support his claim to legitimacy.

mobilisation, the celebration of a legacy of communist militancy and the proclamation of a perceptibly Islamic identity—all reflected in the exhortative rhetoric of this article.

Such critiques of the colonial state did not emerge from strictly doctrinaire positions, such as the Islamic rejection of infidel rule or the Marxist condemnation of imperialism. Rather, they were part of a *pergerakan* tradition of resistance to the colonial state that had existed since the 1910s and was both intellectually and spiritually eclectic. This milieu was accommodating of plurality, and the confluence of Islamic identity and Marxist ideas was but one of many novel ideological combinations. Marxism was valued for the analytical tools it provided to critique the colonial state; Islam was valued as an integral part of Indies Muslims' identity. Both were relevant to the *pergerakan* and could be invoked without recourse to formal Islamic jurisprudence (*fiqh*) or to Comintern doctrine. The *pergerakan*'s genius lay in its creative, if sometimes overly optimistic, adaptations of foreign ideas to suit DEI conditions. As seen in *Api Ra'jat*, this strand of *pergerakan* discourse remained wedded to an Islamic world view but drew on socialist strategies of resistance to combat colonial policy. Other Pendidikan newspapers made no secret of their willingness to adapt Marx's ideas to the DEI wherever they were deemed relevant. This supple intellectual dynamism characterised much *pergerakan* political thinking of the 1930s, and the confluence of Islam and Marxism would be evident after independence was proclaimed (in 1945) as well.

The Persatuan Muslim Indonesia (Permi)

As a counterweight to the relatively elite Pendidikan, it is helpful to consider the discursive tenor of avowedly Islamic *pergerakan* organisations. The Pendidikan was not an anomaly. Rather, it emerged from an intellectual milieu in which creative adaptation was widely accepted. This environment facilitated the adaptation of foreign ideas to suit Indonesian purposes, and Islamic activists were full participants in this process as well. Examining the most prominent Islamic *pergerakan* organisations of the 1930s, it quickly becomes obvious that socialism had significant appeal and the adaptation of Marxist ideas was commonplace. Of all the major Muslim modernist movements of the 1930s, none was more open to Marxist ideas than Permi. Permi was founded in 1930 by former students and faculty of the Sumatra Thawalib schools. They had organised their own union, the Persatuan Sumatera Thawalib, in 1928, after the arrest and flight of both Islamic and Marxist radicals in 1926–27. The Sumatra Thawalib Union reorganised itself as Permi in 1930, during its third annual congress.[86] As a direct descendent of the Sumatra Thawalib, Permi inherited its ideological mantle, including its divergent impulses. As with the Sumatra Thawalib student body, not all members of Permi were sympathetic to communism, but it would be safe to say they were drawn towards a vision of Islam that combatively arraigned itself against the impositions of the extractive colonial state, and that aggressively embraced a policy of noncooperation with a view to eventual independence.

The congruence between the Persatuan Sumatera Thawalib and Permi was evident in the location of Permi's first headquarters: it was founded in Padang Panjang, the home of the original and most radical of the five Sumatra Thawalib schools, at which the Islamic communist Haji Datuk Batuah had taught. Permi members themselves openly admitted, in speeches like the one given by Haji Abdul Majid at the second Permi conference in September 1932, that Permi was a direct continuation of the Sumatra Thawalib student movement.[87] By 1930, Permi had grown into one of the more prominent *pergerakan* organisations, with branches in Tapanuli, East Sumatra, Aceh in the far north-west and Bengkulu in South Sumatra. It was prolific in publishing anticolonial newspapers and pamphlets, running schools, founding scouting organisations and holding public rallies.[88] At its peak in December 1932, Permi claimed more than 7,700 members, 3,000 of whom were women.[89] Unlike the PSII, it avoided electoral politics (that is, putting up candidates for election to the Volksraad), but neither did it claim to be apolitical as Muhammadiyah and Nahdlatul Ulama tried to be. Instead, its activism found expression in autodidactic education and organising cooperatives outside the realm of formal politics.

---

86   Audrey R. Kahin, *Rebellion to Integration: West Sumatra and the Indonesian Polity* (Amsterdam: Amsterdam University Press, 1999), 53.
87   Haji Abdoel Majid, 'Ringkasan Pidato Pemboekaan Konperensi PMI Ke 2 [2nd PMI Conference Opening Speech Summary]', *Medan Ra'jat*, 10 September 1932.
88   Ingleson, *Road to Exile*, 230.
89   ibid.

Permi was effectively neutered by the colonial security apparatus in December 1932, when executive board member Rasuna Said was arrested, sparking a series of arrests of core Permi leaders like Rasimah Ismail, Muchtar Lutfi, Iljas Jacoub and Djalaluddin Thaib throughout 1933. Lutfi, Jacoub and Thaib were key Sumatra Thawalib figures, having taught at various Sumatra Thawalib schools and published newspapers like *Medan Ra'jat* ('*The People's Field*') throughout the 1920s and early 1930s. After being put on trial, many were subjected to house arrest or incarceration, while others were exiled to Boven Digoel. This notorious penal colony housed numerous PKI members exiled after the 1926–27 uprisings, including many Islamic communists with Sumatra Thawalib connections. While Permi continued to exist until 1937 under the leadership of Muhammad Sjafei, it had ceased to be a meaningful force in *pergerakan* activism by 1934.[90]

At the national level of *pergerakan* interparty politics, Permi was open to limited cooperation with Sukarno's Partindo. Permi leaders travelled frequently to Java to meet with Sukarno, and even participated in Partindo rallies, ultimately signing a document establishing that each party would refrain from competing with the other in their respective strongholds.[91] This was typical for the 1930s: the aforementioned Soekiman's splinter faction of the PSII, the Partai Islam Indonesia (Indonesian Islamic Party), looked set to sign a memorandum of cooperation with the Pendidikan in August 1933, before the arrest and exile of Sjahrir and Hatta put paid to those plans.[92] Soekiman and Hatta were personal friends, both deeply pious and had similar political leanings, and this may have facilitated the two organisations working together. In both cases, the Pendidikan's clearly Marxist inspiration and Partindo's blatant adaptation of Marxist analytical categories (*Marhaenisme*) did not constitute a serious barrier to cooperation. That said, there were certainly those in both parties who opposed working with nationalists who did not prioritise Islam as the fundamental basis for an independent Indonesia.

Permi's newspaper, *Medan Ra'jat*, began in 1931 under Iljas Jacoub's editorship and was published three times a month in Padang. It was a distinctly regional paper, circulating mainly in West Sumatran towns

---

90   Rémy Madinier, *Islam and Politics in Indonesia: The Masyumi Party between Democracy and Integralism*, Jeremy Desmond, trans. (Singapore: NUS Press, 2015), 49.
91   Ingleson, *Road to Exile*, 197.
92   ibid.

like Payakumbuh, Padang Panjang, Kerinci, Padang, Manindjau and Bukittingi. It was remarkably strident in its explicit support for an independent Indonesia, to such an extent it is entirely unsurprising it attracted colonial suppression in late 1932. Tellingly, it often published short articles tracking Hatta's movements on his return from Europe and was clearly comfortable with his Marxist sympathies. By that point, Hatta's sympathies were well publicised in *Kedaulatan Ra'jat* and were also evident in his involvement with the Perhimpunan Indonesia and the Comintern in organising the League Against Imperialism.[93] *Medan Ra'jat* also regularly expressed sympathy for and solidarity with known communists such as Sardjono, Alimin and Musso of the PKI, as well as Rustam Effendi of the Communist Party of the Netherlands.[94] It did not limit itself to rhetoric, and took concrete steps like soliciting donations to pay the legal fees for *pergerakan* activists in trouble with the law. Beneficiaries included Sukarno, Abdul Manaf (aka Achmad Soebardjo), M. Yamin, Muchtar Lutfi, Iljas Jacoub, Amir Sjarifoeddin and Ki Sarmidi Mangunsarkoro, most of whom were known for their Marxist sympathies.[95]

As Permi's main press organ, *Medan Ra'jat* was explicit in its twin critiques of capitalism and imperialism, which clearly drew inspiration from Lenin's *Imperialism: The Highest Stage of Capitalism* (1919) and Karl Kautsky's *Imperialism and the War* (1914). An article by Loetan Gani argued that imperialism was a *kolot* ('hackneyed') system, while nationalism was 'modern' and strongly implied to be more rational.[96] While this was a simplistic and teleological approach to history, the modern/*kolot* dichotomy mirrors the bifurcation embraced by modernist Muslims, and also maps directly on to *pergerakan* assumptions about Islam being the restrained and *akal* ('rational') alternative to the *nafsu* ('rapaciousness') of imperialism and capitalism. Loetan Gani argued that '*nafsoe Imperialisme*' was driven by a quest for profits. He acknowledged imperialism's *kepandaian* ('dynamism') but condemned it as acquisitive and covetous. He accused imperialism of continually seeking 'more territory to conquer,

---

93 Stutje, *Campaigning in Europe for a Free Indonesia*, 94–133.
94 Anonymous, 'Berita Dari Belanda [News from Holland]', *Medan Ra'jat*, 10 September 1932. This article made a point of praising Rustam Effendi for rebutting the Dutch attorney-general's derogatory comments about the DEI.
95 Anonymous, 'Indonesia Berdjoang [Indonesia Fighting]!', *Medan Ra'jat*, 1 November 1932. Among this list, only Muchtar Lutfi and Iljas Jacoub—both key Permi leaders—could conceivably be said to be non-Marxist.
96 Loetan Gani, 'Perdjoangan Imperialisme dan Nationalisme [Struggle for Imperialism and Nationalism]', *Medan Ra'jat*, 10 September 1932.

aided by yet more machines and factories, which in turn incentivize the acquisition of more territory and business opportunities'.⁹⁷ Loetan Gani also argued that imperialism incentivised war, citing the examples of World War I and the recent Japanese invasion of China.

Tellingly, Loetan Gani's article embraced the rhetoric of internationalist anti-imperial solidarity; it discussed and praised anti-imperial movements and their leaders in Egypt (Saad Zaghloul), Iraq (Sultan Pasha al-Atrash), Turkey (Atatürk), Bolivia (José de San Martín and Simón Bolívar) and the Philippines (José Rizal and Manuel L. Quezon) in significant detail.⁹⁸ Other articles even praised Turkey's 1932 decision to join the League of Nations while maintaining good diplomatic relations with the USSR by signing a treaty of mutual recognition and friendship, striking a clearly sympathetic tone towards the USSR.⁹⁹ Evidently, Permi's points of reference, or interlocutors, were not merely European Marxists but also fellow anticolonial movements in the Islamic world and in South-East Asia.

Permi's critiques of colonialism and capitalism were not only theoretically engaged with Marxism, they also proposed concrete solutions that evinced a strong awareness of socialist praxis in Europe and America. One article by M. Dang Jogja argued that because capitalism and imperialism went hand-in-hand, Indonesia had much to learn from Gandhi's *Swadeshi* ('self-sufficiency') movement. It explained how *kaoem kapitalisten* ('capitalists') extracted profits from Indonesia not merely by exploiting its *grondstoffen* ('natural resources') cheaply, but also through creating a captive market in which processed goods could be sold without competition, while simultaneously raising revenue through export duties.¹⁰⁰ Another article in *Medan Ra'jat* cited Surah al-Qasas 76 of the Koran to support its argument that God required Muslims to look not only to the afterlife but also to this life, exhorting them to not forget the welfare of one's fellow man in this world. In that vein, it went on to proudly proclaim that Permi had set up a *dewan peroeashaan* ('business council') to support Indonesian businesses, which it explicitly distinguished from *peroesahaan kapitalis* ('capitalist businesses'), because the Indonesian businesses it supported

---

97 ibid.
98 ibid.
99 Anonymous, 'Turkie dan Volkenbond (LON) [Turkey and League of Nations]', *Medan Ra'jat*, 10 September 1932. The treaty in question was likely to be the Soviet–Turkish non-aggression pact originally signed on 17 December 1925, and subsequently prolonged twice.
100 M. Dang Jogja, 'Pergerakan Swadeshi [Swadeshi Movement]', *Medan Ra'jat*, 20 September 1932.

operated as cooperatives, the profits of which were distributed among the cooperative's members.[101] Unsurprisingly, capitalist businesses were explicitly associated with *nafsu Imperialisme* multiple times.[102] The article concluded that 'true *suci* [lit., 'holy'] nationalism' opposed capitalism; Indonesian business endeavours needed to be organised in a *cooperatief* way, such that they would not give birth to capitalist enterprises.[103] Such articles evinced a sophisticated awareness that colonial capitalism was not simply a matter of colonial exploitation, but also a fundamentally inequitable, paradigmatic economic system.

Other articles published in *Medan Ra'jat* revealed a discernible willingness to learn from the experience of European and American socialists, while proposing concrete solutions adapted to DEI needs. Aziz Thaib argued for the creation of peasant cooperatives, which would allow farmers to stop relying on flour merchants who 'suck the blood of the people and who demand more profit than is appropriate'.[104] Drawing on the example of nineteenth-century English cooperatives, he argued that peasant cooperatives could be set up with as little as £325 in communal capital.[105] These cooperatives would purportedly ease the problem of limited access to credit, because farmers rarely had the connections or collateral to obtain loans from urban banks and relied instead on rural moneylenders who charged exorbitant interest rates. Without providing a specific example, Dang Jogja claimed capitalists in the contemporary United States were grumbling because they had 'met their match' in farmers' cooperatives and 'could no longer do as they pleased'.[106] An editorial note appended to the article even made a point of stating that cooperatives with 'capitalist characteristics' were in opposition to 'our *pergerakan*' and called on cooperatives to guard against the creeping infiltration of capitalist practices by reminding them of their Islamic moral obligations.[107]

---

101 Dt. Penghoeloe [pseudonym], 'Sifat Toedjoean dan Asas PMI [The Nature of PMI's Goals and Principles]', *Medan Ra'jat*, 20 September 1932.
102 ibid.
103 ibid.
104 Aziz Thaib, 'Menoendjoe Cooperatie Ra'jat Indonesia [Towards People's Cooperatives]', *Medan Ra'jat*, 1 November 1932.
105 ibid.
106 ibid. It seems likely the author was referring to the Socialist Party of America (formed in 1920) and its predecessors, with their strong links to trade unions and rural cooperatives. They achieved significant local and regional electoral success in the first quarter of the twentieth century under the leadership of Eugene V. Debs.
107 Thaib, 'Menoendjoe Cooperatie Ra'jat Indonesia'.

Similarly, a series of articles in late 1932, Dang Jogja wrote glowingly of Marx and his various interpreters, even going so far as to quote Joseph Stalin (in English) and translate the quotation into Bahasa Indonesia.[108] Intriguingly, the various strains of Marxism were described by Dang Jogja as *tarekat* (Sufi brotherhoods built around saintly and scholarly lineages, pl. *turuq*)—an excellent example of how Marxism was indigenised or made relevant within an Islamic vernacular. The analogy was a useful one: different *turuq* made different claims to spiritual power based on the mythos of each *tarekat*'s founding *sheikh*, but all remained siblings in the family of Islam—the global community of Muslims known as the *ummah*. Finally, the article also discussed the USSR and the various German social-democratic parties of the interwar period, exhorting the *pergerakan* to learn from their experiences.[109] These articles in *Medan Ra'jat* were visibly 'translating' Marxism to Indonesia—whether literally translating Stalin's words or more indirectly making sense of Marxist movements in other parts of the world—and were doing so in a way that relied on Islamic vocabulary and ethical justifications.

Permi's relationship with socialism emerged most explicitly in a slim pamphlet titled *Tabligh Oemoem*, which was clearly meant to be circulated among members and potential recruits. *Tabligh Oemoem* translates roughly as 'the public propagation of faith'. The term '*tabligh*' has specific proselytising connotations, which often take the form of a public or private meeting at which attendees are exhorted to Islamic orthopraxy.[110] Consistent with its title, this pamphlet functioned less as a didactic text than as a devotional one; it was presented as though the reader was attending a *tabligh* meeting, opening with the full suite of Islamic greetings and the confession of faith, and ending with a recitation of Surah al-Fatihah, the opening surah of the Koran.[111] *Tabligh Oemoem* reads almost like a Christian order of service, or a Sufi *wird*, as though a social and pedagogical experience had been crystallised in print form so one might carry that experience in one's pocket and be edified repeatedly by it. The pamphlet is organised in three parts: the first section is historical, dealing with the basics of the Islamic faith and its early history.

---

108 Dang Jogja, 'Nasionalisme dan Islamisme [Nationalism and Islam]', *Medan Ra'jat*, 1 December 1932.
109 ibid.
110 'Tabligh', in *The Oxford Dictionary of Islam*, John L. Esposito, ed. (Oxford, UK: Oxford University Press, 2003), available from: www.oxfordislamicstudies.com/article/opr/t125/e2295.
111 Permi, *Tabligh Oemoem* (Medan: Badan Perwakilan Dewan Penjiaran dan Pertahanan Islam Permi, 1930), 1, 19.

The second is titled 'Islam dengan Kemadjoean' ('Islam with Progress'), and is dominated by justifications from *fiqh* ('jurisprudence') and *tafsir* ('Koranic exegesis'), which explains why Islam is not inimical to progress or change. The third and final section, however, is the most telling of all, titled 'Socialisme Dalam Islam' ('Socialism in Islam').[112]

This section relates an eponymously titled speech given on this topic, presumably at a *tabligh* meeting, by M. Ali Tholib Siregar. Siregar's argument was straightforward and closely mirrored Oemar Said Tjokroaminoto's in his 1924 work, *Islam and Socialism*. Siregar claimed Islam was, in fact, socialism. For him, the principles of socialism were inherent in Islam, not in the various European formulations of socialism: '*socialisme sedjati*' ('true socialism') was '*socialisme tjara Islam, boekan tjara Barat*' ('Islamic socialism, not the socialism of the West').[113] Specifically, he identified the principles promoted by socialism as '*perikemanoesiaan adalah menjadi satoe persatoean*' ('the unity of mankind') and '*wajiblah kita mentjapai keselamatan bagi mereka semoeanja*' ('the obligation to ensure each other's welfare'), among others.[114] Siregar argued these principles were congruent with Islamic goals such as '*permerintah jang se-adil adilnja*' ('the establishment of a just government'), and '*orang mendjalankan agama Islam haroeslah dengan roekoen dan damai*' ('the implementation of Islam necessarily means promoting harmony and peace').[115] A number of *hadith* and Koranic verses were quoted to support these assertions, although specific references were not provided.

This was not merely a knee-jerk reaction against all things Western by asserting the moral superiority of Muslim societies over European decadence. It was a call to action consistent with the ethos of *tabligh*; Siregar readily admitted 'our social realities have strayed far from what the Qur'an teaches, for both men and women'.[116] Permi as an organisation, even in its most accessible literature, was openly engaging with socialism. It did so despite the waves of arrests and exiles that followed the 1926–27 uprisings, after which Marxist discourse became increasingly taboo. This was not the explicit Islamic communism of Nathar Zainuddin and Haji Datuk Batuah, but it was one among many outgrowths of Sarekat Islam's entanglement with Marxism in the 1920s, and it would continue in

---

112 ibid., 16–18.
113 ibid., 18.
114 ibid., 17.
115 ibid., 18–19.
116 ibid., 17.

various permutations beyond the 1930s.[117] Permi's newspapers expressed solidarity with anti-imperial movements in the Middle East and Asia as well as a variety of Marxist movements in Europe and America, seeking to learn from their collective experiences. At the same time, a thoroughly Islamic ethical framework pervaded Permi's discourse, and sometimes Marxist ideas were rendered in an Islamic idiom. It is probable Permi members, much like the Pendidikan, recognised Marxism was not a comprehensive new faith; rather, it provided valuable insight in terms of understanding the world and its injustices. Rather than being a conduit for Moscow's imperatives, Marxist analysis afforded them analytical clarity. Permi members incorporated these insights into their own struggle, on their own terms, and this struggle was framed in nationalistic and Islamic terms as much as it was in the terms of class struggle.

Conclusion

As Opper and Galway note in the Introduction to this volume, the anticolonial activists examined here, like Sjahrir and Hatta, did not simply learn to parrot the prestigious lexicon of European philosophy and Marxist theory. They were adept agents of adaptation, empowered by an education that exposed them to (in Mannheim's words) 'opposing tendencies in social realities'—notably, languages, syntaxes and critical interpretative paradigms, which allowed them 'to attach themselves to classes to which they originally did not belong … to choose their affiliation' as they saw fit. The affiliations they chose sometimes easily correlated to the 'proletariat' (as with Sukarno's identification with *marhaen* or Tan Malaka's identification with *murba*), but often they took the ideas of Marx, Engels, Lenin, Kautsky and many others besides, incorporating them into expansive visions for Indonesian justice, equity and prosperity. Some of these chosen identities were exclusionary (with no room for Chinese and Eurasians) while others were more aspirational than realistic (making Indonesians of the population of the entire archipelago, even unwilling participants such as the Timorese and Papuans). Nevertheless, theirs was a genuine effort to not only adapt and translate the knowledge of imperial

---

117 For Sarekat Islam's symbiotic but tempestuous relationship with communism, see McVey, *The Rise of Indonesian Communism*, 76–124.

and revolutionary metropoles, but also synthesise the experiences of other Asian anticolonial movements—a process John Sidel has identified occurring across Indonesia, Vietnam and the Philippines.[118]

The Pendidikan and Permi activists whose writings have been examined here were part of a rich 'synthetic' Indonesian intellectual tradition that continued to flourish beyond independence. This openness to synthesis—learning from the best the world had to offer—suffused the Indonesian political milieu during the revolutionary (1945–49) and parliamentary democracy (1950–59) periods. Soedjatmoko, a core member of Sjahrir's postwar political party, the Partai Sosialis Indonesia (Socialist Party of Indonesia), was unequivocal in celebrating Indonesia's hybridity and adaptiveness:

> The development of Western European culture was the result of its contact with Islamic civilization during the crusades. The Renaissance emerged from Northern Italy's reacquaintance with the culture of classical Greece. The glory of Islamic civilization was itself the result of a meeting between Hellenistic culture, and after some time, the Turkic and Mongol cultures that had been integrated into Indian culture. In Indonesia, the development of Hindic culture and its later meeting with Islamic culture is evidence of the great benefits and progress that accrue from the meeting of one culture with another. The capacity for a culture to digest and adapt [*mencerna dan menyesuaikan*] elements of another culture in accordance with its own needs is evidence of the vitality of a nation's culture.[119]

This *Weltanschauung* animated the *pergerakan* of the 1930s as well, moving them to use Marx's conceptual lenses selectively. Some of the most prominent activists incorporated these ideas within a broader field of anticolonial discourse that also included Islam. This freewheeling openness to adapting Marx, European socialism or even the revolutionary experiences of Sun Yat-sen, Atatürk and José Rizal was evident in all the newspapers examined here. This was a predecessor of the cosmopolitan world view Soedjatmoko embraced in the 1950s.

---

118 John T. Sidel, *Republicanism, Communism, Islam: Cosmopolitan Origins of Revolution in Southeast Asia* (Ithaca, NY: Cornell University Press, 2021).
119 Soedjatmoko, *Kebudayaan Sosialis* [*Socialist Culture*], Muhidin M. Dahlan, ed. (Jakarta: Melibas, 2001), 65.

Indonesia's rich tradition of intellectual hybridity, and the centrality of Marxist analytical tools within it, is now almost forgotten. The 1965–66 anticommunist massacres that resulted in the needless deaths of hundreds of thousands have burdened Indonesians with collective guilt, which has in turn necessitated the blanket of silence covering the past. Any meaningful discussion of the role of Marxist theory in informing the Indonesian anticolonial movement—especially outside the PKI—has been smothered by the need to demonise communism, which justifies the egregious bloodshed of 1965–66. The idea that some of the most revered anticolonial politicians and organisations—like Hatta, Sjahrir, the Pendidikan or Permi—could have imbibed and adapted Marxist theory would be considered sacrilegious by most Indonesians today. In highlighting the boldly adaptive and synthetic impulses of the Indonesian anticolonial movement, this chapter has attempted to restore Marxism to its rightful place in Indonesian history: as an essential ingredient in Indonesia's political maturation, even when shorn of its association with the PKI.

2

'The most dissolute and dishonest' Khmer to aid China: Hu Nim and indigenising the Maoist ideological system, 1955–77

Matthew Galway

Khyal disa pūbea taeṇtae jhneaḥ khyal disa paccim jeanicc
[The East wind always triumphs over the West wind]

Ekreāj mceās'kār ṇeāp' kap' khloeneṇ
[Be masters of your own destiny! The dead must bury themselves!][1]

— Two Communist Party of Kampuchea slogans

The ideology of the Communist Party of Kampuchea (CPK) has eluded scholarly description over the years. Members of the party centre have claimed that the CPK was 'not following any model, either Chinese or Vietnamese … the Cambodian situation does not fit any existing model

---

1   Henri Locard, *Pol Pot's Little Red Book: The Sayings of Angkar* (Chiang Mai, Thailand: Silkworm Books, 2004), 69, 81.

and thus requires original policy'.² Contrary to some academic appraisals of the party as antimodern, bereft of cultural and intellectual sophistication and communist in name only, its paramount leader, General Secretary Pol Pot, revealed for the first time in a September 1977 speech that the CPK was a Marxist-Leninist party. 'In light of [our] experiences,' he proclaimed:

> [T]he committee worked out a draft proposal for the Party's political line, based upon Marxism-Leninism and the principles of independence, sovereignty, and self-reliance, [to] be masters of our own destiny, *applying Marxism-Leninism to the concrete realities of Kampuchea and Kampuchean society.*³

Because of the CPK's vocabulary, syntax and praxis in Democratic Kampuchea (DK), scholars have been quick to trace convenient, often facile, threads between it and Maoist China. Supporters of this description identify similarities in rhetoric, strategy and socialist transformation, but fail to explain how and why Maoism, which they never define, arose as a fit for the CPK leadership, and largely sidestep relevant Khmer or Chinese-language sources.⁴ If it is truly unquestionable that the CPK founders were Maoist, or if the depths of their understanding and particular interpretations of the Marxist-Leninist canon are lacking, the issue is less about whether the CPK was Maoist than about *how* and *why* it was

---

2   *Far Eastern Economic Review*, [Hong Kong], 30 September 1977, 26; '*Der Spiegl* Interview with Ieng Sary', May 1977, reprinted in *News from Kampuchea* 1(3) (August 1977): 1–3; Roel A. Burglar, *The Eyes of the Pineapples: Revolutionary Intellectuals and Terror in Democratic Kampuchea* (Saarbrücken, Germany: Verlag Breitenbach, 1990), 59; and Michael Vickery, *Cambodia: 1975–1982* (Boston, MA: South End Press, 1984), 288–89.
3   Pol Pot, 'Discours prononcé par le camarade Pol Pot, secrétaire du comité du parti communiste du Kampuchéa au meeting commémorant le 17è anniversaire de la fondation du parti communiste du Kampuchéa et a l'occasion de la proclamation solennelle de l'existence officielle du parti communiste de Kampuchéa [Speech by comrade Pol Pot, Secretary of the Central Committee of the Communist Party of Kampuchea at a meeting commemorating the seventeenth anniversary of the founding of the Communist Party of Kampuchea and on the occasion of the solemn proclamation of the official existence of the Communist Party of Kampuchea]', Phnom Penh, 27 September 1977, 16. Emphasis added. On such an appraisal, see Stephen J. Morris, *Why Vietnam Invaded Cambodia: Political Culture and the Causes of War* (Stanford, CA: Stanford University Press, 1999), 17.
4   See V. Simonov, *Crimes of the Maoists and their Rout* (Moscow: Novosti Press Agency Publishing House, 1979); Wilfred Burchett, *The China–Cambodia–Vietnam Triangle* (Chicago, IL: Vanguard Press, 1981); Kenneth M. Quinn, 'Origins and development of radical Cambodian communism' (PhD diss., University of Maryland, College Park, MD, 1982), 180–215; Daniel Snyder, 'Life After Death in the Kampuchean Hell', *Executive Intelligence Review* (September 1981): 19–31; and Karl D. Jackson, 'Intellectual Origins of the Khmer Rouge', in *Cambodia 1975–1978: Rendezvous with Death*, Karl D. Jackson, ed. (Princeton, NJ: Princeton University Press, 1989), 241–50. A most intriguing description is that the CPK was 'hyper-Maoist'. Morris, *Why Vietnam Invaded Cambodia*, 13, 17, 39, 229.

Maoist. One ought to begin, then, with the would-be Maoists themselves and trace their passages through spaces intellectual and geographic, transforming and transformed.

I challenge arguments that claim Paris-educated CPK leaders were 'non-entities', mere 'figureheads' and merely 'exploited by the Communists to give their movement a misleading public face'.[5] This chapter provides a genealogy of how future CPK Central Committee member and DK Minister for Information and Propaganda Hu Nim (aka Bhoās, 1932–1977) encountered, engaged with and indigenised Maoism—an 'ideological system' that is at once a 'critical interpretive paradigm, ideological discourse, and practical strategy for waging political and protracted struggle'.[6] It tracks his ideological development from his studies in 1950s Paris and 1960s Phnom Penh to his time as a radical politician, activist-critic, guerilla and CPK leading figure. I selected Hu Nim because of his important roles as the following: a member of the Paris Group of Cambodian Communist intellectuals, alongside his mentors Hou Yuon (1930–1975) and Khieu Samphan (1931–); a politician in Norodom Sihanouk's National Assembly Cabinet on his 1957 return from Paris; a leftist activist-critic whose Maoist economics dissertation on land tenure and social structure informed CPK policy and whose political profile provided a credible, familiar 'face' to the faceless CPK when many Cambodians knew it only as Angkar or Angkar Paṭivatt (the Organisation, or Revolutionary Organisation, 1967–75); and a CPK Central Committee member whose outspoken criticism of the Pol Pot regime led to his 1977 demise at Tuol Sleng (S-21) prison.[7]

---

5   Khieu Samphan, *L'historie récente du Cambodge et mes prises de position* [*Cambodia's Recent History and the Reasons behind the Decisions I Made*] (Paris: L'Harmattan, 2004), 67–68; and Steve Heder, *Cambodian Communism and the Vietnamese Model: Imitation and Independence, 1930–1975* (Chiang Mai, Thailand: White Lotus, 2004).
6   Matthew Galway, *The Emergence of Global Maoism: China and the Cambodian Communist Movement, 1949–1979* (Ithaca, NY: Cornell University Press, 2022), 6–7. See also Matthew Galway, 'Boundless revolution: Global Maoism and communist movements in Southeast Asia, 1949–1979' (PhD diss., University of British Columbia, Vancouver, 2017), 1–29, doi.org/10.14288/1.0349136.
7   Ben Kiernan, *How Pol Pot Came to Power: Colonialism, Nationalism, and Communism in Cambodia, 1930–1975*, 2nd edn (New Haven, CT: Yale University Press, 2004), 27–29, 119, 181, 197, 204–5, 209–10; David Chandler, *The Tragedy of Cambodian History: Politics, War, and Revolution since 1945* (New Haven, CT: Yale University Press, 1991), 95, 98, 128, 153, 167–71, 201, 263, 286, 293; Ian Harris, *Buddhism in a Dark Age: Cambodian Monks under Pol Pot* (Honolulu: University of Hawai'i Press, 2013), 39–40, 48–49, 53; and Craig Etcheson, *The Rise and Demise of Democratic Kampuchea* (Boulder, CO: Westview Press, 1984), 51–52, 177–79.

As I argue, Hu Nim was a networked individual whose engagement with Maoism *intellectually* and then *in practice* stands as an example of how he 'responded to crises' in the Cambodian rural sector and political sphere.[8] He sojourned in the rural periphery, where he experienced the plight of those in the agricultural sector at first hand, and in the national core of Phnom Penh and then in Paris. After his 1955 arrival in the 'anti-imperial metropole' of Paris,[9] he fostered connections and read progressive materials with which he engaged for most of his academic and political life. He responded to crises of post-independence underdevelopment and political corruption, capitalist imperialism and Cambodia's urban/rural divide by first engaging with Maoism as theory, then applying Maoism as praxis in his political and revolutionary tenures in Cambodia.

Indigenising Maoism in Cambodia: A framework

Maoism was not merely grafted on to the Cambodian situation. A close textual exegesis of Hu Nim's doctoral dissertation and examination of his political career reveal that his reception of, and engagement with, Maoism was dialogic. He applied what he found especially useful to Cambodia's historical situation as he saw it, and adapted it where he thought necessary.[10] Hu also held ranking positions in several major Cambodian political organisations from which to put his ideas into practice: Prime Minister Norodom Sihanouk's Saṅgam Rāstr Niyam (hereinafter Saṅgam; Popular Socialist Community) government; the China-curious, arguably Maoist Association d'Amitié Khmero–Chinoise (AAKC, Samāgam Mittphāp Khmer–Chin, Khmer–Chinese Friendship Association), which was established in September 1964; the Front uni national du Kampuchéa (FUNK, Raṇasirs Ruopruomjāti Kampuchea, National United Front of Kampuchea) and Gouvernement royal d'union nationale du Kampuchéa

---

8   Thomas S. Kuhn, *The Structure of Scientific Revolutions*, 2nd edn (Chicago, IL: University of Chicago Press, 1970), 66–76, 90–91.
9   See Michael Goebel, *Anti-Imperial Metropolis: Interwar Paris and the Seeds of Third World Nationalism* (Cambridge, UK: Cambridge University Press, 2015).
10 Hu Nim, 'Les services publics économiques au Cambodge [The economic public services in Cambodia]' (PhD diss., Université Royale Khmère/Sākalvidyālay Bhūmind Khmer, Phnom Penh, 1965). Translated excerpts are available under the title 'Land Tenure and Social Structure in Kampuchea', in Ben Kiernan and Chanthou Boua, eds, *Peasants and Politics in Kampuchea, 1942–1981* (London: Zed Books, 1982), 69–86.

(GRUNK, Rājraṭhābhipāl Ruopruomjāti Kampuchea, Royal Government of the National Union of Kampuchea) of the CPK movement (1967–75); and the CPK Central Committee in Democratic Kampuchea until his death in 1977.[11]

Plate 2.1 Head of state Norodom Sihanouk (second from right) with Communist Party of Kampuchea members, including ministers Hu Nim (far right) and Khieu Samphan (centre left), during his 1973 inspection tour of the liberated zone.
Source: A special issue of *China Pictorial* (No. 6, 1973).

---

11   Vita Chieu 周德高, with Zhu Xueyuan 朱學淵, Wo yu Zhonggong he Jiangong: Jianpuzhai gongchandang xingwang zhuiji/我與中共和柬共：柬埔寨共產黨興亡追記 [*My Story with the Communist Parties of China and Kampuchea: A Record of the Rise and Fall of the Communist Party of Kampuchea*] (Hong Kong: Tianyuan Shuwu, 2007), 20. On the AAKC's establishment, see 'La naissance de l'Association d'amitié Khméro–Chinoise [The Birth of the Khmer–Chinese Friendship Association]', in *Revue trimestrielle de l'Association d'amitiée khmero-chinoise* [*Quarterly Review of the Khmer–Chinese Friendship Association*], Ministry of Information, No.1 (January 1965): 15. Hou Yuon was acting first secretary general-adjunct in May 1961 and Hu Nim was then a councillor. On the Beijing-based China–Cambodia Friendship Association (established in 1961), see: 'Jian–Zhong youhao xiehui zhangcheng cao'an 柬－中友好協會章程草案 [China–Cambodia Friendship Association Draft Charter]', *Mianhua ribao* 棉華日報 [*Sino-Khmer Daily*], 29 May 1961.

Throughout his career, Hu was not completely uprooted (*déraciné*); he devoted himself to altering Cambodian society without the total erasure of its political system. His outlook changed, however, with the outbreak of the 1967 Samlaut Rebellion: uprisings by disgruntled peasants in Battambang Province that served as the prelude to the 1970–75 Cambodian Civil War. At this time, Hu recognised that the Maoism-as-theory he wrote about in the pages of his dissertation had not made any ground in implementation within the system. As Sihanouk targeted him personally for his association with other leftists, but most famously representatives of Maoist China, he broke with Sihanouk and fled to join the *maquis* (bands of rural Cambodian communists). From the countryside, he and his comrades strove through protracted struggle, then in power (from 17 April 1975 to his arrest on 10 April 1977), to execute nationwide the party's brand of Maoism-as-praxis.

I contend that his reception of, and serious engagement with, Maoism was therefore central to the production of *Cambodian Maoism*. The imperfection of Hu Nim's first effort to execute in practice his Maoist-inspired ideas from his doctoral work, and the repressive Cambodian political scene from 1966 to 1967, ultimately compelled him to band with the CPK guerilla to apply more radical and violent components of Maoism-as-praxis nationally.

The first section traces Hu's passage through intellectual spaces in Cambodia and Paris and his subsequent exposure to Maoist texts in French Marxist reading circles. The second section explores his intellectual engagement, or indigenisation-on-paper, with Maoism through a close textual exegesis of his 1965 doctoral dissertation. The third section brings us to Hu's practical adaptation of Maoism whereby he spent years in pursuit of a political path to put his dissertation's proposals into practice. After Sihanouk's threats against him because of his popularity and the public perception that he was a 'positive role model', especially among Sino-Khmers, Hu Nim abandoned this effort and joined his Paris comrades in the Maoist struggle for state power.[12]

---

12 Chandler, *The Tragedy of Cambodian History*, 142–44, 160.

2. 'THE MOST DISSOLUTE AND DISHONEST' KHMER TO AID CHINA

The French connection: Rural origins and the path to Paris, 1949–65

Before Hu Nim engaged with Maoism, few may have guessed someone of such humble origins could ascend to national prominence so quickly. Unlike his future CPK contemporaries Pol Pot (born Saloth Sar, 1925–1998) and Khieu Samphan, he did not come from a wealthy background. He was born in Korkor Village, Kompong Siem District, Kompong Cham, in 1930 to mixed Sino-Khmer lineage.[13] His father, Hou, died in 1936 and his mother, Sorn, a poor peasant, cared for him alone by offering household services to wealthier people throughout Kompong Cham. More than 40 years later, Hu described the situation in his forced confession:

> My mother and I wandered aimlessly from place to place, selling our labour … She made *akao* cakes and exchanged them for rice to feed our stomachs. Later, she was remarried, to a poor peasant … Because her husband was poor, she sent me to live in Mien pagoda [Vatt Mien]. An old monk named Nhep Nauv brought me up and looked after me like a son from that time on.

Mien pagoda, as Hu recalled, 'created favourable conditions for my studies', and instilled in him an appreciation for monks, even if decades later he was behind the party that sought to eradicate them.[14]

Much of Hu Nim's world view was shaped by his education. A talented student, he won admission in 1942 to a prestigious junior high school in Kompong Cham, Collège Norodom Sihanouk, where only 'twenty boys were selected as the first class'.[15] Against French designs to cultivate

---

13   Hu Nim, 'Camlœy Hu Nim hau Phoas Krasouṅ Ghosnākār aṃbi Pravatti Paks Se Aī Aā [Confession of Hu Nim, aka Phoas, Ministry of Propaganda/Information, on his time with the CIA]', (Tuol Sleng Prison, 2 May 1977), Documentation Centre of Cambodia [hereinafter DCCAM], Document No.D00067, 1. See also Hu Nim, 'Planning the Past: The Forced Confessions of Hu Nim, Tuol Sleng Prison, May–June 1977', Chanthou Boua, trans., in *Pol Pot Plans the Future: Confidential Leadership Documents from Democratic Kampuchea, 1976–1977*, David P. Chandler, Ben Kiernan and Chanthou Boua, eds and trans, Monograph Series 33 (New Haven, CT: Yale University Southeast Asia Studies, 1988), 233; and 'The selected 31 biographies of Khmer Rouge leaders' (January 1996), DCCAM, EAO/CORKR, D13969.
14   Hu, 'Confession of Hu Nim', 1–2. See also Timothy Carney, 'Biographical Sketches', in *Communist Party Power in Kampuchea (Cambodia): Documents and Discussion*, Timothy M. Carney, ed., Southeast Asia Program Data Paper No.106 (Ithaca, NY: Department of Asian Studies, Cornell University, 1977), 64; and Kiernan, *How Pol Pot Came to Power*, 27–28.
15   James Tyner, *The Killing of Cambodia: Geography, Genocide, and the Unmaking of Space* (Burlington, VT: Ashgate, 2008), 35. Tyner states this cohort 'included Saloth Sar. Others who attended [were] Hu Nim, Khieu Samphan, and Hou Yuon, all of whom would become important Communist leaders.'

a class of obedient, homegrown civil servants with strong attachments to French thought and achievement, Hu developed nationalist sentiments through his shared experiences as a student reading French classics about revolution, romance and emancipation. As one attendee who also joined the CPK years later recalled of the curriculum at Collège Norodom Sihanouk, those lessons on the French Revolution had lasting effects on his thinking:

> [H]istory and geography were my 'Ingres' violin' [violon d'Ingres, to denote an activity done regularly in one's leisure time for pleasure] with a predilection for the contemporary era. I was passionate about the 1789 French Revolution of which I espoused the three-part motto: Liberty, Equality, and Fraternity. I read with avidity all that touched on it, with a preference for the Jacobins, whose leader Robespierre was my hero and idol. My passion for the 1789 Revolution was hardly altered by my [later] adherence to Marxism. *A Short History of the French Revolution* by Albert Soboul, my professor at the Sorbonne, will long be my bedside book. In particular, I gravitated toward the idea of the revolutionary transformation of society, the importance of the role of the masses, and the need for a people's dictatorship. My passion for reading, together with activism, has contributed much to the formation of a solid ideological conception and to the shaping of a radical political attitude, rejecting in principle any idea of compromise. Dedication, selflessness, loyalty, and sacrifice, these are the key terms that inspire me and will push me to action. For all these reasons, I am deeply attached to the city of Kompong Cham and its College, which is now a high school.[16]

Such sentiments followed Hu in 1950 to Lycée Sisowath, a secondary school in Phnom Penh established in 1935 by the author of 'How to Be a Khmer Civil Servant', Résident Supérieur du Cambodge (Governor-General of Cambodia) Achille Louis Auguste Silvestre (1879–1937). The school's mission—per the French approach to instruction at the time—was to nurture the first generation of protectorate-born civil servants in obedience and service to French interests.[17]

---

16 Suong Sikœun, *Itinéraire d'un Intellectuel Khmer Rouge* [*Itinerary of a Khmer Rouge Intellectual*] (Paris: Éditions du Cerf, 2013), 38–39.
17 M. Humbert-Hesse, 'Rapport General sur l'Enseignement au Cambodge (Janvier 1923) [General report on instruction in Cambodia, January 1923]', 10 January 1923, Archives Nationales d'Outre-Mer, Résident Supérieur du Cambodge 304, Aix-En-Provence, Provence-Alpes-Côte d'Azur, France; and Penny Edwards, *Cambodge: The Cultivation of a Nation* (Honolulu: University of Hawai'i Press, 2007), 76–77.

Yet the significance of Lycée Sisowath was that it brought together young minds, gave them 'a rare freedom of association and discussion, and helped to forge a sense of connection that was far from imagined in its physical immediacy'.[18] A school that was, by the time of Hu's enrolment, already the 'training centre for the Khmer educated class',[19] Lycée Sisowath housed students who were the first to participate in anticolonial demonstrations (in 1936) and Buddhist demonstrations (in the 1940s), later forming the left-leaning Democratic Party (Krum Prajādhipteyy). Students also made up much of the Khmer educated class, with many forming the country's political class. Future CPK Minister for Foreign Affairs Ieng Sary (1925–2013), for one, attended Lycée Sisowath, where he spearheaded the 'Liberation of Cambodia from French Colonialism' group.[20] Lycée Sisowath was also where Hu, who now lived in Unnalom temple (Vatt Uṇṇālom) in Phnom Penh because he could not afford to board, fixed his gaze towards activism and politics.

Hu joined the People's Movement (Prajājan calneā), or Thanhists, led by republican nationalist Sơn Ngọc Thành (1908–1977), in 1952 and subsequently participated in anti-government demonstrations.[21] As Hu recalled, People's Movement members 'included Tep Hong Kry, Chhut Chhoeu, Srei Rithy, Chan Youran, Leav Theaa Im, and myself. By the end of 1952, the situation intensified. The movement members were forced to move into the jungle.' Hu then worked as a schoolteacher at a local junior high school 'to recruit more operatives with a view to enlarging our movement'.[22] Instead of fostering the movement's growth, however, Hu sought opportunities to advance his education. He left for Paris in 1955 by grace of a Democratic Party policy that facilitated study in France for gifted students. As Hu recalled, 'Plek Phœun had helped me to go and

---

18   Edwards, *Cambodge*, 224.
19   Kiernan, *How Pol Pot Came to Power*, 28. According to an editorial in *Le Khmer*: 'Old Cambodians saw a near future where all the posts in the French administration would be occupied by … graduates of the *Lycée Sisowath*' who would augment administrators' 'understanding of the true Khmer soul.' 'Une irréparable faute politique [An Irreparable Political Fault]', *Le Khmer*, 18 May 1936, 1, quoted in Edwards, *Cambodge*, 224.
20   Elizabeth Becker, *When the War Was Over: The Voices of Cambodia's Revolution and Its People* (New York, NY: Simon & Schuster, 1998), 69.
21   Kiernan, *How Pol Pot Came to Power*, 157. That year, as well as graduating from Lycée Sisowath, he married his close friend Kim Lang (aka Comrade Yeat in his confession) in nearby Tonle Bet. In observance of Khmer tradition, he settled in Phnom Penh. Hu, 'Confession of Hu Nim', 3; and Solomon Kane, *Dictionnaire des Khmer rouges: Édition revisée et augmentée [Khmer Rouge Dictionary: Revised and Expanded Edition]* (Bangkok: L'Institut de recherché sur l'Asie du Sud-Est contemporaine, 2011), 156.
22   Hu, 'Confession of Hu Nim', 3.

study in France … [and] took me to see Mau Say', after which Hu won a bursary 'with help from Plek Phœun'. Another man, Um Sim, then told Hu to 'see Hing Kunthel at the Law School in Paris'.²³

In Paris, Hu joined dozens of Cambodian university students—including Hou Yuon, whom Hu met even though he 'was about to return home'— in pursuit of degrees to obtain Cambodian government positions.²⁴ Hu began his studies as a customs officer at the National School of Customs (École nationale des douanes) in the Paris suburb of Neuilly-sur-Seine, but also enrolled in law school (likely the Université de Paris).²⁵ He recalled in his 1977 'confession'—a document to be used with great scrutiny, but that nonetheless contains useful information about his early life—that he often travelled 'several hours by metro to reach law school' from Neuilly. A dedicated student, Hu attended classes for his degree in the morning while taking afternoon and night classes in law, and even received a work placement in Marseille on completion of his second year examinations. The study schedule was gruelling. As Hu recalled:

> I had classes in the morning, which gave me time to go to the Law School in the afternoon (I had to take the metro right across Paris) … For most of the time, I was very busy with my studies, which were very hectic. In the Law School I had to sit for the third year exams (to obtain the Licence), and at the School of Customs, I had to sit for an exam for the higher certificate.²⁶

In between, he abstained from 'political activities' because his studies 'required so much attention'.²⁷ Such studies and discussions with colleagues led him to identify several crises in Cambodia that required a response from its elites: non-agricultural economic life was an outsider-dominated affair, the French dual administrative system favoured neighbouring Vietnamese and dependence on France prevented significant economic modernisation.

---

23 Hu, 'Planning the Past', 237–38; and Hu, 'Confession of Hu Nim', 4. Hu met anticommunist Hing Kunthel, Sihanouk's finance minister in his conservative 1966 cabinet. 'General Elections—Cabinet Changes—Communist Revolt—Recognition of Cambodia's Frontiers by Foreign Governments—Incidents on South Vietnamese and Thai Frontiers', in *Keesing's Record of World Events. Volume 13* [September 1967] (Reno, NV: Keesing's Worldwide, 1931–2006), 22283, available from: web.stanford.edu/group/tomzgroup/pmwiki/uploads/1230-1967-09-Keesings-a-SHP.doc.
24 Hu, 'Planning the Past', 237; and Hu, 'Confession of Hu Nim', 4.
25 Hu, 'Confession of Hu Nim', 2; and Suong, *Itinerary of a Khmer Rouge Intellectual*, 40–41.
26 Hu, 'Planning the Past', 237; and Hu, 'Confession of Hu Nim', 4.
27 Hu, 'Confession of Hu Nim', 3.

This led Hu Nim to join the Union des Etudiants Khmers (UEK, Khmer Students Union), the successor organisation to the nationalist Association des Étudiants Khmers (AEK, Samāgam Nissit Khmer, Khmer Students Association). The UEK brought together students from a wide spectrum of social milieus with a common interest in Cambodian political reform, though unlike the AEK, it was led by leftist students. It was within the UEK that Hu and his comrades first encountered the Marxist-Leninist canon. Their 'exegetical bonding' in the French capital reading such materials against the backdrop of the Second Indochina War (1955–75) led them to devote themselves to radical activism.[28]

Hu's predecessors Hou Yuon, Khieu Samphan, Pol Pot and Ieng Sary had laid the groundwork for his espousal of radical thought.[29] Participation in the Marxist Circle (Cercle Marxiste)—a secret cell within the AEK, and then the UEK, with links to 'language groups' (*groupes des langues*), established in 1949 by the Parti Communiste Français (PCF, French Communist Party)—was an important shift in this transformation. The Marxist Circle, one member averred, 'secretly controlled the student movement from within … by Communist Party members whose … membership was kept secret' to protect them from losing their scholarships, or even from imprisonment for subversive activities.[30] Pol Pot's one-time mentor, Cambodian linguist Keng Vannsak (1925–2008), was a radical thinker, student mentor and Democratic Party supporter with established links to Parisian leftist networks.[31] He hosted student meetings until 1952 at his Rue de Commerce (15th arrondissement) apartment to discuss Cambodian independence and reform.[32] Initially an antimonarchist

---

28 On exegetical bonding, see David Apter and Tony Saich, *Revolutionary Discourse in Mao's Republic* (Cambridge, MA: Harvard University Press, 1994), 263–93. Vergès was active in student circles in the PCF at this time and served as Khieu Samphan's defence lawyer decades later during the Extraordinary Chambers in the Courts of Cambodia trials against CPK leaders.
29 On Pol Pot's early political writing and engagement with Maoism, see: Matthew Galway, 'From Revolutionary Culture to Original Culture and Back: "On New Democracy" and the Kampucheanization of Marxism-Leninism, 1940–1965', *Cross-Currents: East Asian History and Culture Review* (24) (September 2017): 132–58, doi.org/10.1353/ACH.2017.0022.
30 David P. Chandler, *Brother Number One: A Political Biography of Pol Pot* (Boulder, CO: Westview Press, 1999), 33. On discussion groups, see Kiernan, *How Pol Pot Came to Power*, 119; and François Debré, *Cambodge: La révolution de la forêt* [*Cambodia: The Forest Revolution*] (Paris: Club français du livre, 1976), 81.
31 Ben Kiernan, *Blood and Soil: A World History of Genocide and Extermination from Sparta to Darfur* (New Haven, CT: Yale University Press, 2007), 543.
32 ibid., 28, 543–44; Kiernan, *How Pol Pot Came to Power*, 119–21; Chandler, *The Tragedy of Cambodian History*, 53; Marie-Alexandrine Martin, *Le mal Cambodgien: Histoire d'une societe traditionnelle face a ses leaders politiques, 1946–1987* [*The Cambodian Agony: A History of a Traditional Society Facing its Political Leaders, 1946–1987*] (Paris: Hachette, 1989), 105; and Philip Short, *Pol Pot: The History of a Nightmare* (London: John Murray, 2004), 51 [Vannsak's address], 63–64.

reading group, the Marxist Circle gravitated towards its namesake because Marx's theories were useful for interpreting Cambodia's global position and for obtaining genuine independence from colonialism/imperialism.[33]

The Marxist Circle had its own politburo and secretariat and distinguished itself from the Vietnamese-led Kampuchean People's Revolutionary Party (KPRP; Gaṇapaks Prajājan Paṭivatt Kampuchea, Parti révolutionnaire du peuple du Kampuchéa) in its rejection of Vietnamese students' Indochina Federation proposal that ceded Cambodian sovereignty to Hanoi.[34] Leading Marxist Circle members were card-carrying PCF members (Rath Samueoun, Ieng Sary, Hou Yuon, Khieu Samphan, Pol Pot and eventually Hu Nim). The Circle held doctrinaire reading groups of radical materials, consisted of individual cells and was strictly clandestine. Members debated the communist canon, ranging from Lenin's 'On Imperialism', Marx's *Das Kapital* and 'Dialectical Materialism', to Engels, *The Communist Manifesto* and Mao Zedong's 'On New Democracy' (French edition: *La nouvelle Démocratie*)[35] and *Selected Works of Mao Tse-tung* (French edition: *Lectures choisies des Oeuvres de Mao*).[36] Marxist Circle members read, interpreted and discussed materials in French because some of the political language in these texts simply did not have Khmer equivalents.[37]

The Cambodian political scene just before and after the nation's independence in 1953, about which Paris-based Cambodians were acutely aware, hastened the radicalisation of Cambodians abroad like Hu Nim. In Phnom Penh, Sihanouk's interference with the democratic process disillusioned those bright-eyed Paris-based students who held hopes for a genuine democracy in independent Cambodia. Many students responded

---

33 Anna Belogurova, 'Communism in South East Asia', in *The Oxford Handbook of the History of Communism*, Stephen A. Smith, ed. (Oxford, UK: Oxford University Press, 2014), 236–51; and Alexander Vatlin and Stephen A. Smith, 'The Comintern', in *The Oxford Handbook of the History of Communism*, 190–99.
34 Thomas Engelbert and Chris Goscha, *Falling out of Touch: A Study of the Vietnamese Communist Policy towards an Emerging Cambodian Communist Movement, 1930–1975* (Melbourne: Centre of Southeast Asian Studies, Monash Asia Institute, Monash University, 1995), 54.
35 Members read the French-language 1951 edition. Mao Tsé-toung, *La nouvelle Démocratie* (Paris: Éditions sociales, 1951) or Mao Tsé-toung, *La nouvelle Démocratie* (Beijing: People's Press, 1952).
36 Chandler, *The Tragedy of Cambodian History*, 54; and Debré, *Cambodge*, 77–95. On French versions of Mao's works as Marxist Circle materials, see Sacha Sher, 'Le parcours politique des khmers rouges: de Paris à Phnom Penh, 1945–1979 [The political journey of the "Khmer Rouge": From Paris to Phnom Penh]' (PhD diss., Université Paris-Nanterre, 2003), 78, 121.
37 Chandler, *Brother Number One*, 32–33.

by taking a particularly radical turn: they joined the PCF in droves.[38] Deeply suspicious of the AEK membership's increasingly leftist orientation, Sihanouk disbanded the association in 1953. The Cambodian leader's heavy-handed move forced AEK members to found the UEK on 26 November 1953, so the group was in place when Hu Nim landed in 1955.[39]

Hu Nim radicalised further to counter Sihanouk's antidemocratic moves in the Cambodian political arena, and he eventually became a politician to effect change. He returned to Cambodia in 1957[40] to work as a customs officer and to pursue an advanced degree in law, eventually pursuing a doctorate in economic sciences with a view to taking the political route. His PhD dissertation represents one of the earliest texts in which he frames his Maoist vision, and it became a foundational national text on which the CPK built Democratic Kampuchea. His post within Sihanouk's government, however minimal, also allowed him to travel throughout Eastern Europe and, after he assumed the position of secretary of state for commerce in 1962, to Beijing (in 1965), at a time when a veritable Mao fever was taking hold of Cambodian progressive circles in Phnom Penh's radical urban climate.[41]

Maoist China was an attractive alternative modernity for Cambodian leftists, including Hu Nim, who would visit the country, much to Sihanouk's consternation. 'New China', one of Hu's contemporaries reflected:

> occupied a special place in our hearts and in our thoughts, symbolized by Mao, the graceful dancers of the Beijing Opera, the fantastic acrobats of the Sheng Yang circus, or the fabulous magicians of Shanghai … I threw myself into reading Mao Zedong's works, the only Marxist books available in Phnom Penh … We built a small library where we found, among others, 'On New Democracy,' 'On Contradiction,' 'On Practice,' 'On the Correct Handling of Contradictions Among the People,' [and] President Liu Shaoqi's 'How to be a Good Communist'.[42]

---

38 Chandler, *The Tragedy of Cambodian History*, 8. On AEK support for the Democratic Party, see Saloth Sar, 'Rājādhipteyy ṝ Prajādhipteyy? [Monarchy or Democracy?]', *Khemara Nissit* [*Khmer Student*] 14 (August 1952): 39. On Sihanouk's 'coup', see Milton Osborne, *Sihanouk: Prince of Light, Prince of Darkness* (Honolulu: University of Hawai'i Press, 1994), 63–66; Chandler, *Brother Number One*, 29; and Kiernan, *How Pol Pot Came to Power*, 72, 121.
39 Kiernan, *How Pol Pot Came to Power*, 121. On the UEK, see: Martin, *The Cambodian Agony*, 106–7.
40 Hu, 'Planning the Past', 238.
41 Matthew Galway, 'Red Service-Intellectual: Phouk Chhay, Maoist China, and the Cultural Revolution in Cambodia, 1964–67', *Journal of Southeast Asian Studies* 52(2) (June 2021): 275–308, esp. 298–99, doi.org/10.1017/S0022463421000436.
42 Suong, *Itinerary of a Khmer Rouge Intellectual*, 57.

Plate 2.2 Front cover of the second issue of the *Revue Association d'Amitié Khmero-Chinoise*, September 1965.

Source: Author's copy and photograph.

Newspapers sponsored by the Chinese Communist Party (CCP) such as the *Sino-Khmer Daily* (*Mianhua ribao* 棉華日報) were all too willing to capitalise on the emergent Maoist enthusiasm among overseas Chinese (*huaqiao* 華僑) in Cambodia, which in turn helped to spur China

2. 'THE MOST DISSOLUTE AND DISHONEST' KHMER TO AID CHINA

curiosity among Khmer leftists.[43] One issue of the paper recounted Hu Nim receiving vocal encouragement from the Beijing-based Chinese–Cambodian Friendship Association in 1961 to found a Phnom Penh–based friendship association, the AAKC.[44] Hu's 'leftist activities' won him favour among Chinese leaders, as he recalled. He led a delegation to China before the Cultural Revolution, during which he met Premier Zhou Enlai and President Liu Shaoqi.[45]

Afterward, Hu was vocally supportive of China and the Maoist path to socialist development. As an article in the AAKC's *Quarterly Review* conveyed, the association, including Hu, regarded China's success as part of Mao's clear-sighted leadership. Its members also regarded American imperialism increasingly as a 'paper tiger'.[46] As Hu once declared in a statement he released in the *Peking Review*:

> US imperialism and its stooges are not all happy to see a close friendship between Cambodia and China. But this is a good thing. *Future developments will further prove the correctness of Chairman Mao Tse-tung's thesis that the East wind is prevailing over the West wind.* The anti-imperialist forces of the East are bound to defeat the imperialist forces of the West.[47]

---

43 Galway, 'Red Service-Intellectual', 275–78, 293–97. The *Sino-Khmer Daily* was founded in Battambang in 1956, two years before formal diplomatic relations between Maoist China and Cambodia were in place and, on its move to Phnom Penh, operated as the PRC Embassy's 'official propaganda outlet' (*shishi tingmin yu Zhongguo dashiguande xuanchuan meiti* 事事昕命於中國大使館的宣傳媒體).
44 'Jian-Zhong youhao xiehui zhangcheng cao'an 柬中友好協會章程草案 [China–Cambodia Friendship Association Draft Charter]', *Mianhua ribao* 棉華日報 [*Sino-Khmer Daily*], 29 May 1961; and Galway, 'Red Service-Intellectual', 291. On Maoist speeches by AAKC leaders, see 'Visite de la Délégation de l'Association d'Amitié Chine-Cambdge, 4–12 Septembre 1964 [China–Cambodia Friendship Association Delegation Visit, 4–12 September 1964]', in *Revue trimestrielle de l'Association d'amitiée khmero–chinoise* [*Quarterly Journal of the Khmer–Chinese Friendship Association*], 23–47.
45 Hu, 'Confession of Hu Nim', 9.
46 'A Son Excellence Monsieur Leng-Ngeth, Président de l'Association d'Amitié Khméro-Chinoise [To His Excellency Mr Leng Ngeth, President of the Khmer–Chinese Friendship Association]', (Beijing, 2 December 1964), in *Quarterly Journal of the Khmer–Chinese Friendship Association*, 40; and Ding Xilin 丁西林, 'Nouvelles victoires du Peuple Cambodgien [New Victories of the Cambodian People]', in *Quarterly Journal of the Khmer–Chinese Friendship Association*, 46. Leng Ngeth was a former Cambodian ambassador to Beijing and, although he was AAKC president, Hu Nim 'led the Association effectively'. Hu, 'Planning the Past', 243.
47 'Premier Chou on Sino-Cambodian Friendship', *Peking Review*, 22 October 1965, 15. Emphasis added. Zhou visited Cambodia months earlier to an 'enthusiastic welcome'. 'Zhou zongli zuochen di Jian shou kongqian relie huanyin 周總理做襖底柬受空前熱烈歡飲 [Premier Zhou Arrived in Cambodia Yesterday Morning and Received an Unprecedented Warm Welcome]', *Mianhua ribao* 棉華日報 [*Sino-Khmer Daily*], 6 May 1960.

Hu's experiences in Cambodia and France led him through various intellectual spaces that shaped his reception of Maoism. His education in the French protectorate compelled him to turn his interest in French arts into overseas studies. There, in the 'powerful, superior, mundane Western mother country', he developed revolutionary ideas, whereas participation in the Marxist Circle meant that he 'read, learned, and debated the meanings of revolution, the strategies involved, and the objectives'.[48] Marxist-Leninist and Maoist theories arose as means by which to interpret, then reverse, Cambodia's plight. Developments in Paris and crises in Phnom Penh then provided the *mise-en-scène* for him to move from debating communist literature to reforming the country via the political route. Now a revolutionary intellectual, he was convinced that Marxism-Leninism and Maoism, if applied to concrete Cambodian realities, could transform Cambodia from a monarchical state into a nation that served the people.

Importantly for our purposes, Maoism arose as *the* dominant leftist trend in Hu's thinking when decolonisation and Soviet revisionism during the 1960 Sino-Soviet Split pushed alternative interpretations of Marxism-Leninism to the fore. As Keng intimated: 'At the beginning, we were very Stalinist … We turned toward China in the late 1950s because the Russians were playing the Sihanouk card and neglecting us … When everyone began to criticize Stalin, we became Maoists.'[49] Mao's writings soon underpinned diagnoses of problems in Cambodia and informed proposals for altering the country radically. Hu Nim's PhD dissertation in law and economic sciences, which he completed in Cambodia at Royal Khmer University (Sākalvidyālay Bhūmind Khmer, RKU), reflects this imprint most vividly.

---

48 Burglar, *The Eyes of the Pineapples*, 188.
49 Martin, *The Cambodian Agony*, 105–6. Also quoted in Matthew Galway, 'Specters of Dependency: Hou Yuon and the Origins of Cambodia's Marxist Vision (1955–1975)', *Cross-Currents: East Asian History and Culture Review* 31 (2019): 137, doi.org/10.1353/ach.2019.0021.

Analysis of the classes in Cambodian society: Hu Nim's economics dissertation, 1965

Hu Nim defended his PhD dissertation in economic sciences on land tenure, socioeconomic inequality and rural social structure in Cambodia before the RKU Faculty of Law on 4 June 1965. It is an essential document for any study of CPK thought. His evaluation committee comprised his adviser, Dr Francis Doré, and jurors doctors Gérard Farjat and Rémy Prud'homme. Hu described his dissertation as taking 'a progressive stand' and, indeed, it provided an outline of his leftist vision for Cambodia.[50] He completed it while serving as undersecretary of state in the office of Prime Minister Sihanouk; he graduated from RKU in 1966.[51]

Although Sihanouk coopted Hu and other leftist officials after crushing the Democratic Party and the socialist People's Group (Krum Prajājon), Hu's dissertation reflects Maoist leanings that crystallised after his trip to Beijing in 1965.[52] A 'work resonant with Maoist voluntarism',[53] his dissertation examines the Chinese, North Korean and North Vietnamese models of socialist development in a favourable, even admiring, light. Hu levels praise, in particular, at the Chinese leadership for the people's communes (*renmin gongshe*, 人民公社), which 'were larger than cooperatives, developed a diversified economy of their own, and were at the same time the basic administrative unit'.[54] Importantly, Hu was also acting vice-president of the Maoist AAKC—that is, until Sihanouk disbanded it in 1967, citing Chinese interference.[55] Hu's ties to China and, later, a Maoist cultural diplomatic association might explain why one scholar described his 1965 dissertation as a 'detailed Maoist analysis of the peasant problem'.[56]

---

50 Hu, 'Planning the Past', 241.
51 Henri Locard, *Pourquoi les Khmers Rouges?* [*Why the Khmer Rouge?*] (Paris: Vendémaire, 2013), 111.
52 On Hu's praise of Sihanouk, see Hu, 'The economic public services in Cambodia', 385.
53 Geoffrey C. Gunn, *Monarchical Manipulation in Cambodia: France, Japan, and the Sihanouk Crusade for Independence* (Copenhagen: Nordic Institute of Asian Studies, 2018), 134.
54 Charles Twining, 'The Economy', in *Cambodia 1975–1978: Rendezvous with Death*, Karl D. Jackson, ed. (Princeton, NJ: Princeton University Press, 1989), 113.
55 Timothy Carney, 'Continuity in Cambodian Communism: Introduction', in *Communist Party Power in Kampuchea (Cambodia): Documents and Discussion*, Timothy M. Carney, ed., Southeast Asia Program Data Paper No.106 (Ithaca, NY: Department of Asian Studies, Cornell University, 1977), 14–15.
56 William Shawcross, *Sideshow: Kissinger, Nixon, and the Destruction of Cambodia* (London: The Hogarth Press, 1986), 240.

This section examines how Hu Nim used Mao's vocabulary, syntax and class categories from his analysis of rural class structure to identify Cambodian economic problems and propose novel alternatives.[57] As Hou Yuon and Khieu Samphan had done before him,[58] Hu tracked the 'structural evolution of the Cambodian economy' in which disproportionate amounts of the country's agricultural land and wealth were concentrated in the hands of a small number of farmers. The concentration of wealth and fragmentation of land resulted in a 'semi-proletariat of rootless, destitute rural dwellers … with few ties to the land'.[59] Here, Mao's original work on peasants, which Hu references[60]—not to mention Mao's denunciation of exploitation by state monopoly capitalism and the bureaucratic bourgeoisie, and his calls for government seizure of the economy—shaped how Hu Nim viewed future Cambodian society.

Hu Nim expanded on previous arguments by his peers that Cambodia's economy was oriented exploitatively around foreign interests.[61] He urged Sihanouk to seize control of foreign trade and finance and contended that autonomous development and agricultural cooperatives that served the workers first *must* replace the private sector and modernise Cambodia. He supported state-sponsored planning mechanisms and specialised state economic organisations, state-directed private trade and industry, industry-supported agricultural development and production of consumer goods instead of manufacturing goods that were unobtainable for most Cambodians. In his view, valuable foreign exchange was essentially 'wasted' in the dependence on imported goods for this modest sector of

---

57   Hu Nim's footnotes: Mao Tsé-toung, *Sur le problème de la coopération agricole* [*On the Problem of Agricultural Cooperation*] (Beijing: Éditions en langues étrangères, 1956); and Li Fou-Tchoun, *Rapport sur le Premier Plan quinquennal pur le développement de l'économie nationale de la République Populaire de Chine* [*Report on the First Five-Year Plan for the Development of the National Economy of the People's Republic of China*] (Beijing: Éditions en langues étrangères, 1956). Others that he did not reference but that influenced his views included Mao Tsé-toung, 'Analyse des classes de la société chinoise [Class Analysis of Chinese Society]', and 'Rapport sur l'enquête menée dans le Hunan à propos du mouvement paysan [Report on an Investigation of the Peasant Movement in Hunan]', both in *Œuvres choisies du Mao Tsé-toung, tome I* [*Selected Works of Mao Tse-tung. Volume I*] (Paris: Éditions sociales, 1955).
58   Hou Yuon, 'Le paysannerie du Cambodge et ses projets de modernisation [The peasantry of Cambodia and its modernisation projects]' (PhD diss., Université de Paris, 1955). On his dissertation, see: Galway, 'Specters of Dependency', 126–61.
59   Gunn, *Monarchical Manipulation in Cambodia*, 141.
60   Hu, 'The economic public services in Cambodia', 410. See also William Willmott, 'Analytical Errors of the Kampuchean Communist Party', *Pacific Affairs* 54(2) (Summer 1981): 209–27, at p.213n.10.
61   Khieu Samphan, 'L'économie du Cambodge et ses problèmes d'industrialisation [The Cambodian economy and its problems of industrialisation]' (PhD diss., Université de Paris, 1959).

urbanite elites. Cambodia's agrarian structure, by contrast, was dominated by a minuscule percentage of well-off rural inhabitants. This, in turn, eliminated any chance of the lower peasant stratum improving their lot.[62]

Hu pointed to the persistence of usury as one of the major obstacles to clear in the amelioration of rural living standards and agrarian production. The 'sale of green crop on credit', he noted, contributed significantly to increasing rates of usury. As he elaborates on such debts and unequal exchange:

> For the majority of the peasants, these sorts of loans are for the purpose of daily consumption, to bridge the food gap or even to celebrate religious festivals or family occasions. The loans are difficult to repay, and the debts accumulate so much that one day the peasant is obliged to abandon his plot of land to the merchants, which explains further the increased number of landless peasants and debt bondsmen. At each sale of agricultural produce, a multitude of middlemen from the bottom to the top—shopkeeper, individual collector, miller, transporter, small wholesaler, exporter—take out exorbitant profits so that a very tiny portion of the salve value at the last exchange gets back to the peasants.[63]

Similarities with Mao's 1927 *Report on an Investigation of the Peasant Movement in Hunan* are evident. Mao claimed:

> When they [peasants] buy goods, the merchants exploit them; when they sell their farm produce, the merchants cheat them; when they borrow money for rice, they are fleeced by the usurers; and they are eager to find a solution to these three problems.[64]

Hu, likewise, held that cooperatives in which peasants could set up their own credit system and work for mutual benefit would free them from debt bondage, sharecropping and payment in kind, thereby raising their standard of living. If the landlords and wealthy peasants had to rely on their own productive labour and most peasants could prosper, the countryside could serve most Cambodians and the nation could move towards autonomous development.

---

62 Etcheson, *The Rise and Demise of Democratic Kampuchea*, 52.
63 Hu, 'The economic public services in Cambodia', 92–93.
64 Mao, 'Report on an Investigation of the Peasant Movement in Hunan'.

Hu then turns to his case studies of the development of public economic services wherein models, stages of development and cooperatives in North Korea, China and North Vietnam are noteworthy. He lauds the North Korean communists for their 'shining example of a successful scientific socialist path based on the principle of "self-reliance" and close economic cooperation between the countries of the socialist camp'. In five short years, he notes, North Korea moved from zero cooperatives to one large, self-reliant cooperative per district. Hu credits North Korean industrial success to the 'active workers' spirit of the Korean people'.[65] Years later, in September 1976, Hu again praised North Korean accomplishments. He said Cambodians were:

> greatly impressed by the ideological and artistic value of the Democratic People's Republic of Korea's sound and progressive new arts which firmly uphold a strong national spirit, the glorious socialist line, and the great *chuche* [Juche] idea of independence and self-reliance advocated by Marshal Kim Il-song, respected and beloved great leader of the Korean people.[66]

Hu commends Maoist China primarily for its communes and for the development of economic public services. He argues that both were a function of the degree of China's systematic socialisation. Hu identifies the First Five-Year Plan (1953–57, the 'Little Leap'), in particular, as indicative of how the CCP worked towards the realisation of its general line and socialist edification. He praises the 'realist spirit' of the Chinese leaders as especially exemplary:

> [They] know best how to combine uncompromising revolutionary spirit and practical and scientific creativity … all measures are and will be taken [by the CCP leaders] to ensure that the socialist road overcomes capitalism, which is to say, expanding the state's role continuously as leader of the national economy … The practical spirit, the desire to respect concrete conditions, led Chinese leaders to adopt the method of rectification of the style of work.[67]

---

65   Hu, 'The economic public services in Cambodia', 51–54.
66   Foreign Broadcast Information Service, 'Hu Nim Reception Speech', *Phnom Penh Domestic Service*, 30 November 1976, and *Daily Report: Asia & Pacific* (FBIS-APA-76-233), 2 December 1976: H5.
67   Hu, 'The economic public services in Cambodia', 46, 48.

Since 1960, Hu notes, the CCP had realised there was no need to follow the Soviet model any further and that it must distance itself from the Soviet linking of industry to agriculture (and vice versa) and depend on its own resources to become self-reliant.

In the second part of his dissertation, Hu Nim combines Maoist class categories with a more substantial statistical base than Hou Yuon and Khieu Samphan used in their works—namely, figures for 1962, which threw into sharp relief Cambodia's unequal land distribution. Hu argues that problems in Cambodia's rural sector were the largest in the nation. He breaks Cambodia's rural sector down into two main thematic parts, the first of which, the rural classes, consisted of five major class groupings. First, he divides Cambodian landowners according to the size of their landholdings and overall yields: 1) landed proprietors, who owned more than 10 hectares of land and depended heavily on exploitative practices such as charging high rent to peasants and forcing those who could not afford it to sharecrop; 2) wealthy peasants, who owned land but depended on wage labour, living comfortably on landholdings that exceeded 5 hectares; 3) middle peasants, who possessed 2–5 hectares on which they worked without help, though they occasionally rented additional land to sustain themselves; 4) poor peasants, who were the great majority, and either owned little to no land (1–2 hectares depending on region) or held smallholdings at the expense of the necessary tools to work it, sustaining themselves through sharecropping or living on another's land; and 5) agricultural wage-earners—a group that held no land and depended on the sale of its labour to maintain the most modest existence (6.6 per cent of the population, or 156,7000 people, according to Hu's 1962 census figures).

Hu determines that more than 250,000 families (30.7 per cent of farming households) held only 126,800 hectares of land (merely 5.18 per cent of the total cultivated area in 1962 by his account). A mere 4 per cent of the population owned more than 4 hectares, or 21.45 per cent of land. Cambodia's farming population—more than 50 per cent of the national population by Hu's account—owned virtually nothing.[68] Population increases meant the number of smallholders rose from 669,000 families in 1956 (92 per cent of 727,000) to 718,000 in 1962 (86 per cent of 835,000). The expansion of rice land, deficient tenure records and

---

68   ibid., 69–86, 88, 96–98.

major discrepancies between figures for land owned and land actually sown, among other statistical anomalies, made it difficult to ascertain the situation.[69] Hu argues that the 1962 census figures on renting and sharecropping 'did not accurately reflect the situation since many of the very small landowners had to rent land or sell their labor in order to subsist', and he estimated that as many as 25 per cent of agricultural families rented or were sharecroppers.[70]

Second, Hu Nim analyses land tenancy in the Cambodian rural sector to emphasise its semifeudal nature. The land rent system, which often depended on sharecropping or rent-in-kind (paddy before rice planting), constituted direct exploitation by landlords and wealthy peasants of Cambodia's poorest farmers. This entrenched semifeudal mode of production was, for Hu, a rigged system in which two conflicting agrarian phenomena of concentration and fragmentation—he cites French colonial agronomist Yves Henri's 1930 analysis to frame the latter[71]—perpetuated Cambodia's agrarian problems.

Concentration, Hu explains, was an agrarian structure in which a minority of landowners possessed almost all the land. Fragmentation, or the dispersion or scattering of plots, occurred when most landowning farmers were smallholders. 'Concentration', Hu continues, was 'accompanied by high exploitation: small owners, poor farmers, and farm employees work for the prosperity of the big landowners'. Fragmentation, by contrast, caused two problems: lower productivity and limited innovation. In Cambodia, Hu observes, the two phenomena combined:

> The agrarian structure in Kampuchea is mixed, that is to say, both fragmented *and* concentrated. It is true that parcellization dominates in all the riverbank land and the fertile rice-growing regions, but for more than a decade there has been a marked tendency toward concentration, not only in the newly opened areas, but also to a limited extent in the fragmented regions themselves.[72]
>
> … [B]oth the parcellized [or fragmented] structure and the trend towards concentration present problems. Concentration, if it is not speculative, can play a role in increasing production,

---

69 Carney, 'Continuity in Cambodian Communism', 15.
70 Hu, 'The economic public services in Cambodia', 96.
71 Gunn, *Monarchical Manipulation in Cambodia*, 129.
72 Hu, 'The economic public services in Cambodia', 83–85, 95.

> providing the opportunity to apply scientific and technical progress. But because [of] Kampuchea's weak development of capitalism, this tendency exists only for the speculation (in the sale of land tenancy, sharecropping, etc). This agrarian structure still varies from one region to another. If concentration is in progress in certain rice-growing provinces like Battambang, fragmentation and the dispersion of holdings is [*sic*] increasing in the riverbank regions, and these are the most fertile regions with the highest population density.[73]

The 'parcellised structure' in Cambodia presented serious problems to development and innovation in the rural sector. The trend towards concentration would, without intervention, add to most peasants' struggles. The 'nature of agrarian structures joined with the social structure of rural life would further aggravate the lives of the peasants and compound the obstacles to modernization and the development of agriculture'.[74]

Yet, Hu cautions that the state must not force reform on its peasants. Because Cambodian peasants were 'quite attached to their plot of land and their right to it must be respected', the state ought to persuade peasants that reform was in their best interest and, by extension, in the national interest.[75] If peasants understood the aims of 'mutual help and cooperative groups', Hu asserts, they would endorse agricultural reforms and cooperatives, for mutual aid was 'the only way to escape the individual poverty cycle'.[76]

Here, another connection to Mao arises. Mao addressed a very similar problem regarding the semi-proletariat (semi-owners and owner-peasants) in his 1926 'Analysis of the Classes in Chinese Society'. As Mao argued, semi-owner peasants were:

> worse off than the owner-peasants, because every year they are short of about half the food they need and have to make up this deficiency by cultivating others' land, working, or engaging in petty trading. In late spring and early summer, when the crop is still in the blade and the old stock is consumed, they borrow money from others at exorbitant rates of interest and buy grain

---

73   ibid., 89.
74   ibid., 92.
75   Twining, 'The Economy', 113.
76   Hu, 'The economic public services in Cambodia', 100, 296.

at high prices. Their plight is naturally harder than that of the owner-peasants, who need no help from others, but they are better off than the sharecroppers.[77]

Alongside the proletariat—who held no land, farming tools or sufficient funds, sustaining themselves solely by selling their labour—the semi-proletariat, poor peasants and *lumpenproletariat* constituted the most revolutionary groups. These groups were ultimately most likely to support widespread industrial and agricultural reform and outright revolution. How to harness this potentially revolutionary vanguard force remained a subject for intense debate—that is, until Mao proposed the 'new-democratic state under the joint-dictatorship of several anti-imperialist classes', which was an idea on which Hou, Khieu and Hu drew to propose state-directed autonomous development *and* mutual aid teams/collectives.

Hu's conclusion urges the Cambodian state under Sihanouk to 'carry the highest possible level of political consciousness of the masses', which mirrors Mao's assessment of peasants as a class of 'brave', albeit 'apt to be destructive', fighters who stood as 'a revolutionary force if given proper guidance'.[78] Here, too, as Mao's homage to Marx reveals: 'It is not the consciousness of men that determines their being, but, on the contrary, their social being that determines their consciousness.'[79] Any state initiative, Hu notes in his conclusion, ought to recognise the peasants' social being as a conduit for positive change in Cambodia's society and economy, rather than perpetuating the status quo by leaving them powerless, destitute and unable to contribute to Cambodia's national growth. Hu considers it was of 'decisive importance' to train Cambodian, not foreign, executives, and established as another priority a 'policy of relying on our own strength so that Cambodia may help itself' to answer the 'primacy to the national accumulation'.[80]

---

77   Mao Zedong, 'Analysis of the Classes in Chinese Society', [1 December 1925], in *Mao's Road to Power: Revolutionary Writings, 1912–1949. Volume 2: National Revolution and Social Revolution, December 1920 – June 1927*, Stuart Schram, ed. (Armonk, NY: M.E. Sharpe, 1992), 256–57.
78   Mao Zedong, 'Report on the Peasant Movement in Hunan', [February 1927], in *Mao's Road to Power*, Vol.2, 430.
79   Mao Zedong, 'On New Democracy', [January 1940], in *Mao's Road to Power: Revolutionary Writings, 1912–1949. Volume 7: New Democracy, 1939–1941*, Stuart Schram, ed. (Armonk, NY: M.E. Sharpe, 2005), 331, quoting Karl Marx, 'Preface to *A Contribution to the Critique of Political Economy*', in *Selected Works of Marx and Engels, English Edition. Volume 1* (Moscow: Foreign Languages Press, 1958), 363.
80   Hu, 'The economic public services in Cambodia', 386–88.

To accomplish both tasks, the state could not ignore its poorest strata, or favour stuffing its own coffers at the expense of benefiting its own populace. Otherwise, Hu concludes forebodingly, the:

> negative impact of the exploiting characteristics of the current economic system would not only cause failure and plunge the country's economy into devastating crisis, but also sharpen the contradictions among workers, peasants and feudal classes, landlords, and capitalists. The only solution [is] revolution.[81]

To summarise, Hu Nim's dissertation reflects the Maoist political economy leanings of its author, with a similar class analysis and solutions to rural problems (cooperatives and self-reliance, among others). He quotes Mao and CCP sources and praises the CCP's Little Leap and North Korean self-reliance. Hu's work proposes novel solutions for restructuring Cambodian society from the top down and the bottom up, yet it avoids an abject call to arms for a communist revolution. At this stage, anyway, he still had faith in reforming the country by political, nonviolent means. He would run for, and win, a host of ministerial political posts within the Cambodian Government and began the process of putting into practice his Maoist proposals from within. But despite Hu's popularity among his rural constituency, Sihanouk's suspicion of leftists led to his ostracism from the government. After a series of threats against his life, Hu joined the *maquis* from 1967 until its seizure of power in 1975.[82]

Comme la paille desséchée dans les rizières ['Like dried straw in the rice paddies']: Political career and flight, 1958–67

The last among his Paris cohort to receive his PhD, Hu Nim returned to Cambodia in 1957 to work in a law office of the Customs Department for three months, and then shifted his focus to politics. He reluctantly joined Sihanouk's Sangam on 30 December of that year on Hou Yuon's advice that to join the National Assembly 'one had to become a member of the

---

81 Hu, 'Confession of Hu Nim', 11.
82 Pol Pot left Paris without a degree in 1953 aboard the SS *Jamaïque* for Saigon, after which 'he entered the top echelons of the Communist Party of Kampuchea earlier as a professional revolutionary and, thus, had a much higher status than his friends who returned home after their studies'. Chieu, *My Story with the Communist Parties of China and Kampuchea*, 22.

Popular Socialist Community first'.[83] Hu won a seat in the 1958 election (and again in 1962 and 1966) as a representative of a district in Kompong Cham Province.[84] He also worked for two leftist newspapers at this time, *Cambodian Realities* (*Réalités Cambodgiennes*) and *Free People* (*Prajājon Serī*), and Sihanouk's private newspaper, *The Nationalist* (*Anakjātiniyam*). A source claims that Hu Nim even 'translated into Khmer the writings of "Mao Zedong Thought"', after which he founded the AAKC in Phnom Penh, in 1964.[85] On the Democratic Party's 1957 dissolution, Hu exhibited an 'openly' leftist political stance that forced him to the *maquis* a decade later.

Hu was an important part of several Saṅgam governments and developed his profile as a prominent leftist politician before he fled the capital in 1967. He was undersecretary of state in the Prime Minister's Department (April–July 1958), undersecretary of state at the Ministry of the Interior for Parliamentary Relations (July 1958 – February 1959) and undersecretary of state at the Ministry of Justice (February–June 1959).[86] Despite his limited mobility to initiate the kind of change that he envisioned, he cultivated a fiercely loyal following among his Kompong Cham constituency. His ties to leftist newspapers also enhanced his reputation as a leftist politician with a genuine commitment to peasant outreach. Because of his self-described 'progressive activities', Hu had close contacts with the embassies of the People's Republic of China, the People's Democratic Republic of Korea and the Democratic Republic of Vietnam. As he recalled, the Chinese 'liked me even more wholeheartedly, because on the one hand *I respected and studied Mao Zedong thought*, and on the other hand *I took a stand against the revisionists—the Soviet Union*'.[87] In 1962, Hu recalled, he attended a conference in Jakarta 'organized by an association of the newspaper *Afrique–Asie* [*Africa–Asia*], with Uch Ven', at which he 'met Nguyen Thi Binh, [the] Vietcong representative who was also representing a Hanoi newspaper'.[88] Hu's meetings with high-profile communists augmented his reputation as a leftist and solidified his internationalist bona fides.

---

83   Hu, 'Confession of Hu Nim', 5; and Locard, *Why the Khmer Rouge?*, 111.
84   Locard, *Why the Khmer Rouge?*, 111.
85   Kane, *Khmer Rouge Dictionary*, 156.
86   Galway, *The Emergence of Global Maoism*, 141; and Chandler, *The Tragedy of Cambodian History*, 98.
87   Hu, 'Planning the Past', 242. Emphasis added. See also Hu, 'Confession of Hu Nim', 5, 8; and Carney, 'Biographical Sketches', 64.
88   Hu, 'Planning the Past', 242.

As a journalist for *The Nationalist*, Hu earned the chance to travel with a delegation to the Soviet Union and throughout Eastern Europe. He claimed that these trips 'gave the delegations a chance to see with their own eyes socialism in practice'. As he recalled, 'the more [leftist] activities I engaged in with socialist countries' embassies, especially China, North Korea, and North Vietnam's, the warmer I felt'.[89] His reputation as a leftist soon preceded him. At a 1965 meeting with Vietnamese Communist Party leader Hồ Chí Minh, Hu was promised a warm reception in Hanoi should Sihanouk's invective intensify.[90] During Hu's trip to Hanoi, Sihanouk, who was growing suspicious of his activities, would remove Hu from his post and sever ties between them.

Hu gradually developed strong feelings of admiration for China, North Korea and North Vietnam, and expressed his praise in the French-language newspaper *The New Dispatch* (*La Nouvelle Dépeche*) and throughout the second part of his PhD dissertation. He visited China frequently—first, in 1963–64 as a foreign journalist invitee on a 15-day visit during which Chinese officials urged him to establish the AAKC. Hu subsequently gained considerable encouragement from high-ranking representatives who, at the commemoration of the AAKC's first anniversary, invited him to visit again in 1965.[91] The Chinese, Hu reminisced, 'felt so secure with my activities' that the China–Cambodia Friendship Association (Jian–Zhong youhao xiehui 柬中友好協會) in Beijing sent its director and CCP Vice-Minister Ding Xilin 丁西林 (1893–1974) to 'participate in the inaugural ceremony of our association, which was held in the Theatre of Phnom Penh'.[92]

Despite the maelstrom of anti-leftism in Cambodian politics, Hu Nim was firm in his convictions that he could reform Cambodia's economy and its citizens' social welfare from within the National Assembly. He served as secretary of state for commerce from August to October 1962 while he pursued his PhD. As he recounted of his writings at this time:

---

89   Hu, 'Confession of Hu Nim', 8.
90   Carney, 'Biographical Sketches', 64; and Kiernan, *How Pol Pot Came to Power*, 204.
91   Hu, 'Confession of Hu Nim', 12–13. See also Ding, 'Nouvelles victories du Peuple Cambodgien [New Victories of the Cambodian People]', in *Quarterly Review of the Khmer–Chinese Friendship Association*, 46–47.
92   Hu, 'Confession of Hu Nim', 10.

> I wrote extensively about the failure of economic reform in Cambodia. I had credible evidence and data to support my argument. SONEXIM [Société Nationale d'Exportation et d'Importation (Cambodia), National Export and Import Company], for example, had lost 700 million riel [Cambodian currency] annually in the exportation of rice since that state organization was formed. I argued that this resulted from the existing exploiting economics system and its relationships of production. I pointed out the current statistics [that] showed confiscation of land by a small number of the feudal landlords and capitalists, resulting in land shortages for farmers, tax burdens, and the losses of SONEXIM, which fell upon the workers and peasants. I concluded that negative impact of the exploiting characteristics of the current economic system would not only cause failure and plunge the country's economy into devastating crisis, but also sharpen the contradictions among workers, peasants, and feudal classes, landlords, and capitalists.[93]

Hu recognised the myriad flaws of Sihanouk's leadership. He put theory into practice in 1965 when he sided with oppressed Kampuchea Krom residents and joined a 'Complaint Commission'—both CPK-linked—that resolved disputes over land claims and confiscations. He also pressed his fellow assembly members to sever all ties with the United States, which he viewed as imperialist.[94] Far from influential within the conservative Saṅgam after 1966, Hu felt the pressure more than ever, as the Chinese Cultural Revolution had caused Sihanouk to repress communist sympathisers. The arrest of 22 supposed leftists by Sihanouk's rightist strongman (and future usurper) Lon Nol again prompted Hu Nim to action.

---

93   ibid., 11.
94   ibid., 13; Carney, 'Biographical Sketches', 64. Hu was also vocal in the National Assembly on behalf of cooperatives, especially in his constituency of Kampong Cham. 'Le député Hu Nim a posé deux questions au Gouvernement [Deputy Hu Nim Posed Two Questions to the Government]', *Echos de Phnom Penh* [*Echoes of Phnom Penh*], 11 July 1960.

2. 'THE MOST DISSOLUTE AND DISHONEST' KHMER TO AID CHINA

Plate 2.3 Norodom Sihanouk, Cambodia's head of state, and other distinguished Cambodian guests arrive in Beijing on 11 April 1973 after an inspection tour of the Liberated Zone of Cambodia and a friendly visit to the Democratic Republic of Vietnam.
They are warmly welcomed at the airport by PRC Premier Zhou Enlai, other Chinese leaders and more than 5,000 people. Massive receptions for important foreign guests, dignitaries and delegations were often greeted with great fanfare.
Source: A special issue of *China Pictorial* (No. 6, 1973).

Disillusioned by Soviet de-Stalinisation and frustrated by Sihanouk's constant repression, Hu looked to China for answers. He visited the country again in 1965 for two weeks as 'leader of a delegation of AAKC members' that included Vann Tip Sovan, Sam Chaing, Ol Chan, Svay Borei, Phy Thean Lay and Eap Kim Phan.[95] He returned home with the Maoist view that the Soviet Union was 'revisionist'.[96] But in that year, Mao's ever-growing popularity in Cambodia, especially after the outbreak of the Cultural Revolution, distressed Sihanouk, who, after nearly a decade of rhetorical support for Mao (whom Sihanouk called the 'great venerated guide of the Cambodian people'), now viewed China's

---

95 Hu, 'Confession of Hu Nim', 12–13; Galway, 'Red Service-Intellectual', 301; and 'China–Cambodia Friendship Association Delegation Visit', 23–47.
96 Etcheson, *The Rise and Demise of Democratic Kampuchea*, 174.

'Maoist foreign policy' as a disruption.[97] Fearful that people were plotting to remove him from office, Sihanouk 'became distressed by news that the *Little Red Book* was popular' and imprisoned or ordered the execution of pro-China students.[98] Aware of the Beijing link to leftist intellectuals in Paris and Phnom Penh, Sihanouk urged Beijing to cease 'meddling' in Cambodia's internal affairs.[99]

Sihanouk suspected AAKC Vice-President Hu Nim most of all.[100] Sihanouk shuttered the AAKC in 1967 for its vocal support of Beijing and, according to one account, because he 'wanted to put an end to the distribution in the capital of Mao's *Little Red Book*'.[101] By one account, Hu oversaw the distribution of French-language translations of *Quotations from Chairman Mao Zedong* (*Mao zhuxi yulu* 毛主席語錄) by AAKC activists during his tenure as vice-president.[102] Along with Hou Yuon and Khieu Samphan, Hu Nim had also drawn Sihanouk's suspicion for his outspoken criticism of Sihanouk's government. Hu wrote in a 1967 edition of *The New Dispatch*, for example, that 'Sihanouk presided over a "national front which responds exactly to the aspirations of the people"', the wording of which irked Sihanouk.[103] Because of Hu's popularity as an intellectual, especially among progressive youths, Sihanouk suspected Hu of 'complicity in anti-regime student disturbances in Siem Reap (February 1963) and

---

97   Norodom Sihanouk, '"Pour nous, Cambodgiens, la Chine est bien notre amie numéro un ..." Déclaration de Samdech Chef de l'Etat à son départ de Pékin au terme de sa Vème Visite à la République Populaire de China, le 6 Octobre 1964 ["For Cambodians, China is Our Number One Friend ..." Declaration of the Head of State on the Occasion of his Departure from Beijing after his Fifth Visit to the People's Republic of China, 6 October 1964]', in *Quarterly Review of the Khmer–Chinese Friendship Association*, 8. On Sihanouk's pro-China stance, see: Norodom Sihanouk, 'Comment nous voyons la Chine [How We View China]', *Anakjātiniyam* [*The Nationalist*], 20 September 1963, 7, National Archives of Cambodia, Box 689, ID6061, also in Box 332, 1–19; '*Xihanuke qinwang zaizhi lianheguo dian zhong zhichu Zhongguo dui baowei Yazhou heping gongxian juda* 西哈努克親王在致聯合國電中指出中國對保衛亞洲和平貢獻巨大 [Prince Sihanouk Recognises China's Huge Contribution to the Defence of Peace in Asia to the United Nations]', *Sino-Khmer Daily*, 13 October 1962; Norodom Sihanouk, 'Message de S.A.R. le Prince Norodom Sihanouk à la radiodiffusion chinoise [Message from His Royal Highness, Prince Norodom Sihanouk, to Chinese Broadcasting]', [1956], National Archives of Cambodia, Box 689, ID unknown, 1–2; and Norodom Sihanouk, 'Rapport de Samdech chef de l'état au peuple khmer [Report from Samdech Head of State to the Khmer People]', [5 October 1964], National Archives of Cambodia, Box 689, ID6060, 1–6.
98   Chandler, *Brother Number One*, 83.
99   Ying Bing and Shi Zeliang, '*Jianpuzhai xiandai shilüe* 柬埔寨現代史略 [Modern History of Cambodia]', *Dongnanya yanjiu ziliao* 東南亞研究資料 [*Southeast Asian Studies*] 1 (1983): 106; and Chandler, *The Tragedy of Cambodian History*, 170.
100 Carney, 'Biographical Sketches', 64.
101 Kane, *Khmer Rouge Dictionary*, 156.
102 Locard, *Why the Khmer Rouge?*, 111–12.
103 Chandler, *The Tragedy of Cambodian History*, 169.

peasant activities [that he] deemed subversive'. Sihanouk's suspicions were accentuated by a 12 May 1964 'anti-American' student demonstration in which protestors, under leftist leadership, chanted slogans such as 'Down with Sihanouk' and 'Down with Saṅgam'.[104]

Sihanouk's suspicions of Hu Nim and other leftists led the Cambodian leader to suspect virtually anyone with links to China. After a Chinese-language newspaper declared 'all Cambodian workers believed in Chairman Mao' and PRC Premier Zhou Enlai pleaded for Chinese 'to display their pride of the Cultural Revolution and their love for Chairman Mao', many of Phnom Penh's *huaqiao* began to mimic Cultural Revolution fervour.[105] As the Samlaut rebellion erupted in April 1967, Sihanouk responded by levelling accusations against local Chinese, pro-China officials (Hu among them) and even Beijing for the rising tide of radicalism in the country. Sihanouk accused *huaqiao* 'who … have remained very Chinese at heart' of 'busily circulating Communist publications in the schools, propagandizing Communism in newspapers, movies, and the arts, and putting up wall posters Red Guard-style that were insulting to [Saṅgam]'.[106] He also charged:

> At present I find that China has made a serious change because she has given up peaceful coexistence and the five principles. China had changed her policy since the Cultural Revolution. There have been a number of Khmer who aid China … *The most dissolute and dishonest is Hu Nim.*

He then urged Hu 'to go over to the other side, as Khieu Samphan and Hou Yuon had done'.[107]

---

104 Gunn, *Monarchical Manipulation in Cambodia*, 411. For a report, with photos of a similar anti–US imperialism protest on 11 March 1965, see 'Mohā pātummneā thṅdī 11 mīneā 1965 nau Phnom Penh procheāṅ niṅ cakbot(r) Āmerikāṅ [Mass Demonstration on 11 March 1965 in Phnom Penh Against US Imperialism]', in *Quarterly Review of the Khmer–Chinese Friendship Association*, 2 September 1965, 28–30.
105 Chandler, *The Tragedy of Cambodian History*, 169.
106 Norodom Sihanouk, *Les Paroles de Samdech Preah Norodom Sihanouk* [*The Words of Samdech Preah Norodom Sihanouk*] (Phnom Penh: Ministère de l'information, 1968), 328–29, quoted in Galway, 'Red Service-Intellectual', 294.
107 Ben Kiernan, 'The Samlaut Rebellion, 1967', in *Peasants and Politics in Kampuchea, 1942–1981*, Ben Kiernan and Chanthou Boua, eds (London: Zed Books, 1982), 181. Emphasis added. Chinese writers were resolute and insisted that renewed Sino-Cambodian relations would 'give the gift of struggle'. Zhang Xizhen 張錫鎮, *Xihanuke jiazu* 西哈努克家族 [*The Sihanouk Family*] (Beijing: Shehui kexue wenpian chubanshe, 1996), 161.

Brother Bhoās: Hu Nim and the CPK Central Committee, 1967–77

Hu Nim did go to the other side, but not without genuine concern for his safety and knowledge that his political strategy was impossible. The Cultural Revolution had struck a nerve with Sihanouk and Cambodian radicals such as Hu did not ignore this development. Sihanouk had long since fallen out of favour among intellectuals over the Saṅgam's years of 'functional corruption' that were 'admitted, condemned, and then ignored', and its suppression of leftist opposition parties to maintain total neutrality in the National Assembly.[108]

By 1967, the political route to reform in Cambodia was a dead end. Sihanouk had grown paranoid by the 1966 elections because of the rising popularity of leftist ministers like Hu Nim, who ran for and won re-election. Right-wing members and commercial representatives within the National Assembly, too, remained recalcitrant and repealed all policies proposed by leading Cambodian leftists. As Khieu, who lost the confidence of the assembly and the government, conceded, there was nothing to salvage from the 'unreformable' state.[109] This revelation and the frustration many felt with the stagnant, Vietnamese-directed KPRP, radicalised Hu Nim. The stage was now set for a two-pronged attack: one from the revolutionary route, with Pol Pot working since 1953 as a covert operative in the rural-based KPRP;[110] and the other from Hu Nim and his fellow leftist ministers, who had steadily built their reputations and earned strong followings among their constituents.

Sihanouk's 'increasingly threatening invective' united the revolutionary and political paths into one, as his anger grew towards leftist ministers such as Hu Nim. Even with Hu reaffirming his loyalty to Sihanouk and rebuffing allegations he and other leftists played a role in peasant unrest, Sihanouk was unmoved. He responded with vitriol and set the now

---

108 Galway, *The Emergence of Global Maoism*, 129; and Galway, 'Red Service-Intellectual', 289, both quoting and citing Osborne, *Sihanouk*, 159. As Osborne notes, Sihanouk admitted to 'great corruption' in all aspects of Cambodian political life, but recognised his powerlessness to stop it, as it emanated from the royal family's inner circle and government downward. See also Ying and Shi, 'Modern History of Cambodia', 106; and Zhang, *The Sihanouk Family*, 161. On Sihanouk's policies, see: 'Jianpuzhai diyige wunian jihua—Xihanuke jihua 柬埔寨第一個五年計畫—西哈努克計畫 [Cambodia's First Five-Year Plan: Sihanouk's Plan]', *Dongnanya yanjiu ziliao* 東南亞研究資料 [*Southeast Asia Studies*] 1 (1960): 111–12.
109 Kiernan, *How Pol Pot Came to Power*, 204–5.
110 On this route, see Galway, *The Emergence of Global Maoism*, 144–58.

2. 'THE MOST DISSOLUTE AND DISHONEST' KHMER TO AID CHINA

conservative-rightist National Assembly to target the former minister. He publicly branded Hu a communist and pro-China sympathiser.[111] In a noteworthy incident, Sihanouk admonished Hu Nim in person on 30 September 1967 at Prey Totoeng High School in front of Hu's constituency:

> 'Companion' Hu Nim is a little hypocrite … a specialist in the art of being all honey on the outside and all venom on the inside. His voice has the tone of a monk at prayer, his words carry the scent of honey, but he hides his claws like a tiger … If you were a sincere and committed communist, if you had the courage of your convictions, if you had any courage at all, if the fire that devours you was not that of ambition but that of the ideology you proclaim, you would not be afraid to struggle in the light of day for the triumph of that ideology, you would have dared to assume full responsibility for it and face all the consequences alone.[112]

Sihanouk continued to berate Hu before his voting base: 'Hu Nim and his associates have excluded themselves from the national community … Your [Hu Nim's] "courage" consists simply in working in the shadows.'[113] Hu Nim fled to the *maquis* on 7 October 1967 to join his Paris cohort of Hou Yuon and Khieu Samphan in the communist movement on instruction from CPK Phnom Penh City Committee head Vorn Vet (born Sok Thuok, 1934–1978).[114]

Announcement of his disappearance led many to speculate that he, Hou and Khieu had been killed on Sihanouk's orders, which turned their loyalists against Sihanouk. Their popularity as representatives of the marginalised within the Saṅgam prompted widespread mourning; in Kandal Province, more than 15,000 students gathered at temples to grieve the 'martyrdom of Hou Yuon and Khieu Samphan'.[115] Thus began the legend of the 'Three Ghosts': ostracised yet popular leftist ministers who reappeared in 1970 as leaders of the CPK.[116]

---

111 Hu, 'Confession of Hu Nim', 18; and Ieng Sary, 'Kingdom of Cambodia National United Front of Kampuchea: Cambodia 1972', [1 January 1970], 16–17, DCCAM, D24010.
112 Sihanouk, *The Words of Samdech Preah Norodom Sihanouk*, 778, quoted in Kiernan, *How Pol Pot Came to Power*, 264.
113 Sihanouk, *The Words of Samdech Preah Norodom Sihanouk*, 752, 761, quoted in Kiernan, *How Pol Pot Came to Power*, 264–65.
114 Carney, 'Biographical Sketches', 64; Kiernan, *How Pol Pot Came to Power*, 265; and Galway, 'Red Service-Intellectual', 289.
115 Chandler, *The Tragedy of Cambodian History*, 167.
116 Suong, *Itinerary of a Khmer Rouge Intellectual*, 40.

EXPERIMENTS WITH MARXISM-LENINISM IN COLD WAR SOUTHEAST ASIA

In fact, they ascended to the highest posts within the CPK. Because of their meticulous analyses of Cambodia's economic problems, each occupied a ministerial post on the CPK Central Committee. Hu Nim served as Minister of Information and Propaganda, first in the FUNK and then in CPK-controlled liberated zones in the GRUNK.[117] A 1973 special issue of *China Pictorial* (*Renmin huabao* 人民畫報; lit., '*People's Pictorial*') covered the since deposed Norodom Sihanouk's inspection tour of the GRUNK, during which he met and talked with his hosts, CPK Central Committee members Hu Nim, Hou Yuon and Khieu Samphan. The issue provides several photographs, including ones in colour, of Sihanouk smiling and participating in a range of activities within the liberated zones. The photos also depict Hu Nim and his Paris comrades as close friends during their stints as Central Committee members.[118]

Plate 2.4 Hu Nim (centre) warmly greets head of state Norodom Sihanouk during his 1973 inspection tour of the liberated zone.
Source: A special issue of *China Pictorial* (No. 6, 1973).

117 ibid., 190–91.
118 'Xihanuke qinwang shicha Jianpuzhai jiefangjun zhuanji 西哈努克親王視察柬埔寨解放軍專輯 [Samdech Sihanouk's Inspection Tour of the Cambodian Liberated Zone]', *Renmin huabao* 人民畫報 [*China Pictorial*] (6) (June 1973).

Yet, only Khieu Samphan survived. As Hu recalled, the Angkar ('Organisation') developed into an increasingly tight circle of 'Brother No.1', Pol Pot, and 'Brother No.2', Nuon Chea, who he claims ordered the plan to evacuate Cambodia's cities on 19 April 1975.[119] By July 1976, the writing was on the wall for Hu Nim. Vietnam News Agency (Thông tấn xã Việt Nam) director Trần Thanh Xuân, a man whom Hu had met in 1974 in Hanoi, recalled that after Hu welcomed him:

> I could see Hu Nim had no power anymore. He was not at ease; he was very friendly, but not his own master. Everything was arranged by [DK Minister for Foreign Affairs] Ieng Sary. Hu Nim just implemented it [CPK policy] and played the official role.[120]

Indeed, the CPK, once in power, systematically purged its critics, including its own intellectual thrust. For instance, Pol Pot ordered Hou Yuon's murder in 1975 for opposing the total evacuation of the cities and abolition of the currency, and had Hu Nim incarcerated, tortured and ultimately killed on 6 July 1977 for similar calls for moderation.[121]

His tragic fate notwithstanding, Hu Nim's influence on the CPK cannot be understated. Before his October 1967 flight to the *maquis*, in late 1966, Hu Nim and Hou Yuon:

> established a secret committee—in which Khieu Samphan played no role—to coordinate dissident activities and consider various options for the overthrow not only of Lon Nol [who deposed Sihanouk in a 1970 bloodless coup], but also of Sihanouk, including political and armed actions.[122]

---

119 Hu, 'Planning the Past', 276; and Ben Kiernan, *The Pol Pot Regime: Race, Power, and Genocide in Cambodia under the Khmer Rouge, 1975–1979*, 3rd edn (New Haven, CT: Yale University Press, 2008), 33.
120 Kiernan, *The Pol Pot Regime*, 122, quoting the author's interview with Tran Thanh Xuan, Ho Chi Minh City, 26 October 1980.
121 Mission du Gouvernement Royal d'Union Nationale du Cambodge [Mission of the Royal Government of the National Union of Cambodia], 'Declaration de MM. Khieu Samphan, Hou Yuon, et Hu Nim [Declaration of MM. Khieu Samphan, Hou Yuon, and Hu Nim]', *Bulletin d'Information*, 16 February 1973, 3–4, National Archives of Cambodia, Box 670; Hu, 'Planning the Past', 304; Chieu, *My Story with the Communist Parties of China and Kampuchea*, 20; and Kiernan, *The Pol Pot Regime*, 59.
122 Heder, *Cambodian Communism and the Vietnamese Model*, 103, citing Nuon Chea, Pravoat Chdlananat Td-sou robdh Kasikdr K/ch Yoeng pi Chhnam 1954 d&l Chhnam 1970 [History of the struggle movement of our C(am)b(odian) peasants from 1954 to 1970] (Phnom Penh: Unpublished ms, n.d.), n.p.

A charismatic orator with a loyal following of activists, students and leftists, Hu provided a public face to the faceless 'Organisation'. He marshalled his public persona as a vocal critic of government corruption and advocated for improvements in the rural sector. In so doing, he established a link between the rural-based CPK movement and urbanite leftists and aided the party's recruitment of peasants.[123] On 26 March 1970, for instance, Hu and his Paris Group CPK leaders responded 'to Sihanouk's appeal with one ostensibly of their own' by 'calling on the Cambodian people to "organize guerilla units and armed forces ... and set up an equitable power" in the country'.[124]

In the five years before Lon Nol's ouster (1970–75), the CPK surrounded Phnom Penh and, from 17 April 1975, initiated its radical Maoist human experiment, drawing heavily, from a policy standpoint, on the Maoist doctoral dissertations of Hu Nim and his Paris colleagues. Hu's dissertation called for collectivisation based on voluntary work and democracy, not forced labour. Yet he valorised Chinese, North Korean and North Vietnamese models of self-sufficiency, grassroots cooperation and situational autarky. Hu also believed, however idealistically, that Cambodian peasants would join new collectivised structures of their own volition. Although somewhat derivative of Hou Yuon's 1955 dissertation, Hu's provided the CPK leadership with some useful blueprints and updated, more rigorous statistics of rural demographics—not to mention Maoist zeal befitting the era in which he authored it—for the party's grand vision of mass peasant communes.[125]

---

123 Heder, *Cambodian Communism and the Vietnamese Model*, 160–61; Chandler, *The Tragedy of Cambodian History*, 207, 228; Willmott, 'Analytical Errors of the Kampuchean Communist Party', 221; and Ben Kiernan, 'The 1970 Peasant Uprising in Kampuchea', *Journal of Contemporary Asia* 9(3) (1979): 314–16.

124 Heder, *Cambodian Communism and the Vietnamese Model*, 161, quoting 'Statement of Support to Prince Norodom Sihanouk by the Three Cambodian Deputies, Khieu Samphan, Hou Youn, Hu Nim', [26 March 1970], in *Cambodia in the Southeast Asia War*, Malcolm Caldwell and Lek Tan, eds (New York: Monthly Review Press, 1973), 396, 398.

125 Locard, *Why the Khmer Rouge?*, 38–41. Locard notes the CPK veered away from the more moderate proposals of Hou, Khieu and Hu by 1973 during the war against Lon Nol (68–69). See also Carney, 'Continuity in Cambodian Communism', 1–2, 12–17, 22–23.

Conclusion

A genealogy of the CPK's Maoism is a long and winding road that at once swings backward to account for the earliest and most formative social experiences and forwards to connect radical ideology to implementation. Men such as Hu Nim who became Maoists took different routes to their radicalisation, for sure, and did not agree monolithically in the same kind of Maoism. Hu gravitated towards Mao's political economy, which he saw as a useful critical interpretative paradigm with which to conceive, then overturn, Cambodia's political instability, underdevelopment and socioeconomic disequilibria.

Before the CPK's genocidal human experiment, Hu and his Paris-trained comrades were passionate students who cared genuinely about liberating their motherland from exploitation and painstakingly went about identifying problems and providing solutions. Hu had tremendous acumen when it came to peasant grievances since he had lived that life before and struggled so mightily to enter a world that had been reserved for the nation's elite. The realisation of the CPK's Maoist vision after 17 April 1975—the day the CPK captured Phnom Penh—was, sadly, the beginning of a four-year project that would set the already downtrodden country back several decades and cost nearly one-third of its people their lives.

As a corrective to facile descriptions of the CPK as Maoists or hyper-Maoists, or other opinions that disregard this aspect of the party's thought entirely, we ought to recentre Maoism in the CPK's ideological equation, with social experiences guiding us through the shaping and reshaping of Maoism to fit the concrete realities of the Cambodian situation. Hu Nim did his best to achieve this, both theoretically and practically, and found success once he abandoned the dead-end of working within the system. His purge from the party in 1977 because he opposed some of Pol Pot's policies notwithstanding, Hu represents part of the CPK's intellectual thrust, with his foundational national text one of the essential cogs in the moving wheel of Cambodian Maoism. The continued omission of Hu Nim and his other Paris Group contemporaries excludes perhaps the most crucial minds behind the DK machine, and to ignore the French connection—learning about Maoism in 1950s Paris—means cutting out the single most formative period in the development of Cambodian Maoism. Hu Nim's travels and written work, among those of his peers, hold one of the keys to the mystery behind the nature of the CPK's political thought, as well as the blueprint for its utopic—and disastrous—vision.

3

Buddhist socialism and national identity in colonial and postwar Burma: An analysis of U Nu's political thought

Khine Thant Su

In 1954, Prime Minister of Burma U Nu (1907–1995) hosted the Sixth Buddhist World Council in what was then the country's capital, Rangoon (Yangon). Spanning two years until 1956, the council was an extravagant event attended by delegates from major Buddhist countries and highly venerated Buddhist monks from Burma. These dignitaries welcomed the event as a revival of Buddhism that had been weakened under colonial rule. In preparation for the council, U Nu spent more than 16 million kyat (about A$3 million at the time) building a pagoda and other religious facilities.[1] Later in 1954, U Nu proposed a new law encouraging religious instruction in public schools. According to this policy, students of different religious backgrounds would be required to take classes on their respective religions. Members of the Buddhist monastic community, the *sangha*, who welcomed the Sixth Buddhist Council, protested this policy, with many seeing it as an attempt by the U Nu government to force Buddhist

---

1   U Ohn Ghine, 'Report on the Chattha Sangayana', *Light of the Dhamma* 2(3) (April 1954): 32–37.

schoolchildren to take classes on non-Buddhist religions.[2] As such, the convention of the Sixth Buddhist Council and the proposal of the religious instruction act—both carried out by the U Nu government in the same year—elicited completely different reactions from the Buddhist monastic community. This illustrates the complicated relationship between U Nu and the Burmese monastic community in the post-independence period arising from tensions among competing political ideologies.

The convention and the religious instruction act were two noteworthy instances among the various religious revival movements undertaken by U Nu's government as part of its effort for moral reform of Burma's postwar society. After suffering massive infrastructural damage due to the scorched-earth policies of the British during World War II, postwar Burma hosted armed ethnic and communist insurgencies that spread nationwide immediately after independence in January 1948.[3]

Lacking the financial and technical resources to effectively deal with these problems, U Nu made extensive use of rhetorical power to sway public opinion towards support for his beleaguered government, embarking on a project of societal moral reform, which he identified as the most crucial aspect of social reform since the colonial period. As a nationalist leader during the colonial period and then as post-independence prime minister of Burma, U Nu authored plays, novels and speeches highlighting moral decline and its deleterious effects on Burmese society.

Why did U Nu focus on moral reform to address Burmese society's political and economic problems? What was the significance of his ideas on morality in the larger context of the Cold War? This chapter traces changes in U Nu's discourse on the relationship between Buddhism and politics starting from the colonial period of the 1930s to the post-independence era of the 1950s. In both periods, U Nu stressed moral reform as an essential aspect of social reform, but his definitions of moral action evolved in response to changing international and domestic political contexts. U Nu's emphasis on moral reform took on a new significance in the Cold War era with the emergence of the threat of indirect involvement by foreign powers in Burmese politics.

---

2   U Nu, 'Clarification on the 1954 Policy of Religious Instruction in Public Schools (National Broadcast)', *U Nu: Collection of Speeches on Religion. Volume 3* (Yangon: Seikku Cho Cho, 2018), 305–6.
3   Frank N. Trager, *Burma—From Kingdom to Republic: A Historical and Political Analysis* (New York, NY: Frederick A. Praeger, 1966), 210.

U Nu's approach

Characterising moral reform as key to political and economic reforms, U Nu adopted and adapted foreign terms like 'democracy' and 'socialism' without replicating the Euro-American and Soviet models of modernisation. U Nu argued that the goals of his modernisation projects were superior to those of capitalist and communist models because these were only concerned with the material conditions of human life while his reforms aimed for spiritual rejuvenation of the people. U Nu criticised both capitalism and communism as immoral—the former for its encouragement of the profit motive and the latter for its advocacy of violent revolt and authoritarian rule. In contrast to these two varieties of modernity, U Nu envisioned a path for Burma on which moral rejuvenation paired with improved material conditions would bring the Burmese closer to spiritual elevation, resulting in the attainment of *nibbāna* or the ideal Buddhist state of 'freedom from desire'.[4]

Emphasis on moral reform had been central to U Nu's nationalist discourse since the colonial period. Even as Burma moved into the post-independence period, he continued to tout the importance of good morals as a means of resisting foreign interference in Burmese society and preserving independence. U Nu's definition of what constituted morality, however, changed in accordance with different political scenarios. During the colonial era, he equated morality with resistance to colonial capitalism and its corrupting impact on people's morals. U Nu criticised the profit-seeking capitalists and Buddhist monks who accepted bribes for political favours as immoral elements in society who were contributing to the entrenchment of colonial rule. After independence, U Nu came to view problems of poverty and insurgency as manifestations of society's continuing moral decline. He began to equate morality with selflessness, and explained the armed insurgencies, continued economic inequality and rampant corruption among bureaucratic officials as problems arising from the selfish pursuit of personal gain.

---

4   The 'desire' in this context encompasses both attachment to a physical existence and psychological desires such as greed, anger and ignorance. In critiquing capitalism and communism as being overly concerned with material life, U Nu thus also critiqued them based on their conduciveness to desires such as greed and anger. Definition of '*nibbāna*' from *Nyanatiloka Buddhist Dictionary*, available from: vdocuments.net/nyanatiloka-buddhist-dictionary.html?page=1.

The post-independence period was also when U Nu articulated morality in terms of religious devotion, which led to his advocacy of moral reform via religious revival. Morals came to constitute a link between the religious and secular realms when U Nu argued that improved morals would not only help solve the secular problems of poverty and political instability, but also bring Burmese society closer to attainment of religious ideals—something that was often defined in Theravada Buddhist terms. This resulted in the complicated relationship between the U Nu government and various religious groups during the post-independence period. U Nu's attempts to create a distinct marker of national identity for the emergent Burmese nation centred on Buddhism even as he was aware of the political necessity to emphasise equality and inclusivity for all so as not to alienate ethnic minorities and push them towards joining the various insurgencies.

The pressing need for independence during colonial rule had produced a tension in U Nu's political thought, leading him to advocate for reforming Burma into an ethnically harmonious nation that would abide by Buddhist notions of morality. Since the colonial period, U Nu had viewed Buddhist morals as a means of resistance against foreign domination. At the same time, he was influenced by modern colonial sensibilities, resulting in his call for a formal separation of religion and politics, and his criticism of the so-called false conflations of Marxism with Buddhism and the resultant 'misconception' of political issues as religious ones.[5] As such, U Nu's political ideology was shaped by the new epistemologies of colonial modernity even as he used indigenous notions of morality to critique colonial rule.

From the colonial to the post-independence periods, U Nu's internalisation of the colonial idea of the separation of politics and religion remained in tension with his tendency to understand politics through Buddhist categories. This tension gave rise to his view that modern reformist ideas such as socialism and democracy provided useful means for the material reform of society, but they were not the ultimate goals of his social reform agenda, which was the spiritual liberation of the people through moral reform. In the colonial period, U Nu partially reconciled Marxism with Buddhism, but maintained that the former could only bring about

---

5   Recent scholarship has pointed out the artificiality of claims for the separation of religion and politics in Burma because the Burmese conception of politics is deeply influenced by Buddhist concepts and practices. See, for example, Juliane Schober, *Modern Buddhist Conjunctures in Myanmar: Cultural Narratives, Colonial Legacies, and Civil Society* (Honolulu: University of Hawai'i Press, 2011), 14.

material liberation from colonial rule and was therefore incapable of providing spiritual liberation. After independence, when he embarked on creating a socialist welfare economy, U Nu argued similarly that socialism was merely a step towards restoring Burmese society to its original prosperity as symbolised by the Buddhist notion of the *Padaythabin* (the 'Tree of Fulfilment').

Moral reform as an important aspect of Buddhist modernism

After independence, U Nu's actions aligned with what have been interpreted as key features of 'Buddhist modernism' in three ways: in his emphasis on Buddhist textual traditions, his emphasis on Buddhist practice as a means of social change and his promotion of meditation among the masses to encourage individual spiritual enlightenment.[6] U Nu's convention of the Sixth Buddhist Council in 1954 was above all an attempt to preserve the Buddhist scriptures and prevent the disappearance of the *Sāsana* ('Buddha's teachings').[7] U Nu also emphasised the link between Buddhist morality and social reform, interpreting socialism as a means of 'removing greed'—one of the three desires leading to moral corruption in the view of Buddhism—while acknowledging that good morals were themselves a necessary precondition for socialism to work. Finally, U Nu promoted *vipassanā* ('insight') meditation among the population, stressing its power to transform the mind as key to producing moral citizens and bureaucrats.[8] Taken together, the three features of U Nu's Buddhist modernism revealed the ways in which he reconstituted Buddhist traditions in the face of changing political conditions. He employed Buddhist thought to make worldly reforms by preserving Buddhist textual traditions to systematise Buddhist practices, linking Buddhist morality to socialism. His promotion of *vipassanā* meditation also emerged in response to central notions of Western modernity such

---

6   'Buddhist modernism' as a phenomenon was first theorised by Heinz Bechert, *Buddhismus, Staat und Gesellschaft. Volume 1* [*Buddhism, State and Society*] (Berlin: Alfred Metzner Verlag, 1966). For a more recent study, see David McMahan, *The Making of Buddhist Modernism* (New York, NY: Oxford University Press, 2008).
7   Chris Clark, 'The Sixth Buddhist Council: Its Purpose, Presentation, and Product', *Journal of Burma Studies* 19(1) (2015): 79–112, at p.82, doi.org/10.1353/jbs.2015.0007.
8   Ingrid Jordt, *Burma's Mass Lay Meditation Movement: Buddhism and the Cultural Construction of Power* (Athens, OH: Ohio University Press, 2007), 30.

as reflexivity and personal agency. In short, U Nu's Buddhist modernist reforms were formed in the context of 'an engagement with the dominant cultural and intellectual forces of modernity'.[9]

To understand the dynamics of Buddhist modernity in postwar Burma, one needs to examine how it took shape in resistance to and interaction with new epistemologies introduced under colonial rule. As Alicia Turner has described for the early colonial period, the initial Burmese response to colonial domination did not centre on the Western-centric idea of a nation-state. Instead, the Burmese imagined themselves as belonging to 'moral communities' that did not take the nation as their organising unit.[10] According to Turner, the creation of 'moral communities' showed how the Burmese laity reconceptualised their responsibilities as Buddhists in the absence of the king, who had traditionally served as the patron of Buddhism. 'Moral community' was thus a modern reinterpretation of how the *Sāsana* might be protected in the context of new colonial conditions. In imagining themselves as part of these 'moral communities', the Burmese laity was concerned not so much with resistance to colonialism as with preserving longstanding Buddhist temporal subjectivities.[11] Turner points out that for the Burmese Buddhists, the social problems plaguing society were only the manifestations of a deeper problem, which was the decline of the *Sāsana*, not just as the product of external colonial impetus, but also stemming from their personal moral failings.[12] The encounter with colonial modernity thus led the Burmese Buddhists to view moral decline as both a symptom and a cause of the decline of the *Sāsana*, and stemming this became the ultimate goal of any material reform.

Turner's observations about the Burmese Buddhists in the early colonial period (1890–1920) provide important context for this chapter, which examines how U Nu's articulations of morality represented both change and continuity with those of Burmese Buddhists during that period. The activities of U Nu's government resembled those of the colonial-era Buddhist lay organisations in terms of designating moral reform as the crucial aspect of social reform. The Burmese Buddhist laity, Turner has shown, employed modern colonial communication and bureaucratic technologies to form these 'moral communities'.[13] Similarly,

---

9   David McMahan, *Buddhism in the Modern World* (New York, NY: Routledge, 2012), 8.
10 Alicia Turner, *Saving Buddhism: The Impermanence of Religion in Colonial Burma* (Honolulu: University of Hawai'i Press, 2014), 2–4.
11 ibid., 9.
12 ibid., 22.
13 ibid., 77–79.

in the post-independence period, U Nu embarked on modern projects of rationalisation, industrialisation and democratisation in the name of re-elevating morals. An important difference was that U Nu's moral reform was carried out when the nation-state had become the norm. How did U Nu continue employing the discourse of morality to articulate a unique Burmese world view in the post-independence period when his economic and political programs aimed to build Burma into a sovereign nation-state of the Westphalian kind? Answering these questions also means exploring whether resistance to Western domination was possible even after nationalist elites in the Third World had absorbed values central to European colonialism.

There have been few general studies of the intellectual life of Burma during the 1950s, and, to date, a detailed study of U Nu's political thought does not exist. As a period of liberal democracy under a civilian government, 1950s Burma was host to a high level of open intellectual activity that was not to reappear until the present. The Burmese intellectual elite of this era, many of whom had participated in the nationalist movements of the 1930s and 1940s, held contested visions of the nation. A study of U Nu's political thought, then, is a step towards constructing a better picture of the intellectual landscape of postwar Burma.

Previous studies of Burma have characterised U Nu as a 'Buddhist nationalist' in contrast with the 'secular nationalists' of Burma like Aung San.[14] Scarce are studies that highlight his early engagement with leftist ideas. U Nu's autobiography, *Saturday's Son*, acknowledges his important role in the 1936 establishment of the avowedly leftist publishing outlet the Nagani ('Red Dragon') Book Club, which became 'a hotbed of radical views' during the colonial period. However, other than acknowledging that he 'founded' the club and the *Nagani Journal* (the *Nagani Daily* newspaper never came to fruition), mention of his early engagement with Marxism-Leninism is scarce to nonexistent, as he shifts immediately to his 1942 imprisonment during the Japanese invasion of Burma.[15] Nor does

---

14   For earlier literature on Burmese Buddhism and politics, see Manuel Sarkisyanz, 'On the Place of U Nu's Buddhist Socialism in Burma's History of Ideas', *Studies on Asia* 2(1) (1961): 53–62; John H. Badgley, 'Burma: The Nexus of Socialism and Two Political Traditions', *Asian Survey* 3(2) (1963): 89–95; Donald E. Smith, *Religion and Politics in Burma* (Princeton, NJ: Princeton University Press, 1965); and Jan Becka, 'The Buddhist Revival in Post-Independence Burma', in *Religion and Society in India and Burma*, Stanislava Vavrouskova, ed. (Prague: The Oriental Institute of the Czechoslovak Academy of Sciences, 1991), 12–38.

15   U Nu, *Saturday's Son*, U Law Yone, trans., U Kyaw Win, ed. (New Haven, CT: Yale University Press, 1975), 80–81.

U Nu reflect or elaborate on his previous engagement with leftist materials in his earlier book, *Burma under the Japanese*, which focuses almost exclusively on his life and experiences from 1942.[16]

Political scientist Robert H. Taylor notes that U Nu was a leader of the People's Revolutionary Party, the predecessor to the Burmese Socialist Party, and was on the Supreme Council of the Anti-Fascist Organisation that resisted Japanese imperial occupation.[17] 'Among the group [that] advocated no cooperation whatsoever with fascists', Taylor states, was U Nu, although he acknowledges this group was divided between Marxists who endorsed a temporary alliance with the British and those who preferred the imperialist powers fight each other.[18] Whether U Nu at that time was an advocate for the first or second approach is unclear. Taylor indicates that during Nu's imprisonment, he tended towards a temporary alliance with the Allies with the proviso that the British grant Burma 'dominion status'.[19] These observations notwithstanding, U Nu's engagement with Marxist-Leninist texts is not a focus of his autobiography or of Taylor's studies.

In recent times, Juliane Schober, Erik Braun and Alicia Turner have pointed out the inaccuracy of viewing nationalism in Burma along the religious–secular binary. They argue instead for the interrelations between Buddhist world views and conceptions of political power.[20] Their studies have illuminated the ways in which modern Burmese Buddhist reformers drew on precolonial practices and reinterpreted them in engagement with new forms of knowledge introduced by colonial rule. Building on these studies, this chapter examines U Nu's Buddhist nationalist reforms to situate this period in the history of Burmese Buddhism. The existing literature on U Nu has not examined how he used the notion of morality to reconcile modern sensibilities such as socialism, democracy and national

---

16 Thakin Nu, *Burma under the Japanese* (London: Macmillan & Co., 1954).
17 Robert H. Taylor, 'Burma', in *Political Parties of Asia and the Pacific*, Haruhiro Fukui, ed. (Westport, CT: Greenwood Press, 1985), 129–30; and Robert H. Taylor, *Marxism and Resistance in Burma, 1942–1945: Thein Pe Myint's Wartime Traveler* (Athens, OH: Ohio University Press, 1984), 38.
18 Taylor, *Marxism and Resistance in Burma*, 9.
19 ibid., 109.
20 See Juliane Schober, *Modern Buddhist Conjunctures in Myanmar: Cultural Narratives, Colonial Legacies, and Civil Society* (Honolulu: University of Hawai'i Press, 2011); Erik Braun, *The Birth of Insight: Meditation, Modern Buddhism, and the Burmese Monk Ledi Sayadaw* (Chicago, IL: University of Chicago Press, 2013); and Turner, *Saving Buddhism*. Schober argues the colonial government's policy of separating state and religion led to secular governance being viewed with suspicion by the populace, who associated secularism with oppressive colonial rule. Aware of this, U Nu as prime minister used Buddhism to present himself as upholding Buddhist kingship models as well as to secure political legitimacy for his regime.

unity with longstanding Buddhist cosmological beliefs. The present study attempts to fill this gap in the current literature on the U Nu period (1948–60).

There have also been attempts to reconsider how closely U Nu replicated the precolonial Buddhist kingship traditions in the post-independence era. Hiroko Kawanami argues U Nu did not wish to restore all features of traditional Buddhist practices indiscriminately. By setting out the impact of modern colonial education on the shaping U Nu's world view, Kawanami highlights instead the 'rationalising' reforms of Buddhist practice carried out by the prime minister. She cites, for example, his rejection of the allegedly 'superstitious' practice of *śamatha* ('focus') meditation in favour of the more 'scientific' *vipassanā* meditation, to highlight that state-sponsored Buddhism under U Nu represented a qualitatively different kind from precolonial models.[21] This is an important point that is often underacknowledged in studies of U Nu. But Kawanami has not put U Nu's thought into the global historical context by examining how he employed his notion of Buddhist modernity to respond to and resist the threat of the hegemonic Cold War powers.

Importantly, as this chapter shows, U Nu reconciled his modernisation projects with reconstituted standards of Buddhist practice to distinguish Burmese modernity from capitalist and communist models. By shifting away from the tradition–modernity binary to understand U Nu, this essay examines how U Nu employed the notion of morality to criticise Euro-American forms of modernity even while he implemented reform projects in Burma to achieve an industrialised economy and a democratic government.

Colonial threat to Burmese Buddhist morality and U Nu's nationalist recommendations

U Nu's views on the link between moral reform, nation-building and social reform developed in the crucible of colonial domination. As has been illustrated by Turner, the Burmese search for identity in the early colonial period revolved around Buddhism rather than the notion of a Burmese

---

21   Hiroko Kawanami, 'U Nu's Liberal Democracy and Buddhist Communalism in Modern Burma', in *Buddhism and the Political Process*, Hiroko Kawanami, ed. (New York, NY: Palgrave Macmillan, 2016), 36–37.

nation. The Burmese nationalist elite mobilised Buddhism as a signifier of *national* identity to create a unique identity for the Burmese vis-a-vis the foreign colonisers. From the time of the slogan 'To be Burmese is to be Buddhist'—a rallying cry of the first Burmese nationalist organisation, the Young Men's Buddhist Association (YMBA, established in 1906)—the subsequent nationalist movements in Burma would continue to designate Buddhism as a central element of Burmese national identity.[22]

The establishment of the Dobama Asiayone (DBA, We Burmans Association) in 1930 marked a generational shift in Burmese nationalism. Formed by young university students frustrated with the colonial government's oppressive education policies and the older generation's YMBA, whom they perceived as too accommodating to the colonial government, the DBA represented a revolutionary turn in the Burmese nationalist movement. Members of the DBA adopted the title *thakin* ('master')—a term hitherto reserved for Europeans in Burma.[23] Although often characterised as a secular nationalist group in contrast with the YMBA, the DBA's members continued the YMBA's practice of forming a national identity around the common majority belief in Buddhism. This is best illustrated by the fact that members of the DBA used Buddhist concepts and categories even in their translations of foreign revolutionary literature published through the Nagani Book Club.

Importantly, according to U Nu's autobiography, the Nagani Book Club 'was modeled on the Left Book Club of Victor Gollancz in England'. An 'immediate success', Nagani served as a channel through which the nationalists could distribute international ideas on anticolonialism, anti-imperialism and national liberation to the Burmese masses, many of which were leftist materials.[24] In attempting to create a revolutionary force out of the people who had been functioning under Buddhist soteriological views, members of the DBA interpreted these foreign ideas through Buddhist language and concepts familiar to their readers.

---

22 Juliane Schober, 'To be Burmese is to be Buddhist: Formations of Buddhist Modernity in Colonial Burma', in *Theravada Buddhism in Colonial Contexts*, Thomas Borchert, ed. (London: Routledge, 2018), 23–25.
23 In taking the title *thakin*, the DBA members claimed Burmese, not Europeans, were the real masters of Burma.
24 U Nu, *Saturday's Son*, 80.

3. BUDDHIST SOCIALISM AND NATIONAL IDENTITY IN COLONIAL AND POSTWAR BURMA

Thakin Nu, as U Nu was known at the time, published several original and translated works through the Nagani Book Club. One of his earliest publications was his collection *Modern Plays*, in 1937. A unifying theme of all six plays in the collection was the issue of moral decay, which was explored in many forms ranging from corrupt 'political monks' to politicians who preached patriotism while neglecting good moral conduct in their personal lives. In the first vein was a play titled 'U Kalein' ('Mr Crook'), which portrays a monk who abuses his religious status by consuming liquor and consorting with women. One day, the monk's actions are discovered by a village youth, who then tries to expose the monk's lack of propriety. However, not only is the youth dismissed by village elders, he is also punished for his attempt to tarnish the reputation of a revered monk. At the end of the play, it is revealed that the monk has been accepting donations from colonial government officials who wished to use his influence to secure votes in the region. Therefore, these politicians had a vested interest in maintaining the monk as an object of reverence in this village. With such unified support behind the monk, the youth cannot bring justice even though the monk is corrupt.[25]

Nu included a foreword to the play detailing his reasons for writing it, urging monks to 'stay out of politics' because monks who had not studied politics would be easily manipulated by politicians seeking to 'gain influence in the country by colluding with monks'. The result would be politicians 'will no longer work hard to bring prosperity to the country; instead they will spend time contriving ways to cheat and deceive'.[26] Here is an example of the ways in which Nu's political consciousness during this period was moulded by the combination of traditional cultural beliefs and new sensibilities introduced by colonialism. The separation of state and religion was a new concept that colonial rule introduced to Burma, where conventionally, the Buddhist conception of merit had been embedded in notions of the political legitimacy of a ruler.[27] In addition, the idea of 'religion' as a category in itself was just starting to take shape in the Burmese consciousness at this time. Nu's recommendation for Buddhist monks to

---

25 Thakin Nu, 'U Kalein', in *Modern Plays* (1938), cited in *Myanmar Literature Project Working Paper No.10*, Hans-Bernd Zöllner, ed., *Austrian Journal of South-East Asian Studies*: 17, 32–58.
26 ibid. The author thanks Tin Hlaing for the Burmese-to-English translation of these quotes.
27 Juliane Schober, 'Buddhism in Burma: Engagement with Modernity', in *Buddhism in World Cultures: Comparative Perspectives*, Stephen C. Berkwitz, ed. (Santa Barbara, CA: ABC-CLIO, 2006), 79–81.

'stay out of politics' suggests he had internalised colonial epistemologies even as he made his proposal in the name of resisting the foreign colonial rule that was undermining Burmese social values such as morality.

Another play, titled 'Naung Daw Chut-Khan' ('Taming the Elder Brother'), is set in the Ava period in Burma in the fifteenth century and follows two brothers who are officials in a Burmese army fighting a Shan ruler. The younger brother finds the older one having an affair with a married woman; he drives the woman away and scolds his brother, lamenting that he would rather take his own life than continue to survive as the brother of an adulterer. Hearing this, the older brother regrets his actions and comes to accept his brother's claim that a corrupt politician is an unreliable one and he vows to change his behaviour.[28] The other plays in the collection similarly explore adultery as a danger to both private and public lives, investigating how families are wrecked and politicians led astray from their rightful duties when they become preoccupied with such an immoral act. It must be noted that these plays were written at a time when Burmese men were highly concerned about European and Indian men taking Burmese women as mistresses. European colonial officers took Burmese women as secret lovers during their time in Burma and abandoned them when they left the country. Chie Ikeya has pointed out that Burmese men objected to such intimate relations between Burmese women and foreign men as a threat to Burma's Buddhist culture.[29] Considered in this context, Nu's stories exploring adultery can be read as a warning to Burmese against following the immoral actions associated with foreign men. In this way, Nu identified societal moral decay as induced by foreign colonial rule.

It is clear the notion of morality in all the stories is derived from the Buddhist notion of the five precepts, which urge people to abstain from killing, stealing, sexual misconduct, lying and intoxication. Taken together, the plays portray the dangers of moral decay from different perspectives, but all have a common suggestion: foreign imperial domination and the attendant corruption of morals created by such oppressive rule can only be overthrown when the Burmese themselves reform their morals. In other words, moral improvement in one's private life was thought to be capable

---

28   ibid., 58–79.
29   Chie Ikeya, *Refiguring Women, Colonialism, and Modernity in Burma* (Honolulu: University of Hawai'i Press, 2011), 120–21. Ikeya references a British report on the 1938 Indo-Burmese riots in her observation that anxiety about such intermarriage constituted a major reason for the riots against the *kala* (Indian) men.

of effecting social change. Such a connection between the private and the public realms anticipated U Nu's emphasis in the post-independence period that the success of his political and economic reform programs depended on the moral reform of every individual in Burmese society.

Marxism and Buddhism: Political freedom versus spiritual liberation

Around the time he published his plays stressing the importance of morality, Thakin Nu wrote short stories exploring the question of whether Marxism was compatible with Buddhist values. One such story, entitled 'I Am a Supporter of Bon Wada', was published through the Nagani Book Club in the late 1930s.[30] Nu made himself a character in the story, called Ko Nu, who debates the character Ko Sein about whether communism dictates actions incompatible with Buddhist values.[31] Ko Nu is initially convinced that implementing *bon wada* ('collectivity') in Burma goes against Buddhist values because the former dictates violence against capitalists while Buddhist teachings prohibit even wishing someone ill. To this, Ko Sein responds by reminding Ko Nu of Buddha's warning of the danger of three evils—*lobha* ('greed'), *dosa* ('anger') and *moha* ('ignorance')—which can trap a person inside endless *saṃsāra* (the cycle of life and rebirth), precluding his or her potential of reaching nirvana. Ko Sein continues, explaining that capitalists 'add fuel to the fire of *lobha* in men' by claiming land and commodities as their private property. In contrast, *bon wada* transforms private property into common property thereby extinguishing the 'fire of *lobha*', which arises solely from the existence of private property.[32] In other words, *bon wada* can restore morals by ridding society of the main causes of moral decline.

---

30   Maung Nu, 'Kya naw Bon Thamar [I Am a Follower of Bon Wada]', in *Bon Wada Hnit Dobama [Bon Wada and Us Burmese]*, Thein Pe Myint, ed. (Rangoon: Pyidawsoe, 1954). *Bon wada* (the 'principle of collectivity') was first used as a Burmese translation of 'communism' by Thakin Than Tun in his foreword to Thakin Soe's book *Socialism*, published through Nagani in 1938. Than Tun and Soe eventually split from the mainstream Burmese nationalist movement that was dominated by socialists in the late 1940s. In the post-independence era, Than Tun and Soe led White Flag and Red Flag communist insurgencies, respectively, against the Nu government.
31   '*Ko*' is roughly equal to 'Mister' but is only used for middle-aged men; those slightly older are called '*U*', although the exact distinction between the two in terms of age is not clear.
32   Nu, 'I Am a Follower of Bon Wada', 56–57.

Ko Sein also goes on to discuss the relationship between the Buddhist idea of *kamma* ('action' or karma) and *bon wada*. He points out that belief in *kamma* does not necessarily mean a passive acceptance of one's poverty in this life. In fact, the poor need to be aware of the rich's ploy to interpret the idea of *kamma* incompletely. The poor need to realise the capitalists only highlight the *effects* of having bad *kamma*, without also acknowledging that Buddha pointed to the *causes* of bad *kamma* and how to avoid them.[33] According to the Buddhist world view, Ko Sein argues, accumulating private poverty is the main way to accrue bad karma because it leads one to become corrupted by the three evils. By consciously omitting this fact from their Buddhist rhetoric, capitalists use Buddhist ideas selectively to justify their continued exploitation of the working class. Ko Sein's explanation satisfies Ko Nu, who, by the end of the story, admits his views on *bon wada* and Buddhism have been changed.

A few noteworthy points emerge from this exchange between the two men. Even though the characters are debating from opposite sides on the issue of communism and Buddhism, they both appeal to Buddhist concepts to support their case. This reflected the intellectual milieu in Burma during the late 1930s, when the aspiring young nationalists first came in contact with foreign revolutionary ideas through literature. Buddhist concepts and categories, which had formed the basis of public education before colonisation, continued to serve as the primary framework through which the Burmese understood the world. Despite the colonial policy of separating state and religion, Buddhism continued to provide a moral basis for the everyday actions of Buddhist Burmese. As someone attempting to introduce foreign revolutionary ideas to Burmese society, Thakin Nu needed to convince the public that communism or *bon wada* was not against religion. Rather, it was conducive to good Buddhist morals and capable of reversing the moral decay brought on by capitalist exploitation. Considered against his earlier plays stressing moral uprightness as a crucial tool in the fight against imperialism, this story can be seen as Nu's attempt to argue in support of the anti-imperialist message of communism through the language of Buddhist morality.

During the colonial period, Nu started to read foreign works on Marxism-Leninism, and his understanding of the various revolutionary ideas was still taking shape. His writings during this period reflect the formative

---

33   Emphases added by author.

stage of thinking about the relationship between Buddhism and modern foreign revolutionary ideas. Ending colonial rule was his primary goal during this period. As such, he demonstrated a willingness to accept a wide range of anticolonial ideologies that would help mobilise people in resistance to colonial rule—something that was common among anticolonial intellectuals across Southeast Asia.[34]

Nu's affiliation with Marxism and communism must be understood within this context. He was attracted to these revolutionary ideas mainly because of their use for political mobilisation, not through an unconditional acceptance of Marxist doctrines. Although he agreed with Marxism in terms of pragmatic political action, he did not agree with its materialism at the philosophical level because it conflicted with the Buddhist notion of impermanence. In reconciling Marxism with Buddhism, one of the challenges for Thakin Nu was how to explain the Marxist dictate of class struggle in Buddhist terms. In the story discussed above, Ko Sein gives only a roundabout response to Ko Nu's point that *bon wada* cannot be compatible with Buddhist teachings because the former prescribes the violent overthrow of capitalists. Ko Sein does not directly address this issue, instead choosing to argue against capitalism using a different aspect of Buddhism—the three evils. Ko Sein's circumvention of this question reflects the author's dilemma regarding this issue. It was only six years later, in a booklet titled *What is Marxism?*, written in 1946, that Thakin Nu again approached the violence inherent to the Marxist approach to revolution.

In this booklet, Thakin Nu admits Marxism prescribes the necessary role of violence in carrying out revolution, and that this might be looked on unfavourably by Burmese Buddhists. Nonetheless, Nu reasoned the communist idea of the violent takeover of capitalist property was only retaliation for the latter's initial crime of robbing the *Padaythabin* and its material abundance from the inhabitants of the world.[35] Thus, communism should be seen not as an initiator of violence but rather as only prescribing violence to the degree necessary to take back what was wrongfully exploited from the masses. To further illustrate this point, Nu cited a Buddhist tale in which the Buddha has been reborn as a crab

---

34 Anna Belogurova, 'Communism in South East Asia', in *Oxford Handbook of the History of Communism*, Stephen A. Smith, ed. (Oxford, UK: Oxford University Press, 2014), 236–51.

35 '*Padaythabin*' ('Padeytha tree') signifies the Burmese equivalent of a cornucopia. U Nu often invoked the myth of the *Padaythabin* in his speeches justifying his government's choice of socialism as a development model for Burma.

in a lake. One day, seeing a crane hunting his fellow crabs, the Buddha crab decides to snip off the crane's neck to preserve the greater good of his fellow crabs even though he knows the action of killing will give him bad karma. Using this Buddhist tale as an example, Nu points out communists must sacrifice their karma by carrying out violent revolution against capitalists to improve the lives of their fellow Burmese who are oppressed by the colonial system. In conclusion to this section, Nu claims communism and its attendant violence mean that acting as a communist can lead one off the path to nirvana, but anyone who wishes to reverse the capitalist oppression of the people should join the communist side.[36]

This snippet from *What is Marxism?* suggests Nu believed that improving one's material life could sometimes hinder one from attaining spiritual salvation. Yet, given the pressing concern of fighting for independence from colonial rule, Nu chose to promote Marxism as an expedient tool to further his pressing goals. In the post-independence period, the threat of foreign intervention changed from direct colonial domination to indirect intervention in Burmese affairs by the Cold War powers. In response to such changing threats, U Nu made a complete turnabout in his stance regarding the relationship between material and spiritual wellbeing. Thus, after independence, he came to argue that secular political and economic programs such as democratic and socialist reforms should not only provide material wellbeing but also serve spiritual goals, such as escape from the three desires of *lobha*, *dosa* and *moha*.

In the next section of his story, Nu criticises the behaviour of those who call themselves 'Marxists'. Addressing the debate between Buddhists and the self-proclaimed Marxists about the relationship between Marxism and Buddhism, Nu points out the conflict arose mainly from the self-identified Marxists' inadequate understanding of Marxism and misguided attempts to interfere in religious matters. To illustrate this, Nu points to the use of the Buddhist terms *rūpa* and *nāma* in the Marxists' political campaigns.[37] He claims Burmese Marxists have wrongly equated the Marxist notion of 'matter' with *rūpa*. Citing a passage from the Pāli Canon, Nu instead argues the true Buddhist notion of *rūpa* refers to a principle, rather than physical matter. As a principle of change, different states of being—such as being hot, cold, hungry, thirsty and so on—cause *rūpa* to appear in

---

36 Thakin Nu, *What is Marxism?* (Yangon: Seikku Cho Cho, 2014), 133–34.
37 '*Yote*' and '*nam*' are Burmese derivations of the Pāli words *rūpa* and *nāma*, referring to the distinction between 'corporeality' and 'mind'. *Nyanatiloka Buddhist Dictionary*.

3. BUDDHIST SOCIALISM AND NATIONAL IDENTITY IN COLONIAL AND POSTWAR BURMA

different forms. As such, the Marxist notion of matter/material cannot be translated as *rūpa* because the former conceptualised matter as an aggregate of atoms, permanently remaining in their form and not affected by contact with different *dhātu* ('elements').[38]

U Nu also criticised Burmese Marxists for equating the Marxist notion of mind or spirit with the Buddhist notion of *nāma*. Nu pointed out that, according to Buddhist belief, *nāma* is a combination of 89 different forms of *sate* (Burmese for the Pali word *citta*, meaning 'consciousness') and 52 different forms of *say ta thate* (Burmese version of the Pali word *cetasika*, meaning mental states that are 'bound up with the simultaneously arising consciousness and conditioned by its presence').[39] Nu argued that the Marxist notion of mind covered only five of the 52 varieties of *say ta thate* and thus the two could not be equated. Such wrongful conflations of Marxist categories of matter and mind with Buddhist notions of *rūpa* and *nāma* gave rise to the debate between Buddhists and Marxists regarding the question of whether *rūpa* or *nāma* came first. In Nu's view, such a debate was ill conceived because both sides were arguing from two different epistemological standpoints. Instead, Nu argued that Buddhism and Marxism were two fundamentally different ideologies. Buddhism shows the way of escape from the material world, which is perpetually associated with *dukkha* ('suffering'), whereas Marxism focuses on eradicating problems of the *lawki* ('the everyday material world'). In conclusion, Nu urged the leftists in Burma to refrain from attacking Buddhism inaccurately to avoid further deterioration of communism's reputation among the Burmese populace. This he deemed an urgent matter because he 'worried that Communism would be rejected by the Burmese even though it has a good purpose'.[40]

Although he prescribed the Marxist idea of political action through violent revolution, Nu declared he personally did not believe in Marxist materialism. He did not explicitly state his reason for disagreeing with materialism, but one could deduce it was due to the Marxist view of matter as permanent, which contradicted the Buddhist view of matter as impermanent. Given this, it is worth noting that Nu identified as a

---

38 Derived from the Pāli word *dhātu*, the 'elements' referred to by *dhāt* included not only physical elements such as earth, water, fire and wind, but also mental elements that constitute the 'conditions of the process of perception'. *Nyanatiloka Buddhist Dictionary*.
39 Nyanatiloka Mahathera, *Manual of Buddhist Terms and Doctrines*. The author is yet to locate the Pāli root for this word.
40 Thakin Nu, *What is Marxism?*, 147.

leftist, claiming a belief in materialism was not a necessary precondition for one to call oneself a 'leftist' nor was it the case that one could only become a leader in the project of establishing communism if one believed in materialism. He defined leftists as 'leaders of the society in establishing Communism', and they need not be believers in materialism. But to qualify as a 'leftist' one must be equipped with good morals and believe that as long as class oppression persisted, there would continue to be *lawki* ('material', 'secular') problems, and therefore they must work to end this system that produced commodities for profit rather than for use.[41] It is significant that in formulating an alternative definition of a leftist, Nu placed good morals at the fore. In proposing a new definition of leftism based on morality, Nu implied morality was not an inherent component of Marxist materialism. Given his distinction between Marxism and Buddhism along the lines of *lawki* ('the material world') and *lawkouttara* ('spiritual things'), it is apparent that from the colonial period, Nu started to view Marxism merely as a political tool to solve the secular problems created by colonial capitalism.[42] But Marxism was incapable of guiding people towards spiritual liberation.

U Nu's post-independence reconceptualisation of morality, Buddhism and politics

U Nu became the prime minister of Burma after the country gained independence from the British on 4 January 1948, after which he continued to emphasise the importance of high morals in Burmese society; however, the purposes for which he employed the morality discourse evolved. In contrast to his definition of morality during the colonial period, U Nu's idea of morality now centred on resistance to intervention by foreign powers during the Cold War. Designating moral reform as the cornerstone of his nation-building project, U Nu critiqued both capitalism and communism while distinguishing his developmental plan from these two hegemonic forms of modernity. Concerns about national unity led U Nu to frame morality in terms of devotion to religion in general, and not just Buddhism. Yet his postwar explanations of why

---

41   ibid., 150.
42   *Lawki* and *lawkouttara* are Burmese derivations of the Pāli words *lokiya* and *lokuttara*, signifying the duality between the 'mundane' and the 'supermundane'. *Nyanatiloka Buddhist Dictionary*.

modern systems such as socialism and democracy were compatible with Burma's situation frequently centred on Buddhist values and categories. His agenda of creating a nation-state built on individual rights and civil liberties resulted in his nominal support of all religions as sources of morality and, as such, important partners in his modernisation. Tension arose, however, from the fact he articulated this vision of a moral and modern society mostly in Theravada Buddhist terms.

U Nu's continued advocacy for the separation of religion and politics after independence was born of his desire for national unity. On 25 September 1954, U Nu spoke to the nation via the Public Broadcasting Station about the recently proposed policy of religious instruction in government-run schools—the policy that had provoked vehement opposition from the *sangha*. To illustrate the fairness of his government's religious policies, U Nu recalled some of his talks with Roman Catholic and Muslim religious leaders during the height of ethnic insurgencies in 1949. He claimed that during these meetings, the Christian and Muslim leaders reaffirmed their faith in his government and assured him their followers were not among the insurgents active in the Karen and Arakan states.[43] From these religious leaders' comments, U Nu pointed out, it was apparent the reason for the ethnic insurgencies was not religious persecution by his government. His policy of religious instruction was merely a 'political' gesture to maintain the goodwill of other religious groups and was not to be confused with an oppressive 'religious' policy against Burmese Buddhists.[44] U Nu thus attempted to keep the issue of ethnic insurgencies from being framed in terms of religious conflict between Buddhists and non-Buddhists by urging people to view 'religion' and 'politics' separately.

At the same time, however, U Nu started to justify many of his political goals using religious language. Signifying a complete departure from his colonial-era discourse, U Nu as prime minister stressed that politics should not only serve material welfare but also facilitate spiritual fulfilment. In such terms, he justified his socialist welfare policies, reconciling socialism with Burmese culture by characterising the former as a system that would bring society back to the age of the *Padaythabin*. As such, his discourse on the relationship between politics and religion had evolved

---

43 This was in reference to two major ethnic separatist movements on the eastern and western borders of Burma at the time. The Karen National Defence Organisation was active along the Burma–Thailand border while Islamic Mujahideen insurgents were active in the western Arakan (Rakhine) region.
44 U Nu, 'Clarification on the 1954 Policy of Religious Instruction', 298–306.

from his colonial-era thinking in two ways. First, socialism was no longer an intermediary step towards communism, but rather a facilitating stage in the creation of an ideal Buddhist society. Furthermore, U Nu's use of Buddhist symbols such as the *Padaythabin* to describe his socialist program showed he now conceived of a more intimate relationship between the mundane world and the spiritual liberation of the people. The goal of material sufficiency was interpreted as reversing moral decline in society by extinguishing the fire of the three desires—*lobha*, *dosa* and *moha*—that accompanied poverty.

In the following excerpt from U Nu's 'Martyr's Day Speech' in 1951, he adapts Marxist-Leninist theories and reinterprets them using Buddhist language. He takes Lenin's theory that imperialism is the highest stage of capitalism and modifies it to argue that imperialism is a consequence of men falling prey to *lobha*, one of the three roots of evil according to Buddhist belief:

> In the beginning, there was a Tree of Fulfillment [*Padaythabin*] from which people could get anything they needed … But men gave in to greed [*lobha*] and started seeking profit out of resources. This led to capitalists colonizing territories. Capitalists who wanted to gain control of the same territories went to war against other capitalists. Thus were generated the *three calamities* of bloody conflicts, famine, and epidemics.[45]

Here again the *Padaythabin* was invoked, along with the three roots of evil (*lobha*, *dosa* and *moha*) and the three calamities—another Buddhist concept predicting disasters thought to occur as *Śāsana* declines. He explained capitalism and imperialism as direct consequences of the decline in morals. Men fall prey to different stages of immorality by first giving in to greed (induced by the profit motive) and move on to commit violence against others (such as capitalists going to war). In the same speech, U Nu explained he did not consider building a socialist country an end in itself but rather a step towards restoring Burmese society to its original prosperity—that is, the time of the *Padaythabin*: 'The root cause of [the three calamities] is the exploitation of man by man born of this system of private ownership. Socialism is primarily concerned with the removal of this cause.'[46]

---

45 U Nu, 'Martyrs' Day Speech', in *Collection of Political Speeches. Volume 1* (Yangon: Seikku Cho Cho, 2016), 92. Emphasis added.
46 ibid.

The logic here was that reform of the material world would result in spiritual elevation of the people. This represented a significant change since the colonial period when he had argued that a Marxist revolution could cause an individual to accrue bad karma. The reason for this change must be understood in the context of Burma's changing political climate.

In the colonial period, U Nu's pressing political concern was to overthrow colonial rule, for which he prescribed Marxism, which he admitted was not entirely compatible with Buddhist belief. After independence, however, his political task changed to resisting foreign intervention in Burma linked to the problems of ethnic and communist insurgencies. Burma as a nominally independent nation was facing threats to its sovereignty. It was in this context that U Nu came to emphasise morality as the link between material and spiritual wellbeing. Using this non-dualistic view of the mundane and the spiritual, U Nu distinguished his programs of material (socialist and democratic) reform as qualitatively different from the developmental models of the Euro-American and Soviet powers.

U Nu's shifting views on the relationship between material and spiritual wellbeing evolved in tandem with his reinterpretation of what morality meant. In contrast to the colonial period, when he equated morality with resistance to colonial capitalism and its corrupting effects on the people, U Nu's postwar definition of morality centred on the idea of selflessness. He criticised the armed insurgents, corrupt officials in the bureaucracy and capitalists in postwar Burmese society as immoral elements in selfish pursuit of personal gain. For example, in a speech in 1951, U Nu lamented the decline of the 'moral pillar' in Burma resulting from the prevalence of those 'who are beckoning distant friends regardless of the consequences' because they 'have not the capacity to look a little beyond their self-interest'.[47] This was a clear reference to the ethnic and communist insurgencies, which the U Nu government suspected had connections to the Cold War powers. But U Nu's criticism was targeted not only at the insurgents. In another speech in 1951, at the founding ceremony of the Bureau of Special Investigation, U Nu declared the bureau's mission was to arrest moral deterioration among the 'three classes of people: government servants, politicians, and traders'.[48] He accused these three

---
47 U Nu, 'Task Before Us (Convocation Address at the University of Rangoon on 22nd December 1951)', in U Nu, *Burma Looks Ahead* (Rangoon: Ministry of Information, 1953), 34.
48 U Nu, 'Bribery and Corruption (Speech delivered at the Swearing-in Ceremony of Members of the Bureau of Special Investigation on 17th December 1951)', in *Burma Looks Ahead*, 23.

groups, respectively, of stealing state property, pocketing state-issued agricultural loans intended for poor farmers and avoidance of income tax. Claiming that obsession with the self was the root of these social ills, U Nu concluded that the bureau's activities would be complemented by programs to 'reeducate people through religious revival'.[49]

The underlying theme in U Nu's speeches was his conception of morality as the link between material and spiritual welfare. Thus, threats to morality were threats to these two forms of wellbeing. U Nu's criticism of the communist insurgents followed this logic. In a rally speech in 1954, he condemned the communist insurgents for 'shooting people at random, robbing and stealing from villages'—the implication being the communists had broken two of the five precepts of Buddhism: killing and stealing. He directly linked communism to moral decline in a government publication promoting his Pyidawtha ('Great Prosperous State') project—a welfare program that included political and economic reforms and religious revival. In this text, he called the communist insurgency a 'moral outrage' and he highlighted its 'destructive and wasteful' impacts on Burmese society.[50] Thus, communism and insurgents rebelling in the name of this ideology constituted a moral threat to Burmese society.

At other times, U Nu was more explicit about communism's dual threats to morality and religion. For example, in a speech in 1952, he warned the public of the communist threat to all religions in Burma:

> [T]he Communists used to accuse religion of being an opiate and that it needed to be abolished. You would remember that they even published a thesis with a sacrilegious title, 'Is there such a thing as omniscient knowledge?'[51] If they have such audacity to insult Buddhism, which is the sacred belief of 85 percent of the citizens, they will have even less compunction in flinging similar insults at the Muslim, Christian, Hindu, and Animist faiths held by the remaining 15 percent of our nationals.[52]

---

49   ibid., 24–25.
50   Government of the Union of Burma (Economic and Social Board), *Pyidawtha: The New Burma* (Rangoon: Department of Information Press, 1954), 3.
51   This was in reference to the 'omniscient knowledge of the Buddha', known in Burmese as *that bay nyu ta nyan* and derived from the Pāli root *sabbaññutá-ñána*. U Nu, 'Pyidawtha Tho [Towards Pyidawtha]', in *Collection of Political Speeches*, 168.
52   ibid., 167.

U Nu chose to highlight the communist threat in terms of its threat to religion, which enabled him to argue that his government was fighting the communist insurgents not merely for the political goal of preserving national unity. Rather, his government deemed it of utmost importance that the insurgent communists be quelled because they posed a bigger problem to Burmese society: they were attacking all religions, and religion formed the basis of social morality.

Throughout the 1950s, U Nu continued to emphasise his support for non-Buddhist religions. In a speech towards the end of his time in office, in January 1958, U Nu reaffirmed that his government—known by then as the Anti-Fascist People's Freedom League (AFPFL)—continued to support the fight against capitalism and the establishment of socialism in Burma. More importantly, he linked socialism, religious freedom and national unity together by asserting that socialist Burma would be a unified state whose citizens would be accorded 'natural rights, financial security, high standards of living, strong morals, and the ability to continue observing one's religion freely'.[53] By linking his proposed socialist governance with religious freedom, U Nu attempted to mobilise ethnic and minority groups in his nation-building project, when the prospects of ethnic secession and communist victory in the civil war remained very real.

From the quotes discussed above, it becomes clear that for U Nu, political and spiritual goals were two sides of the same coin. His proclaimed support for non-Buddhist religions suggested political freedom to these minorities at the same time as it conformed with his goal of moral improvement through religious revival. This suggests a non-dualist relationship between 'religion' and 'politics' influenced U Nu's thought even as he talked about the separation of the two in imitation of colonial rationalism. In other words, while he proclaimed modernity by speaking in the language of Western rationalism, U Nu continued to be influenced by precolonial Buddhist cosmological conceptions. The ways in which he reconciled these competing epistemologies lay at the heart of U Nu's post-independence political project. Understanding this helps one see that attempts to evaluate U Nu as either a sincere champion of religious freedom or 'an erratic zealot' are misplaced.[54] Such inquiries replicate the

---

53 U Nu, '1958 Speech at the AFPFL Meeting', in *Collection of Political Speeches*, 229.
54 See Tilman Frasch, 'The Relic and the Rule of Righteousness: Reflections on U Nu's *Dhammavijaya*', in *Buddhism, Modernity, and the State in Asia: Forms of Engagement*, John Whalen-Bridge and Pattana Kitiarsa, eds (New York, NY: Palgrave Macmillan, 2013), 129–30.

artificial colonial separation of 'religion' and 'politics' and fail to see that U Nu's thought in the post-independence period cannot be explained in such simplistic, dualistic terms.

Buddhist modernity in contradistinction with capitalism and Marxism

Studies of U Nu's modernist reforms have not examined the ways in which he employed his notion of Buddhist modernity to distinguish Burma's development from the capitalist and communist models. For example, Hiroko Kawanami has characterised U Nu as a Buddhist modernist, citing his rejection of what he saw as 'superstitious' and 'mystical' Buddhist practices such as *samatha* meditation and his support instead for the 'rational' and 'modern' *vipassanā* method.[55] However, Kawanami's argument takes for granted certain meanings of rationality without considering the ways in which U Nu reinterpreted what it meant to be 'rational' using longstanding Burmese cultural concepts. By redefining certain central notions of Western modernity, U Nu formulated a Buddhist modernist resistance to the Euro-American and Soviet powers of the Cold War.

U Nu's postwar definition of morality as 'selflessness' provides a useful starting point to examine how he distinguished his modernisation agenda from those of the Euro-American and Soviet models. From his speeches examined in the previous section, we can see U Nu used the notion of 'selfishness' to critique not only the insurgents but also capitalists and corrupt bureaucrats. Attachment to the 'self' also contradicted the Buddhist belief of *anicca* ('impermanence'), which U Nu would later claim was supported by the latest scientific discoveries about the ever-changing nature of matter. It is worth noting that the *vipassanā* meditation U Nu promoted seeks to gain 'insight' into such impermanence. Changes in U Nu's definition of morality—from resistance to colonialism to selflessness—occurred in the context of his modernisation projects, which were transforming Burma into a modern state with demarcated territorial boundaries, an industrialised economy and a functioning bureaucracy. In justifying these modernist reforms based on Buddhist notions of morality, U Nu attempted to formulate a unique development path for Burma.

---

55   Kawanami, 'U Nu's Liberal Democracy and Buddhist Communalism in Modern Burma', 36–37.

3. BUDDHIST SOCIALISM AND NATIONAL IDENTITY IN COLONIAL AND POSTWAR BURMA

In what follows, I examine how U Nu employed Buddhist language and categories to critique aspects of capitalist modernity and Marxist thought. I will illustrate how U Nu appealed to Buddhist temporal views and ideas about the nature of matter to critique the notion of 'evolution', which he viewed as fundamental to both capitalist and Marxist world views. Not only did U Nu point out the differences between Buddhism and these two Western epistemologies, he also argued for the superiority of his Buddhist modernist world view over capitalist and Marxist principles.[56]

According to U Nu, the 'fulfilment' he sought for Burma lay not in a distant future but had already defined the lives of the Burmese before the arrival of colonial rule. It was colonialism that had disrupted this state of fulfilment, leading to poverty and moral decline. Since Burmese society had already enjoyed material abundance and social harmony before the colonial disruption, to return to this state, the Burmese did not need to follow the development models of Western industrialised countries; they just had to rediscover Buddhist teachings. In the process of such a rediscovery, the Burmese would incorporate new organisational ideas such as socialism, but these would be merely political means to the spiritual ends. In so doing, the Burmese would not only achieve the same level of material welfare as promised by capitalism and communism, but also receive the benefit of spiritual liberation.

The following excerpt illustrates the characteristics of U Nu's Buddhist modernist thought. U Nu brought up the *Padaythabin* myth time and again in his speeches in the post-independence period. His invocation of this myth was important not only because he used it to reconcile foreign ideas such as socialism with Burmese Buddhism, but also because it enabled him to invoke a unique Buddhist temporality:

> In the beginning, there was a *Padeythabin* ['Tree of Fulfilment'] from which people could get anything they needed. But men gave in to *lobha* ['greed'] and started seeking profit out of resources. This led to capitalists colonizing territories. Capitalists who wanted to gain control of the same territories went to war against other

---

56   I do not wish to suggest that capitalism and Soviet Marxism represented qualitatively distinct forms of modernity. Scholars have reassessed the extent to which communist ideas and practices represented an alternative to capitalist forms of development. Postone, for example, has argued that Soviet socialism was merely a local manifestation of the globally dominant 'state-centric capitalism'. Here, I make the distinction between capitalism and Marxism simply to indicate that there were two foreign development ideologies to which U Nu was responding during this period. See Moishe Postone, 'Critique and Historical Transformation', *Historical Materialism* 12(3) (2004): 54, doi.org/10.1163/1569206042601765.

> capitalists. Thus were generated the three calamities of bloody conflicts, famine, and epidemics ... The root cause of [the three calamities] is the exploitation of man by man born of this system of private ownership. Socialism is primarily concerned with the removal of this cause.⁵⁷

The *Padaythabin* myth here represents a different mode of seeing time. In both capitalism and Marxism, time develops in a linear direction; society progresses from relative backwardness to development. Such a conception gave rise to the notions of evolution and social Darwinism that drove Western imperialism—a hallmark of capitalist modernity. Linear conceptions of the development of history also informed Marx's historical materialism, which outlined a stagist developmental path for societies. U Nu was responding to such linear views of history when he invoked the *Padaythabin* story about the loss of a prior utopian society. According to this story, the Burmese lost their utopian social harmony due to colonial intervention. To return to this utopian state, they would use modern political methods like socialism, not with the goal of building communism but to reverse the moral decline that had accompanied colonial capitalism. The *Padaythabin* story and its cyclical view of history also allowed U Nu to rescue Burma from the linear developmental trajectory outlined by the modernisation theory popular during the 1950s and 1960s, and to argue instead that Burma did not have to follow the same pattern of development as the West.

U Nu also critiqued the evolutionary view of social development as it pertained to Marxist thought. In January 1958, he gave a lengthy speech to the All Burma AFPFL Conference. This speech is well cited in the literature as a landmark event signifying U Nu's final split from Marxism, with which he had a troubled relationship during the 1950s. What is less often noted, however, is the fact that, in this speech, U Nu criticised Marxist dialectical materialism, citing its incompatibility with the latest scientific discoveries. First, he pointed out the difference in Marxist and Buddhist views of matter:

> Dialectical materialism maintains that all living and non-living things can be returned to their original atomic form, and that these atoms exist forever. But according to our Buddhist belief, nothing in the world is permanent. Living and non-living inhabitants of the thirty-one abodes are subject to *thinkata dat*

---

57 U Nu, 'Martyrs' Day Speech', 92.

['principle of impermanence'] and can only escape this when they reach *nibbana* ['nirvana'] governed by *athinkata dat* ['principle of permanence'].

Having set up this distinction between Buddhist and Marxist views on matter, U Nu went on to demonstrate that scientific findings since the time of Marx had proven the inaccuracy of Marxist materialism while increasingly converging with Buddhist beliefs about the impermanence of matter. Tracing in detail the results of scientific experiments from the time of J.J. Thomson and Pierre and Marie Curie to that of Louis de Broglie, U Nu reasoned that 'as science develops further, it began to corroborate more and more closely Buddha's theory that there exists no such thing as permanent material or matter'.[58]

In the latter part of the speech, U Nu also questioned the evolutionary model of societal development outlined by historical materialism. Here again, U Nu appealed to Western science to support his case against Marxist dialectics. He argued that the Marxist idea of the stagist development of societies was based on scientific knowledge of Marx's time, in which the world was 'conceptualized … as a machine'.[59] This 'mechanical' world view posited that every event was governed by the law of cause and effect, that each was a consequence of an event that preceded it. To reject this Marxist view, U Nu raised the quantum theory discovered by Max Planck in the twentieth century: 'Just as how quantum theory has shown that events in nature happen randomly and not according to predetermined laws, societies also develop randomly and not in a stagist manner as outlined in historical materialism.'[60]

Juxtaposing Buddhism's compatibility with science with Marxist dialectical materialism's lack of scientific accuracy, U Nu implied the superiority of Buddhism over Marxism using the modern language of science.

The excerpts above illustrate that U Nu recruited aspects of modern thought, such as science, to critique modernity in its Western forms. Another example of how U Nu invoked liberal sensibilities to critique negative elements of modernity could be seen in the ways in which he invoked 'individual freedom' to criticise interventions by the Cold War powers in Burmese affairs. In his speeches in the post-independence

---

58   U Nu, 'Speech at the 1958 All Burma AFPFL Conference', 265.
59   ibid., 269.
60   ibid., 270.

period, U Nu often criticised the armed insurgents for their attempts to wrest political power by force. In a public speech in 1952, U Nu pointed out that such violent policies of the insurgent leaders indicated their 'authoritarian' bent, making them enemies of the 'democracy' symbolised by his own AFPFL government.[61] In 1954, U Nu wrote a booklet titled *Protect Democracy*, in which he emphasised that Buddhism, like democracy, encouraged individual freedom and the independent search for knowledge whereas 'authoritarian communism' limited individual freedom.[62] U Nu thus carried out a modern reinterpretation of Buddhism by highlighting its emphasis on individual freedom—a central notion of Western modernity. At the same time, he used this newly constituted relationship between Buddhism, democracy and individual freedom to critique communism, whose limitation of freedom was cast as an antimodern quality. In criticising the armed insurgents as 'authoritarian', U Nu also implied the Euro-American and Soviet powers behind these insurgents were not abiding by their proclaimed respect for freedom.

U Nu's promotion of *vipassanā* meditation among the Burmese populace developed in tandem with his argument that Buddhism emphasised social equality. During the 1950s, U Nu's government sponsored the monk Mahasi Sayadaw (1904–1982), a leading figure in the Sixth Buddhist Council, who taught the *vipassanā* method to laypeople at the Thathana Yeiktha meditation centre, which was built under U Nu's direction in 1950.[63] Recent scholarship has noted how U Nu's promotion of *vipassanā* meditation formed a crucial aspect of his modernising reforms of Buddhism, which were intended to contribute to his nation-building agenda. State sponsorship of *vipassanā* meditation elevated it as the legitimate form of Buddhist meditation due to its perceived 'scientific' nature. At the same time, its rival *samatha* meditation was marginalised when its mystical elements did not align with the U Nu government's notion of modern Buddhism.[64] U Nu urged government officials to practise the modern *vipassanā* meditation until they achieved the first stage of *sotāpanna* ('awakening') so they would become incorruptible in working to establish a socialist state.[65]

---

61 U Nu, 'Towards Pyidawtha', 173.
62 U Nu, *Protect Democracy* (Yangon: Seikku Cho Cho, 2018), 3.
63 E. Michael Mendelson, *Sangha and State in Burma: A Study of Monastic Sectarianism and Leadership*, John P. Ferguson, ed. (Ithaca, NY: Cornell University Press, 1975), 265.
64 Schober, *Modern Buddhist Conjunctures in Myanmar*, 78–79.
65 Jordt, *Burma's Mass Lay Meditation Movement*, 30.

U Nu also advertised *vipassanā* meditation internationally. Throughout the 1950s, he delivered many lectures on Buddhism in India, the United Kingdom and the United States. In July 1955, U Nu gave a speech entitled 'What is Buddhism?' to a lay American audience at New York University, in which he gave a detailed description of how *vipassanā* meditation should be practised and the different stages of insight that could be attained. He even requested the American people put Buddhism to the test in the same way they would test a scientific theory. He invited 10 US citizens to travel to Burma to practise the required course of spiritual exercises, claiming such an experience would prove his points about Buddhist meditation to Americans, who 'only believed what could be empirically proven'.[66] In this manner, U Nu declared to a Western audience that Buddhist practices could withstand the test of scientific scrutiny; they had been bringing spiritual welfare to the Burmese, who now wanted to share the benefits with Westerners who had not yet experienced this spiritual liberation.

Conclusion

From the colonial to the post-independence periods, U Nu as a nationalist saw moral reform as the key aspect in reforming Burmese society to resist foreign domination and intervention. However, his definition of morality evolved over the two periods in response to the different political challenges in each era. As an anticolonial nationalist during the 1930s and the early 1940s, Thakin Nu identified colonial capitalism as the source of the moral corruption of the Burmese. In prescribing Marxist revolutionary action as a useful political tool in overthrowing colonial rule, Thakin Nu reconciled Marxism's support for egalitarianism with Buddhist morals. Meanwhile, he regarded Marxism only as a useful political tool, not as an ideology that could guide him towards his ultimate wish: spiritual liberation in Buddhist terms.

As Thakin Nu became U Nu, the prime minister of Burma, in 1948, he modified his earlier discourse on morality as well as that on the compatibility of Marxism/communism and Buddhism in response to the changing political context. After independence, the immediate tasks

---

66 U Nu, 'What is Buddhism, New York University, New York, 1955', in *U Nu: Collection of Speeches on Religion. Volume 3* (Yangon: Seikku Cho Cho, 2018), 12.

for U Nu were to preserve Burma as a sovereign nation-state while resisting interventions by the hegemonic Cold War powers. He continued to stress moral reform as essential for social reform, but he now characterised morality as devotion to religion in general, not just Buddhism. U Nu argued for the interrelationship of material and spiritual wellbeing, while identifying moral reform as the link between the two. Articulation of such a link allowed U Nu to distinguish his modernisation project in Burma from the Euro-American and Soviet models. He invoked central elements of modern thought—such as scientific inquiry and individual freedom—to critique Western modernity. In characterising his modern political projects of socialist and democratic reform as merely intermediary steps in the process of attaining spiritual liberation, U Nu implied that his Buddhist modernism was not only different but also superior to the capitalist and Marxist modernisation projects.

In examining how U Nu's discourse of moral reform intersected with his nation-building agenda in the post-independence period, this chapter has attempted to deepen present understandings of Buddhism and politics in Burma. Building on Alicia Turner's idea of 'moral communities' in early colonial Burma, it has explored the complications involved in U Nu's attempts to superimpose the nation on to these preexisting 'moral communities'. One line of further inquiry suggested by this chapter's conclusions is to investigate what forms of Buddhist and non-Buddhist subjectivities in postwar Burma became marginalised by U Nu's promotion of his idea of Buddhist modernity. As Dipesh Chakrabarty has pointed out, the nation-state and its accompanying institutions often replicate colonial forms of violence on the subaltern in carrying out modernisation based on Enlightenment rationalism.[67] Thus, it will be worthwhile to explore what forms of domination persisted and what new kinds of oppression emerged under the U Nu government's Buddhist modernisation project even as it claimed resistance to the hegemony of capitalism and Marxism.

---

67   Dipesh Chakrabarty, *Habitations of Modernity: Essays in the Wake of Subaltern Studies* (Chicago, IL: University of Chicago Press, 2002), 32.

4

Heavier than Mount Banahaw: 'Five Golden Rays' and the 'Filipinisation' of Maoism

Ramon Guillermo, Teo Marasigan, Amado Anthony G. Mendoza III and Dominic Sy[1]

The global dissemination of the revolutionary ideas of Mao Zedong has recently been the subject of much research. This includes study of the history of translation, dissemination, publication and reception of *Quotations from Chairman Mao Zedong* (the '*Little Red Book*') as well as the *Selected Works of Mao Tse-tung*.[2] However, a small collection of writings by Mao that also exerted a substantial and lasting influence on the Maoist Communist Party of the Philippines (CPP) has thus far seemingly escaped scholarly scrutiny. The text in question is a collection of Mao's short essays entitled *Lao wupian* 老五篇 ('*Five Old Articles*', 1967) that was printed in English as *Five Articles* in 1968.[3] The first part of this chapter will give a general account of the origin, formation and constitution of this collection, which originally contained just three essays and was known

---

1   The authors are grateful to Jose Ma. Sison and Hersri Setiawan, without whose knowledge and insights this chapter would not be possible. The authors would also like to thank Carol Hau and Tom Talledo for their invaluable comments, ideas and references.
2   Oliver Lei Han, *Sources and Early Printing History of Chairman Mao's 'Quotations'* (New York, NY: The Bibliographical Society of America, 2004), available from: bibsocamer.org/BibSite/Han/; and Xu Lanjun, 'Translation and Internationalism', in *Mao's Little Red Book: A Global History*, Alexander C. Cook, ed. (Cambridge, UK: Cambridge University Press, 2014), 76–95.
3   Jennifer Purtle and Elizabeth Ridolfo, *Reading Revolution: Art and Literacy during China's Cultural Revolution* (Toronto, ON: Coach House Press, 2016).

as the *Lao sanpian* 老三篇 ('*Three Old Articles*' or '*Three Constantly Read Articles*', 1967). The changing meaning and significance of this collection will be situated within the shifting historical contexts of the Chinese Revolution and the Cultural Revolution. The next section will discuss the extraordinary Philippine reception, dissemination and translation of the *Five Old Articles* under the new Philippine title, *Five Golden Rays*. The final section will conclude with a brief comparison of the Philippine reception of these articles with their spread in Southeast Asia. Doing so will emphasise further the distinctive role these articles have played in the development of Maoism outside China.

The 'Five Old Articles' in China

On 18 September 1966, Lin Biao gave a speech to high-ranking officers of the People's Liberation Army (PLA) in which he advocated the deepening of revolutionary consciousness among the people. This would be achieved, he proposed, by putting together three popular articles by Mao: '*Wei renmin fuwu* 为人民服务' ('Serve the People', 1944), '*Jinian Bai Qiu'en* 纪念白求恩' ('In Memory of Norman Bethune', 1939) and '*Yugong yishan* 愚公移山' ('The Foolish Old Man Who Removed the Mountains', 1945). These works were published as the *Three Old Articles* soon after in the well-known red-book format. Less than six months later, two earlier works by Mao were added to the set: '*Fandui ziyouzhuyi* 反对自由主义' ('Combat Liberalism', 1937) and '*Guanyu jiuzheng dangneide cuowu sixiang* 关于纠正党内的错误思想' ('On Correcting Mistaken Ideas in the Party', 1929). This new collection was given the title *Five Old Articles* and made required reading throughout the Cultural Revolution.[4]

The five articles were written at different periods in the context of the development of both Mao's thought and the Chinese Communist Party (CCP). More than 15 years separates the oldest article from the most recent. Another 22 years separates that final piece from its eventual publication in a book. Over those four decades, the CCP managed to escape destruction, establish a base at Yan'an, hold off the Japanese, defeat Chiang Kai-shek's Guomindang (GMD), found the People's Republic of China (PRC) and begin the process of constructing a socialist state and

---

4   Guo Jian, Song Yongyi and Zhou Yuan, eds, *Historical Dictionary of the Chinese Cultural Revolution* (Lanham, MD: Scarecrow Press, 2006), 96, 284.

society. At the same time, Mao fought his way to the top of the party, developed what would be called 'Mao Zedong Thought', had those ideas enshrined as the official ideology of the CCP, lost power and prestige after the errors committed during the Great Leap Forward and regained control of the party during the Cultural Revolution.

Contrary to how Mao's thought has sometimes been presented, Stuart Schram argues that there were indeed changes in Mao's thinking across these four decades. This is particularly evident when it comes to the question of how to build socialism in China, with Mao having initially endorsed, shortly after the founding of the PRC, models of economic development that were more centralised, technocratic and urban-centred than the agricultural collectivism of the Great Leap Forward or the radical class-levelling initiatives of the Cultural Revolution.[5] With regard to other themes, however, there is more consistency. Schram notes, for example, that Mao always placed importance on what in Marxist terminology might be called 'subjective' and 'political' attitudes. In other words, Mao consistently emphasised the capacity of the people to overcome and change their 'objective' economic conditions, especially through proper conscious action and struggle.[6] Elements of this line of thinking pervade many of his works, including the original 'Three Old Articles', which extol service and self-sacrifice ('Serve the People', 'In Memory of Norman Bethune') and perseverance ('The Foolish Old Man Who Removed the Mountains'). Interestingly, this emphasis on conscious action and struggle is also formulated in these three texts in a way that harkens back to the Chinese tradition of moral education via the emulation of exemplars or models[7] who are held up as virtuous examples of how to be a revolutionary (that is, Zhang Side, Norman Bethune and the eponymous 'Old Man', respectively).

Despite the continuity in this aspect of Mao's thinking, it is impossible to ignore the influence of changing contexts in the reading of these texts. Promoting these articles at the onset of the Cultural Revolution involved a drastic change in both audience and the overall sociopolitical situation within which prospective readers might respond to Mao's writing. This degree of change is most apparent in the oldest of the five articles.

---

5   Stuart R. Schram, *The Thought of Mao Zedong* (Cambridge, UK: Cambridge University Press, 1989), 97–103, 110–13.
6   ibid., 54–55.
7   See Børge Bakken, *The Exemplary Society: Human Improvement, Social Control and the Dangers of Modernity in China* (Oxford, UK: Oxford University Press, 2000), 173–74.

'On Correcting Mistaken Ideas in the Party' was written in 1929 as the first section of the *Gutian huiyi jueyi* 田会议决议 ('Gutian Congress Resolution') adopted by the Ninth Congress of the CCP in the Fourth Red Army. In that period, the party leadership was still debating the precise nature of armed revolution—its form, location (for example, urban versus rural) and overall strategies. Mao, meanwhile, was struggling not only to have his ideas accepted by the party leadership, but also for his military and political authority to be recognised across the countryside.[8] While this struggle for political and ideological supremacy may have parallels with the contentious political situation of the mid-1960s, Mao's overall position in both the party and the military had shifted dramatically. In the late 1920s, Mao, expelled as an 'alternate' member of the Central Committee, was an isolated and often rebellious commander of the Red Army, at odds not only frequently with the party leadership but also occasionally with Zhu De, his fellow commander.[9] But in the mid-1960s, despite his power having receded following the Great Leap Forward, Mao remained chairman of the party and wielded considerable influence. Thus, while pushing for their own models of economic development, Liu Shaoqi and the other members of the Politburo always tried to compromise with any issues Mao raised.[10]

Meanwhile, in the military, through Lin Biao's influence as minister for defence, simplified versions of Mao's works formed the basis of the ordinary soldier's political education, which had itself become one of the central aspects of life in the PLA.[11] It was in this context that first the *Little Red Book* and, later, the *Three Old Articles* were published and disseminated. The articles soon became compulsory reading for young students as well as 'mandatory recitation material' for the whole population.[12] Officially, these texts were meant to provide a shortcut for general readers to understand the core principles of Marxism-Leninism and Mao Zedong Thought. Critics of Lin Biao, however, both during and after the 1960s,

---

8   Stuart R. Schram, ed., *Mao's Road to Power: Revolutionary Writings 1912–1949. Volume III: From the Jinggangshan to the Establishment of the Jiangxi Soviets, July 1927 – December 1930* (London: M.E. Sharpe, 2004), xxi–xxii.
9   ibid., xxvi–xxviii, xliii–xliv.
10 Kenneth Lieberthal, 'The Great Leap Forward and the Split in the Yan'an Leadership, 1958–1965', in *The Politics of China: Sixty Years of the People's Republic of China*, Roderick MacFarquhar, ed., 3rd edn (Cambridge, UK: Cambridge University Press, 2011), 144–45.
11 ibid., 114–15, 125–30.
12 Rebecca E. Karl, '"Serve the People": An Exemplary Chinese Socialist Text of 1944', in *Reading the Postwar Future: Textual Turning Points from 1944*, Kirrily Freeman and John Munro, eds (London: Bloomsbury, 2019), 228n.2.

argued that this campaign, which often involved the rote memorisation of texts, led to the 'vulgarisation' of both the Marxist tradition and Mao's own writings.[13] This campaign is also understood as one of a number of strategies Lin employed to both expand the relative power of the PLA within the party and promote a personality cult around Mao, both of which in turn consolidated Lin's own power.[14] By the time 'On Correcting Mistaken Ideas in the Party' was reprinted in the 28 January 1967 issue of the *People's Daily*—and then included a few months later in the *Five Old Articles*—the Cultural Revolution was well under way. Read at this time, therefore, what could originally be thought of as a resolution on how to work out problems of party discipline and education within the Red Army had transformed into—in the words of the editorial note of the *People's Daily*—a call for '[p]roletarian revolutionaries [to] unite and seize power from the handful of persons in the Party who are in authority and taking the capitalist road'.[15]

The significance of such a shift becomes even more evident when looking at how Mao's writings had already been used by different groups in the PRC to justify their positions in ideological debates. For example, Christos Lynteris has shown how, throughout the 1950s and 1960s—as the CCP grappled with the best way to balance the need for technical expertise to modernise China with the danger that such expertise would serve as the foundation for continued class inequality—contrasting interpretations of 'In Memory of Norman Bethune' were used to forward two competing models of the proper relationship between the self, the state and revolution. One model aligned itself with Liu Shaoqi's neo-Confucian formulation of becoming a 'good communist' through proper self-cultivation. The other, which would become dominant during the Cultural Revolution, forwarded a concept of complete 'selflessness'.[16]

---

13   Lowell Dittmer, *China's Continuous Revolution: The Post-Liberation Epoch 1949–1981* (Berkeley, CA: University of California Press, 1987), 38.
14   Lieberthal, 'The Great Leap Forward and the Split in the Yan'an Leadership', 125–30.
15   Translated in Mao Zedong, 'On Correcting Mistaken Ideas in the Party', *Peking Review* 6 (3 February 1967): 5–10.
16   Christos Lynteris, *The Spirit of Selflessness in Maoist China: Socialist Medicine and the New Man* (London: Palgrave Macmillan, 2013), 117.

It is beyond the scope of the current research to probe into every possible shift in the discourses produced as each of the 'Five Old Articles' was written, collected and disseminated within China. What matters here is simply the recognition not only that these shifts occurred but also that they were unavoidable, especially given the highly contentious and rapidly changing social and political environment within which the reading of the articles occurred. Such changes were even more drastic as Mao's writing was translated, shipped overseas and integrated into other people's movements—movements that each had their own cultures, contexts and characteristics. In fact, as the discussion below shows, the 'Three Old Articles' and 'Five Old Articles' have taken root outside China not exclusively in the context of a 'vulgarisation' of Marxist and/or Maoist texts, but also within the context of movement (re)building during periods of the popularisation, emergence and/or emergency of revolutionary movements.

The Philippine reception and translation of the 'Five Golden Rays'

The significance of the *Five Golden Rays* (hereinafter *FGR*) in the history of Philippine Maoism cannot be overemphasised. According to the founder of the CPP, Jose Maria Sison:

> *Malaki at mapagpasiya ang kahalagahan ng LGS sa pagtutuon sa diwang rebolusyonaryo at komunista na magsakripisyo para puspusang mapaglingkuran ang sambayanang Pilipino at dapat bakahin ang pagkamakasarili upang itaguyod ang mga karapatan at kapakanan ng masang anakpawis at isakatuparan ang pagkakaisa, kolektibong pagkilos at kapakanan ng lahat ng mamamayan.*

> [The *FGR* is of great and decisive importance in emphasising the revolutionary and communist spirit of sacrifice and wholehearted service to the Filipino people and the need to struggle against selfishness in fighting for the rights and welfare of the working classes and to uphold the unity, collective action and welfare of the people.][17]

---

17 Authors' interview with Jose Maria Sison, online, 6 January 2021.

The story of how the 'Five Old Articles' entered the Philippines begins with its English translation. The first English edition of the 'Five Old Articles', entitled *Five Articles*, was published in China in 1968 by the Foreign Languages Press.[18] It was a product of an active campaign to 'export Chinese revolution to the world' by means of translation.[19] However, according to Sison, the Filipino cadres first learned of these articles from their republication with accompanying commentary in the *Peking Review*.[20] He recalls it was around this time that the Propaganda and Education Bureau of the Kabataang Makabayan (Nationalist Youth) took charge of translating the articles into Tagalog and then printing and disseminating them in the Philippines. Given the timeline of the publication of the relevant issues of the *Peking Review* (February and March 1967), it is possible the popularity of these articles had already begun to take root in groups like the Kabataang Makabayan even before the founding of the CPP, which officially broke away from the older Soviet-oriented Communist Party of the Philippines (now self-styled as the Partido Komunista ng Pilipinas-1930, PKP-1930) in December 1968.[21] The CPP Central Publishing House subsequently produced mimeographed editions and master copies of the articles for distribution to the various regions. The party's Translation Bureau also made translations into various other Philippine languages such as Ilokano, Cebuano, Bikolano, Ilonggo and perhaps a few others.[22]

---

18   See Mao Zedong, *Five Articles*, 1st vest-pocket edn (Peking: Foreign Languages Press, 1968). Also see Mao Zedong, *Five Articles* (Peking: Foreign Languages Press, 1968); Mao Zedong, *Five Articles*, 1st edn (Peking: Foreign Languages Press, 1972); Mao Zedong, *Five Articles*, 2nd edn (Peking: Foreign Languages Press, 1972); Mao Zedong, *Five Articles*, 2nd vest-pocket edn (Peking: Foreign Languages Press, 1972); Mao Zedong, *Five Articles* (Peking: Foreign Languages Press, 1982). The Foreign Languages Press also published in other languages, including French, as can be seen in Mao Zedong, *Cinq articles* (Pékin: Éditions en langues étrangères, 1972).
19   Xu, 'Translation and Internationalism', 77.
20   See Mao Zedong, 'In Memory of Norman Bethune', *Peking Review* 8 (1967): 5–6; Mao, 'On Correcting Mistaken Ideas in the Party'; Mao Zedong, 'Serve the People', *Peking Review* 2 (1967): 6–7; and Mao Zedong, 'The Foolish Old Man Who Removed the Mountains', *Peking Review* 12 (1967): 8–19. The authors of this chapter are currently unable to verify whether 'Combat Liberalism' was ever published in the *Peking Review*. Regardless, it is possible the source of its English translation in the *FGR* was not the *Peking Review*, but the *Selected Works* or another anthology of Mao's writing. If so, this might also be the reason 'Combat Liberalism' is the only article in the *FGR* that is not accompanied by an extended 'commentary' (which were also, it seems, taken from the *Peking Review*). Conducting a more in-depth study of the different editions of the *FGR* would be necessary to resolve this conundrum.
21   Interestingly, Sison recollects there were no reading materials analogous to the *FGR* during his time as a member of the PKP-1930.
22   Unlike in the case of Thailand, as will be discussed further below, Sison is not aware of any Philippine-language translations of the *FGR* done by the Chinese comrades themselves.

On the matter of the change of title from *Five Articles* (in the Foreign Languages Press edition) to *Five Golden Rays* (or *Limang Gintong Silahis* in Tagalog), Sison recalls the pamphlet was renamed to emphasise its qualities as a *maningning* ('shining') guide for proletarian revolutionaries. According to Sison:

> *May pormal na desisyon ng Party group ng KM na gamitin at palaganapin ang LGS bilang babasahin at aralin ng mga abanteng aktibista para ihanda silang maging kandidatong-kasapi ng Partido Komunista dahil sa simple, malaman, interesante at mabisa ang limang artikulo sa pagpapaliwanag at pag-inspira ng diwa at moralidad ng komunista: paglilingkod sa bayan, proletaryong internasyonalismo, pagpupursigi sa pakikibaka, paglaban sa liberalismo o indibidwalismo at pagtutuwid sa mga maling ideya sa loob ng Partido.*
>
> [There was a formal decision by the party group of the Kabataang Makabayan to disseminate the *FGR* as reading and study material for advanced activists to prepare them to become candidate members of the Communist Party because the five articles were simple, pithy, interesting and effective in explaining and inspiring the spirit and morality of a communist: service to the people, proletarian internationalism, perseverance in the struggle, combating liberalism and individualism, and correcting wrong ideas within the party.][23]

Due to its popular appeal, the *FGR* was increasingly used by activists and even more widely disseminated by the party. The 'Political Report to the Second Plenum of the First Central Committee of the Communist Party of the Philippines' in 1970 already mentions that both the *FGR* and the *Little Red Book* should be read alongside the basic documents of the CPP.[24] According to the same document:

> In all study courses as well as during practical work, the *Five Golden Rays* and the *Quotations from Chairman Mao Zedong* should be used extensively and often referred to in the ideological remoulding of entire units and individual members of the Party.[25]

---

23 Sison, Interview.
24 Jose Ma. Sison, *Foundation for Resuming the Philippine Revolution: Selected Writings 1968 to September 1972* (The Netherlands and The Philippines: International Network for Philippine Studies and Aklat ng Bayan Inc., 2013), 281.
25 ibid., 289.

Similarly, in 1972, the party report, entitled 'Summing up Our Experience after Three Years', stated:

> We have reopened in an unprecedented way the great treasury of Marxism-Leninism–Mao Zedong Thought to Filipino revolutionaries. We have made available to them as constant reference in their daily work the *Five Golden Rays* and *Quotations from Chairman Mao Zedong* and as texts for more extensive and profound study Chairman Mao's works under the seven headings of philosophy, class analysis and social investigation, party building, armed struggle, united front, economic work and land reform, and culture.[26]

Interestingly, for various reasons, the *Little Red Book* eventually fell out of general use in the Philippines. Sison surmises this was primarily due to criticisms by Filipino comrades of the dogmatic style of the quotations, which sounded like sermons or recitations of statements taken out of context and without any accompanying explanations.[27] In contrast, Sison estimates the inclusion of the *FGR* as the first part of the larger volume of readings known as *Araling Aktibista* ('*Activist Reading Materials*') could have begun as early as the 1980s, where it remains to this day.[28]

Beyond simply its longevity, it is also undeniable the *FGR* is one of the most memorable texts for activists in the Philippines. Former CPP member Joel Rocamora writes that, compared with both the *Little Red Book* and *Five Golden Rays*: 'It might even be argued that Mao Zedong's theoretical work played less of a role in the politicization of the first generation of CPP leaders.'[29] Another former activist, Jose 'Butch' Dalisay, who became a professor of English literature at the University of the Philippines, recalls:

---

26   ibid., 376.
27   Sison, Interview. The main reason for the relative neglect of the *Red Book* may, however, be because it is not included in the basic curriculum of activists known as the Pambansa-Demokratikong Paraalan (PADEPA, National-Democratic School). See, for example, the 'Manwal sa Gawaing PADEPA ng ANAKBAYAN', which is available from: aklatangtibak.wordpress.com/category/padepa/. The authors are aware there is still some evidence of its contemporary use in criticism and self-criticism sessions among activists.
28   See Communist Party of the Philippines—National Education Department [hereinafter CPP-NED], *Activist Study: Araling Aktibista (ARAK)* (Paris: Foreign Languages Press, 2020). The second edition of *ARAK* (published in 1999) includes the CPP-authored essays 'What is Revolutionary Study and Proper Analysis', 'The Mass Line' and 'Democratic Centralism'.
29   Joel Rocamora, *Breaking Through: The Struggle within the Communist Party of the Philippines* (Pasig City, Philippines: Anvil, 1994), 21.

> We devoured a plethora of works by Mao Tse-Tung, chiefly his red-covered *Quotations* and a booklet of morale-boosting selections called *Five Golden Rays*. One of those golden rays was 'Serve the People,' which became the motto of a generation that would be known in the Philippines as First Quarter Stormers.[30]

Meanwhile, a Filipino former activist based in the United States recounts: 'In terms of growing up in the movement, all I remember is Norman Bethune, *Five Golden Rays*.'[31] Similarly, Antonio Zumel, former president of the National Press Club of the Philippines and chairperson of the National Democratic Front of the Philippines, singles out the *FGR* as a work that 'inspired many people'.[32] Although many Filipino activists probably read the *FGR* in English, the impact of its various translations into different Philippine languages should not be underestimated, and they were a crucial element behind the receptivity of a wide range of Filipino readers to this text. Even more importantly, any study of the reception and interpretation of this text in a specifically Philippine context cannot ignore the matter of translation and the way in which translation changes one's reading of material. In fact, the following discussion will try to show that what is arguably the most popular Maoist text in the Philippines is a striking example of what one scholar has termed the 'Filipinisation' of Maoism.[33]

Our analysis of the Tagalog (or, more precisely, Filipino) translation of the *FGR* will focus on the first three most read, and perhaps most memorable, essays. Because they are often read and studied together, they will be treated, despite their differences, as a single discursive totality experienced as an integrated textual whole and not in isolation from one another. The three Chinese texts will be assigned the following codes: 'Serve the People', STP; 'In Memory of Norman Bethune', MNB; and 'The Foolish Old Man Who Removed the Mountains', FOL. Each sentence in the original Chinese text will be assigned a number according to its order of appearance. The following discussion will indicate the location of

---

30 Jose Dalisay, jr, 'Memoirs of a Street Marcher', *Phi Kappa Phi Forum* 88(2) (2008): 12–13.
31 John Gershman and Walden Bello, *Reexamining and Renewing the Philippine Progressive Vision: Papers and Proceedings of the 1993 Conference of the Forum for Philippine Alternatives* (Quezon City, Philippines: Forum for Philippine Alternatives, 1993), 208.
32 Antonio Zumel, *Radical Prose: Selected Writings* (Quezon City, Philippines: Friends of Antonio Zumel and the First Quarter Storm Movement, 2004), 233.
33 Matthew Galway, 'Boundless revolution: Global Maoism and communist movements in Southeast Asia, 1949–1979' (PhD diss., University of British Columbia, Vancouver, 2017), 365.

pertinent words according to the Chinese text by code and sentence number—for example, 'STP 10' will refer to the tenth sentence of 'Serve the People'.

This kind of sentence-by-sentence comparison between translations is useful in revealing nuanced differences between the texts that may not be clear on a surface reading. For example, a comparison with the English translation and the Chinese original shows the Tagalog version is a relay translation from English. More interestingly, comparative analysis reveals a potentially insightful point of entry into understanding the reception of the *FGR* by its Tagalog readers: the conceptual pair '*pagmamalasakit*' and '*pagpapakasakit*'.

Pagmamalasakit and *pagpapakasakit* are both central to the moral-ethical imagination of Tagalog speakers. In the *FGR*, *pagmamalasakit* is generally used to translate the English 'concern' and 'care' (*guanxin* 关心).[34] On the other hand, *pagpapakasakit* is used as the translation for 'sacrifice' (*xisheng* 牺牲).[35] These two words derive from the root-word *sakit*, which generally means 'sickness' or 'pain'. However, the prefix *mala-* joined to *-sakit* forms *malasakit* (noun), which roughly means 'having a sense of compassion' or an attitude of 'caring for the wellbeing of another'. It is used to allude to a sense of empathy for the 'pain' or 'suffering' felt by another. *Malasakit* also appears in another form as *magmalasakit*. The prefix *mag-* joined to *malasakit* to form *magmalasakit* (verb) means an 'act of caring for the wellbeing of another'. Finally, the Tagalog prefix *pag-* joined to *malasakit* with the first syllable *ma-* reduplicated to form *pagmamalasakit* (noun) basically means the same as *malasakit* but with perhaps a heightened sense of intensity. On the other hand, the root-word *sakit* combined with the prefix *pagpaka-* with the second syllable reduplicated as *pagpapaka-* results in *pagpapakasakit*, which means 'sacrifice', 'suffering', 'perseverance' and 'abnegation'. A close synonym of this is *pagpapakahirap* ('to endure'; 'to persevere') from the root-word *hirap* ('difficulty'; 'suffering').

It should be observed that the Tagalog *pagmamalasakit*, as a sense of empathy for the pain and suffering of others, is not simply an internally felt emotion but something that is necessarily acted on to help a person in need. It is not a purely psychological state of empathy in which one merely gazes passively at the suffering of another; such a person would

---

34 'Serve the People' [hereinafter STP], 22, 23.
35 ibid., 19, 21; 'The Foolish Old Man Who Removed the Mountains' [hereinafter FOL], 13.

have *walang pagmamalasakit* (or be 'without *pagmamalasakit*') despite any emotions he or she may outwardly display. In addition, *malasakit*, unlike other modes of social reciprocity, seems to genuinely connote a selfless sense of giving without expectation of any personal return. However, acting to alleviate or end the suffering of other people is not always a simple matter and often requires sacrifice and perseverance on the part of those who feel *malasakit*. This is where *pagpapakasakit* ('sacrifice'; 'perseverance') comes in.

In other words, *pagmamalasakit* already implies *pagpapakasakit*; however, there are degrees of *pagpapakasakit*. The most intense and idealised type of *pagmamalasakit* in the *FGR* is one that involves *walang pag-iimbot* ('no self-interest at all'), which is translated from the English 'selfless' and from the Chinese original, '*haowu lijide dongji* 毫无利己的动机'.[36] Canadian doctor Norman Bethune's spirit of selflessness was made even more striking by the fact that, being *waiguoren* 外国人 (an 'outsider/ foreigner')[37] from a faraway country, he appeared to have nothing at stake in the victory of the Chinese Revolution for which he puzzlingly gave his life. The sacrifice of a foreigner in *guojizhuyide jingshen* 国际主义的精神 (the 'spirit of internationalism') therefore became the highest ideal and paradigmatic example of selfless sacrifice in the *FGR*.[38]

Transplanted to another context, this narrative of selflessness could easily be reimagined to refer to Filipino student activists coming from the intelligentsia and petty bourgeois strata *na lumubog sa masa* ('who immerse themselves among the masses') and work as full-time cadres of the revolution. Communities sometimes see them as *dayuhan* ('foreigners') or *dayo* ('someone who comes from elsewhere') because of their often distinctive appearance, manner, ethnic origin and language (at least initially) and because they seem to have given up every comfort and privilege to serve the poor and impoverished in remote and far-flung areas. Coming from relatively better off classes in the urban areas, they nevertheless throw in their lot with the lives and struggles of the masses.

---

36 'In Memory of Norman Bethune' [hereinafter MNB], 3.
37 ibid., 3.
38 Mao also underscores this spirit of internationalism by pointing out that, despite the war with Japanese imperialists, the Japanese people themselves were allies in the war against imperialism: 'We must unite with the proletariat of all the capitalist countries, with the proletariat of Japan, Britain, the United States, Germany, Italy and all other capitalist countries, for this is the only way to overthrow imperialism, to liberate our nation and people and to liberate the other nations and peoples of the world.' ibid., 7.

Like Bethune, therefore, they strive to embody the *tunay na diwang komunista* ('the true communist spirit'; *gonchangzhuyi zhede jingshen* 共产主义者的精神)[39] or *diwa ng ganap na di makasarili* ('spirit of absolute selflessness'; *haowu zisili zhi xine jingshen* 毫无自私自利之心的精神).[40]

Such themes may seem all too familiar to Tagalogs immersed in the world of daily moral-ethical discourse. The usages of *pagmamalasakit* and *pagpapakasakit* shown above have a long history in Philippine radical politics and mass mobilisation. The Sakdalistas, for example, one of the most prominent nationalist mass movements in the 1930s, frequently used both terms/concepts in their writings calling for independence, a more just and equitable society and unity among the poor and oppressed. As just one example, in a passage that was often repeated in the *Sakdal* weekly newspaper, the main publication of their movement from 1930 to 1938, the Sakdalistas wrote:

> *Maglingkod ka sa Bayan nang hindi magiimbot ng anumang katungkulan, biyaya o ganting-pala, pagka't ang tunay na pagmamahal ay ang pagbibigay nang walang hinihintay, pag-ibig nang walang kapalit, pagpapakasakit ng sarili para sa kabutihan ng lahat. Ang mga katungkulan ay nakasisira ng loob, nakagigising ng pagsasamantala, naguudyok sa pagdaya at paglinlang sa kababayan. Samantalang wala kang sarili ay magtiis ka sa iyong kalagayan. Ang paninilbihan sa iba ay pagpapahaba lamang ng panahon ng iyong pagkaalipin.*
>
> [Serve the people without looking for any office, blessing or reward, for true love is giving without expectation, love without reciprocation, sacrificing oneself [*pagpapakasakit ng sarili*] for the good of all. Serving in office destroys the moral sense, arouses exploitation, leads to the cheating and deceiving of fellow countrymen. For while you have no self you will continue to suffer in your state. Serving others only prolongs your servitude.][41]

---

39 ibid., 4, 19.
40 ibid., 27. In this vein, the centrality of the notion of *jingshen* 精神 ('spirit'; 'soul') (3, 4, 10, 19, 27, 29) in the Chinese original can be remarked on. This is evidently an important concept that strongly correlates with notions of selflessness and sacrifice. However, the Tagalog word used consistently to translate *jingshen*, '*diwa*' (likely borrowed from Sanskrit through Malay, *jiwa*), which means 'spirit' in the sense of 'attitude', apparently does not have the same complex meaning and historical weight as the Chinese term.
41 'Maglingkod ka sa Bayan [Serve the People]', *Sakdal*, 2 July 1932, 2. This same passage is repeated in eight further issues of *Sakdal* from July to October 1932, and again in four issues from July to August 1936.

In the above passage, the Sakdalistas implore their readers to reject selfishness and rewards, the highest form of which is serving in 'office', by which they mean the colonial government (a source of wealth and power). Instead, they ask everyone to sacrifice themselves (*pagpapakasakit ng sarili*) for the good of all, without thinking of what they might get in return. Meanwhile, the last two sentences of the passage, which might seem contradictory at first glance, are a reminder that they need to love their country (the 'self' or, more precisely, 'what is your own') and not serve foreign, colonial interests (the 'others' in 'serving others').

The use of *pagmamalasakit* and *pagpapakasakit*, in other words, draws on an existing matrix of moral-ethical discourse that itself is deployed in the political arena. What distinguishes the *FGR*, however, from previous moral arguments like those that appear in the *Sakdal*, is the way these values—usually directed towards an undifferentiated *kapwa* ('fellow human')[42]—are reinterpreted along lines drawn by historical social relations in class struggle.[43] In MNB, *kapwa* is therefore given a very different meaning in the phrase '*lubos na pagmamalasakit sa kapwa nang walang pagsasaalangalang sa sarili*' (translated from the English 'utter devotion to others without any thought of self' and from the Chinese '*haobu liji zhuanmen liren* 毫不利己专门利人').[44] The notion of *kapwa* that usually pertains to one's fellow humans abstracted from all other aspects of social or cultural identity now refers exclusively to a member of the oppressed classes. This can be contrasted with the previous quotation and general concept of sacrifice in the *Sakdal*, where the injunction to serve your countrymen and defend the poor does not link up with any systematically defined notions of classes of oppressors and oppressed, especially among Filipinos.[45]

---

42 See Virgilio Enriquez, *From Colonial to Liberation Psychology* (Quezon City, Philippines: University of the Philippines Press, 2008).
43 A complementary reformulation might have also taken place in the original Chinese texts. Just as Filipino notions of *pagpapasakit* towards an undifferentiated *kapwa* are realigned in the *FGR* towards the specificity of relations in class struggle, 'Serve the People' as it was originally formulated in 1944 may have also been reinterpreting previous notions of 'service' within the context of Confucian filial piety—that is, in support of *a priori* constructions of social hierarchy—towards an awareness of the relations between individual action and attitude, the concrete historical context/situation and the desire to create a more egalitarian society. See Karl, "'Serve the People'", 215–30.
44 MNB, 10.
45 For a comparison of notions of class, oppression and imperialism between the Sakdalistas and Philippine communists during the 1930s, see Dominic Sy, 'Anak ng Bayang Dukha: Isang Kwantitatibong at Kwalitatibong Pagsusuri ng Diskurso ng Lapiang Sakdalista [Child of the poor: A quantitative and qualitative analysis of the discourse of the Sakdalista Party]' (MA thesis, University of the Philippines, Diliman, 2021), 167–224.

Both *pagmamalasakit* and *pagpapakasakit* should be directed to *sambayanan* (the 'people') and not towards local and foreign oppressors. The *liyi* 利益 ('interest') of the nation and of the oppressed classes should be the main consideration in all one's actions. Every effort should be for the *interes ng sambayanan* ('people's interest'; '*renminde liyi* 人民的 利益'),[46] for the *kapakanan ng sambayanan* ('benefit of the people'; '*rénmín de lìyì* 人民 的 利益')[47] and *alang-alang sa sambayanan* ('for the sake of the people'; '*wei renmin liyi* 为人民利益').[48] In fact, the most popular and universally recognisable slogan among Filipino activists is '*Paglingkuran ang sambayanan*' ('Serve the people'; '*wei renmin fuwu* 为人民服务'). While the referent of *kapwa* has been made more precise, the meaning of *pagmamalasakit*, which has humanitarian connotations of feeling empathy towards and providing immediate relief to people in need, has been expanded, especially in connection with *pagpapakasakit*. In the last, it now means much more than giving food to the poor, for example; it now also means fighting to change socioeconomic structures and challenging class rule. This is a bridging of the distinction between a saint in religious discourse and a communist in political discourse hinted at by the Latin American practitioner of liberation theology, Brazilian Archbishop Hélder Câmara in his famous quote: 'When I feed the poor, they call me a saint. When I ask why so many people are poor, they call me a communist.'

Another dimension of *pagpapakasakit* that should be underlined is that of 'perseverance' or 'endurance in suffering'. One must be able to go the distance in sacrificing for others. This is what the *FGR* emphasises in such phrases as '*walang takot sa pagpapakasakit*' (translated from the English 'unafraid of sacrifice', from the Chinese '*bùpà xīshēng* 不怕牺牲')[49] and '*mapangingibabawan nila ang lahat ng kahirapan*' (from 'surmount every difficulty', from '*paichu wannan* 排除万难').[50] *Pagpapakasakit* also implies an almost religious sense of faith and fidelity to one's purpose, which is often misinterpreted by unsympathetic observers as 'dogmatism'.[51]

---

46 STP, 2.
47 ibid., 13, 20.
48 ibid., 6, 7.
49 FOL, 13.
50 ibid., 13.
51 Joshua Moufawad-Paul, *Continuity and Rupture: Philosophy in the Maoist Terrain* (Winchester, UK: Zero Books, 2016), 76.

A person who pursues this purpose to the end is someone who does not swerve from their conviction, '*hindi natitinag sa kanyang paniniwala*' (from 'unshaken in his conviction', from '*haobu dongyao* 毫不动摇').[52]

It should not be surprising, then, that the concepts of *pagmamalasakit* and *pagpapakasakit* are also deeply and irrevocably immersed in the Catholic religious ideology and popular Christology of the Philippines. Indeed, Mercado merges both terms under a single concept of sacrifice in the Catholic religious sense.[53] In addition, the religious tenor is not eased but compounded by the story in FOL (no matter how metaphorical) of a 'god' who takes pity and sends two 'angels' from the heavens to help the persevering earthly revolutionaries overthrow feudalism and imperialism.[54] In a way, these types of discourse may partly explain why the Maoist movement has developed particularly strong roots among liberation theologians and religious congregations of various denominations in the Philippines.[55] In the *FGR*, the Maoist revolutionary is called on to enact, on the path to national liberation, an almost spiritual narrative of *pagmamalasakit* and *pagpapakasakit*. It is only the seemingly innocuous injunction to activists and revolutionaries to avoid *di-kinakailangang pagpapakasakit* ('unnecessary sacrifices'; *bu biyaode xisheng* 不必要的牺牲),[56] which in practice allows for a wide enough latitude of interpretation, that prevents this secular 'selflessness' from becoming a saintly asceticism and a demand for complete self-abnegation.

In the extreme case that one's *pagpapakasakit* leads to the ultimate sacrifice of one's life, the *FGR* states that though death is only natural and comes to everyone, the only *makabuluhang kamatayan* ('meaningful' or 'worthy' 'death'; *sideqisuo* 死得其所)[57] is in the service of the people. As the classic

---

52 FOL, 23.
53 Leonardo N. Mercado, *Filipino Popular Devotions: The Interior Dialogue between Traditional Religion and Christianity* (Manila: Logos Publications, 2000).
54 ibid., 24. The use of 'God' and 'angels' in the *FGR*, which are translated as '*Diyos*' and '*anghel*' in the Tagalog version, comes from translations made not by Filipino activists but by the original translators of Mao's texts into English, who sought for English equivalents to *shangdi* 上帝 and *shenxian* 神仙, respectively. That the words chosen should resonate so well with a predominantly Catholic Filipino audience was probably never imagined by the original translators.
55 See Jose Maria Sison, 'The Role of the Church in Social Change', in *On the Philosophy of Marxism-Leninism-Maoism*, Julieta de Lima, ed. (The Netherlands: International Network for Philippine Studies, 2021), 99–101.
56 STP, 21.
57 ibid., 20. The Chinese word *qisuo* 其所 means, literally, 'appointed place'. Arguably then, the Filipino *makabuluhang kamatayan* puts even more emphasis on the agency of the person in choosing to sacrifice and possibly encounter a 'worthy death'.

aphorism from the *FGR* says, '*ang mamatay alang-alang sa sambayanan ay higit na mabigat kaysa bundok Tai, subalit ang maglingkod sa mga pasista at mamatay para sa mga nagsamantala at mga nang-aapi ay higit na magaan kaysa isang balahibo* [to die for the people is weightier than Mount Tai, but to work for the fascists and die for the exploiters and oppressors is lighter than a feather; *wei renmin liyi er sijiu bi Taishan hai zhong ti faxisi maili ti boxue renmin he yapo renminde ren qu sijiu bi hongmao haiqing* 为人民 利益 而 死 就 比 泰山 还重替法西斯卖力替 剥削人民和压迫人民的人去死就比鸿毛还轻]'.[58] Filipino Maoists, who may not necessarily know where the real Mount Tai is (in Shandong Province), use this aphorism to this day to give the highest honour to their comrades who have died in the struggle or served it to the end of their lives. For example, after the passing on 23 July 2020 of Fidel Agcaoili, head of the National Democratic Front of the Philippines' Negotiating Panel, a tribute from a legal democratic umbrella organisation revised and indigenised the aphorism by likening his death to the Sierra Madre—not a mountain, but a mountain range, and in fact the longest in the Philippines—to highlight the heaviness of his death. Another tribute, meanwhile, from an underground organisation of revolutionary teachers, declared: '*Ang pagpanaw ng mga kumprador, ang pagpakamatay ng mga berdugong pasista ay mas magaan pa sa balahibo ng ibon. Ngunit ang pagpanaw ni Ka Fidel ay mas mabigat pa sa bundok ng Banahaw* [The passing of compradors, the deaths of fascist executioners are lighter than the feathers of a bird. But the passing of Comrade Fidel is heavier than Mount Banahaw].'[59] The choice of mountain here is important; Mount Banahaw is an active volcano on the island of Luzon with great cultural and historical significance for Filipinos. Like Mount Tai, one of the sacred mountains of China, Mount Banahaw is linked with folk traditions of spiritual power. Mount Banahaw is also associated by some with the Philippine revolutionary tradition, both because it was used as a camp for revolutionaries in the war against Spain and because the mountain is still seen by some religious

---

58 STP, 6.
59 Katipunan ng mga Gurong Makabayan [Association of Nationalist Teachers], 'Pagpupugay sa mga dakilang aral na pinamana ni Kasamang Fidel Agcaoili, kasamang rebolusyonaryo ng mga gurong nagsusulong ng armadong rebolusyon [Tribute to the Great Lessons We Have Learned from Comrade Fidel Agcaoili, Revolutionary Comrade of Teachers in Armed Struggle]', *PRWC Newsroom*, 8 August 2020, available from: prwcinfo.wordpress.com/2020/08/08/1899/.

groups as 'the altar of brave Filipino heroes like José Rizal, Andres Bonifacio, Emilio Aguinaldo, Gregorio del Pilar, Agapito Illustrisimo, and Bernardo Carpio'.[60]

If *kapwa* is redefined in the *FGR* to pertain only to members of the oppressed nation and classes, even *kamatayan* ('death') is given a new meaning; the bare fact of death in STP 'divides into two' (*yifenwei'er* 一分为二) along the lines of historical class struggle, one meaningless and another meaningful. There is a kind of life after death in the revolutionary imagination wherein *ang mga martir ng rebolusyon* ('the revolutionary martyrs') are given the highest respect and recognition. The wording of the *FGR* that foregrounds the sacrifices of those who fought and sacrificed their lives against foreign and local oppressors unavoidably resonates with the nationalist commemoration of the heroes of the Philippine anticolonial revolution of 1896 against Spain. Such national heroes as Andres Bonifacio (1863–1897), Antonio Luna (1866–1899), Apolinario Mabini (1864–1903) and José Rizal (1861–1896), as well as the nameless masses who have continued to fight since that time for the ideals of the 'unfinished revolution',[61] become imbricated in the textual density of the *FGR*.[62] One can even argue that selfless sacrifice is a foundational virtue for the Philippine revolutionary and nationalist traditions, as exemplified by the climactic self-sacrifice of the character Elias in Rizal's novel *Noli Me Tangere* (*Touch Me Not*), which helped inspire the Philippine revolution.[63]

---

60   Vitaliano R. Gorospe, 'Mount Banahaw: The Power Mountain from Ritualism to Spirituality', *Philippine Studies* 40(2) (1992): 204–18. For more on the relationship between Philippine folk and revolutionary traditions, see the classic study by Reynaldo Ileto, *Pasyon and Revolution: Popular Movements in the Philippines, 1840–1910* (Quezon City, Philippines: Ateneo de Manila University Press, 1979). See also an important critique of Ileto's ideas in Jim Richardson, *The Light of Liberty: Documents and Studies on the Katipunan 1892–1897* (Quezon City, Philippines: Ateneo de Manila University Press, 2013), 452–65.
61   Ileto, *Pasyon and Revolution*.
62   According to Floro Quibuyen, Rizal read Thomas à Kempis's *La imitacion de Cristo* (*The Imitation of Christ*, 1418–27) in the days before his execution by firing squad by the Spanish Army on 30 December 1896. This, as well as other actions by Rizal, opened the way for various interpretations of his life and death as the 'Tagalog Christ'. Kempis's book was translated into Tagalog as *Pagtulad kay Cristo* (1880). Though quite different in almost all respects from *Limang Gintong Silahis*, à Kempis's famous work was also translated into many languages and seemed to offer Rizal a way to understand the meaning of his martyrdom. Floro Quibuyen, 'Rizal and the Revolution', *Philippine Studies* 45(2) (1997): 247. Filipino activists, unsurprisingly, have a long history of drawing on the stories of the sacrifices of the heroes of the Philippine Revolution. The CPP, similarly, continues to celebrate the anniversary of the birth of Andres Bonifacio.
63   In this vein, the Chinese tradition of moral education through the emulation of exemplars (for example, Norman Bethune) parallels similar traditions of character and values education in the Philippines that have roots in the pedagogical practices of Catholicism, American colonialism and twentieth-century Philippine nation-building.

Thus, activists and mass revolutionaries who read the *FGR* can imagine themselves as the genuine heirs of the Philippine national revolutionary tradition. It is fitting that, according to Walter Benjamin, the image of their enslaved forefathers remains the most powerful source of hatred and capacity for sacrifice of the oppressed classes whose historical mission is to finish the work of liberation in the name of previous defeated and downtrodden generations.[64]

This deeply felt lived connection with history therefore serves to further deepen the commitment of Filipino Maoists to persevere through the decades in the face of setbacks, difficulties and innumerable attempted refutations of their revolutionary project. Sison writes:

> *Angkop pa ang paggamit ng mga halimbawa tulad nina Chang Szu-teh, Norman Bethune, at ng pabula ng 'Matandang Hangal' bilang mga halimbawa ng katapatan, paninindigan at taos-pusong paglilingkod sa kasalukuyang panahon. Pero totoo naman na sa hinaba ng ating pakikibaka at dinami ng mga parangal natin sa ating mga Pilipinong martir at bayani, matagal nang puede tayong maglikom at pumili ng mga parangal para sa inspirasyon ng mga kasama at mga aktibista. Matagal nang angkop na gamitin natin ang mga halimbawa mula sa karanasan ng kilusang rebolusyonaryo sa Pilipinas.*

> [It is still appropriate up to the present time to use Chang Szu-the, Norman Bethune, and the fable of the 'Foolish Old Man' as examples of fidelity, firmness, and whole-hearted service. But it is true that in the many years of our struggle and the many tributes we have given to Filipino martyrs and heroes, it has been some time since we could have collected and chosen tributes for the inspiration of comrades and activists. It has been a long time since we could use examples from the Philippine revolutionary movement.][65]

Beyond the *FGR*, the importance of the term and idea of *pagpapakasakit* in modern Philippine revolutionary discourse is also highlighted by its prominence in a revolutionary song titled 'Ang Gabay' ('The Guide').

---

64   Walter Benjamin, *Illuminations* (New York, NY: Harcourt, Brace & World, 1968), 260.
65   Sison, Interview. Some individuals from the Philippine revolutionary movement (for example, Lean Alejandro, Lorena Barros, Edgar Jopson and Emmanuel Lacaba) are recognised as martyrs even in mainstream publications. See Asucion David-Maramba, *Six Young Filipino Martyrs* (Pasig City, Philippines: Anvil, 1997); and Benjamin Pimentel, *U.G.: An Underground Tale—The Life and Struggle of Edgar Jopson*, 3rd edn (Pasig City, Philippines: Anvil, 2019). See also the website *Bantayog ng mga Bayani* [*Monument to the Heroes*], available from: www.bantayog.org/.

The song is attributed to 'Ka [Comrade] Arting', a fighter of the New People's Army, and a book of revolutionary songs indicates 'Cagayan Valley, 1979' as the place and year of the song's composition.

The song, a lullaby that ends on a high note, with the cadence of a march, draws on the country's tradition of religious-nationalist imagery. Like the title *Five Golden Rays* itself, the song's lyrics are filled with metaphors for light: *sikat* ('ray'), *liwanag* ('light'), *ningning* ('radiance'), *sinag* ('beam'), *ginto* ('gold'), *luningning* ('brilliance') and *bukang-liwayway* ('dawn'). Known in some regions as 'Awit ng Partido' or 'Song of the Party'— already an important designation in a movement that featured the 'Song of a Farmer', 'Song of a Worker' and other such 'songs'—it likens the Communist Party to a messiah that will 'liberate' the poor whose persona is singing the song. It is said that in celebrations of the anniversaries of the Communist Party, the song is a constant presence, sung standing by attendees like the 'Internationale'. The song's last lines, during which the marching cadence sets in, are: 'You are our true hope, Communist Party/ That will liberate us/How sweet it is to live on this land/If in sacrifice [*pagpapakasakit*], we will be free.' Here, *pagpapakasakit* is used to signify everything the poor do to support and advance the revolution:

> **Ang Gaba**
> *Tumatagos sa diwa ang iyong pagsikat*
> *Nagsisilbing gabay ang iyong liwanag*
> *Sa balat ng lupa ang ningning mong sinag*
> *Katumbas ay ginto sa aming mahihirap.*
> *Kung sa aming buhay ay di ka dumating*
> *Di namin malilikha mga gintong awitin*
> *Binulag man kami ng mga ganid at sakim*
> *Ang mga sinag mo ang tunay na nagpaluningning.*
> *Tulad mo ay butil na hinasik sa bukid*
> *Tumubo't namulaklak sa aming anakpawis*
> *Ang lambong ng gabi'y iyong pinapalis*
> *Na nagpapalaya sa isipang napiit.*
> *Pag-asa kang tunay sa pagbubukang-liwayway*
> *Na sa amin ay gintong sumilay*
> *Anong tamis pala ang sa lupa mamuhay*
> *Kung sa pagpapakasakit ay may tagumpay.*
> *Pag-asa kang tunay Partido Komunista*
> *Na sa amin ay magpapalaya*
> *Anong tamis pala ang mamuhay sa lupa*
> *Kung sa pagpapakasakit, tayo'y lalaya.*)

[*The Guide*
Your rays penetrate the soul
Your light serves as a guide
On the surface of the earth, your shining rays
Are like gold for us who are poor
If you did not come into our lives
We would be not able to write this golden song
We may have been blinded by the greedy and selfish
Your rays have bathed everything in light
You are like a seed that has been sown in the field
Which has grown and flowered for us workers
You have banished the veil of darkness
And liberated the imprisoned mind
You are a genuine hope as the sun rises
Like gold shining upon us
How sweet it is to live on this land
If in sacrifice there is victory
You are our true hope, Communist Party
That will liberate us
How sweet it is to live on this land
If in sacrifice, we will be free.]

It was unavoidable that the secular, internationalist and proletarian perspectives of Philippine Maoism would overlap with the accumulated layers of meaning of the popular idioms used to translate Mao's works. Despite the complex stratified nature of Philippine languages, the uniquely Filipino and peculiar mélange of religious and moral idioms, rhetoric and languages of nationalism, and the discourses of class struggle point to the intimate dialectic of ideological formation between intellectuals and the masses that takes place in the *FGR*.[66] One Filipino historian, invoking leaders of the country's revolutionary movements from the 1896 revolution to the early 1970s, describes the opposing poles of this dialectic—an opposition he deems it necessary to transcend—as such: '[E]very period needs a "brain" and an "executive," which are symbolized in our consciousness by a Jacinto/Rizal for a Bonifacio, Mabini for an Aguinaldo, Lava for a Taruc and Guerrero for a Dante.'[67]

---

66   Floro C. Quibuyen, *A Nation Aborted: Rizal, American Hegemony, and Philippine Nationalism* (Quezon City, Philippines: Ateneo de Manila University Press, 1999), 220.
67   Jaime B. Veneracion, 'Panimula', *Philippine Social Sciences Review. Special Issue: Ang Kilusang Masa sa Kasaysayang Pilipino* [*The Mass Movement in Philippine History*] *(1900–1992)* (January–December 1994).

The point, however, is not to conflate Philippine Maoism with religious or ethical-moral discourse. Rather, what the *FGR* shows is the complex interplay in tension and non-reductive intermingling of these languages within a living social movement.[68] The translated texts combine traditional Tagalog moral concepts, the genre of the religious exemplum, the history of the unfinished Philippine revolution and the political manifesto of class struggle. The Tagalog translation demonstrates how moral-ethical and political idioms are not necessarily contradictory but can deeply intertwine with one another. These rich layers of meaning may explain why this 'dusty relic' from the Chinese Cultural Revolution seems to have found a durable home in the Philippines. It is no longer simply an alien text but one that resonates within a new context. The convergence of Catholic and nationalist idioms of heroism and sacrifice may also explain why sectors of the petty bourgeois intelligentsia, including youth and students, are particularly drawn to the *FGR*. After all, these are the natural adepts of the dominant religious ideology and the nationalist secular religion of the state.

Conclusion

This chapter began with a look at how the writing, collection, interpretation and dissemination of the *Five Old Articles*, even within China, passed through changes in social and historical context. To conclude, it may prove useful to digress briefly into a few other countries in Southeast Asia, particularly Indonesia, to show how the Philippine case is distinctive in its use of Mao's writing, especially the *Five Old Articles*.

It is interesting to note, given the continued existence of the Filipino Maoist movement, that the translation and dissemination of Mao's writing seems to have occurred throughout much of Southeast Asia before the Philippines. In Vietnam, 1949 was the year of both the Conference of Debate in Viet Bac—where the VCP unanimously resolved to uphold

---

68 There has been a tendency in the scholarship of movements in Philippine history to either define them using rigid and positivist categories or to assume, ultimately, that every movement has at its core the same 'indigenous' Filipino character (which is often portrayed as some form of syncretic millenarianism). Reynaldo Ileto's classic study, *Pasyon and Revolution*, has played an important role in criticising the former tendency, but it has also ironically often promoted the latter. Unfortunately, classifications of either sort ignore the complex and conflicting nature of social movements, mass mobilisation and cultural transformation. For a lengthier discussion of the problem, see Sy, 'Child of the poor', 14–57.

the slogan 'Revolutionise ideology and popularise activities'[69]—and the translation of Mao's 'Talks at the Yenan Forum', which solidified what King Cheng[70] and David Marr have dubbed the 'Chinese influence' in the VCP.[71] The translation of this essay led to the translation, publication and dissemination of many of Mao's other works in North Vietnam during the 1950s.[72] Each of the five articles was included among the works of Mao that were promoted at this time. After an influx of young cadres following the Việt Minh's victory in Dien Bien Phu, the newly established Ministry of Culture launched both a special education program for cadres and a mass literacy program for all citizens.[73] In the program for cadres, all five articles were included in the required reading. For the mass literacy program, meanwhile, both 'In Memory of Norman Bethune' and 'Serve the People' were included among the materials.[74]

---

69   Tuan Ngoc Nguyen, 'Socialist realism in Vietnamese literature: An analysis of the relationship between literature and politics' (PhD. diss., Victoria University, Melbourne, 2004), viii.
70   King Chen, *Vietnam and China, 1938–1954* (Princeton, NJ: Princeton University Press, 1969), 155–212, 218.
71   David Marr, *Vietnam 1945: The Quest for Power* (Berkeley, CA: University of California Press, 1995), 255.
72   Such translations were also facilitated by the long history of Chinese-language use among the Vietnamese educated and elite. For more on the Maoist influence in Vietnam in the 1950s, see Hoaøng Vaên Hoan, *Gioït Nöôùc trong Bieån Caû* [*A Drop in the Ocean*] (Portland, OR: N. Tran, 1991).
73   Alexander Woodside, 'The Triumphs and Failures of Mass Education in Vietnam', *Pacific Affairs* 56(3) (1983): 416.
74   Perhaps this inclusion should come as no surprise, given how political attitudes like those seen in the five articles were already being propagated in the writings of the Việt Minh and the Vietnamese Communist Party (VCP) during their successive military campaigns against the Japanese and the French (1938–54). For example, in two of Truong Chinh's seminal works at the time—*Cách mạng Tháng Tám* [*The August Revolution*] (1946) and *Kháng chiến nhất định thắng lợi* [*The Resistance Will Win*] (1947)—the value of self-sacrifice, serving the interests of the masses and self-effacement (especially for intellectuals) were consistently emphasised. For a look at how these ideas were integrated with the cultural policies of the VCP, as well as an examination of the cultural anticommunist response it generated both within the party and externally among groups inside and outside Vietnam, see Amado Anthony G. Mendoza III, 'Ang Anti-Komunistang Diskursong Pampanitikan sa Timog-Silangang Asya sa mga Antolohiya, Kritisismong Pampanitikan, Polemikong Pampanitikan at Opisyal na Dokumento mula sa Indonesia, Pilipinas, at Vietnam [Anticommunist literary discourse in Southeast Asia in anthologies, literary criticism, literary polemics, and official documents from Indonesia, the Philippines, and Vietnam]' (Master's thesis, University of the Philippines, Diliman, 2019), 127–97. After the 'failure' of the land reform campaign in the mid-1950s and in the wake of the Nhan Van Giai Pham Controversy, the VCP (with the Ministry of Culture) focused its energies on consolidating its authority and stifling ideological unorthodoxy. This change in priorities led the VCP to hasten the institutionalisation of 'Hồ Chí Minh Thought' like that of Maoist Thought in China. One corollary of this process was a decline in the propagation of Maoist materials. This effectively spelled the end of the dissemination of Mao's writing, including the *Five Articles*, in Vietnam. See Kim Ngoc Bao Ninh, *A World Transformed: The Politics of Culture in Revolutionary Vietnam, 1945–1964* (Ann Arbor, MI: University of Michigan Press, 2002), 164–203.

In Thailand, the initial translations of Mao's works were carried out by those of ethnic Chinese descent, who made up a majority of the members of the Central Committee of the Communist Party of Thailand. As Kasian Tejapira shows, each of the five articles was included among the various texts by Mao that were translated into Thai.[75] However, unlike in Vietnam, the motivation for these translations seemed to be mostly intellectual and did almost nothing to influence the concrete practices of the Communist Party of Thailand.[76]

Perhaps the most interesting case to compare with the Philippines, however, is Indonesia. While much of the current scholarship on the Communist Party of Indonesia (PKI) dates its 'Maoist turn' to the tumultuous 1960s,[77] Hersri Setiawan, a former alternate member of the PKI's Central Committee and former head of the Yogyakarta chapter of the Lembaga Kebudayaan Rakyat (Institute of People's Culture), claims the dissemination of Mao's writing in Indonesia began much earlier. As early as 1951, just a few years after reconstruction of the party began following the Madiun Affair of 1948, PKI members who were fluent in Chinese read many of Mao's works, including most, if not all, of the five articles. They then translated and distributed these writings among select party officials and cadres. This move, according to Setiawan, was initiated by the party leadership to *membaja ketetapan hati* ('steel their resolve') through the painstaking process of resurrecting revolutionary fervour in the consciousness of the Indonesian people.[78]

A potentially illuminating example in this regard is D.N. Aidit's speech entitled 'Menempuh Jalan Rakyat [Taking the People's Way]'.[79] In this speech, delivered on 23 May 1952 during commemoration of the thirty-second anniversary of the PKI, Aidit emphasised the party's important

---

75 Kasian Tejapira, *Commodifying Marxism: The Formation of Thai Radical Culture, 1927–1958* (Kyoto, Japan: Kyoto University Press, 2001), 34–36.
76 Perhaps as an ironic twist of fate, some of the key anticommunist texts produced in the first half of the twentieth century, the literary works of Rama VI, used similar themes of selflessness and self-sacrifice to attack what he claimed was the fake utopianism of communists. See Rama VI, *Uttarakuru: An Asiatic Wonderland* (Bangkok: Siam Observer Press, 1913), 1–34.
77 See Harold Crouch, *The Army and Politics in Indonesia* (Jakarta: Equinox Publishing, 1978); Rex Mortimer, 'The Downfall of Indonesian Communism', *The Socialist Register* 8 (1969): 189–217; Ulf Sundhausen, *The Road to Power: Indonesian Army Politics* (Kuala Lumpur: Oxford University Press, 1982).
78 Authors' interview with Hersri Setiawan, online, 21 January 2021. All translations in this study are provided by the authors.
79 D.N. Aidit, *Menempuh Djalan Rakjat [Taking the People's Path]* (Jakarta: Jajasan Pembaruan, 1952), 11–18.

role in advancing and serving the interests of the people. As in most speeches of this kind, Aidit also stressed the duty of both the party and the people to safeguard the revolutionary legacies of the August Revolution, for by doing so they would serve the interests of all oppressed classes in both Indonesia and the world.[80] When asked about 'Menempuh Jalan Rakyat' and to what extent the Five Articles may have influenced Aidit, Setiawan notes:

> *Aidit, Njoto, dan petinggi partai lainnya, tetapi terutama Aidit, menganggap 'Melayani Rakyat', 'Untuk Mengenang Norman Bethune' dan 'Sang Bodoh, Orang Tua yang Memusnahkan Pegunungan' sebagai karya yang menanamkan baik tua maupun muda kader pentingnya iman yang teguh pada rakyat dan revolusi. 'Tentang Mengoreksi Ide-ide yang Salah dalam Partai' dan 'Memerangi Liberalisme' menjadi penting selama tahun 1960-an, ketika Partai mencoba membikin daftar bacaan untuk rekrutan dari militer. Bahkan dalam perdebatan anggota CC setelah 1965, artikel-artikel tersebut sering dikutip atau digunakan untuk membenarkan argumen dan posisi politik tertentu.*
>
> [Aidit, Njoto, and other high-ranking party officials, but especially Aidit, considered 'Serve the People', 'In Memory of Norman Bethune' and 'Foolish Old Man Who Removed the Mountains' as works that instil in both young and old cadres the importance of unwavering faith in the people and the revolution. 'On Correcting Mistaken Ideas in the Party' and 'Combat Liberalism' became crucial during the 1960s, when the party was trying to come up with a reading list for recruits from the army. Even in debates of CC [Central Committee] members after 1965, these articles were often quoted or used to justify certain arguments and political positions.][81]

Setiawan's confirmation of the much earlier dissemination of Mao's writings among PKI members—both during its reestablishment and ascent in the 1950s and at its peak (and dissolution) in the 1960s—explains certain gaps in the extant literature on the political and ideological shifts happening within the PKI. This, for instance, partly explains why the importance of Mao Zedong Thought would be consistently emphasised in many of the PKI's most important documents (even in the party's so-called *otokritik* or 'self-criticism') from 1965 to 1971.

---

80   ibid., 20–22.
81   Hersri Setiawan, Interview.

Most notable among these is the 1971 document *Tegakan PKI yang Marxis-Leninis Untuk Memimpin Revolusi Demokrasi Rakjat Indonesia* ('*Uphold a Marxist-Leninist PKI in Order to Lead the Democratic Revolution of the Indonesian People*'). Aside from the expected outline and delineation of the PKI's prospects after Suharto's rise to power, the introduction to the document boldly declares the PKI is a Marxist-Leninist party that also upholds *pikiran Mao Tjetung* ('Mao Zedong Thought').[82] This earlier spread of Mao's texts—including the different works that would become the *Five Old Articles*—may also help to explain the emphasis the PKI's cultural arm, the Lembaga Kebudajaan Rakjat (People's Cultural Institute), placed on self-effacing attitudes when it came to serving the masses. This is particularly exemplified by its '*turun ke bawah*' (lit., to 'go under' or 'go down') method, which exhorted cultural workers—intellectuals, writers and cadres—to learn from the masses.

It is beyond the scope of this chapter to discuss why the Philippine translation and dissemination of Maoist writings took place much later than in countries like Vietnam and Indonesia. A provisional hypothesis, however, may be that the spread of Maoism was hindered by the strained relationship between the PKP-1930 and the 'Chinese Bureau'—a branch of the CCP that was based in the Philippines. Interestingly, members of this Chinese Bureau were already reading Mao's texts as early as the 1930s. These texts had not, however, been translated into local languages.[83] It is possible the belated translations were in part a result of state suppression of communists in the late 1940s and 1950s, which included increased state surveillance of the Chinese community in the Philippines. The intensity of the suppression of both communists and Chinese was such that the leaders of the PKP-1930 and their armed wing, the Huks, lost contact with the Chinese Bureau for many years. In addition, there were always tensions between the PKP-1930 and the Chinese Bureau over the issue of the latter's autonomy in the Philippines.[84] Such tensions may

---

[82] Politburo CC-PKI [Political Bureau of the Central Committee of the Communist Party of Indonesia], *Tegakkan PKI jang Marxis-Leninis Untuk Memimpin Revolusi Demokrasi Rakjat Indonesia: Lima Dokumen Penting Politburo CC PKI* [*Build the PKI Along the Marxist-Leninist Line to Lead the People's Democratic Revolution in Indonesia: Five Important Documents of the Political Bureau of the CC PKI*] (Jakarta: Delegation of the CC PKI, 1971), i.

[83] Armando Liwanag, *Marxism-Leninism-Mao Zedong Thought as Guide to the Philippine Revolution* (Communist Party of the Philippines, 6 November 1993), available from: www.marxists.org/history/philippines/cpp/liwanag/1993/mlmzt-guide.htm.

[84] Jesus Lava, *Memoirs of a Communist* (Pasig, Philippines: Anvil Publishing, 2002), 169–70.

have precluded the kind of deep interpersonal exchange that would have allowed an earlier communication of Maoist ideas and writings to non-Chinese communists in the country.

On the more important point of what these comparisons can show us about the dissemination of the *Five Old Articles*, the most interesting finding is the fact that, in the Philippines and also possibly in Indonesia, during periods of the popularisation of and emergency for revolutionary movements, the *Five Articles* (and Mao's writing as a whole) played a role not in 'vulgarising' Marxism through dogmatic memorisation (as may perhaps have happened in China) but in a genuine (re)building of parties and movements. As mentioned above, from as early as 1951, members of the PKI fluent in Chinese had already read and translated at least some of the *Five Articles*. They had reportedly found these useful to *membaja ketetapan hati* ('steel their resolve') in the coming struggles. This Indonesian reception is similar to the Philippine interpretation. '*Ketatapan hati*' in Tagalog is *lakas ng loob* ('strength of the will')—a phrase that occurs in the Tagalog text of the *FGR* in a passage from the commentary attached to 'The Foolish Old Man':

> *Ang itinuturo ni Tagapangulong Mao na 'maging matatag, huwag matakot sa pagpapakasakit at pangibabawan ang lahat ng kahirapan upang magtagumpay' ay nangangahulugan, sa huling pagsusuri, ng pagbibigay diin sa salik ng tao, ng panghihikayat sa atin para palargahin nang husto ang ating suhetibong inisyatiba, ng pagiging walang-takot sa mga kagipitan at kahirapan, at ng lakas ng loob para makibaka at magtagumpay.*
>
> [What Chairman Mao teaches us, 'be resolute, do not fear sacrifice [*pagpapakasakit*] and overcome all difficulties in order to be victorious' means, in the final analysis, to give emphasis to the human factor, to encourage us to unleash our subjective initiative, of having no fear in the face of repression and difficulty, and to have the strength of the will [*lakas ng loob*] needed to fight and win.][85]

---

85 Mao Zedong, *Limang Gintong Silahis: Limang Artikulo ni Mao Zedong na may mga Komentaryo* [*Five Golden Rays: Five Articles by Mao Zedong with Comments*], Central Committee of the Communist Party of the Philippines, trans. (Manila: Central Committee of the Communist Party of the Philippines, 2013), 60–61.

Furthermore, in the Philippines, as this study has shown, the *FGR* has become part of an 'ethical technology' that is 'aimed at the formation of a "Filipino" subject of moral and political knowledge and action'.[86] It should be emphasised that this process of subject formation does not gesture towards the creation of a 'new man' as seen in the revolutionary imaginaries of the past,[87] including that of Rizal's notion of '*hombres nuevos*'.[88] In fact, the idea of the *bagong tao* ('new man') does not figure at all in Philippine Maoist phraseology.

The *FGR* is, then, an ethical technology that appeals instead to the capacity of each Filipino for *pagmamalasakit* and *pagpapakasakit*, reinterpreted in the service of the oppressed classes. Indeed, the strong imprint of this popular revolutionary ethic may be part of the reason, despite the errors and excesses it has acknowledged, the CPP–New People's Army is distinguished both by its longevity and by the fact that, even despite strident anticommunist propaganda, it has not devolved into a patently 'gangster' or 'terrorist' organisation.[89]

If Mao constantly insisted on the Sinicisation of Marxism, the reception, creative reinterpretation, translation and dissemination of the *FGR* and other revolutionary texts in the Philippines point to the 'Filipinisation' of Maoism. This process of vernacularisation[90] underlines the potential universality of Maoism while drawing attention to the extremely unique, almost contingent and inimitable qualities of some of its effects. Nevertheless, the recent reprints of the *Five Old Articles* in other countries under its Philippine title, *Five Golden Rays*,[91] as well as the printing of the compilation known as *Activist Study Material* (*Araling Aktibista*, to preserve its Tagalog title),[92] which includes the *FGR*, are significant as a symbolic return of a text from the global Maoism of the 1960s that, having found its home in the Philippines, has come back to an international readership in the twenty-first century.

---

86 Caroline Sy Hau, *Necessary Fictions: Philippine Literature and the Nation, 1946–1980* (Quezon City, Philippines: Ateneo de Manila University Press, 2000), 26–30.
87 See Cheng Yinghong, *Creating the New Man: From Enlightenment Ideals to Socialist Realities* (Honolulu: University of Hawai'i Press, 2009).
88 Ramon Guillermo, 'Moral Forces, Philosophy of History, and War in Jose Rizal', *Philippine Studies: Historical & Ethnographic Viewpoints* 60(1) (2012): 5–32.
89 Arif Dirlik, 'Mao Zedong Thought and the Third World/Global South', *Interventions: International Journal of Postcolonial Studies* 16(2) (2014): 233–56, doi.org/10.1080/1369801X.2013.798124.
90 Teodor Shanin, *Late Marx and the Russian Road* (New York, NY: Monthly Review Press, 1983), 256.
91 Mao Zedong, *Five Golden Rays* (Austin: Fourth Sword Publications, 2017); Mao Zedong, *Five Golden Rays* (Utrecht, Netherlands: Christophe Kistler, 2017).
92 CPP-NED, *Activist Study*.

5

Partai Republik Indonesia: Communist exiles and their noncommunist approaches to anticolonialism

Kankan Xie

From November 1926 to January 1927, a series of insurrections broke out in several districts across the Dutch East Indies (DEI) (now Indonesia). Starting in the capital city of Batavia, the revolt soon spilled over to the rural areas of the nearby region of Banten and finally reached the west coast of Sumatra at the turn of the year. Behind the movement was the Partai Komunis Indonesia (PKI, Communist Party of Indonesia), the earliest communist party in Asia. Lacking adequate coordination, the rebellions played out in a highly disorganised manner. The Dutch authorities managed to crush each insurrection within a few days. The revolts provided the authorities with ideal justification for full-scale suppression of the PKI and affiliated organisations. In the aftermath, the colonial government arrested 13,000 people for their direct involvement in the uprisings and 5,000 more for displaying 'communist tendencies'. They also banished 1,308 alleged communist leaders to a remote penal colony in Boven Digoel, Netherlands New Guinea.[1] The anticommunist repression destroyed the party organisation, marking the end of the first

---

1 Ruth McVey, *The Rise of Indonesian Communism* (Ithaca, NY: Cornell University Press, 1968), 353; J. Th. Petrus Blumberger, *De communistische beweging in Nederlandsch-Indië* [*The Communist Movement in the Dutch East Indies*] (Haarlem, Netherlands: Tjeenk Willink, 1935), 111.

phase of the communist movement in Indonesia. Despite attempts to reorganise the party in the late 1920s and throughout the long 1930s, the PKI would not play a significant role in Indonesian politics until its reestablishment after World War II (WWII).

The DEI authorities' full-scale suppression dealt a crushing blow to the PKI. The party lost its entire leadership in the DEI due to the ceaseless arrests, imprisonments and banishments. However, the PKI movement was by no means dead. While the party dissolved in the DEI due to the crackdown, hundreds of PKI members managed to escape to nearby British Malaya. Moreover, although just a handful of individuals, the party leadership in exile remained largely intact. Despite escalating pressures, the PKI liaison office in Singapore was still operating under revolutionary leader Tan Malaka and his inner circle. Alimin and Musso were on their way to join the Singapore group from Moscow. PKI leaders such as Semaun and Darsono stayed in Europe, where they sought to influence the Dutch Government by working with the Communist Party of Holland and Indonesian students in the Netherlands. Meanwhile, Dutch and British colonial authorities had not yet formed a close working relationship to fight communism. A question thus arises as to whether the PKI leadership overseas took the opportunity to try to reinstate the party. If so, why were they unsuccessful?

The existing literature commonly attributes the PKI's failure to the ruthless suppression of the DEI Government and suggests communism ceased to play a crucial role in Indonesian politics until its revival after WWII.[2] While such observations reflect certain truths from the perspective of domestic politics, they tend to downplay the fact that many PKI fugitives carried on the anticolonial struggle overseas in various forms throughout the remainder of the colonial era.[3] It is also problematic to regard the PKI as a clandestine movement from 1927. Due to the heated debates over who should be responsible for the poorly organised uprisings and, consequently, the party's disintegration, PKI fugitives split into many factions. While all claimed to be legitimate successors of the PKI, there was no central party leadership to speak of. At least three PKI factions coexisted outside the DEI with limited interactions between them: the Tan

---

2   McVey, *The Rise of Indonesian Communism*, 353–54; Harry Benda and Ruth McVey, *The Communist Uprisings of 1926–1927 in Indonesia: Key Documents* (Ithaca, NY: Cornell University Press, 1960), xviii; George McT. Kahin, *Nationalism and Revolution in Indonesia* (Ithaca, NY: SEAP Publications, Cornell University, 2003), 86–87.
3   Takashi Shiraishi, 'Policing the Phantom Underground', *Indonesia* (63) (1997): 1–3.

Malaka group formed the Partai Republik Indonesia (PARI, Indonesian Republican Party) and carried on clandestine struggles against Dutch colonialism. Alimin and Musso, two ardent advocates of the rebellion, fell out with the Tan Malaka group but stayed close with the Comintern course throughout the interwar period. By contrast, Semaun and Darsono gradually distanced themselves from Moscow but still sought to influence Indonesian politics in the metropole.

This chapter explores PARI's clandestine activities outside the DEI in the aftermath of the 1926–27 uprisings. While distancing themselves from Comintern-sanctioned international communism, PARI operated mainly in neighbouring countries and sought to infiltrate the DEI through various religious and nationalist networks. However, throughout its active years, PARI remained a propaganda group of limited size and with insignificant presence in the public sphere.[4] As a result, historians usually only mention the organisation in passing in their writings about Indonesia's nationalist movement, as it never grew into the mass movement envisioned by its founders. The scarcity of surviving materials also makes investigations into the clandestine organisation particularly difficult. Nevertheless, as Helen Jarvis points out, PARI was a 'golden bridge' that spanned the chasm between the failed PKI uprisings of 1926–27 and Indonesia's eventual independence in the late 1940s. PARI's significance lies in its efforts to carry on militant anticolonial activities—characterised by its continuous calls for immediate and complete independence—while the colonial state became increasingly repressive in the aftermath of the PKI uprisings. Moreover, what distinguished PARI from other Indonesia-based nationalist groups at the time was its leadership. With clear visions of the domestic and global situations, a group of former PKI leaders in exile adopted inverted approaches to anticolonialism.[5] PARI networks spanning Southeast Asia thus profoundly affected Indonesia's struggle for independence in the remainder of the colonial era.

---

4   Takashi Shiraishi, *The Phantom World of Digul: Policing as Politics in Colonial Indonesia, 1926–1941* (Singapore: NUS Press and Kyoto University Press, 2021), 160–61.
5   Helen Jarvis, *Partai Republik Indonesia (PARI): Was it 'The Sole Golden Bridge to the Republic of Indonesia'?* (Townsville, Qld: James Cook University Press, 1981), 20–22.

PARI: A PKI reincarnation?

In his study of the Vietnamese communist movement, Christopher Goscha has explored how Vietnamese activists went to neighbouring countries to build revolutionary bases that served as a critical part of the extensive Vietnamese revolutionary network during the late colonial period. Southern China and north-eastern Thailand were ideal places for such purposes for two main reasons: first, the existence of large Vietnamese communities; and, second, their strategic location—'close to Vietnam but … just beyond the reach of the omnipresent French Sûreté'.[6] Goscha's work demonstrates how Vietnamese revolutionaries established themselves among immigrants in Thailand and how they continued to organise anticolonial activities against the French through layered intraregional networks.[7] PARI's regional networks shared many similarities with its Vietnamese counterparts. Nevertheless, its activities went far beyond one territory. The leaders of PARI—first started in the Siamese (Thai) capital of Bangkok in 1927—soon moved, along with party operations, to Singapore, Malaya, Borneo, southern China and the Philippines. PARI activists frequently penetrated Indonesia from these places, establishing contacts on both Java and the Outer Islands. Before delving into PARI's revolutionary practices, it is essential to discuss the backdrop against which the party was founded.

Shortly after the failed PKI uprisings, in May 1927, Tan Malaka gathered with his two loyal associates, Subakat and Djamaluddin Tamin, in Bangkok. There were several reasons for choosing Bangkok as their new hideout. Apart from the fact that Siam was relatively safe because it was not a Western colony, Malaka and Tamin also knew many people in the city through their West Sumatran network.[8] From his Sumatra Thawalib connections, Tamin heard that two *ulamas*, Sjech Taher and Sjech Ahmad Wahab, lived in the city and were sympathetic towards anticolonial

---

6   Sûreté is the detective branch of the French civil police force. See Christopher E. Goscha, *Thailand and the Southeast Asian Networks of the Vietnamese Revolution, 1885–1954* (London: Curzon Press, 1999), 65.
7   ibid., 8.
8   Djamaluddin Tamin studied and taught at the Islamic school Sumatra Thawalib in Padang Pajang, where communist ideas were widespread in the early 1920s. Tamin co-edited a progressive newspaper, *Pemandangan Islam [Islamic View]*, and joined the PKI in 1922. Audrey Kahin, 'The 1927 Communist Uprising in Sumatra: A Reappraisal', *Indonesia* (62) (1996): 25–26, doi.org/10.2307/3351390.

struggles.⁹ Without much difficulty, Tamin connected with Sjech Taher, who introduced him to Sjech Ahmad Wahab, a leader of 20,000 Wahhabi Muslims in Bangkok who ran several *pesantren* ('Islamic boarding schools') in the city.¹⁰ Sjech Ahmad Wahab arranged accommodation for Tamin and Subakat, but they decided not to connect him to Tan Malaka for reasons of safety.

In Bangkok, the three PKI veterans finally had the chance to reflect on the party's failure and to analyse their situation. They concluded that, as of January 1927, the DEI Government had utterly crushed the PKI movement in the wake of the abortive revolts. According to Tamin, a Comintern document was crucial in the three PKI leaders' discussion. Alimin brought this document from Moscow and handed it to a Singapore-based PKI member before his arrest by British police.¹¹ The document confirmed that the Comintern regarded the PKI's plan to rebel (the so-called Prambanan Decision) as a mistake and was opposed to what it considered a suicidal revolt. The document also reaffirmed Tan Malaka's leadership role as a Comintern representative. Finally, the document showed only the Trotskyists supported the Prambanan Decision, while the Stalinists, who had more influence over the Comintern, opposed the plan.¹²

The most crucial outcomes of the discussion were two documents— a manifesto by Tan Malaka and a statute by Subakat—which the three PKI fugitives used to declare the establishment of the PARI on 1 June 1927. DEI authorities seized the two key documents when they arrested Subakat in Bangkok in 1929 with the help of the Siamese Government. The original 1927 version of the manifesto is no longer available. What remains in Dutch archives is a summary of a 1929 version produced by Tan Malaka in Amoy (Xiamen) and brought back to Indonesia by Mardjono, a PARI member who visited Tan Malaka in China in

---

9   According to Tamin, there were five famous religious teachers in Bangkok at that time, three of whom were well known for their pro-Dutch stance; only Sjech Taher and Sjech Ahmad Wahab were potential supporters. See Djamaluddin Tamin, *Sedjarah P.K.I.* [*PKI History*] (Jakarta: Pustaka Antara, 1957), 59.
10 Audrey Kahin, *Rebellion to Integration: West Sumatra and the Indonesian Polity, 1926–1988* (Amsterdam: University of Amsterdam Press, 1999), 301n.68, citing Djamaluddin Tamin, 'Sedjarah PKI. Djilid 1 [PKI history. Volume 1]' (Typescript, n.d.), 59–60.
11 Alimin and Musso fell out with the Tan Malaka group in Singapore after their release by the British police. The two then opted to leave Singapore for Moscow via China. See Tamin, *PKI History*, 55–56.
12 Tamin wrote his memoir in 1957; the PKI leadership at the time accused Tan Malaka of being a Trotskyist. It is highly possible Tamin emphasised this by pointing out they were not to defend PARI and Tan Malaka. See Tamin, *PKI History*, 60.

the same year. A Dutch intelligence officer summarised the 30-page document in nine and a half pages, noting that Tan Malaka had analysed the global communist movement based on the English translation by Max Eastman of Leon Trotsky's *The Real Situation in Russia*.[13] The book included a document Trotsky had presented at a meeting of the All-Union Communist Party in September 1927, but the English version was not published, in New York and London, until 1928. Therefore, it is unlikely Tan Malaka's original draft talked much about the international situation in the way he did in the 1929 version.[14] However, the summary did shed important light on PARI's stance on the PKI's weaknesses and the failures of the 1926–27 uprisings.

First, the manifesto addressed 'supporters of the Comintern in Indonesia' and suggested the Indonesian people must now accept the 'inglorious collapse' of the PKI, which had not one but many causes. Chief among them was the fact that the party was not sufficiently disciplined. Despite its popularity among the masses, the PKI 'fulfilled not the most elementary criteria of a communist party'. While the party accepted people from all walks of life, it was not 'organisationally a homogeneous machine', as many sections remained independent from each other. Additionally, qualified leaders were too few in comparison with Indonesia's population of 60 million and only a tiny proportion of workers were organised under unions. The PKI also significantly underrated Dutch imperialism, and the revolts carried out were 'not equal to a revolution; not even to a general strike'.[15] Furthermore, the manifesto indicated the more fundamental problem was deeply rooted in 'the psychology of the people', who had 'misplaced hopes' for assistance from outside. Indonesian people still believed in Ratu Adil (the 'Just Queen' of Javanese mythology) and Mahdi (a messianic figure in Islam), who would restore justice and order in times of hardship. In a way, the PKI riots of 1926–27 were 'in essence a copy of those in Aceh and Jambi, only on a smaller scale. The same in Bantam, but there too they thought they had joined a communist revolution.'

---

13 Leon Trotsky, *The Real Situation in Russia*, Max Eastman, trans. (New York, NY: Harcourt, Brace & Co., 1928).
14 Helen Jarvis, *Partai Republik Indonesia*, 5.
15 'Korte Inhoud van het Manifest der Partij Republiek Indonesia (PARI) [Brief Contents of the Manifesto of the Republic of Indonesia Party]', 2.10.36.06-446x/1936, Geheime Mailrapporten [Secret Mail Reports] [hereinafter GMR], Ministerie van Koloniën [Ministry of Colonies], Nationaal Archief [National Archives of the Netherlands; hereinafter NA-NL], Den Haag. Reproduced in Jarvis, *Partai Republik Indonesia*, Appendix 2, 1–6. Also see Shiraishi, 'Policing the Phantom Underground', 31.

5. PARTAI REPUBLIK INDONESIA

Related to this point, Tan Malaka discussed in detail the 'indifference and ignorance' of the Comintern. Specifically, he criticised the bureaucratic leadership of Moscow, which cared only about the interests of Russia:

> With examples from Germany, Italy, and Bulgaria, it demonstrated that the Moscow leadership has failed for other countries. The entire Third International is built up in the Russian interest, and young Eastern leaders, in particular, will be inclined to go over to worship and to lose their independence, with the result that they will lack contact with their own masses, who have different impulses from the Russian people.[16]

It is also noteworthy that, by the time PARI was established in June 1927, the Comintern's China policy had failed because of Chiang Kai-shek's nationwide anticommunist purge in the aftermath of the Shanghai Massacre.

Although it is unclear whether Tan Malaka wrote his criticism in the original draft of the PARI manifesto or added the lines to the new version after witnessing the political situation in China for himself, his point about breaking away from the Comintern was well articulated:

> Following China's example, Stalin would send his Borodins, Van Gelens, Cheka, military and other innumerable advisers to a revolutionary 'Indonesia.' The Third International would have nothing to say in the choice of the individuals, and everything would remain secret from this body. They consider that it would be in the interests of imperialism, and not in the interest of the Indies if Stalin made himself master of an eventual revolutionary movement in the Netherlands-Indies.[17]

Therefore, the PARI trio decided not to reactivate the PKI, as there would be 'serious drawbacks' if people continued relating the new party to Moscow.[18]

Instead, Tan Malaka pointed out the urgent need to establish a new party that served the true interests of Indonesians:

> A soviet, naturally completely adjusted to local conditions, is, in the opinion of the writers, not only conceivable but would be the best form of government for Indonesia, taking into account its

---

16 'Brief Contents of the Manifesto of the Republic of Indonesia Party', GMR, NA-NL.
17 ibid.
18 Shiraishi, 'Policing the Phantom Underground', 30.

> cultural and economic development ... The people of the Indies have enough to do without waiting around for the conclusion to the fight between Stalin and Trotsky. They have their own pressing problems that require a solution. PARI is a revolutionary-workers instrument that tries to deal with these problems on the basis of its own insight.[19]

The manifesto concluded by stating that the PARI group wished to remain internationalists but held different views from the Comintern on how to achieve the ultimate goal—'Not from above to below, but the reverse', Tan Malaka noted.[20]

PARI's statute by Subakat is available in full in colonial archives with parallel Dutch and Indonesian texts. While the tone was similar to Tan Malaka's manifesto, the statute made no mention of the PKI and international communist movements at all. It claimed PARI was 'independent and free from leadership or influenced by any other party or force, either within or outside of Indonesia'. The statute set PARI's objective as:

> [To] achieve full and complete independence for Indonesia as soon as possible, and thereafter to establish a Federal Republic of Indonesia on principles that accord with the country's economic, social and political conditions, with the customs and character of its inhabitants, and which, furthermore, are designed to advance the physical and mental well-being of the Indonesian people.[21]

Despite the statute's well-formulated statements, Helen Jervis suggests 'the exact nature of PARI, and what its founders intended it to be are shrouded in confusion'.[22] While many historians regard PARI as a complete break from international communism because it acted independently of the Comintern, others see it as a reincarnation of the destroyed PKI with continuities in many aspects of its communist ideology and organisational strategies.

In Tan Malaka's memoir, *From Jail to Jail*, he says little about PARI. A crucial reason for this was that when he wrote the memoir in prison around 1947, Tan Malaka was still engaged in heated debates with leaders

---

19 'Brief Contents of the Manifesto of the Republic of Indonesia Party', GMR, NA-NL.
20 Jarvis, *Partai Republik Indonesia*, 10.
21 'Statuten der Partij Republik Indonesia (PARI) [Statutes of the Republic of Indonesia Party]', 446x/1936, GMR, NA-NL, Reproduced in Jarvis, *Partai Republik Indonesia*, Appendix 1, 1.
22 Jarvis, *Partai Republik Indonesia*, 3.

5. PARTAI REPUBLIK INDONESIA

of the reestablished PKI over the legitimacy of the party leadership.[23] It is likely Tan Malaka deliberately avoided this topic so his rivals could not use the narrative against him by claiming PARI was not communist. Instead, he provided a rather vague statement:

> Now, twenty years later, the results of the actions taken in Bangkok by the three of us are clear to all. We wanted to see continuity in the Indonesian peoples' and workers' movement through a time of great difficulty. We felt that this continuity could best be ensured first by relying on our own strength and secondly by marching independently but on a parallel course with the international proletarian movement—*getrennt marschieren, vereint schlagen* (march separately but strike together). We feel that the content and form of the situation and the struggles of 1945–1947 confirm in large part the position we took then, but it is not yet the time to reveal in detail the role played by PARI from its founding in July [*sic*] 1927 until now (July 1947).[24]

This implies PARI operated on its own and was independent of Comintern-sanctioned international communism.

In his 1946 *Thesis*, however, Tan Malaka gave a more nuanced description of the party's objective in response to new PKI leaders who accused PARI members of being Trotskyists:

> Party names are not so important and are easy to change as long as the contents remain. The Russian Communist Party itself has changed names three times! The important thing is [to retain] the revolutionary essence at every level and situation of struggle. Do not engage in counterrevolutionary actions, provocations, or opportunism. Marxism is not a dogma or a study of memorization, but a guideline for class struggles. And it is a method of dialectical materialism that must be carried out in accordance with the time and place. Since 20 years ago, PARI has possessed the quality

---

23 In May 1946, a committee of the reinstated PKI decided to hand over the party leadership to the 1926 generation. Sardjono, the PKI chairman in 1926 and a major advocate of the Prambanan Decision, took over control of the party. According to Tamin, Sardjono and Achmad Sumadi sabotaged the goodwill of this committee and excluded 75 former leaders of the PKI from the New PKI during the 1920–26 period. Alimin and Musso later joined the group after they returned to Indonesia. As a result, the PARI group was essentially alienated from the New PKI. See Tamin, *PKI History*, 56.
24 Tan Malaka and Helen Jarvis, *From Jail to Jail. Volume 1* (Athens, OH: Ohio University Press, 1991), 141–42.

> of Marxist philosophy with Leninist tactics. [PARI] is heading towards national and social revolutions, and towards socialist and communist societies throughout the world.[25]

Compared with the rather ambivalent position taken in his memoir, the statement in *Thesis* showed the leadership intended PARI to remain a Marxist-Leninist party in essence but carry on Indonesia's national and social revolutions on its own terms.

Tan Malaka continued, providing four reasons PARI had to be established in the way it was: first, most PKI leaders had been either jailed or banished to Boven Digoel in the aftermath of the two abortive revolts. While reflecting on the failure of the PKI movement was necessary, using the old name was not conducive to the correction of past mistakes. Second, PKI fugitives outside Indonesia lost contact with those inside the colony, and it was difficult to revive the party under the harsh government suppression. Meanwhile, due to the PKI's popularity among the masses, many people attempted to continue the movement under the same name. The PARI group saw these people as lacking a basic understanding of communist principles and their actions as nothing but dangerous provocation. Third, the PKI was so popular it led to widespread fanaticism, especially among illiterate people. Such fanaticism towards communism and Russia, as Tan Malaka suggested, was reminiscent of the groundless belief during past rebellions in Sumatra that Turkey would send warships to help Indonesian Muslims. Therefore, using the PKI name tended to reinforce people's unrealistic expectations that the Comintern would step in to help the Indonesian revolution and would 'push revolutionaries to the brink of opportunism, fascism or putsch'.

Finally, Tan Malaka reiterated that the Comintern had appointed him as a representative of what he called the 'Aslia' region, which encompassed continents and islands across East Asia and Oceania (including Australia). While Aslia countries shared many similarities in terms of 'environment, ethnicity, economy, and psychology', the common imperialist enemies, headed by the British with Singapore as their centre 'for trade and strategy', further strengthened the unity of this region. Tan Malaka thus believed the peoples of Aslia should pursue their common interests by taking an

---

25   Tan Malaka, 'Tuduhan Trotskyisme [Indictments of Trotskyism]', in *Thesis* (Djakarta: Moerba, 1946), available from: www.marxists.org/indonesia/archive/malaka/1946-Thesis.htm.

international 'proletarian revolutionary' path. 'One should not wait for gold to fall from the sky,' he emphasised, 'we should keep our eyes while walking on this rough field.'[26]

Despite Tan Malaka's efforts to establish PARI as an 'independent' communist party, the lack of clarity around its nature became one of his greatest political weaknesses.[27] After the PKI reemerged as a major political force in the postwar national revolution, Tan Malaka's opponents—now leaders of the new PKI—launched fierce attacks on him by branding him a 'Trotskyist'. They accused Tan Malaka of sabotaging the Indonesian revolution by rejecting the Prambanan Decision, trying to stop the revolts and establishing PARI, which operated outside the purview of the Comintern.[28] Sakirman, who worked with Tan Malaka in his Persatuan Perjuangan (Struggle Front) in early 1946 and joined the PKI shortly after, wrote a booklet entitled *Menindjau Perdjoeangan PARI* ('*Reviewing PARI's Struggles*') in 1947. In this booklet, he claimed PARI members should be regarded as 'enemies of Soviet Russia' because the party had 'opposed the Comintern's line of struggle and organisation', 'fraudulently used the name "communist"' and their 'ideals and the course of struggle are in contradiction to Marxism-Leninism'.[29]

As well as Sakirman, chief among the accusers were Alimin and Musso, who had held personal grudges against Tan Malaka since 1926. In response to Tan Malaka's 1946 *Thesis*, Alimin published his *Analysis* in 1947, in which he defended his position in the 1926–27 revolts and reiterated the 'Trotskyist' accusation. The feud between Tan Malaka and Alimin deserves careful study in its own right, but we should bear in mind that PKI members' verbal attacks on PARI emerged mostly in the late 1940s, and were more closely associated with the politics of Indonesia's national revolution than with what PARI really was in the 1920s and 1930s. Therefore, it is necessary to first investigate PARI's operation in the years after its establishment.

---

26   Malaka, 'Kesimpulan [Conclusion]', in ibid.
27   Jarvis, *Partai Republik Indonesia*, 10.
28   Kahin, *Nationalism and Revolution in Indonesia*, 85.
29   Sakirman, *Menindjau perdjoeangan PARI* [*A Review of the PARI Struggle*] (Djakarta: Soeara Lasjkar, 1947), 3. As quoted in Jarvis, *Partai Republik Indonesia*, 4.

Active penetration

Tamin pointed out in his memoir that despite the collapse of the PKI, left-wing forces in Indonesia had not entirely lost hope in their struggle against the Dutch Government around the time of PARI's establishment. As the authorities continued radical crackdowns on the PKI and affiliated organisations, news about communist activities was still all over the press in mid-1927. Although PKI members were not necessarily the ones plotting conspiracies, some of the news was encouraging from the perspective of the PKI fugitives, as it suggested the momentum of the PKI movement had not been entirely lost. For example, Tamin learned that the DEI Government had unearthed a conspiracy by former soldiers to organise a rebellion in West Java in July 1927. Although the government later found out the PKI was not involved in the incident, they arrested many nationalist leaders such as Dr Tjipto Mangoenkoesoemo, Sukarno's political mentor, who allegedly lent the soldiers moral and material support. Dr Tjipto received similar treatment to the PKI leaders and was banished to the Banda Islands in the east of the archipelago.

More exciting than the abortive uprising was the establishment of Sukarno's Perserikatan Nasional Indonesia (PNI, Indonesian National Association) on 4 July 1927.[30] Sukarno, who would rise to become Indonesia's first president 20 years later, claimed the PNI would adopt a noncooperative approach in its struggle for independence. The three PARI founders in Bangkok were delighted to hear this news, which reminded Tan Malaka that Sukarno had sent him a letter asking for guidance a year earlier. The trio thus came to realise PARI could use the PNI as a viable channel to influence Indonesia's nationalist movement.

Tan Malaka reacted immediately to the creation of the PNI by writing an article entitled 'PARI dan Kaum Intelektuil Indonesia [PARI and the Intellectuals of Indonesia]', which became one of the party's most important policy statements. As no copies of the document seem to be available today, we have only a general idea from Tamin's summary:

---

30 The Indonesian National Association changed its name to the Indonesian National Party in May 1928.

I. Suggestions to Sukarno and all the intellectuals: please join hands with us so that all the patriots and fighters could achieve Indonesia's 100% independence. The primary objective of the Party Republic of Indonesia (PARI) is to establish a 100% Republic of Indonesia, be it in political, economic, or social domains;

II. Books such as *Naar de Republiek Indonesia* [*Towards the Republic of Indonesia*], which had entered Indonesia in mid-1924, *De Jonge Geest* or *Semangat Muda* [*Youth Spirit*], in mid-1925, and *Massa Actie* [*Mass Actions*], at the end of 1926, should become guidance for intellectuals. Hopefully, they could also become the guidance for workers, farmers, youths, and national economic development in the fields of society, arts, culture, and education. Intellectuals will come to realize that patriots and fighters are living among the masses and will lead them to achieve the sacred ideals of independence;

III. Try to work with religious, socialist, and other nationalist groups as much as possible;

IV. Wake up and take over workers', farmers', and youths' movements. Try our best to approach the masses and unite them under organizations in which their leaders hold true leadership roles.[31]

PARI's three founders elected themselves members of the Central Executive Committee, with Tan Malaka as chairman, Subakat as secretary and Tamin as commissioner. The party's leadership decided to part ways shortly after its establishment and to run it from different locations. Subakat remained in Bangkok for two years. Although it is unclear what his specific job was, he maintained close contact with Tan Malaka until his arrest in 1929. Tan Malaka left Bangkok for Manila, but the Philippine Government arrested him within a few days of his arrival at the request of the DEI authorities. Under pressure from the colony's sympathetic nationalist leaders, however, the Philippine Government deported Tan Malaka to Amoy, where he would stay until 1929. Living far from the rest of his party members, Tan Malaka worked more like a theoretician than the party chairman, as he was mostly busy writing articles rather than directing PARI activities.[32] I will elaborate on Tan Malaka's experience in a later section, but for now, it is important to note Tamin played

---

31 Tamin, *PKI History*, 62.
32 Shiraishi, 'Policing the Phantom Underground', 31–32.

a more crucial role in the daily operation of PARI in the following years. Tamin returned to Singapore in August 1927 and began work almost immediately via the old PKI network.

There were obvious advantages to choosing Singapore as the base for PARI's operations. First, PKI activities had left a relatively good foundation in the city and, as PKI fugitives continued to come to Singapore after the failed revolts, Tamin could find many reliable disciples with whom to work. Additionally, there was an extensive Indonesian network in Singapore; PKI fugitives could not only evade surveillance by hiding inside the Indonesian community, but also ask for assistance such as accommodation and employment. Moreover, Singapore was close to Indonesia. While penetrating Indonesia was always an option, PARI activists also frequently used their personal networks to distribute propaganda materials. Singapore was an important hub for the Muslim pilgrimage, with many Indonesians passing through Singapore on their way to and from Mecca. Tamin noted many of Tan Malaka's books would *naik haji* ('rise to Haji'—make the pilgrimage to Mecca) before entering Indonesia.

Finally, Singapore is a port city with abundant employment opportunities for seamen. Many PKI fugitives took refuge in seamen's dormitories when they first arrived in the city and soon became sailors or mechanics themselves through introductions by their countrymen. Tamin's disciples Kandur and Djamaluddin Ibrahim, for example, took advantage of their jobs as seamen and frequently helped smuggle PARI publications to Indonesia. Tan Malaka's *Semangat Muda* ('*Youth Spirit*') and *Massa Actie* ('*Mass Action*') seemed to have enjoyed an extensive readership as many PNI-affiliated intellectuals would quote his words in their speeches and writing. Tamin was also pleased to discover that some Surabaya-based newspapers often cited articles and passages from PARI documents.[33]

Running PARI from Singapore also had its downside. The Straits Settlements authorities tightened their surveillance of communist activities in 1927. The shift in British policy was closely related to political events in China and the DEI at the time; the ongoing nationalist revolution in China polarised the politics of the Malayan Chinese. Under the influence of left-wing forces, Singapore saw a rapid rise of anti-British sentiment during 1926–27. A violent clash between supporters of the Guomindang's

---

33 Tamin, *PKI History*, 63.

left wing and the police—the so-called Kreta Ayer Incident—broke out in March 1927 and led to the death of six people and protracted protests in following months.

The two abortive PKI uprisings prompted the DEI Government to call for closer international cooperation in policing communist activities. Due to geographical proximity and the fact that Singapore had been serving as a PKI overseas centre, Dutch and British authorities gradually came to agree that anticommunist cooperation was of great significance. Although the British handling of the Alimin–Musso case was somewhat disappointing from the Dutch perspective, the two governments regarded communism as a common threat and expressed their willingness to deepen their cooperation.[34] Moreover, police officials on both sides established a close working relationship, which laid a good foundation for cross-border policing in subsequent years.[35] As a result, PARI faced much heavier pressure from British surveillance than the PKI.

To evade this surveillance, Tamin and his followers relied on the seamen's network. As mentioned earlier, Tamin had helped many PKI fugitives find accommodation and jobs by connecting them to Indonesian sailors in Singapore. This meant PKI fugitives could not only make a modest living, but also enjoy some other benefits of the party's operations. Colonial authorities certainly did not pay much attention to the activities of such a marginal group. Even if they had intended to, keeping track of the seamen's whereabouts was extremely difficult, as the highly mobile group was often absent from the city and sailors frequently changed from one ship to another.

The seamen played several crucial roles in PARI's operations: first, they were central to the dissemination of books and other propaganda materials. Tamin and his disciples mostly printed Tan Malaka's writings in Singapore in large volumes and sent them to Indonesia through the sailors' secretive channels. Kandur and Djamaluddin Ibrahim were two

---

34 See Consul-General Batavia's [Crosby] No. 47 Secret of 14 April 1927, CO 273/535, Straits Settlements Original Correspondence, The National Archives, Kew, United Kingdom.
35 For instance, M. Visbeen, assistant commissioner of the Batavian police, came to Malaya in December 1926 and stayed until July 1927. During this time, he formed close ties with his British counterparts such as Harold Fairburn, the inspector-general, and Rene Onraet, the chief of the Criminal Investigation Department (CID). See Takashi Shiraishi, 'A New Regime of Order: The Origin of Modern Surveillance Politics in Indonesia', in *Southeast Asia over Three Generations: Essays Presented to Benedict R.O'G. Anderson*, James Siegel and Audrey Kahin, eds (Ithaca, NY: Cornell University Press, 2003), 68.

of the most active PARI couriers and often smuggled books to Indonesia. While Kandur went back and forth between Singapore and Sumatra, Djamaluddin Ibrahim frequently travelled between Batavia, Singapore, Pekan Baru and Padang.[36] Second, PARI relied on the seamen to approach nationalist group leaders such as Sukarno, Singgih and Dr Soetomo.[37] A common tactic was to connect with local branches of the PNI and recruit members for PARI activities.[38] Moreover, the seamen's network was essential to maintaining contact between PARI members dispersed in different locations. PARI activists considered postal services insecure as the colonial authorities often intercepted letters, so the party often delivered messages through the seamen's network, both inside Indonesia and beyond, by concealing letters and documents inside newspapers.[39]

Suitable couriers were not always available, however, and Tamin had to figure out other methods to keep in contact with Tan Malaka. Tamin thus sent several batches of young PARI activists to China in hopes they could reconnect with the party chairman while gaining knowledge and experience. For instance, Tamin sent Mardjono and Arief Siregar to Amoy in 1927. Djamaluddin Ibrahim and Sarosan went on the same journey a year later.[40] When Tamin sensed danger in Singapore in 1928, he had to move from one lodging house to another but usually stayed with his seamen friends. In August 1930, Tamin began working as a sailor himself aboard the *Darvel* of the Singapore–Zamboanga–Mindanao line. When the ship ran aground near Sandakan, in British Borneo, Tamin took the opportunity to enter the city, from where he managed to reestablish contact with Tan Malaka.[41]

As time passed, some PARI members became well established in Singapore. Umar Giri, for instance, opened a cigarette shop in the city's Geylang area with his comrades Subandi and Djamaluddin Ibrahim. By selling cigarettes and cigars smuggled from Indonesia, the business significantly improved the party's financial situation. Towards the end of 1928, most party members had secured higher incomes by taking stable jobs or

36 Tamin, *PKI History*, 64.
37 ibid., 68; and Shiraishi, 'Policing the Phantom Underground', 34.
38 Jarvis, *Partai Republik Indonesia*, 14.
39 'De Partij Republiek Indonesia (PARI) [The Republic Party of Indonesia]', 509x/1931, GMR, NA-NL; and Jarvis, *Partai Republik Indonesia*, 13–14.
40 According to Tamin, he initially only wanted to send Djamaluddin Ibrahim to Amoy and asked him not to reveal the plan to anyone due to the high cost. However, Sarosan heard about it and insisted on joining the trip. Tamin, *PKI History*, 64.
41 ibid., 69–70.

running private businesses. In addition to sustaining their daily lives, PARI members could now contribute a good amount of money to the party's operations and even provide financial assistance to Tan Malaka in China.[42] A major drawback of having more established lives in Singapore, as Tamin pointed out, was some PARI activists gradually lost their desire to get involved in dangerous activities and risk their comfortable lives. While PARI members continued to send books and newsletters to Indonesia, Tamin thought some of them were no longer passionate and confident about continuing the struggle against Dutch colonialism.[43]

The indolence of these members aside, PARI did manage to send activists back to Indonesia in hopes of influencing the nationalist movement there. Mardjono and Sarosan were the most active among the PKI fugitives who successfully penetrated Indonesia while maintaining close contact with the Singapore head office. Mardjono and Sarosan had known each other in Semarang, where they were both active in the PKI-affiliated Indonesian Scout Organisation.[44] In May 1926, Mardjono and Sarosan moved to Banjarmasin, where they worked for the local newspaper, the *Borneo Post*. After the PKI revolts, they escaped to Singapore and worked for the Al Ikwan Press, owned by Arab entrepreneur Said Djen Alsagaff. The two PKI fugitives met Tamin and joined PARI in Singapore. In late 1927 and early 1928, Mardjono and Sarosan went to Amoy successively, where they received training from Tan Malaka. Mardjono returned to Banjarmasin in early 1928, followed by Sarosan, who worked briefly as a sailor on the Singapore–Australia line.[45] While teaching at a private school run by his old comrade Moenandar, Mardjono established a PARI liaison office through which he maintained close contact with Singapore under the guise of a local postman.[46]

---

42 ibid., 67.
43 ibid., 68.
44 Mardjono was Tan Malaka's student at the Sekolah Rakyat (People's School) in Semarang, which was established in 1921 to train party members. With its great success, the school expanded to many other places in the DEI. The People's School is also known as Tan Malaka's School. See Helen Jarvis, 'Tan Malaka: Revolutionary or Renegade?', *Critical Asian Studies* 19(1) (1987): 42. Sarosan graduated from a Dutch Native School in Purworejo and worked for PKI organ *Sinar Hindia*. Subsequently, he became a student nurse at the Semarang Central Hospital, where he participated in strikes and lost his job. He then joined the PKI organ *API* under Subakat's leadership. See Shiraishi, 'Policing the Phantom Underground', 35.
45 M. Visbeen and Mohamad Halid, 'Proces Verbaal [Police Report] (July 1930)', 2.10.36.06, 509x/1931, GMR, NA-NL; and Shiraishi, 'Policing the Phantom Underground', 35–36.
46 Tamin, *PKI History*, 67.

While Mardjono was busy reestablishing the liaison office in Banjarmasin, Sarosan went to Java, in April 1928. Through the introduction of Soedarmo, Mardjono's brother and a clerk from the Nederlandsch-Indische Spoorweg Maatschappij (NIS, Dutch East Indies Railway Company), Sarosan got in touch with Danoewirjo, an NIS conductor and former member of the PKI-affiliated Vereniging van Spoor-en Tramwegpersoneel (VSTP, Association of Railway and Tram Workers) who was still active in trade unionism. Danoewirjo then joined PARI and introduced Sarosan to his NIS co-workers, including Soetedjo and Tjokrosoebono, both from Cepu, and Ngadimin from Semarang. As Shiraishi has noted, there were obvious advantages in spreading propaganda among railway workers. Before the 1926–27 PKI revolts, the VSTP was one of the most potent and best-organised trade unions under the communist leadership, with 77 branches and 8,293 members in November 1925.[47] The VSTP was destroyed in the government's wholesale clampdown on communism, yet many workers had hopes of reviving the militant trade union movement and were willing to carry out propaganda for PARI among their 'old friends'.[48] According to Tamin, the group carried out successful campaigns in Central and East Java, and mobilised 350 railway workers within the first three months.[49]

Merantau: The Minangkabau network

With the arrest of Subakat in Bangkok on 8 October 1929, the *Kongsi Tiga* ('PARI Triumvirate') lost an indispensable pillar. Within the party's division of labour, Subakat's role might not have been as significant as that of his two comrades—he was neither a gifted theorist like Tan Malaka, who drafted most of the important party documents, nor a well-rounded executive like Tamin, who almost single-handedly rebuilt a party network from the shambles of the PKI—but his contribution was by no means trivial. His post in Bangkok functioned as a secret hub connecting Tan Malaka, PARI's chief strategist in China, and Tamin, the chief activist overseeing the party's operation across the DEI and British Malaya.

---

47 Shiraishi, 'Policing the Phantom Underground', 13.
48 ibid., 36.
49 Tamin attributed the success of the propaganda campaign to Mardjono, who was at that time still in Banjarmasin. Tamin's recollection contradicts the official records based on the police interrogations of PARI activists. The official records show it was Sarosan who recruited the railway workers through Danoewirjo. Mardjono came to Java in March 1929. See Visbeen and Halid, 'Police Report', July 1930; Shiraishi, 'Policing the Phantom Underground', 36.

As mentioned earlier, due to the increasingly stringent measures taken by both Dutch and British authorities, Tan Malaka usually mailed his writings to Bangkok wrapped in newspapers, which would be brought to Tamin and his disciples via trusted seamen travelling the Singapore–Bangkok route. Because it was not a colonial state, Siam was presumed to be safer than Malaya and Indonesia, but Subakat's arrest and ultimate extradition seemed to suggest otherwise. PARI members had apparently underestimated the capabilities of the DEI Government. The colonial intelligence and policing apparatus could easily extend its arms to foreign lands through international cooperation. Subakat's hideout in Bangkok had acted as something of a repository for crucial party literature. With the seizure of Subakat's archives, many PARI secrets were exposed.

Through Tamin, Hadji Djalaluddin, a famous Bangkok-based Islamic teacher from Bukit Tinggi, Sumatra, sold out Subakat to Siamese and DEI authorities. PARI activists in Singapore felt the impact of Subakat's arrest almost immediately, as Hadji Djalaluddin attempted to help Dutch officials make more arrests there by contacting people he knew in the PARI network. Having noticed the Hadji's intention, Tamin and his followers managed to conceal themselves temporarily from police surveillance, but they knew space in Singapore had become increasingly *sempit dan sulit* ('tight and difficult'). PARI members sensed the growing pressure from all sides, especially after hearing of the crackdown on the Sarekat Kaoem Boeroeh (Indonesian Workers' Union) in mid-1929, followed by the arrests of Iwa Koesoema Soemantri in July, Subakat in October and Sukarno and his PNI co-founders in December. As Tamin said, 1929 was a year when PARI and anticolonial struggles suffered *pukulan-pukulan yang dahsyat berat benar-benar* ('heavy and crushing blows');[50] and 1930 turned out to be no better. In February 1930, PARI members heard Subakat had killed himself in Glodok Prison in Batavia. Six months later, Dutch authorities crushed the PARI network in Central and East Java thanks to Sarosan's betrayal. From the interrogation of PARI activists, the DEI intelligence service learned that most of the party's documents entered Indonesia from Singapore through Mardjono, Soenarjo and Sarosan.[51] Singapore

---

50 Tamin, *PKI History*, 70.
51 'Procureur-generaal (R.J.M. Verheijen) aan gouverneur-generaal (De Graeff) [Attorney-General R.J.M. Verheijen to Governor-General De Graeff]', [21 March 1931], GMR 509x/1931, in *De Ontewikkeling van de Nationalistische Beweging in the Nederlandsch-Indië* [*The Development of the Nationalist Movement in the Dutch East Indies*], R.C. Kwantes, ed. (Groningen, Netherlands: Wolters-Noordhoff, 1981), 549.

once again became the thorn in the side of the DEI Government, and they could only expect to pull it out by establishing a closer working relationship with the British authorities across the Malacca Strait.

As Tamin recalled, he felt the atmosphere in Singapore turn even more intense shortly after the Dutch clampdown on the Mardjono–Soenarjo group in July 1930. Batavian police chief M. Visbeen—who had travelled to Singapore in 1927 for the arrest of Alimin and Musso—returned to the Straits Settlements in August 1930 to reconnect with his police counterparts such as Inspector-General Harold Fairburn, Criminal Investigation Department (CID) Chief Rene Onraet and Chief Inspector Prithvi Chand, with whom he had previously cooperated.[52] The Singapore police looked so busy that Pak Said, a retired CID officer who had been secretly protecting PKI fugitives since the uprisings, advised Tamin to be careful although he was unaware of what had happened in Java.[53] So intense was the atmosphere for PARI members in Singapore that Tamin came to realise the city was no longer an ideal place to hide. With the introduction of a bosun friend named Karim, Tamin became a seaman aboard the *Darvel* in August 1930.[54] From this point, heightened policing measures in both the DEI and British Malaya forced Tamin and many of his PARI followers to move from place to place, switching from job to job, and, as a result, they frequently lost contact with one another.

Many of the PARI activists had their origins in Minangkabau, an area centred on Sumatra's west coast.[55] The so-called *Alam Minangkabau* ('Minangkabau World') consists of two regions: *darek*, the inner highlands, and *rantau*, the coastal frontiers. Perhaps no term could better describe PARI members' unstable lives and wandering than the idea of *merantau*— an important cultural tradition in Minangkabau's matriarchal society.[56] In a rite of passage, a young male needs to *merantau* (leave his home village and the Minangkabau World) in pursuit of a career, knowledge and experience. Either pursuing a specific goal or simply wandering around, *merantau* is critical in the making or breaking of a man. As Taufik Abdullah puts it, '*merantau* is, according to *adat* ['custom'] philosophy,

---

52 For Visbeen's previous visit, see Shiraishi, 'A New Regime of Order', 68.
53 Tamin, *PKI History*, 68.
54 In his memoir, Tamin recalled he started his job as a seaman in August 1929, but this does match the arrest of PARI members in Java, which happened in July 1930. Tamin's recollection of the date was most likely wrong. His starting time should be August 1930. See Tamin, *PKI History*, 69.
55 Shiraishi, *The Phantom World of Digul*, 141–42.
56 Tsuyoshi Kato, 'Rantau Pariaman: The World of Minangkabau Coastal Merchants in the Nineteenth Century', *The Journal of Asian Studies* 39(4) (1980): 729–52, at p.730, doi.org/10.2307/2055180.

one way to fulfill that Principal Law which charges the individual to "subject himself" to the largeness of the world'.[57] While wandering the world, *anak perantau* ('youths who *merantau*') stay connected through their Minangkabau bonds, are introduced to one another, offered timely assistance and keep their lives going despite various hardships. The PKI fugitives' first *merantau* was in the aftermath the 1926–27 uprisings when the DEI Government's wholesale crackdown forced them to leave the Dutch colony.

Yet, PKI fugitives did not feel much different in Malaya than in the Minangkabau World, as the extensive Minangkabau network offered enormous help to get them settled in the Malay States and Straits Settlements. Now with the British implementing more stringent measures against them, Tamin and his PARI followers were pressured to have their second *merantau*—this time, mostly on their own.

Tan Malaka and Tamin reestablished direct contact more than a year after Subakat's arrest.[58] Around the same time, Tamin also received a letter from Daja bin Joesoef alias Alyasin, a PKI fugitive from West Sumatra who had been staying in Negeri Sembilan since 1927. Negeri Sembilan is known as a unique Malay state of Minangkabau tradition, which has maintained close ties with the Minangkabau homeland in West Sumatra since early settlers began migrating to the area in the sixteenth century.[59] Daja told Tamin he had to leave his family behind because Abdullah bin Hadji Isa, a new CID officer in the Federated Malay States, had spotted him and revealed his PKI identity. As a result, Negeri Sembilan's local rulers had rejected Daja's petition to take refuge in the area. Daja thus begged Tamin to help him escape to Singapore so he could become a seaman. However, Singapore had become increasingly dangerous for PARI activists and the CID seemed to be making extra efforts to track Tamin down. Tamin described his situation in a rather pessimistic tone:

> Singapore does not seem to allow me to set foot on its land anymore. In a matter of a few days, I will certainly be forced to leave my traveling home in the ocean. And I will land at a place that I cannot determine and answer now.[60]

---

57 Taufik Abdullah, *Schools and Politics: The Kaum Muda Movement in West Sumatra (1927–1933)* (Ithaca, NY: Cornell Modern Indonesia Project, 1971), 20; and Rudolf Mrázek, 'Tan Malaka: A Political Personality's Structure of Experience', *Indonesia* 14 (1972): 1–48.
58 Tamin, *PKI History*, 68–71.
59 Michael G. Peletz, 'Comparative Perspectives on Kinship and Cultural Identity in Negeri Sembilan', *Sojourn: Journal of Social Issues in Southeast Asia* 9(1) (1994): 2.
60 Tamin, *PKI History*, 71.

PARI was hitting dead-ends in all directions. According to Tamin, the CID had tightened surveillance of postal services between Singapore and Chinese cities such as Shanghai, Amoy and Hong Kong. Although emergent nationalist and communist activities among Malayan Chinese may have contributed to the change, PARI activists were forced to send their letters to Tan Malaka from cities such as Kuala Lumpur or Ipoh via seamen and merchants. Similarly, Tan Malaka would send his replies to a Hainanese coffeeshop in Sandakan so Tamin could pick them up when passing by. Tamin never mentioned to what extent such methods had helped PARI to overcome the hurdles, but we can imagine the party's operations must have been very difficult during this period, as Tamin felt PARI had encountered 'obstacles here and hindrances there, as well as the omnipresent surveillance since 1930'.

Besides external pressures imposed by colonial authorities, PARI was always short of manpower and the arrest in Java only exacerbated the situation. The Singapore headquarters lost contact with many of its previous Sumatran activists. Kandur, who had been very active in smuggling PARI literature to Sumatra after the PKI uprisings, ceased reporting to Tamin and seemed to be hiding from the Singapore group in Bukit Tinggi, West Sumatra. Tamin suspected Kandur had cut ties with PARI on purpose; Kandur could have contacted PARI members in Singapore easily if he wanted, as numerous Bukit Tinggi merchants came to Singapore every day. By contrast, Tamin's righthand man, Djamaluddin Ibrahim, remained active and was ready to return to Indonesia at any time. Given the circumstances, however, Tamin decided Djamaluddin should not go; he felt PARI could not afford to lose any more members and must wait until opportunities presented themselves.[61]

Tamin switched to another ship, the *Kistna*, of the Singapore–Bangkok line, in early 1931. The trip frequency of the *Kistna* was almost identical to that of the *Darvel*—namely, three round trips every two months. The main difference was the *Darvel* stopped many times along the coast of British North Borneo, whereas the *Kistna* provided a direct connection between Singapore and Bangkok—a city where Tamin sought to reconnect with the West Sumatran network Subakat had left behind.[62] Tamin managed to meet Sjech Ahmad Wahab, the Islamic leader who had hosted Subakat

---

61 ibid., 72.
62 On Vietnamese revolutionary networks in Siam during the same period, see Goscha, *Thailand and the Southeast Asian Networks of the Vietnamese Revolution*.

before his arrest. Sjech Ahmad Wahab invited Tamin to stay in Bangkok, but Tamin turned down the offer and decided to return to Singapore to lead the PARI movement. On landing back in Singapore in July 1931, Tamin noticed a CID inspector named Gulam Ali was actively searching for him. Once again, he narrowly escaped arrest but realised that his job as a seaman would no longer guarantee his safety.[63]

One of the few options that remained was to hide in the Malayan hinterland. Tamin's first destination was neither Johor, the Malay state adjacent to Singapore, nor Negeri Sembilan, where he could easily have blended into the Minangkabau community. Rather, he chose to go to Selangor to seek refuge with a group of Muslim scholars whom he had befriended when he was *mengelilingi* ('wandering around') Malaya for the first time in the guise of a journalist in early 1926. These scholars belonged to the *Angkat Tua* ('Old Forces') or the so-called *Alim Ulama dan Tjerdik Pandai* (lit., 'wise and knowledgeable Muslim intellectuals'), who followed the Kaum Muda Movement of West Sumatra.[64] Tamin's *Alim Ulama* friend Hadji Abbas and Djafar Ali, an officer of Kuala Lumpur's Electricity Bureau, hosted him in Rawang, Selangor. Tamin's *Alim Ulama* friends then introduced him to the more renowned intellectuals, the *tjendikiawan* ('pundit') group. Initially, Tamin was hesitant about getting too close to the *tjendekiawans*, as he thought many of them were 'politically illiterate' and generally harboured a 'pro-British, anti-politics, and anti-communist' attitude.

Tamin's perception of the group gradually changed after meeting a *tjendekiawan* named Mohammad Jassin Abdullah, who expressed his concerns about British colonialism and hopes for Malaya's independence; Tamin regretted that Mohammad Jassin Abdullah died at a very young age. Another *tjendekiawan*, Haji Abdul Majid, a senior police officer, accidentally saved Tamin at the end of August. Outside his police job, Abdul Majid had close personal ties with Tamin's two hosts: he was Djafar Ali's uncle and had been a friend of Hadji Abbas since their school years. When a group of Singapore-based CID officials came looking for Tamin

---

63 Tamin, *PKI History*, 73.
64 The Kaum Muda Movement was started by a group of Middle East–educated Islamic scholars influenced by the Pan-Islamic Movement. Its main participants were students of two Islamic school systems: Thawalib, in which Tamin used to teach, and Dinijah. For more details about the movement, see Abdullah, *Schools and Politics*.

in Selangor, Abdul Majid unintentionally leaked this information to Djafar Ali and Hadji Abbas, who urged Tamin to leave Malaya as quickly as possible.[65]

Tamin left Selangor immediately but decided to try his luck in Ulu Beranang, Negeri Sembilan, a place he had visited in 1926 and where he sent Daja bin Joesoef in 1927. As Tamin anticipated, PKI fugitive Daja had left, but many villagers remembered him and treated him with great respect.[66] During his stay between September and December 1931, Tamin cultivated a close relationship with residents by teaching the Koran and contributing to communal work. Due to safety concerns, Tamin had initially planned to interact only with a small circle of trusted people, but many villagers ended up becoming acquainted with him and recognised him as a religious teacher from Sumatra. Instructed by his superiors in Singapore, police officer Abdul Majid continued to search for Tamin in the area, and even came to Ulu Beranang himself. To Tamin's surprise, some of the village chiefs were distant relatives of Abdul Majid and could have exposed Tamin if they had known his true identity. Fortunately, Tamin soon found such worries were unnecessary, as Abdul Majid concluded his search hastily and launched no further investigations.[67]

Towards the end of 1931, Tamin received some good news from Singapore: PARI activists Arief Siregar and Daja bin Joesoef had secured jobs at an oil well of the Nederlandsch Koloniale Petroleum Maatschappij (NKPM, Dutch Colonial Petroleum Corporation) in Sungai Gerong, South Sumatra.[68] Meanwhile, PARI's Singapore headquarters started to send literature to Batavia and West Sumatra again. More importantly, several people expressed interest in joining PARI, potentially ameliorating the party's cadre shortage. Among the most eager candidates was Ahmad Padang alias Djaus, Dawood or Davidson, an Indonesian-European from Tapanuli, North Sumatra, who had been working and living with PARI

---

65   Tamin, *PKI History*, 74–76.
66   As Tamin noted, villagers addressed him as '*tuan*', a honorific for senior officials or intellectuals. See ibid., 77.
67   ibid.
68   Arief Siregar first found a job as a clerk at NKPM in April 1930. After working there for seven months, he wrote a letter to Singapore, asking Tamin to send him an assistant. This happened to be the time when Tamin received Daja bin Joesoef's letter from Negeri Sembilan, asking for help to find him a job in Singapore. Tamin then sent Daja to Sungai Gerong to help Arief Siregar; the two had met previously in Singapore. See 'Proces Verbaal [Police Report] (Mohamad Arief Siregar), (6 October 1932)', 2.10.36.06, 963x/1933, GMR, NA-NL; Shiraishi, 'Policing the Phantom Underground', 40.

members in Singapore for five to six years. Tamin regretted that PARI members had excluded Djaus from the party for many years, not because of his capability or character but because of his skin colour.[69]

From Tamin's perspective, Djaus was an activist with great potential as he not only had a record for being trustworthy, but also was an experienced mechanic (which would allow him to find good jobs) and fluent in Dutch and English, as well as dialects of the Minangkabau and Mandailing regions. Djaus's recruitment was in stark contrast with Tamin's rejection of Limin, a PKI fugitive from Silungkang, West Sumatra, when Tamin was still working as a seaman. Limin had arrived in Singapore shortly after the 1926–27 uprisings, but Tamin believed people like Limin only cared about their own safety and had very shallow understandings of political theories and practices, which made them unqualified to join PARI's struggles.[70] Although Tamin did not elaborate on how he evaluated someone's 'understanding', he apparently had his standards for who should be allowed into the PARI inner circle; he needed to be the one to dictate the process, even if he was not always available while the party was short of personnel.[71]

Tamin returned to Singapore in December 1931 to pick up work on what he had left behind. Indeed, PARI saw some positive changes after Tamin's return. Sukarno's recent release seemed to have reactivated the revolutionary atmosphere in Java and Sumatra.[72] Enthusiasm for Indonesian independence was burgeoning among intellectuals, workers and the public. As a result, demands for PARI literature increased rapidly. In terms of party operations, Tamin and his followers were in a much better position than a year earlier. With the money saved from his modest life in the Malay States and his new job at a timber mill, Tamin managed to send Djaus to Shanghai in February 1932 to train with Tan Malaka. In March, Tamin met his old Thawalib friend Adam Galo, who was visiting from Padang Panjang. After a lengthy conversation, Tamin convinced Galo his revolutionary course was not 'anti-religion and anti-God' but aimed at Indonesia's full independence. Galo promised to support PARI's

---

69 Tamin speculated that Djaus might have been abandoned by his European father when he was young; it was understandable that Djaus did not know his place and date of birth. See Tamin, *PKI History*, 78.
70 ibid., 72, 78.
71 ibid., 72–76.
72 Sukarno was sentenced to four years of imprisonment in 1930 but was released early on 31 December 1931 due to pressure from liberals in both the DEI and the Netherlands.

struggles by helping with the distribution of its literature in Indonesia, sending cadres to Singapore for training and connecting PARI to the West Sumatran network of the Partai Sarekat Islam Indonesia (PSII, Islamic Association Party of Indonesia).

From May, Tamin noticed the police had started to follow him again. He suspected that Salim Sutan Malinggang, a PKI fugitive whom he had helped settle in Kota Tinggi, had informed the CID of his return to Singapore.[73] As he had experienced many times before, Tamin understood Singapore was not safe. However, he decided not to leave the city this time, as the momentum he had been hoping for the PARI movement was just picking up; he had to be in Singapore to hold absolute control over the party. Tamin's key strategy to evade police surveillance was to keep moving from place to place. According to Tamin, he had six to seven hideouts in Singapore, with the safest being CID retiree Pak Said's house, where he also stored numerous books and PARI documents. Tamin learned a lesson the hard way in April 1931, when PARI activist Umar Giri, who had been running a cigarette shop in Singapore to support the party's operations, was arrested in the nearby Indonesian town of Tanjung Uban on Bintan Island. Umar Giri's arrest cost PARI not only a primary source of income, but also Giri's house, which had been an important PARI meeting place and was where they produced most of their propaganda materials. As the police surveillance became more noticeable, Tamin stopped going to Pak Said's place in June 1932. He felt the CID could arrest him at any time but, first, he wanted to ensure the party's archives were safe.

Safety concerns aside, PARI was making unusual progress by mid-1932. Kandur, the PARI propagandist who had been hiding in West Sumatra for about three years, reemerged in Singapore in July with some good news. Kandur told Tamin he had gone to Batavia, where he got in contact with nationalist leaders of Minangkabau origin such as Mohammad Yamin and Assaat Datuk Mudo.[74] He then returned to West Sumatra and established connections with PSII leaders such as Djalaluddin Thaib and Gani Sjarif. Tamin reacted to Kandur's report with excitement, as he saw great potential to cooperate with the PSII through the Minangkabau

---

73 Shiraishi, 'Policing the Phantom Underground', 39.
74 Mohammad Yamin was born in Sawahlunto, West Sumatra, and was a well-known poet. He later became a career politician and played a key role in drafting Indonesia's first constitution in 1945. Assaat Datuk Mudo was born in Agam, West Sumatra. He was the provisional president of the Yogjakarta-based Republic Indonesia between December 1949 and August 1950 and led a rebellion against Sukarno in Sumatra in the late 1950s.

network. Tamin's plan became even more promising a month later, when Adam Galo carried out his promise and sent Lutan Sutan Basa and Lutan Madjid to Singapore for cadre training. Tamin encouraged the two to *menanam benih PARI* ('plant PARI's seeds') within the PSII and recruit new cadres from among Thawalib students. After enduring all sorts of hardships since Subakat's arrest in 1929, PARI members could finally see a viable path to reestablish the party back in Indonesia; they could certainly start with the Minangkabau network of West Sumatra.

Around the same time, Tamin heard that Mohammad Hatta, Indonesia's future vice-president, was about to return to Indonesia via Singapore. A Minangkabau himself, Hatta had by then already achieved fame by leading the Perhimpoenan Indonesia (Indonesian Union), a progressive student nationalist movement in the Netherlands. While PARI activists were thrilled at the prospect of meeting the renowned nationalist leader, Tamin worried Hatta's every move would be under the watchful eye of the CID. With a presentiment of trouble ahead, Tamin eventually gave up on the idea of meeting Hatta in Singapore.[75]

With PARI activities going so well and the pressures of the CID surveillance—and his potential arrest—becoming so intense, Tamin finally decided to return to Indonesia. He bought a ticket on a ship and was set to leave for Batavia on 15 September 1932. Two days before his departure, however, Tamin's worst hunch came true as CID Chief Inspector Prithvi Chand broke into his hideout and arrested him. In addition to Tamin, the police also arrested 12 other men, including Lutan Sutan Basa and Lutan Madjid, who were caught red-handed producing propaganda materials. Subsequently, Chand conducted a thorough search of the premises and seized many incriminating documents.

On 17 September, Tamin was brought to court and he and his comrades were charged with organising an illegal political party intended to rebel against the British Government. Tamin protested by going on a hunger strike, claiming he had never formed any political organisation against the British. The hunger strike earned Tamin an opportunity to talk to the new CID director, Arthur Harold Dickinson, who, according to Tamin, showed great sympathy for Tamin's struggles and appeared very impressed that Tamin was able to run the organisation without the assistance of

---

75 Tamin, *PKI History*, 79–83.

Moscow.[76] Tamin and his comrades were brought back to court two days later. This time, although the court dropped the previous charges of forming an illegal party against the British, they rearrested eight PARI activists under a new law passed in 1931 that subjected foreign politicians establishing political parties in British territories to imprisonment or repatriation to their place of origin. On 22 September 1932, British authorities handed Tamin and his followers over to police officers from the DEI, who brought Tamin back to Batavia for further investigation.[77]

Tamin's arrest in Singapore was the prelude to a much larger, coordinated police operation against the *perantaus* of the PARI network. As mentioned earlier, Arief Siregar had been working as a clerk with the NKPM in Sungai Gerong, South Sumatra, since April 1930; Daja bin Joesoef joined him seven months later but was in Batavia at the time of Tamin's arrest.[78] By investigating the documents seized during Tamin's arrest, the CID learned he had been in close contact with the two activists. The CID immediately notified their Dutch counterparts in Java and Sumatra, who captured the two activists on the same day, along with PARI literature and photographs in their possession.[79]

The PARI network collapsed after the arrests of Tamin and his followers. Dutch authorities conducted a thorough investigation of Tamin in Batavia and eventually interned him, together with his disciples Arief Siregar and Daja bin Joesoef, in Digul in August 1933.[80] Tamin remained in Digul until the outbreak of WWII, when the Japanese invasion prompted the Dutch Government to transfer them to Australia. PARI activities did not cease entirely, however, as younger activists such as Djaus and Sukarni carried on the work, although not necessarily under PARI's name. While some achieved political success by attaining influential positions in legal youth groups, more would be arrested and banished like the party veterans to Digul in the following years.[81]

---

76 Dickinson assumed the position of CID director in February 1932. Before this, he was the chief police officer in Malacca. See 'Mr. A.H. Dickinson', *The Straits Times*, [Singapore], 5 February 1932, 12.
77 Tamin, *PKI History*, 84–87.
78 Shiraishi has conducted an intensive study of Arief Siregar's activities and his connections to Tamin and Daja based on Arief's interrogation record, which shows the two activists made very little progress in expanding PARI's influence among nationalist groups. See Shiraishi, 'Policing the Phantom Underground', 38–44.
79 The ARD also tracked down Kandur in June 1933 by using the information it had obtained from Arief's and Daja's arrests.
80 Tamin, *PKI History*, 84–87.
81 Kahin, *Nationalism and Revolution in Indonesia*, 85–86.

By 1932, the Dutch–British policing cooperation had reached an unprecedented level, paralysing PARI's clandestine network. The *ad hoc* cooperation we see in Alimin and Musso's arrests in 1927 gradually evolved into a multilayered system, which included greater gubernatorial consensus, smoother institutional communication, more effective intelligence sharing and closer personal ties among relevant officials. However, it is worth noting that such cooperation was not limited to the colonial governments of the DEI and British Malaya. Nor did the PARI network operate only in the two colonies. For instance, Tan Malaka's presence outside the two colonies extended the meaning of PARI's *perantau* network, further complicating how the pan–East Asia policing network would operate to counter it.

Conclusion

This chapter has shown that although PARI played a limited role in shaking the foundations of Dutch colonial rule, its operations outside the colony exerted a crucial and lasting impact on Indonesian politics. Like the regional networks of the Vietnamese communist movement during the same period, PARI grafted its revolutionary networks on to the kinship, occupational and religious networks of Indonesian immigrants across many Southeast Asian port cities and smaller towns in the hinterland. In relying on such networks, PARI activists managed to penetrate Indonesia and shape colonial politics by smuggling in anticolonial literature, recruiting new members and cooperating with various nationalist and religious groups.

However, PARI's revolutionary practices differed from those of its Vietnamese counterparts, especially in its relationship with the international communist movement. With the backing of the Comintern, Hồ Chí Minh established Vietnam's earliest communist organisations in southern China in 1925 and then grafted them on to existing anticolonial networks of Vietnamese immigrants in Thailand.[82] Such connections would later become 'the western bulwark of a larger Vietnamese revolutionary network' that connected the Asian bases such as Canton, Hong Kong and Singapore to the European communist headquarters in Moscow,

---

82   Goscha, *Thailand and the Southeast Asian Networks of the Vietnamese Revolution*, 64–68.

Berlin and Paris.[83] PARI, by contrast, broke from the Comintern and adopted a more nationalistic approach to its anticolonial struggle. As a consequence, PARI's operations in Southeast Asia were largely independent of concurrent anticolonial activities by former PKI members in the Soviet Union and Western Europe.[84] Although communism subsided inside the DEI under full-scale suppression, PARI activists continued their militant anticolonial struggle through multilayered noncommunist networks. When communism regained its prominence during Indonesia's national revolution after WWII, the ideological debates between Tan Malaka and the Alimin–Musso groups, which dated back to the PKI's split after 1926, remained central to the power struggles for the legitimacy and leadership of the new communist movement.

As Shiraishi points out, PARI was a small revolutionary party that never succeeded in establishing a significant presence in Indonesian nationalist politics. It was a network of Tan Malaka's disciples, akin to a group of 'commissioned traveling salesmen', whose main task was to distribute his writings.[85] While the hope was to educate millions of competent followers to aid in the attainment of Indonesia's independence, Tan Malaka and his righthand man, Tamin, managed only to train no more than 30. As a result, the threat PARI posed to the colonial order was minimal.[86]

From a policing perspective, however, PARI was not insignificant as it was the closest thing to a reincarnation of the PKI, which had posed an enormous threat to the colony's *rust en orde* ('peace and order') by plotting rebellions against the Dutch Government while maintaining close ties with international communism. The DEI authorities thus had sufficient reason for the mass arrests, imprisonments and internments of anyone reminiscent of the PKI. More importantly, as PARI's network operated mostly outside the DEI's borders, domestic policing appeared insufficient to tame the seemingly ever-growing communist beast—generating a fear that boosted the demand for joint efforts between colonial powers to tackle the 'red menace'. The disappearance of Tan Malaka—Indonesia's most capable and legendary communist leader—further intensified such anxiety. As Tamin wrote:

---

83 ibid., 8.
84 Klaas Stutje, *Campaigning in Europe for a Free Indonesia: Indonesian Nationalists and the Worldwide Anticolonial Movement, 1917–1931* (Copenhagen: NIAS Press, 2019), 114–18.
85 Shiraishi, *The Phantom World of Digul*, 160.
86 Shiraishi, 'Policing the Phantom Underground', 43–45.

> In the British intelligence circle in India and all over the British colonies, Tan Malaka has indeed become a great specter. They were always worried, always suspicious, that Tan Malaka might have been in India already. They were not able to find any trace of Tan Malaka ever since he vanished at the Amoy Port in November 1932. Maybe Tan Malaka is in India, maybe in Iran, maybe in Egypt, maybe in Rangoon, maybe in Malaya … For this reason, the Dutch and British intelligence services needed closer cooperation.[87]

The tone may seem exaggerated, but the essence of the message is clear: the collapse of the PARI network in 1932 did not mark the end of the policing cooperation between colonial powers. In fact, the episode drew the partnership closer. Director Dickinson of the Singapore CID, who had just finished handling Tamin's extradition and Tan Malaka's deportation, visited Batavia in early 1933 to strengthen cooperation between the British and Dutch intelligence services.[88] The following March, Governor of Hong Kong William Peel proposed amending the colony's Deportation Ordinance, pointing out that 'very notorious' communists such as Hồ Chí Minh and Tan Malaka had not committed extraditable crimes and could not be deported to their own countries. Peel argued it was no longer possible to 'consider red communist agitators political offenders against their own country only [because] "red communism" has become a matter of international concern'. Therefore, British authorities should stop allowing foreign revolutionaries to take refuge in their territories.[89] The amendment was subsequently approved in London.[90] As Foster rightly suggests, officials from Dutch, British, French and US colonies in the region shared similar concerns, and it was this consensus that drew the four colonial powers closer than ever. It strengthened their political cooperation, which would persist throughout the interwar period and eventually into the Cold War.[91]

---

87   Tamin, *PKI History*, 89–90.
88   'Letter of Consul-General in Batavia, 1 March 1933', Foreign Office (FO) 371/17403/W 3745/66, The National Archives, Richmond, UK; Harry Poeze, *Tan Malaka: Strijder Voor Indonesië's Vrijheid* [*Tan Malaka: Fighter for Indonesia's Freedom*] (Leiden, Netherlands: Brill, 1976), 433.
89   'Deportations, 1933', in Treaty Department and Successors: General Correspondence from 1906, Foreign Office (FO) 372/2913/02762, as quoted in Jarvis, *Partai Republik Indonesia*, 50.
90   ibid., (FO) 372/2913/303; Poeze, *Tan Malaka*, 433.
91   Anne L. Foster, *Projections of Power: The United States and Europe in Colonial Southeast Asia, 1919–1941* (Durham, NC: Duke University Press, 2010), 41.

Part Two

6

Forging the masses in Malaya: Mass mobilisation, the united front and revolutionary violence in Malaya, 1939–51

Marc H. Opper

One of the most significant challenges, both theoretical and practical, the Malayan Communist Party (MCP) faced was how to mobilise Malaya's civilian population in support of the party. In the absence of a land revolution like that taking place in China, which delivered immediate, tangible results to the peasant population, the MCP's leadership had to craft an ideological and political program that overcame the reluctance of the masses to commit to the revolution. This chapter shows that when confronted with the imperative of leading a revolution in a relatively developed capitalist colony, the MCP initially adopted a united-front strategy, but later discarded it and developed a novel Marxist-Leninist social ontology that held that violent struggle could forge resolute supporters of the MCP from often reluctant civilians.

From its establishment, the MCP faced two major challenges, both theoretical and empirical: leading a revolution in a colony that was 1) relatively prosperous and 2) ethnically diverse. The first years of the MCP's existence were characterised by the search for a type of revolutionary theory that could reconcile the demands of revolution in a multiethnic colony with the fact that most of the party's members were ethnic Chinese.[1] The MCP was founded in British Malaya in 1930 under the aegis of the Comintern and drew its membership primarily from the ethnic Chinese community. The MCP's leadership and a not insignificant portion of its high-ranking cadres had fled to Malaya after the armed struggle by the Chinese Communist Party (CCP) began in 1927.

The CCP struggled in its own way to awaken the class consciousness of workers in cities and peasants in the countryside, but the CCP–Guomindang (GMD) conflict and the sharp contradictions in the Chinese countryside provided ample opportunities for the CCP to mobilise peasants against the rural political economy. The CCP could elicit political participation by previously quiescent peasants by leading a land revolution that delivered tangible results. However, the experience of China could not be mechanically applied to Malaya given the significant differences between the two places and it fell to the MCP's leaders to adapt Marxism-Leninism to the local context.

Cultivating class consciousness is both the end and the means by which the proletariat (or any other group targeted by communist parties for recruitment) comes to understand its place and commits to active and voluntary participation in the revolution. Often, communist theorists focused on a mixture of education and witnessing or participating in political agitation to cultivate class consciousness.

This chapter examines the evolution of the MCP's theoretical understanding of how to mobilise support behind the party and shows that, from 1939 to 1951, it focused on how direct experience of politics (active or passive, peaceful or violent) could forge the masses into active participants in the Malayan revolution. This chapter takes as its focus the period during which the MCP adopted and then discarded a united-front program in favour of a program of violent revolution. While the methods of revolution differed, a common thread ran through both bodies of theory: a belief that the masses could, in the absence of immediate tangible material benefits, be forged in political struggle and transformed into active supporters of the revolution.

---

1   See Anna Belogurova, *The Nanyang Revolution: The Comintern and Chinese Networks in Southeast Asia, 1890–1957* (Cambridge, UK: Cambridge University Press, 2019), doi.org/10.1017/9781108 635059.

The analysis presented in this chapter differs from previous scholarship on the MCP's ideology in two important ways. The first concerns its evidentiary basis: this chapter draws on a large body of Chinese-language materials that have been overlooked by existing scholarship on the MCP. The MCP was an overwhelmingly ethnic Chinese organisation and the party conducted its business (and its members their lives) almost entirely in Chinese, and much existing research on the MCP relies primarily on English-language translations of MCP documents made by British authorities during the Malayan Emergency.[2] The materials include contemporaneous documents written by the MCP's leadership, as well as memoirs of participants in the party's long political and armed struggle against the Malayan Government.

A second important way in which this analysis differs from existing scholarship is that it takes as its primary subject the theoretical approach the MCP adopted to understanding its political environment and how it sought to adapt Marxism-Leninism to the unique conditions of Malaya. As with communist revolutionaries elsewhere, the MCP's theoreticians closely integrated theory and practice. However, this chapter seeks to focus on the former to highlight how the MCP's leadership conceptualised their environment and charted a path forward for the revolution. In so doing, it adds detail to existing knowledge of the history of the MCP and shows that ideology played an important and underappreciated role in driving the party's political behaviour.

A Malayan united front

The first true attempt to adapt Marxism-Leninism to Malaya came from the MCP's leader from 1939 to 1947, Lai Teck. Lai (1909–1947), born Trương Phước Đạt 張福達 in Phan Rang, Annam, French Indochina, joined the Thanh Niên, the forerunner of the Vietnamese Communist

---

2   Anthony Short, *In Pursuit of Mountain Rats: The Communist Insurrection in Malaya*, Reprint (Singapore: Cultured Lotus, 2000 [1975]); Richard Stubbs, *Hearts and Minds in Guerilla Warfare: The Malayan Emergency, 1948–1960* (Singapore: Eastern Universities Press, 2004); Christopher Alan Bayly and Timothy Norman Harper, *Forgotten Wars: Freedom and Revolution in Southeast Asia* (Cambridge, MA: Harvard University Press, 2007); John Coates, *Suppressing Insurgency: An Analysis of the Malayan Emergency, 1948–1954* (Boulder, CO: Westview Press, 1992); Karl Hack, '"Iron Claws on Malaya": The Historiography of the Malayan Emergency', *Journal of Southeast Asian Studies* 30(1) (March 1999): 99–125, doi.org/10.1017/S0022463400008043; Kumar Ramakrishna, *Emergency Propaganda: The Winning of Malayan Hearts and Minds 1948–1958* (Richmond, UK: Curzon Press, 2002).

Party, in 1929.³ Lai Teck was possessed of a keen intellect and was an avid reader of Marxist-Leninist texts. In March 1930, he became a member of the Indochinese Communist Party (ICP) Saigon City Provisional Executive Committee; he was arrested in November of the same year and fled to Hong Kong. There, he met Hồ Chí Minh, who told him he was being sent to Moscow to study to develop talent for the revolution. On his way to the Soviet Union, Lai Teck was arrested in Suifenhe 绥芬河, on the Sino-Soviet border, in March 1931; he was released in early 1932, arrested in Shanghai in April 1933 and deported back to French Indochina. There, the French secret police, the Sûreté Générale, offered to spare Lai prison time if he acted as their agent in the ICP. Threatened and having already lost faith in communism, Lai Teck agreed. Unfortunately, Lai was well known in Saigon and was quickly unmasked as a spy. No longer of use to the French, Lai was handed to the Malayan Special Branch and, by late 1934, he had made contact with the MCP, claiming he was a representative of the Comintern.

Lai Teck rose to become head of the MCP by 1939, not only by virtue of his forged credentials, but also because he could 'walk the walk' of a Marxist-Leninist theorist. The MCP's radical labour agitation of the early to mid-1930s failed to resonate with large numbers of Malayan mine and factory workers. When Lai took control of the party in 1939, he undertook a fundamental reorientation of the MCP's political line and codified the central place of the united front.

Though the MCP had previously declared Malaya's revolution was of a bourgeois democratic nature, it never actually said the bourgeoisie should be included in any form (let alone as a class), stating only that the revolution had to occur under the leadership of the proletariat. The resolution of the sixth plenum stated explicitly that the national bourgeoisie should be part of the MCP's revolution—that 'in Malaya, where capitalist development is backward and still in its infancy, the reformist views [of nationalists] represent the Malayan bourgeoisie', which made them progressive rather than reactionary.⁴

---

3   This paragraph is based on the account of Lai Teck's life in Marc H. Opper, *Counter/Revolutionary Hero: Lai Teck and the Communist Revolution in Southeast Asia* (forthcoming).
4   21 shiji chubanshe bianjibu 21世紀出版社編輯部 [21st Century Press Editorial Department], ed., 'Malaiya gongchandang diliuci zhongyang kuoda huiyi jueyi 馬來亞共產黨第六次中央擴大會議決議 [Resolution of the Sixth Enlarged Plenum of the Malayan Communist Party]', in *Zhanqian dixia douzheng shiqi [er]: Fan faxisi, yuan-Hua kang-Ri jieduan* 戰前地下鬥爭時期(二): 反法西斯、援華抗日階段 [*The Period of Prewar Underground Struggle (2): The Anti-Fascist, Support China, Anti-Japan Stage*] (Kuala Lumpur: 21 shiji chubanshe, 2010), 17.

This was an explicit rejection of *guanmen zhuyi* 關門主義 ('closed-doorism')—the tendency of the MCP (and other communist parties) to recruit only proletarian elements and favour or join only organisations that were explicitly modelled on a communist party itself.[5] Furthermore, the resolution said, 'if we make use of pleasant-sounding "leftist" slogans among the broad, backward masses, the Party will become divorced from the masses [*tuoli qunzhong* 脫離羣衆] and isolated'. The MCP had to focus on attracting the masses and forging and *xunlian* 訓練 ('training') them through a period of legal and semilegal struggle.

For Lai Teck, the revolution would prioritise inclusion over exclusion and making allies over attacking enemies. The masses, for their part, would be involved in the political process and, through that, they would develop the consciousness necessary to become active supporters of the MCP.

A party divided: The MCP after World War II

When World War II abruptly ended in August 1945, the MCP was confronted with a novel challenge: reconciling its own goals for a postwar Malaya with those of the British. During the war, the MCP received logistical and material support from the Allies (the British specifically) and was nominally in alliance with them. The MCP's official policy for the immediate postwar period was promulgated on 25 August 1945 and was titled 'The Eight Point Democratic Program of the Malayan Communist Party'. In it, the MCP, headed by Lai Teck, laid out a list of objectives that were to form the core of the postwar MCP program. They included an alliance with the Allied Powers, bringing about a democratic government and the improvement of people's livelihoods in Malaya.[6] Though this was somewhat radical by the standards of prewar Malayan politics, this program was not the stuff of revolutionary communism. This program

---

5   The Constitution of the Malayan Communist Party promulgated at the sixth plenum allowed workers, soldiers and peasants to join the party—as was to be expected—but also admitted a number of groups previously not allowed to enter the party or who would have been targets of MCP violence: handicraft workers, *shimin* 市民 ('city residents'), intellectuals, students and the petty bourgeoisie. 'Malaiya gongchandang zhangcheng 馬來亞共產黨章程 [Constitution of the Malayan Communist Party]', in 21st Century Press Editorial Department, *The Period of Prewar Underground Struggle (2)*, 23.
6   21 shiji chubanshe bianjibu 21世紀出版社編輯部 [21st Century Press Editorial Department], ed., 'Malaiya gongchandang dangqian ba da zhuzhang 馬來亞共產黨當前八大主張 [The Eight-Point Program of the Malayan Communist Party]', in *Zhanhou heping shiqi (yi): erzhan shengli yu kang-Rijun fuyuan* 戰後和平時期(一)：二戰勝利與抗日軍復原 [*The Postwar Period of Peace (1): Victory in the Second World War and the Demobilisation of the Anti-Japanese Army*] (Kuala Lumpur: 21 shiji chubanshe, 2012), 31.

broke with the MCP's wartime policy, the 'Nine-Point Anti-Japanese Program', by eliminating the call for the establishment of an independent Malaya, seeking instead self-government and eventual independence.[7]

The decision to discard the call for immediate independence was based on Lai Teck's perception of how the war had changed both Malaya and the international environment. In an accompanying document, he concluded that the political struggle was *zhongxin* 中心 ('of primary importance') and armed struggle was *ciyao* 次要 ('of secondary importance'). The people of Malaya supported the MCP because it opposed the Japanese and because they wanted the Allies to return and improve people's livelihoods. According to the document:

> If we were to adopt armed struggle immediately we would become isolated and alienated from the people. This is a kind of extreme leftist Blanquist revolutionary action that is not suitable for the present circumstances[8] … The high tide of national liberation

---

[7] The 'Nine-Point Anti-Japanese Program' was promulgated by the MCP's Central Committee on 20 February 1943. The nine points were: 1) expel the Japanese and establish a Democratic Republic of Malaya; 2) establish a government elected through universal suffrage; 3) absolute freedom of speech, the press, organisation and religion; 4) provide assistance to those in need and abolish high taxes and high-interest loans; 5) make the Malayan People's Anti-Japanese Army the armed forces of Malaya; 6) establish universal, free, vernacular education; 7) confiscate and nationalise the property of the fascist powers and their collaborators; 8) implement national control of tariffs and establish treaties of friendship and trade with neighbouring countries; and 9) unite with the Soviet Union and China, support the oppressed peoples of the Far East and join in the struggle against Japanese fascism. 21 shiji chubanshe bianjibu 21世紀出版社編輯部 [21st Century Press Editorial Department], ed., 'Malaiya gongchandang wei haozhao shixian kang-Ri gangling gao quan Ma ge minzu tongbao shu 馬來亞共產黨爲號召實現抗日綱領告全馬各民族同胞書 [Proclamation by the Malayan Communist Party Calling on All Races in Malaya to Realise the Anti-Japanese Program]', in *Kang-Ri zhanzheng shiqi (yi): dang jun wenjianji* 抗日戰爭時期(一): 黨軍文件集 [*The Anti-Japanese Period (1): Party and Army Documents*] (Kuala Lumpur: 21 shiji chubanshe, 2011).

[8] Blanquism:

> advocates the use of clandestine methods and strict discipline to organise a small number of intellectuals and workers to undertake a sudden armed uprising to overthrow capitalist governments, establish revolutionary regimes and implement a dictatorship of the minority. Blanquists do not realise that the proletariat is the truly revolutionary class and as a result do not understand the necessity of organising a workers' revolutionary political party and the importance of relying on the broad worker masses and carrying out class struggle. At the same time, they did not formulate a specific and concrete revolutionary program to educate the masses, make them aware of their interests, and drive them to unite and struggle. Marx and Engels praised the great revolutionary spirit of the Blanquists, but also sternly criticised their sectarianism and their adventurist tactics.

Wang Yaomin 王耀民, *Zhuyi cidian* 主義詞典 [*Dictionary of Ideologies*] (Hohehot, China: Yuanfang chubanshe, 2003), 54. Engels articulated the first major critique of Louis Auguste Blanqui and his methods in Friedrich Engels, 'The Program of the Blanquist Fugitives from the Paris Commune', Der Volksstaat (73) (26 June 1874), available from: www.marxists.org/archive/marx/works/1874/06/26.htm. Rosa Luxemburg condemned the Leninist approach to revolution as Blanquist, in Rosa Luxemburg, 'Organizational Questions of the Russian Social Democracy (Part 1)', [1904], *Marxists Internet Archive*, available from: www.marxists.org/archive/luxemburg/1904/questions-rsd/ch01.htm.

> cannot be brought about through armed struggle. Instead, we must [adopt] a national united front ... in the spirit of New Democracy. Only then can we bring about a high tide of national liberation. The development of democracy in Malaya and achieving the complete liberation of the Malayan people are inseparable and are a prerequisite to bringing about a [democratic] republic [of Malaya]. The national united front policy ... encourages a democratic movement and alliance among Chinese, Malays, and Indians that serves as the main political, economic, and military force [of the national liberation movement]. The national united front is made up of not just revolutionary mass organisations, but of organisations that represent the interests of the masses ... In other words, all ethnic organisations should reflect the democratic wishes of all strata and parties and work together in the struggle [for national liberation].[9]

The insistence that political rather than armed struggle should take precedence indicates Lai Teck understood the limitations imposed on the party by the postwar environment, but he believed the prospects for a revolution and national liberation were good as long as the party did not go beyond what the objective circumstances allowed.

We also see in this document the first admission of a split between Lai Teck and a group of unnamed radicals who insisted on taking a more militant approach against the British. While the true scope of opposition to Lai remains unclear, even in the days immediately after the war, it reached a level that required a direct refutation in a document promulgated by the party's leadership. At least one group of radicals was in Kedah and was led by Chin Loh 陳魯 (Chen Lu, also known as Ah Woh 阿和 [Ah He] or Chin Khai 陳凱 [Chen Kai]), Chin Koh 陳古 (Chen Gu) and Chong Yoon 張雲 (Zhang Yun). In their capacity as leaders of the Kedah State Committee, these three decided to implement the Nine-Point Anti-Japanese Program and rename the MCP's armed forces from the Malayan People's Anti-Japanese Army (MPAJA) to the Malayan Liberation Army. Lai Teck handled the situation by dispatching Chin Peng to oversee the abolition of this newly created 'Liberation Army' and the reassignment of all its commanders to prevent them from attempting to reestablish an anti-British force. Chin resolved the issue without bloodshed and dispatched several men from his party apparatus in Perak to take over

---

9   21st Century Press Editorial Department, ed., 'Malaya gongchandang zhongyang yijian 馬來亞共產黨中央意見 [Views of the Central Committee of the Malayan Communist Party]', in *The Postwar Period of Peace (1)*, 35.

command of forces in Kedah.[10] Though rumbling continued among the MCP leadership, Lai Teck's political line carried the day and the party apparatus set about implementing it.

Lai argued the MCP's armed struggle must acknowledge Malaya's period of historical development and that only through the development of a *guangfan minzu tongyi zhanxian* 廣泛民族統一戰綫 ('broad national united front') that appealed to as large a constituency as possible could the MCP muster the strength necessary to challenge the British. After the initial split in the party was resolved, Lai Teck's argument was accepted by the leadership and considered appropriate given the conditions in Malaya.[11] As a means of reinforcing the importance of the united front, Lai undertook a systematic enumeration of the MCP's history, emphasising the role of the united front. The result of Lai's efforts was *Nandao zhi chun* 南島之春 ('*Spring in the Southern Islands*'), the first official history of the party, which sought to demonstrate the correctness of the united front during the war against Japan.[12] It was the correctness of the united front and its concrete results both during and after the war that made the MCP the 'headquarters of Malaya's national liberation struggle'.[13]

---

10   Xin-Ma qiaoyou hui 新馬僑友會 [Singapore–Malaya Overseas Chinese Friendship Association], *Malaiya renmin kang-Ri jun* 馬來亞人民抗日軍 [*The Malayan People's Anti-Japanese Army*] (Hong Kong: Witness Publishing Company, 1992), 372–73; Kuo Jen-te 郭仁德 [Guo Rende], 'Shenmi Lai Te 神秘萊特 [The Mysterious Lai Teck]', in *Ma Xin Kang-Ri Shiliao* 馬新抗日史料 [*Historical Materials of Malay(si)a and Singapore on the Anti-Japanese War*] (Johor Bahru, Malaysia: Caihong Chuban Youxian Gongsi, 1999), 271–72; C.C. Chin [Chen Jian 陳劍], 'In Search of the Revolution: A Brief Biography of Chin Peng', in *Dialogues with Chin Peng: New Light on the Malayan Communist Party*, C.C. Chin and Karl Hack, eds (Singapore: Singapore University Press, 2004), 352. The Kedah leadership incident took place on 21 August 1945; the promulgation of the Eight-Point Program, Lai Teck's explanation of it and his refutation of the radicals took place on 25 August 1945. Despite Chin Peng's important role in this intraparty dispute, he made no mention of it in his memoir or during any of his interviews.
11   This was the verdict of Chin Peng, who by this time had been elevated to the Central Committee. Chin and Hack, *Dialogues with Chin Peng*, 118.
12   Though the practical applications of these documents are outside the scope of this chapter, the codification of a leader's ideology requires that others in the organisation study it, understand it and reference it in their own writing and proposals. Furthermore, such documents serve as introductory materials for new recruits into the party. Cheah Boon Kheng 謝文慶, *From PKI to the Comintern, 1924–1941: The Apprenticeship of the Malayan Communist Party—Selected Documents and Discussion* (Ithaca, NY: Southeast Asia Program, Cornell University, 1992), 101.
13   Lai Te 萊特 [Lai Teck], 'Wei minzu tuanjie, minzhu ziyou, minsheng gaishan er douzheng 為民族團結, 民主自由, 民生改善而鬪爭 [Struggle for National Unity, Democracy, Freedom and Improving People's Livelihoods]', in 21st Century Press Editorial Department, *The Postwar Period of Peace (1)*, 128–29.

There is compelling evidence of a split in the MCP leadership after the war, but what of the rank and file? There appears to have been a widespread perception among soldiers and commanders in the MPAJA that the Japanese surrender presented the MCP with a golden opportunity to take control of the country. The demobilisation order and its accompanying instruction to turn weapons over to the British were met with puzzlement by some of the soldiers who believed that such a policy amounted to an act of *zihui changcheng* 自毀長城 ('supreme self-destruction'). To show their displeasure, they fired off their remaining ammunition and destroyed their guns before turning them over to the British, determined they could not be used against them in the future. The MCP's better weapons were hidden for later use either by the party itself or by soldiers who refused to fully comply with the MCP orders.[14] All demobilising MPAJA soldiers were given 350 Malayan dollars, the Burma Star medal and 1939–1945 Star ribbons.[15] To show their dissatisfaction, some soldiers simply threw their ribbons in the street like trash and, even as they kept the Burma Star, some regarded it as little more than a token of 'imperialist charity'.[16]

Members of the MCP who demobilised and returned home became the core of the MCP organisation throughout Malaya. However, working within the limits of the law took a toll on the organisation and its members. In 1946, there were two intraparty disputes, both of which involved state-level party apparatuses voicing opposition to Lai Teck's political line. The first of these took place early in the year and was called the Bei-Rou Zuzhi Weiji 北柔組織危機 (Northern Johore Organisational Crisis). The second took place in the autumn and was called the Xuezhou Zuzhi Weiji 雪州組織危機 ('Selangor Organisational Crisis'). According to Shan Ru-hong, a Negeri Sembilan state-level official dispatched to Selangor to undertake a *zhengdun* 整頓 ('rectification') of the organisation there, organisational crises were defined by 'a diminution of the revolutionary zeal of Party members, a weak concept of organization, individualism,

---

14   Kuo, 'The Mysterious Lai Teck', 275–76; Shan Ruhong 單汝洪 [A'Hai 阿海; A'Cheng 阿成], *Cong 'ba kuo' dao kang-Ying zhanzheng: Ma gong zhongyang zhengzhiju weiyuan A'Cheng huiyilu* 從「八擴」到抗英戰爭：馬共中央政治局委員阿成回憶錄 [*From the Eighth Enlarged Plenary Session to the Anti-British War: The Memoirs of A'Cheng, Member of the Politburo of the Malayan Communist Party*] (Kuala Lumpur: 21 shiji chubanshe, 2006), 6.
15   Harry Miller, *The Communist Menace in Malaya* (New York, NY: Frederick A. Praeger, 1954), 60.
16   Chong Chor 張佐 [Zhang Zuo], *Wode banshiji: Zhang Zuo huiyilu* 我的半世紀：張佐回憶錄 [*My Half-Century: The Memoirs of Chong Chor*] (Kuala Lumpur: Zhang Yuan, 2005), 228–29.

liberalism, and laxity in work'—all of which he and his colleagues believed could be traced to low morale resulting from the decision to demobilise the MPAJA.[17]

Gerald de Cruz, who was intimately involved in MCP activities in Singapore and Malaya, said there was 'a large groundswell of frustration amongst the rank-and-file over the difficulties of the "peaceful united front" struggle'.[18] He stated that, by December 1946, 'voices had been raised' at the MPAJA Ex-Servicemen's Association annual meeting 'demanding a return to the jungle and armed insurrection'.[19] MCP cadres working in the field felt the pressure from other party members as well as ethnic Chinese workers who demanded armed action in response to British pressure on organised labour and nationalist organisations.[20] Even so, the men and women in the MCP and Ex-Servicemen's Association were highly disciplined and largely followed their orders—in this case, to *jiejia guitian* 解甲歸田 ('cast off their armour and return to their fields'). Whatever confusion, anger or resentment they had towards the MCP's policies, they returned to their homes and families and sought to earn a living, much as they had before the Japanese invasion.

The united front repudiated

As the previous section showed, the decision to demobilise the MCP's armed forces after the war and pursue the party's goals within the bounds of British-ruled Malaya was a controversial one within the MCP. Dissatisfaction with Lai Teck's policies led members of the Central Committee to plot his downfall. In October 1946, Chin Peng and Yeung Kuo (Yang Guo 楊果) decided to indirectly confront Lai over what they perceived to be inconsistencies between his evaluation of the international situation and his handling of party funds. Cowed by criticism from

---

17   Shan, *From the Eighth Enlarged Plenary Session to the Anti-British War*, 24–31; Chin Peng 陳平, *My Side of History*, Ian Ward and Norma O. Miraflor, eds (Singapore: Media Masters, 2003), 165.
18   Michael R. Stenson and Gerald de Cruz, *The 1948 Communist Revolt in Malaya: A Note on Historical Sources and Interpretation and a Reply* (Singapore: Institute of Southeast Asian Studies, 1971), 29.
19   ibid., 29.
20   San Loh Hong 单汝洪 [Shan Ruhong], *Senmeilan kang-Ri youji zhanzheng huiyilu* 森美蘭抗日游擊戰爭回憶錄 [*Recollection of the Anti-Japanese Guerilla War in Negeri Sembilan*] (Hong Kong: Nandao chubanshe, 1999), 174; Cheah Boon Kheng 謝文慶, *Red Star Over Malaya: Resistance and Social Conflict during and after the Japanese Occupation of Malaya, 1941–46* (Singapore: NUS Press, 2012), 243.

Chen Yong and the rest of the Central Committee, Lai Teck said he was unwell and would take a vacation to recuperate and improve his Chinese. According to Chin Peng, at this time, Lai took Chin into his confidence, telling him he was a diligent worker and capable leader, and apparently suggesting Chin should be acting secretary-general in Lai's absence.[21]

Though Lai Teck remained in power in 1946, his position was increasingly tenuous. After a brief meeting of the Central Committee on 28 February 1947 at which he was confronted by other members about how he ran the party and his own lifestyle, he decided to flee Malaya—just before a subsequent meeting of the Central Committee on 5 March 1947.[22] Chin Peng and Yeung Kuo then undertook an investigation of Lai's history because both had a *sixiang zhengzhi shuiping he geming jingtixing bijiao gao* 思想政治水平和革命警惕性比較高 ('relatively high-level understanding of political theory and revolutionary vigilance'). It was they, but especially Yeung, who raised questions about Lai Teck's political line and led others to doubt it even before Lai fled.[23]

The repudiation of Lai Teck began in earnest in March 1948 at the Fourth Plenum of the Ninth Enlarged Plenary Session of the Central Committee as the party completed its internal reorganisation and tensions with the British increased. Chin and Yeung condemned the MCP's postwar

---

21 Chin, *My Side of History*, 167–73.
22 Chin Peng states a meeting took place in January 1947 at which Lai Teck was supposed to appear but did not, sparking the manhunt and subsequent investigation. Chin, *My Side of History*, 174–75. This is incorrect according to statements by other MCP members and scholars who have examined this part of the MCP's history. Lo Su Moh 羅須麼, 'Lai Te shizong qianhou 萊特失蹤前後 [The Disappearance of Lai Teck]', in *Zhanhou heping shiqi (san): neijian Lai Te shijian jiemi* 戰後和平時期(三)：內奸萊特揭秘 [*The Postwar Period of Peace (3): Revealing the Traitor Lai Teck*], 21 shiji chubanshe bianjibu 二十一世紀編輯部 [21st Century Press Editorial Department], ed. (Kuala Lumpur: 21 shiji chubanshe, 2012), 319; Kuo, 'The Mysterious Lai Teck', 310. Short is the only scholar who provides a precise date for the February meeting. Short, *In Pursuit of Mountain Rats*, 41. He is certainly correct; a late-February meeting and a brief recess would have made Lai Teck's disappearance such a shock. Short and Comber differ as to the date of Lai's disappearance, with Short dating it 6 March and Comber, 5 March. Leon Comber, '"Traitor of All Traitors"—Secret Agent Extraordinaire: Lai Teck, Secretary-General, Communist Party of Malaya (1939–1947)', *Journal of the Malaysian Branch of the Royal Asiatic Society* 83(2) (2010): 15n.60, doi.org/10.1353/ras.2010.0005. Both are correct. According to the party's official documents on Lai Teck, he departed on the evening of 5 March and his disappearance was noticed on 6 March. 'Yue shijian jianche he baogao 岳事件檢查和報告 [Investigation and Report of the Yueh Incident]', 101, 118, 'Lai Te shijian wengao 萊特事件文告 [Statement on the Lai Teck Incident]', 168, and 'Neijian Lai Te shijian de jingguo 內奸萊特事件的經過 [How the Incident of the Traitor Lai Teck Unfolded]', 190, all in 21st Century Press Editorial Department, *The Postwar Period of Peace (3)*.
23 21st Century Press Editorial Department, 'How the Incident of the Traitor Lai Teck Unfolded', 189–90.

political line as a *youqing touxiang zhuyi de luxian* 右傾投降主義的路綫 ('right deviationist capitulationist line') and a *shiqu jieji lichang de youqing jihui zhuyi luxian* 失去階級立場的右傾機會主義路綫 ('right opportunist political line devoid of a class standpoint'). This manifested in the MCP's political line 'lagging behind the objective situation and the demands of the masses'—specifically, in abandoning movement towards independence, 'unprincipled compromise' with British imperialism, 'unprincipled appeasement of reactionary political parties, unprincipled subservience to the petty bourgeoisie, an unwillingness to lead the masses, and an unwillingness to unleash [*fadong* 發動] a mass struggle'.[24]

With Chin Peng in charge, he and the other members of the Central Committee promulgated a new political line designed to bring about the changes they sought. The revolution, they said, should be led by the proletariat in a united front that brought together all forces with whom it was possible to unite. However, the leadership of the proletariat in the movement was not open to question. Specifically, the proletariat must have leadership within the *shangceng* 上層 ('upper levels') of political parties affiliated with the struggle and leadership of the organisations and movements at *xiaceng* 下層 ('lower levels'). Only by exercising comprehensive leadership of the movement could the proletariat be said to truly lead it. As for the bourgeoisie and petty bourgeoisie, the leadership of the proletariat would 'naturally' prod them into becoming part of the movement.[25]

The fall of Lai Teck came as a surprise to the MCP's rank and file and, while morale did fall among some, the shift in policy appears to have met with widespread approval. De Cruz recalled of that period: 'I am certain that when the change in policy came it was hailed by [frustrated ex-MPAJA servicemen] as both correct and welcome.'[26] Chong Chor, then an MCP district-level cadre, recalled the increasingly militant tone of MCP proclamations was greeted with enthusiasm among the party membership, who felt under serious pressure from the British authorities.[27]

---

24   21 shiji chubanshe bianjibu 21世紀出版社編輯部 [21st Century Press Editorial Department], ed., 'Muqian xingshi yu dang de zhengzhi luxian 目前形勢與黨的政治路綫 [The Present Situation and the Party's Political Line]', in *Zhanhou heping shiqi (er): erzhan shengli yu kang-Rijun fuyuan* 戰後和平時期(二): 戰後的自治獨立運動 [*The Postwar Period of Peace (2): The Postwar Self-Government and Independence Movement*] (Kuala Lumpur: 21 shiji chubanshe, 2012), 140.
25   ibid., 146–47.
26   Stenson and de Cruz, *The 1948 Communist Revolt in Malaya*, 29.
27   Chong, *My Half-Century*, 259.

After the fall of Lai Teck, the MCP embarked on a more aggressive approach to organising labour. As MCP-led strikes paralysed Malaya in mid to late 1947, Chinese businessmen and merchants increasingly felt the MCP was directing its efforts not at the British, but at them. Chang Ming Ching (Zhang Mingjin 張明今), the MCP's representative in Singapore, heard as much personally from prominent businessman Lee Kong Chian (Li Guangqian 李光前). In a meeting with Tan Kah Kee (Chen Jiageng 陳嘉庚) and Hu Yuzhi 胡愈之, Lee, himself a member of the CCP, told Chang 'the MCP leadership's strike movement is committing a leftist error by not uniting with all possible forces [in Malaya] and are [*sic*] alienating the national bourgeoisie'.[28]

The MCP's abandonment of the united front in general and the Chinese bourgeoisie in particular was complete by the time the Malayan Emergency unfolded in earnest. In June 1949, the MCP stated that the 'middle and upper strata of the national bourgeoisie' were traitors and 'our basic attitude is to resolutely and ruthlessly attack them … to attack them politically and economically, or attack them using armed force. We can change our tactics as necessary, but our basic attitude is to attack them.'[29]

An important part of the MCP's June 1949 directive was a call for an increase in revolutionary violence. The document, drafted largely by Yeung Kuo with contributions from Lee An Tung (Li Andong 李安東) stated that rubber plantations and trees were to be destroyed, 'so that it will be impossible for them to restore production', as was infrastructure, including roads, railways, bridges, trucks and powerlines. The MCP believed such operations would *qianzhi* 牽制 ('slow') and *miluan* 迷亂 ('confuse') the British and, by destroying its communication and infrastructure links,

---

[28] Kuo, 'The Mysterious Lai Teck', 307–8. Hu Yu-chih (Hu Yuzhi 胡愈之) was dispatched to Singapore in July 1940 by Zhou Enlai. While in Singapore, he befriended Tan Kah Kee and became editor of *Nanyang Siang Pau* 南洋商報 ('*South Seas Commercial Daily*'). He spent the war in Sumatra and returned to Singapore in late September 1945. Soon after, he reestablished communication with the CCP in Singapore and was directed to stay on to engage in educational and propaganda work. The fruits of his efforts included *Nan Chiau Jit Poh* 南僑日報 ('*Straits Chinese Morning Post*') and *Feng Xia* 風下 (*Land Below the Wind*). Yu You 于友, *Hu Yuzhi* 胡愈之 (Beijing: Qunyan chubanshe, 2013), 243–88; Bayly and Harper, *Forgotten Wars*, 197–98.

[29] 21 shiji chubanshe bianjibu 21世紀出版社編輯部 [21st Century Press Editorial Division], ed., 'Muqian de xingshi he renwu 目前的形勢和任務 [The Present Situation and Tasks]', in *Kang-Ying zhanzheng shiqi (yi): dangjun wenjian ji* 抗英戰爭時期(一): 黨軍文件 [*The Anti-British War (1): Party and Army Documents*], Reprint (Kuala Lumpur: 21 shiji chubanshe, 2015 [1949]), 116.

increase economic and fiscal pressure on the government, diminish and further disperse its forces and make it more difficult to carry out large-scale counterinsurgency operations against the MCP.[30]

These operations were to be carried out by both the *zhuli* 主力 ('main forces') of the Malayan National Liberation Army (MNLA) and the guerilla forces, for whom this *bixu ba zhe yi renwu dangwei benshen de zui zhuyao de renwu* 必須把這一任務當爲本身的最主要的任務 ('must be their primary mission'). The Min Yuen, the MNLA's civilian branch, was also enlisted in this mission and instructed that it should be *richang huodong zhiyi* 日常活動之一 ('among [their] daily tasks'). MCP members at the *qu* 區 ('district level') or in *zhibu* 支部 ('local cells') were to lead them *qinshen* 親身 ('personally').[31]

Even in this relatively early stage of the Emergency, the MCP was experiencing difficulties in eliciting compliance from civilians. The MCP stated this was a product of the *zisi* 自私 ('selfishness') of the masses and reflected their *luohou* 落後 ('backwardness') (as opposed to *jinbu* 進步 ['progressiveness']). The MCP leadership stated this was a temporary problem and could be overcome:

> The masses achieve progress through a tortuous and winding process, a process of struggle and forging [*duanlian* 鍛煉] [through struggle]. This struggle and forging is [*sic*] inseparable from the resolute political and military leadership of the Party and the Liberation Army.[32]

This forging through struggle applied to violence emanating from both the British and, more importantly, the MCP itself. In the context of Malaya and of other Marxist-Leninist parties more generally, this is a novel social ontology, one that emphasises the role of violence as not just a motivator of immediate action, but also the catalyst for a longer-term devotion to the revolution.

The MCP's change in course and adoption of a strategy focused on violent political struggle fundamentally changed the relationship between it and the masses. A united-front program in Malaya, as in China, required the party to focus its energies on gaining an understanding of the masses and

---

30 ibid., 133.
31 ibid., 132.
32 ibid., 113.

their interests and finding a way to reconcile those with the desire of the party to establish a socialist state; if the party acted in the interests of the masses, the latter would develop some form of political consciousness and support the party. The violent program adopted under Chin Peng put the MCP firmly in control; the party did not need to understand the masses because its leadership—schooled in the works of Marx, Lenin, Stalin and Mao—knew what was best for the masses. Cultivating political consciousness among the masses was no longer a concern.

It is important to emphasise here that the MCP's leadership sought to draw on the same logic deployed by Lai Teck 10 years earlier: the masses could be made into willing and active participants in the revolution if they were introduced to the revolution by the party. However, a crucial difference is that Lai Teck envisioned the masses' period of stewardship as one in which they were active in largely legal and non-lethal politics. By contrast, the MCP's 1949 political line reflected a belief that the masses could be made into supporters by being subjected to violence.

The MCP's centrally promulgated policies were quickly put into practice throughout Malaya. The slashing of rubber trees was deeply unpopular, as was the firebombing of buses. However, the result of these operations, to quote one MCP commander at the time, Chong Chor, was often to 'harm the interests of the masses', as rubber tappers, bus drivers, ticket sellers and others lost their jobs while the largest shareholders or owners lost relatively little because many had insurance.[33]

The MCP's policy of confiscating identification (ID) cards from civilians was also deeply unpopular but was nevertheless implemented, even in the face of civilian resistance. Chong recalled that after his unit successfully captured part of Bidor, they confiscated the ID cards of all the civilians they could find 'and explained our reasons for doing so. However, explaining it was one thing; whether the masses accepted it was something else entirely … Whether it was the correct [policy] or not was something [for us] to think about later.'[34] Another guerilla, Tseng Han-tien, operating in another part of Perak, also recalled that civilians had a deep dislike of the

---

33   Chong, *My Half-Century*, 319–20.
34   ibid., 310.

MCP's policies during this time, especially the confiscation of ID cards.[35] Refusal by civilians to comply with the MCP's demands had serious consequences. Individual villagers were sometimes murdered and, in rare circumstances, entire villages were burned to the ground.[36]

The overwhelmingly negative reaction of civilians to the MCP's policies led it to reevaluate its strategy in late 1951. The result, the October 1951 Resolutions, stated the MCP's primary mistakes had resulted in the party committing leftist errors and, because these errors emanated from the party centre, they were reflected in the party's work throughout Malaya. The MCP admitted it did not properly balance the interests of the masses and of the revolution and, as a result, demanded too much from the masses. Echoing Mao Zedong's dictum, the MCP stated the revolution should be waged in a way that was *youli, youli, youjie* 有理有利有節 ('reasonable, beneficial and restrained'). No struggle should take place without careful consideration of the costs and benefits of strategies in which the masses would suffer losses.[37] The MCP also admitted its handling of the classes in Malaya was incorrect and it had erred in declaring the entire bourgeoisie to be its enemy.

The October Resolutions stated for the first time since Lai Teck controlled the party that the MCP must guard against 'leftist' deviations and that such deviations posed the greatest threat to the revolution.[38] The resolutions

---

35 Tseng Han-tien 曾漢添, 'Zhuanzhan bianqu 轉戰邊區 [Shifting Battles in the Border Region]', in *Man Man Lin Hai Lu* 漫漫林海路 [*Journey Through the Boundless Greenwood*], Jianzheng congshu bianweihui 見證叢書編委會 [Editorial Committee of the Witness Series], ed. (Hong Kong: Xianggang jianzheng chubanshe, 2003), 114.

36 For an account of a particularly brutal murder, see 'Yi Keji Jiaogong Canzao Baotu Dushou 一客籍膠工慘遭暴徒毒手 [Hakka Rubber Tapper Violently Killed by Bandits]', *Nanyang Siang Pau* 南洋商報 [*South Seas Commercial News*], 12 October 1952, 11. The most well-known instance of this kind of collective punishment was when the MCP destroyed the village of Simpang Tiga in Sitiawan, Perak. 'Shizaoyuan Santiaolu Jiechang Baotu Conghuo, Jin Qian Nanmin Shisuo, Pile Shujiao Gonghui Juan Wubaiyuan Jiuji, Mahua Fenhui Huyu Inzhong Juanzeng Yiwu 實兆遠三條路街場暴徒縱火近千難民失所吡叻樹膠公會捐五百元救濟馬華分會呼籲民眾捐贈衣物 [Bandits Set Fire to Simpang Tiga, Sitiawan, Nearly 1,000 Homeless, Perak Rubber Tapper's Association Donates $500 Dollars in Aid, Local Chapter of the Malayan Chinese Association Calls on People to Donate Clothing, Daily Necessities]', *Nanyang Siang Pau* 南洋商報 [*South Seas Commercial News*], 5 February 1950, 10. 'The Village the Bandits Can't Destroy', *The Straits Times*, [Singapore], 10 February 1950, 5.

37 21 shiji chubanshe bianjibu 21世紀出版社編輯部 [21st Century Press Editorial Department], ed., 'Wei zhengqu zhanzheng gengda shengli er douzheng 爲爭取戰爭的更大勝利而鬪爭 [Struggle to Achieve a Greater Victory in the Revolutionary War]', in *Kang-Ying zhanzheng shiqi (er): Dangjun wenjian ji (xu)* 抗英戰爭時期(二): 黨軍文件(續) [*The Anti-British War (2): Party and Army Documents (Vol.2)*] (Kuala Lumpur: 21 shiji chubanshe, 2015), 24–29.

38 ibid., 47.

stated the party needed to increase its understanding of the masses and their beliefs through concerted investigation and *diaocha yanjiu* 調查研究 ('research') and if the masses did not accept the MCP's views or policies, they should be changed and brought back to the masses.[39] If these revisions violated the spirit or letter of the MCP's policies, the MCP should talk to the masses again. If they still did not agree, the MCP should cease implementation of those policies and contact higher levels of the party for advice.[40]

Though the MCP existed in a plural society, it did not devote substantial attention to matters of race. The only comprehensive statement on the matter from the MCP came in 1952.

For the MCP under Chin Peng, even though there were differences among the races—with ethnic Malays considered the most *luohou* 落後 ('backward')—it was argued the interests of the proletarian class of each race were identical. Consequently, all the races stood to benefit from the revolution, which was a matter of general principle, a *pubian zhenli* 普遍眞理 ('universal truth'). The party was organised around a *guoji zhuyi* 國際主義 ('internationalist') proletarian ideology, not ethnic *minzu yuanze* 民族原則 ('nationalist principles'). The MCP sought the creation of a proletarian vanguard, proletarian mass organisations, a proletarian fighting force led by the MCP and the establishment of a proletarian regime in Malaya, not a country starkly divided along racial lines.[41]

39　To facilitate this transformation, in 1952, the MCP reprinted and distributed a book titled *Zenyang zuo diaocha yanjiu gongzuo* 怎樣做調查研究工作 (*How to Carry out Investigation and Research Work*), which was originally published in 1947 in China as *Diaocha yanjiu rumen* 調查研究入門 (*Primer on Survey Research*) by Bai Tao 白韜 (Dai Botao 戴伯韜), an educator and researcher working with the CCP. Bai Tao 白韜, *Zenyang zuo diaocha yanjiu gongzuo* 怎樣做調查研究工作 [*How to Carry out Investigation and Research Work*] (Johore, Malaya: Hongxingbao she, 1952).

40　21 shiji chubanshe bianjibu 21世紀出版社編輯部 [21st Century Press Editorial Department], ed., 'Malaiya gongchandang zhongyang zhengzhiju guanyu zhixing "dang de poqie renwu" de gongzuo zhishi 馬來亞共產黨中央政治局關於執行「黨的迫切任務」的工作指示 [MCP Central Politburo Directive on the Implementation of "The Party's Urgent Tasks"]', in *The Anti-British War (2)*, 67.

41　21 shiji chubanshe bianjibu 21世紀出版社編輯部 [21st Century Press Editorial Department], ed., 'Malaiya gongchandang zhongyang weiyuanhui guanyu Ma, Yin gongzuo de zhengce wenti de jueyi 馬來亞共產黨中央委員會關於馬、印工作的政策問題的決議 [Malayan Communist Party Central Committee Resolution on Problems in Malay and Indian Policy]', in *The Anti-British War (2)*, 91–109.

Conclusion: Ideology in the Malayan revolution

Both Lai Teck and the post-Lai leadership saw the MCP as a steward of the masses in the Malayan revolution. Where the two differed, however, was how they envisioned the conditions under which the masses would come to support the revolution. For Lai, the masses would be 'forged' through struggle, to be sure, but a struggle that sought to allow the masses to dictate its tempo and nature, led by the MCP. This dialectic, Lai would probably say, ensured a balance between the demands of the revolutionary elite and the demands of the masses.

By contrast, the post–Lai Teck leadership believed violence could and should be used to induce the masses to embrace the revolution. In this conception, the MCP possessed a sagacity that enabled it to see beyond the narrow interests that so often dictated the actions of the masses. The MCP, seeing the reluctance of the masses to participate in the revolution, committed itself to forcing them; if the masses did not see the full picture, they would be made to see it; if the masses did not consider the longer-term interests of Malaya, they would be made to consider them. In the context of the Malayan Emergency, the best way to make the masses participants in the revolution was the application of violence. It did not matter whether that violence came from the MCP or the British; either way, the MCP's leadership believed, the masses would see there were two sides in the war and armed struggle with the MCP was the only way out.

Though Lai Teck was a spy for the forces of counterrevolution (France, the United Kingdom and Japan) and became disillusioned with communism, he nevertheless retained an aptitude for (and probably an enjoyment of) composing new types of political theory. Whatever his motivations, Lai's united-front approach to the revolution echoed that of other communist parties—notably, that of the CCP from 1935 to 1949 under Mao Zedong, where the pursuit of a broad united front enabled the CCP to survive and thrive even when targeted by the Japanese military or Chinese Nationalist forces.

By contrast, the MCP's Emergency-era program of forging the masses through violent struggle appears most like the approach adopted more than 20 years later by the Shining Path under Abimael Guzmán, who believed continuous mass violence could transform Peruvian peasants into active supporters of the revolution. While the initial decision to take up arms against the British in 1948 may not have been dictated by the MCP's ideology, its political strategy—most notably, the campaign of economic sabotage and its coercion of civilians—was a direct product of the MCP's attempts to apply an ideology of Marxism-Leninism to Malaya. Practically all previous scholarship on the Emergency documents the brutality of the MCP's polices from 1949 until 1951 but leaves unexplored the MCP's theoretical understanding of its political environment and the ideological justification it crafted for its policies.

A focus on the theoretical underpinnings of the MCP's political ideology adds to the understanding of both the MCP's history and the unique role ideology can play in civil wars, insurgencies and contentious politics more generally. With a few notable exceptions, there has been little focused examination of the MCP's political ideology.[42] As a result, the MCP appears in much academic research as an ideologically motivated *communist* party without a carefully articulated or considered ideology. This is very likely because the MCP's premier theoretical heavyweight, Lai Teck, was a spy and his 'theoretical contributions' were merely a tool to weaken the MCP. Yet another possible explanation is the MCP's ideology did not seem to gain much traction among Malaya's citizens, leading to the MCP's defeat by the British.

The lack of space given to the MCP's ideological development may also be a result of organisational dynamics within the MCP itself. Throughout the party's history, those who used political theory to advance their positions (or alternative policies) were often violently purged from the organisation. One of the MCP's first and most promising theoreticians was Boo Chih Fu 鄔熾夫 (Wu Chifu), who articulated a theoretically sophisticated objection to the MCP's relatively radical policies of the early 1930s. The split Boo induced was resolved by none other than Lai Teck, who used the purge of Boo to prove his own bona fides as a Comintern agent.[43] Lai Teck, the party's most advanced theorist between the late

---

42 Ban Ah Kam 萬家安 [Wan Jia'an], *Yu lisih duihua (er): zhanhou Magong celue de tantao* 與歷史對話(二): 戰後馬共策略的探討 [*Dialogue with History (2): An Exploration of the MCP's Postwar Tactics*] (Kajang, Malaysia: Dangdai bentu shiliao yanjiushi, 2008); Belogurova, *The Nanyang Revolution*; Marc Opper, *People's Wars in China, Malaya, and Vietnam* (Ann Arbor, MI: University of Michigan Press, 2019), 174–83; Yong C.F. [Yong Ching Fatt 楊進發], *The Origins of Malayan Communism* (Singapore: South Seas Society, 1997).
43 Marc Opper, 'Boo Chih Fu and the First Malayan Communist Party Split', *Journal of the Malaysian Branch of the Royal Asiatic Society* 92(1) (8 July 2019): 41–66, doi.org/10.1353/ras.2019.0004.

1930s and mid-1940s, was purged when his political line fell out of favour with other members of the MCP's leadership. Yet another relatively sophisticated theoretician, Siew Lau 小劉 (Xiao Liu), was purged for his opposition to the radicalism of the MCP's post–Lai Teck political line.[44] After Siew's death, the party's most capable theorists were Lee An Tung and Wu Tien Wang 伍天旺 (Wu Tianwang), neither of whom ever used their understanding of Marxism-Leninism to advance an alternative approach to the revolution or even penned anything in their own names (unlike Boo, Lai and Siew). The absence of one (or a small group of) leading MCP theorist after the 1950s speaks to the MCP's capacity for collective leadership. However, the absence of theoretical deliberation among the party's leadership may have also inhibited the emergence of a political line that would have been more effective in the MCP's mission of overthrowing the Malayan Government and remaking Malayan society.

If practice is the sole criterion of truth, the failure of the MCP to take power in Malaya cannot lead to anything other than a negative verdict on the utility of the MCP's ideology as the driver of a proletarian revolution in Malaya. However, the MCP's failure should not distract us from the importance of analysing the ideology on its own terms and seeing it as part of broader debates that were part of the international communist movement from its inception between advocates of a moderate approach to revolution and advocates of a more forceful, violent approach.

---

44 For a discussion of the Siew Lau incident, see Short, In Pursuit of Mountain Rats, 311–13; Ma Lim 馬林 [Ma Lin], 'Xiao Liu shijian: Magong lishi shang de yige beiju 小劉事件: 馬共歷史上的一個悲劇 [The Siew Lau Incident: A Tragedy in the History of the Malayan Communist Party]', in Fuqu huichen de jiyi 拂去灰塵的記憶 [Brushing Off the Dust of Old Memories] (Hong Kong: Zuyin chubanshe, 2014), 10–15.

7
Recycling violence: The theory and practice of reeducation camps in postwar Vietnam

Hoang Minh Vu

When the tanks of the People's Army of Vietnam rolled into the Independence Palace in Saigon on 30 April 1975, it marked the end of a very long, bloody and fratricidal war. While in the immediate aftermath there were no bloody reprisals against the Saigon population, in the subsequent months, 200,000 to 250,000 people who had served in the fallen regime were ordered to report for *cải tạo* ('reeducation').[1] These 'students' were held against their will in secluded camps for anywhere between a week and more than two decades, depending on many factors including their role and rank in the fallen regime, their family background and connections and their actions in the camp.[2] Activities in the camps included both political classes and manual labour. Their low rations, poor health care, the difficult terrain and the harshness of the work and punishments meant many died in the process. Graduates carried their

---

1   Edward P. Metzner, ed., *Re-education in Postwar Vietnam: Personal Postscripts to Peace*, Texas A&M University Military History Series 75 (College Station, TX: Texas A&M University Press, 2001), xiii; Frank Snepp, *Decent Interval: An Insider's Account of Saigon's Indecent End Told by the CIA's Chief Strategy Analyst in Vietnam*, 1st Vintage Books edn (New York, NY: Vintage Books, 1978), 476.
2   Lê Hữu Tri, *Prisoner of the Word: A Memoir of the Vietnamese Re-education Camps* (Seattle, WA: Black Heron Press, 2001), 18; Nghia M. Vo, *The Bamboo Gulag: Political Imprisonment in Communist Vietnam* (Jefferson, NC: McFarland & Co., 2004), 207.

past with them and were denied certain vocational and educational opportunities in the new socialist society. Many ended up emigrating and writing detailed memoirs, which I have consulted to construct an account of political reeducation in Vietnam.

These political reeducation camps have always been a puzzle for me as a historian of Vietnam coming from a family that has served the Communist Party for generations, because they appear in retrospect so unnecessary and wasteful. Unnecessary, because there was no appreciable threat of a counterrevolution against communist rule. The last American combat troops were withdrawn in 1973 in the face of massive antiwar protests from a war-weary public and, during the final Hồ Chí Minh Campaign, the US Congress declined to provide air support to the rapidly collapsing Army of the Republic of Vietnam (ARVN), indicating that further foreign intervention was highly unlikely. The last South Vietnamese president, Dương Văn Minh, had ordered his troops to lay down their arms and, by mid-May, there was no anticommunist armed resistance of any significance remaining.[3] It was wasteful because, while there were many in the South who disliked the communists, the majority of those who remained behind were ready to cooperate and move on with their lives. Those sent to the camps included skilled specialists like teachers, doctors and engineers who were sorely needed for reconstructing the nation after decades of war. Even after graduation, the *lý lịch* ('background') classification system that excluded them and their family from many opportunities also closed the door to true rehabilitation and national reconciliation.[4] My study of the liberal foreign policy Vietnam adopted in the late 1970s before the Third Indochina War leaves me further baffled as to why the government pursued apparently contradictory policies at home and abroad.[5]

There has also been comparatively little Western scholarship dedicated to Vietnamese reeducation camps. Two of the most important monographs on Vietnamese Communist Party (VCP) history in the past decade barely mention the camps at all.[6] Only Huy Đức's *The Winning Side* dedicates

---

3   Huy Đức, *Bên Thắng Cuộc: Giải Phóng* [*The Winning Side. Volume 1: The Liberation*] (Los Angeles, CA: OsinBook, 2012), 3–21.
4   Ann Marie Leshkowich, 'Standardized Forms of Vietnamese Selfhood: An Ethnographic Genealogy of Documentation', *American Ethnologist* 41(1) (1 February 2014): 143–62, doi.org/10.1111/amet.12065.
5   Hoang Minh Vu, 'The Third Indochina War and the making of present-day Southeast Asia' (PhD diss., Cornell University, Ithaca, NY, 2020), doi.org/10.7298/q44e-7k02.
6   Tuong Vu, *Vietnam's Communist Revolution: The Power and Limits of Ideology* (Cambridge, UK: Cambridge University Press, 2017); David W.P. Elliott, *Changing Worlds: Vietnam's Transition from the Cold War to Globalization* (Oxford, UK: Oxford University Press, 2012).

a chapter to the reeducation camps, revealing the process by which people were brought to the camps in the immediate aftermath of reunification and their plight in the system. While it is an extremely valuable work drawn from interviews with both internees and policymakers, Đức's journalistic account does not reflect deeply on the theoretical underpinnings or process of reeducation itself.[7] Much of the recent scholarship that explicitly mentions reeducation is written from the perspective of the overseas Vietnamese community and focuses on its effects on Vietnamese-American issues like diasporic anticommunism and family reunification, rather than closely examining reeducation in theory and practice.[8] In fact, some of the best reflections on Vietnamese reeducation have appeared in popular fictional works by diasporic writers like Viet Thanh Nguyen and Nguyễn Phan Quế Mai.[9]

This chapter argues that Chinese influence on the reeducation system was more direct and practical whereas Soviet influence was less direct and more theoretical, but in its final shape, the Vietnamese reeducation system was a product mostly of local circumstances. In drawing from the National Library of Vietnam's collection of theoretical works that underpin reeducation, I trace the genealogy of Vietnamese reeducation from its Soviet and Chinese roots. My reconstruction of the reeducation camp experience relies largely on the Cornell University Library's collection of memoirs published by graduates of reeducation who have resettled in the United States, the overwhelming majority of whom were former ARVN officers. By bringing together surviving theoretical texts and firsthand accounts of those who underwent reeducation, this chapter will hopefully bring new insights into the understudied but important topic of reeducation in Vietnam. My conclusion is that Vietnamese reeducation camps earnestly set out on a pedagogical mission to create new socialist men and women by making them go through an imperfectly reconstructed wartime experience of the communist guerillas. In arriving at this conclusion, I highlight the role of the local cadres, whose interpretation of government directives most decisively shaped the lived experience of

---

7 See Huy Đức, *The Winning Side*.
8 Tuan Hoang, 'From Re-education Camps to Little Saigons: Historicizing Vietnamese Diasporic Anticommunism', *Journal of Vietnamese Studies* 11(2) (2016): 43–95, doi.org/10.1525/jvs.2016.11.2.43; Sam Vong, '"Compassion Gave Us a Special Superpower": Vietnamese Women Leaders, Re-education Camps, and the Politics of Family Reunification, 1977–1991', *Journal of Women's History* 30(3) (2018): 107–37, doi.org/10.1353/jowh.2018.0032.
9 Viet Thanh Nguyen, *The Sympathizer* (New York, NY: Grove Press, 2016); Nguyễn Phan Quế Mai, *The Mountains Sing* (Chapel Hill, NC: Algonquin Books, 2020).

reeducation, as well as contextualise the conditions in the camps as yet another episode in the cycle of political violence in Vietnam stretching back to the colonial era.

Reeducation as theory

While 'reeducation' is the most widely used translation of the Vietnamese term *cải tạo* (a direct translation of the Chinese *gaizao* 改造), it does not capture the meaning and connotations of the term very well. *Cải* denotes a repeated action, while *tạo* is best translated as 'creation'. *Cải tạo* is thus a complete remaking, reforming, remoulding or renovation of something or someone. It was applied in the postwar years to all aspects of society: the economy, the land, hospitals and even the masses who had supposedly been long oppressed by the puppet Saigon regime. *Cải tạo* thus originally carried the positive overtone of the postwar idealism to reform all aspects of society to build a brighter socialist future. Indeed, *cải tạo kinh tế/ cải tạo xã hội chủ nghĩa* ('economic and socialist reformation') were the most common applications of the term 'reeducation' in the speeches and publications by Vietnamese leaders in the aftermath of reunification.[10] Yet, it was primarily because of its association with coercive government policies towards people that *cải tạo* came to acquire ominous connotations. That something or someone needed to go through *cải tạo* implied a deficiency in their character, and the state's ability to act as the doctor for their condition emphasised its omniscience and omnipotence. While there were many different types of reeducation camps, including those still running today for drug addicts and former prostitutes, this chapter focuses on the experiences of those interned for political reeducation in the aftermath of reunification.

Reeducation camps have become a taboo subject in Vietnam, and even at the height of their operations in the 1970s and 1980s, there was little public official discourse on the subject. Nghia M. Vo terms reeducation camps 'bamboo gulags', highlighting the fact that, like many other Vietnamese policies, reeducation camps were influenced by precedents in

---

10 Tố Hữu, *Xoá Sạch Bóc Lột Đoàn Kết Nông Dân Lao Động Đưa Phong Trào Hợp Tác Hoá Nông Nghiệp Tiến Lên Mạnh Mẽ* [*Completely Eliminate Exploitation, Uniting the Working Peasantry to Advance under the Campaign of Communalising Agriculture*] (Hanoi: Sự Thật, 1979); Lê Duẩn, *Cải Tạo Xã Hội Chủ Nghĩa ở Miền Nam* [*Socialist Reform in the South*] (Hanoi: Sự Thật, 1980); *Chính Sách Đối Với Công Thương Nghiệp Tư Bản Tư Doanh ở Miền Nam* [*Policy towards Private Industry and Capitalist Businesses in the South*] (Hanoi: Nhà xuất bản Lao động, 1978).

the Soviet Union and the People's Republic of China.¹¹ He classifies them simply as death camps—a position evoking Hannah Arendt's attempt to understand communism as just another iteration of totalitarianism, under which the reeducation camps are a tool of repression and control.¹² While that is doubtless true on some level, it would be overly simplistic to stop there, because one would miss the defining characteristic of communist totalitarianism versus national socialist totalitarianism. Slavoj Žižek asks us to 'consider the fact that, on Stalin's birthday, prisoners would send him congratulatory telegrams from the darkest gulags: it isn't possible to imagine a Jew in Auschwitz sending Hitler such a telegram'.¹³ There is thus a humanist aspiration hidden in the communist ideology that drives the reeducation camps: by having the bourgeoisie experience the lives of peasants and workers, they learn to empathise with the hardships of the working class and thus become committed to the socialist project.

Despite Nghia Vo's comparison, Stalin's gulags were created in a very different historical context from Vietnam's reeducation camps, and I have not found any documents in Vietnamese showing the Soviet gulags were ever directly studied as a model. This is not surprising: in 1956, Soviet premier Nikita Khrushchev spoke vigorously against Stalin's cult of personality and, in the following years, worked systematically to dismantle the gulag system as part of his de-Stalinisation program.¹⁴ With the Soviet Union a key patron in brewing the Second Indochina War, Vietnamese leaders would not have been especially keen to replicate a model Soviet leaders had disavowed. The extremely few Soviet texts on political reform and reeducation translated into Vietnamese focused instead on high Marxist theory and rhetoric, such as Georgy Fyodorovich Aleksandrov's pamphlet *The Rhetorical Method of Marxism is the Only Scientific Method to Examine the World and Reform the World through Revolution*.¹⁵

---

11 Vo, *The Bamboo Gulag*, 1–4, 58.
12 Hannah Arendt, *The Origins of Totalitarianism* (New York, NY: Harcourt, Brace & Co., 1951), 460–79.
13 Slavoj Žižek, 'The Two Totalitarianisms', *London Review of Books*, 17 March 2005.
14 Nikita Khrushchev, 'Speech to 20th Congress of the CPSU', 24–25 February 1956, available from: www.marxists.org/archive/khrushchev/1956/02/24.htm; A.P. van Goudoever, *The Limits of Destalinization in the Soviet Union: Political Rehabilitations in the Soviet Union since Stalin* (New York, NY: St Martin's Press, 1986).
15 Georgy Fyodorovich Aleksandrov, *Phương Pháp Biện Chứng Của Chủ Nghĩa Mác Là Phương Pháp Khoa Học Duy Nhất Để Nhận Thức Thế Giới và Cải Tạo Thế Giới Bằng Cách Mạng* [*The Rhetorical Method of Marxism is the Only Scientific Method to Examine the World and Reform the World through Revolution*], Phan Nam, trans. (Hanoi: Sự Thật, 1955).

Maoist China exerted much more significant and direct influence on Vietnamese reeducation theory and practice. Mao Zedong had been blindsided by Khrushchev's 'Secret Speech', perceiving it as indirect criticism of his own cult of personality and an unacceptable intervention in Chinese domestic affairs.[16] Meanwhile, Mao was undertaking the Hundred Flowers Campaign in 1956–57, encouraging intellectuals to freely criticise the failings of the party, before quickly shutting the campaign down and arresting those who had spoken out.[17] The Democratic Republic of Vietnam was going through a similar process in the 1950s with the shuttering of the free-thinking magazines *Nhân Văn* ('*Humanities*') and *Giai Phẩm* ('*Masterpieces*') in 1958 and the arrest of the prominent artists and intellectuals who contributed to the movement associated with them, and the execution or reeducation of landlords as part of land reforms.[18] Coupled with China's close physical and cultural proximity, it is perhaps no surprise there were many Chinese books on reform and reeducation of intellectuals and other 'reactionary elements' translated into Vietnamese in the 1950s and 1960s, forming the theoretical basis for the development of Vietnamese reeducation.

The Vietnamese translation of a major Chinese discourse by Lương Duy Trực (Liang Weizai?) on the reeducation of intellectuals, published in the wake of the 1950s land reforms, is an example of early Chinese influence on Vietnamese reeducation discourse. Lương observed that intellectuals generally came from bourgeois backgrounds, and even those who followed the revolution had little faith and were prone to thinking along 'super-social' lines. He prescribed they undergo self-reeducation through reading Marxist theory and practice.[19] Another key Chinese text, by Ngải Tư Kỳ (Ai Siqi?), warned cadres against punishing students harshly and rejecting their ideas and beliefs out of hand. Instead, cadres should hear out their charges' viewpoints and seek common ground.[20] Several memoirs of

---

16 Lorenz M. Luthi, *The Sino-Soviet Split: Cold War in the Communist World* (Princeton, NJ: Princeton University Press, 2008).
17 Roderick MacFarquhar, *The Hundred Flowers Campaign and the Chinese Intellectuals* (New York, NY: Praeger, 1960); Hongda Harry Wu, *Laogai, the Chinese Gulag* (Boulder, CO: Westview Press, 1992).
18 Kim Ngoc Bao Ninh, *A World Transformed: The Politics of Culture in Revolutionary Vietnam, 1945–1965* (Ann Arbor, MI: University of Michigan Press, 2002); Alex-Thai D. Vo, 'Nguyễn Thị Năm and the Land Reform in North Vietnam, 1953', *Journal of Vietnamese Studies* 10(1) (2015): 1–62, doi.org/10.1525/vs.2015.10.1.1.
19 Lương Duy Trực, *Bàn về Cải Tạo Trí Thức* [*On the Reeducation of Intellectuals*] (Hanoi: Sự Thật, 1957), 7–9, 11, 14–16.
20 Ngải Tư Kỳ and Lữ Giang, trans, *Vấn Đề Cải Tạo Tư Tưởng* [*On Reeducation*] (Việt Bắc: Tổng cục Chính trị, 1951), 34–35.

Chinese intellectuals who had 'volunteered' for reeducation by going to the countryside and experiencing the hard lives of farmers and labourers also treated reeducation as a voluntary personal journey of self-reform and enlightenment.[21] Even a report on the reform of intellectuals following the Hundred Flowers Campaign concluded that 'the victory against the right-wingers not only pushed forward our rectification campaign but also increased the determination of the upper classes to undertake self-reeducation for socialism'.[22] Of course, these were theoretical propaganda texts that did not truly reflect the experiences of those intellectuals arrested in the purges. Yet, it is still important to acknowledge that the Chinese texts from which Vietnamese cadres learned about reeducation overwhelmingly emphasised the positive and voluntary aspects, took their pedagogical mission seriously and promised full reintegration into society for graduates.[23]

In the face of obvious disparities between theory and practice, and the lack of public discourse on the subject, survivors have advanced their own theories about reeducation. Huỳnh Sanh Thông acknowledges the positive philosophical underpinnings of reeducation as a process of creating new socialist men, but argues it failed in practice by incentivising greater individualism and heightening disaffection with the government.[24] This criticism is similar to Claude Lefort's distinction of the totalitarian practice of communism versus its ideology, when he clarifies he is 'in no way suggesting that the socialist movement bears the seeds of totalitarianism within itself … It is only too clear that totalitarianism implies the destruction of this movement.'[25] In contrast, Lê Hữu Tri takes a poststructural approach and argues the structures of control in the camps were successful in inculcating in the prisoners the kind of self-discipline that would allow graduates to resume a politically chaste

---

21 Hà Lan and Ngô Cảnh Siêu, *Tham Gia Phát Động Quần Chúng Đã Cải Tạo Tư Tưởng Tôi* [*Participating in the Mass Movement has Reformed My Thoughts*] (Việt Bắc: Sự Thật, 1953).
22 Nguyễn Ngọc Kha, *Cuộc Đấu Tranh Chống Phái Hữu và Cao Trào Thi Đua Tự Cải Tạo Tư Tưởng ở Trung Quốc* [*The Struggle against the Rightists and the Climax of the Reeducation Competition in China*] (Hanoi: Sự Thật, 1958), 52–58.
23 See Minh Tranh and Hoài Nhân, trans, *Cải Tạo Học Tập* [*Reeducation*], 2 vols (Việt Bắc: Sự Thật, 1950).
24 Huỳnh Sanh Thông, ed., *To Be Made Over: Tales of Socialist Re-education in Vietnam*, Lạc-Việt Series No.5 (New Haven, CT, and Boston, MA: Council on Southeast Asia Studies, Yale Center for International and Area Studies and William Joiner Center, UMass, 1988), vii–xiii.
25 Claude Lefort, *The Political Forms of Modern Society: Bureaucracy, Democracy, Totalitarianism* (Cambridge, MA: MIT Press, 1986), 281.

but economically productive role in the new society.²⁶ This position is in turn similar to Michel Foucault's governmentality theory, in which the modern state's power rests on inculcating in its citizenry a self-critical ethos to follow social expectations.²⁷ The ideal graduate of reeducation should become as Václav Havel's famous greengrocer, whose hanging of a positive-sounding communist slogan outside his shop that he does not believe in helps him disguise the true power relations behind his action, and allows him to go on with his daily life as a productive and content, if politically repressed, citizen.²⁸

Reeducation as policy

So how did high-minded Soviet rhetoric and Chinese positivity translate into what was ultimately a very coercive and violent Vietnamese reeducation system? Vietnamese texts on reeducation in the 1950s were much like the Chinese ones in their positive tone and gentler methods (on paper).²⁹ The answer lies primarily in the adaptation of these theories to the local context of the Second Indochina War in the 1960s and early 1970s, which gave rise to the need to efficiently reeducate prisoners of war and those in newly conquered or contested territories. While noting that most subjects of reeducation were cooperative or 'not yet cooperative', reeducation guidebooks from 1963 called for 'severe punishment' to be meted out to those who actively resisted reeducation.³⁰ By 1972, legal experts were advocating life sentences and revocation of citizenship for 'traitors to the revolution'.³¹

---

26 Lê, *Prisoner of the Word*, 11–12.
27 See Michel Foucault, *Discipline and Punish: The Birth of the Prison* (New York, NY: Vintage Books, 1995).
28 Václav Havel and John Keane, eds, *The Power of the Powerless: Citizens against the State in Central-Eastern Europe* (Armonk, NY: M.E. Sharpe, 1985), 10–29.
29 *Thanh Niên Học Tập và Cải Tạo Tư Tưởng* [*Study and Intellectual Reform for Youths*] (Việt Bắc: Trung ương Đoàn Thanh niên Cứu quốc Việt Nam, 1951).
30 *Tài Liệu Học Tập về Công Tác Giáo Dục Cải Tạo* [*Manual on Carrying Out Reeducation*] (Sơn Tây, Việt Nam: Ty Công an Sơn Tây, 1963); *Đề Cương Học Tập về Công Tác Cải Tạo Thường Xuyên Cho Cán Bộ, Nhân Dân, và Các Đối Tượng Trong Diện Cải Tạo* [*Program Outline for the Regular Reeducation of Cadres, the Populace, and those Requiring Reeducation*] (Nghệ An, Việt Nam: Ty Công an Nghệ An, 1964); *Tài Liệu Hướng Dẫn Giáo Dục Cải Tạo* [*Manual on Reeducation*] (Ninh Bình, Việt Nam: Ty Công an Ninh Bình, 1964); *Về Công Tác Cải Tạo Những Người Cần Phải Tiếp Tục Cải Tạo Tại Chỗ* [*On the Reeducation of Those Who Must Remain Detained*] (Thái Bình, Việt Nam: Công tư Hợp doanh Thái Bình, 1966).
31 Viện Luật học, *Một Số Vấn Đề về Nhà Nước và Pháp Luật Việt Nam* [*Issues in the Government and Laws of Vietnam*] (Hanoi: Nhà xuất bản Khoa học Xã hội, 1972), 120–21.

The war also brought a new influence for Vietnamese reeducation: the Republic of Vietnam's own penitentiary system. Infamous for its widespread arbitrary arrests, torture and indefinite imprisonment without trial in tiny and disease-ridden 'tiger cages', the South's penal system saw communist soldiers and cadres experience at first hand a new kind of hell.[32] To counteract international outrage at reports of the squalid conditions in its prisons, the Republic of Vietnam's propaganda machine pumped out beautiful coffee-table books alleging good treatment and gainful reeducation were their mission. By disingenuously lowering the bar of reeducation to that of their dismal penitentiary system, the leaders of the Republic of Vietnam made an unwitting negative contribution to their own fate after 1975.[33]

In retrospect, it is clear the communist government faced no organised threat to its power after the victory of April 1975. However, one ought to be careful not to project this certainty on to revolutionaries who had fought for many years in the jungle and witnessed what they regarded as certain victory snatched from their hands in 1968 and 1972.[34] Indeed, the few party directives that deal with political reeducation at the national level were made in the years immediately after the liberation of Saigon, and their foremost concern was security. Promulgated on 18 April 1975 during the liberation of Central Vietnam and with the collapse of the Saigon Government in sight, Secretariat Directive 218-CT/TW instructed:

> As to prisoners of war: they should be treated humanely according to our policy … In dealing with officers: all must be rounded up, taken into custody, and be educated and perform labour; later on, depending on individual progress they will be classified and dealt with on a case-by-case basis … As for thugs, intelligence elements, military security, psychological warfare officers, pacification operatives, ringleaders of reactionaries, regardless of whether they are troopers, non-commissioned or commissioned officers, all must be rounded up for long-term reeducation, held in a safe and secluded location and be monitored closely.[35]

---

32 Nick Turse, *Kill Anything that Moves: The Real American War in Vietnam* (New York, NY: Metropolitan Books/Henry Holt & Co., 2013); Juan M. Vasquez, 'House Unit's Report on Vietnam Termed "Whitewash" by Aide', *The New York Times*, 8 July 1970, available from: www.nytimes.com/1970/07/08/archives/house-units-report-on-vietnam-termed-whitewash-by-aide-house-unit.html.
33 Vietnam Uỷ-hôi Quôc-gia Thông-tin, *The Republic of Viet Nam Penitentiary System and the Civilian Prisoner Question* (Saigon: National Commission for Information, Republic of Việt Nam, 1973).
34 Marilyn Young, *Vietnam Wars 1945–1990* (New York, NY: Harper Perennial, 1991).
35 Đảng cộng sản Việt Nam [Communist Party of Vietnam], *Văn Kiện Đảng Toàn Tập* [*Complete Document Series of the Party. Volume 37*] (Hà Nội: Nhà xuất bản Chính trị quốc gia, 1998), 121–25, accessed from: dangcongsan.vn/cpv/Modules/News/ListObjectNews.aspx?co_id=30063 [page discontinued], as cited in Vu, 'The Third Indochina War and the making of present-day Southeast Asia', 35.

Directive 219-CT/TW further clarified the classification scheme based on rank, and set out the objectives of reeducation:

- to put them through thought reform
- to mine them for information
- to find out the entire organisational structure and operations of the enemy
- to prevent them from returning to the anti-revolutionary route and open the way for them to make amends for their past actions
- if any of them can be used for converting enemy troops or for security roles then let the Provisional Government pursue their services, but they must be carefully monitored.[36]

The imperatives behind the initial policy of reeducation were mainly security related. Evidently, from the beginning, party leaders envisioned a long process of reeducation for high-ranking ARVN officers, but still one that had the goal of reintegrating them into society in a politically diminished role in which they would look after themselves as per Lê Hữu Tri's argument. While later directives reviewed and refined the process, the fundamental principles behind the policy remained intact.

We should also take a step back and view the reeducation camps in the broader context of state-building. All states desire some degree of control over and security for their citizens, but the Vietnamese state of the late 1970s–80s placed a special premium on social stability. In part, this was born of the difficulty inherent in the unification of two hitherto separate and bitterly opposed halves of the country under a single system; in part, it was a response to new challenges abroad. After 1975, Vietnam became increasingly drawn into the Sino-Soviet Split, resulting eventually in Vietnam's occupation of Cambodia from late 1978 to 1989, a brief border war with China in 1979 and international isolation. The collapse of communism in Eastern Europe towards the end of the 1980s and the resultant instability after the withdrawal of Soviet aid further necessitated the maintenance of a high alert posture throughout the period.[37] The continued operation of some reeducation camps into the late 1980s must be understood in this context.

---

36 Communist Party of Vietnam, *Complete Document Series of the Party*, Vol.36, 142–50.
37 Keith Weller Taylor, *A History of the Vietnamese* (Cambridge, UK: Cambridge University Press, 2013), 561–619. See also Vu, 'The Third Indochina War and the making of present-day Southeast Asia'.

Reeducation camps were also a key factor in another component of state-building: socialist development. More than 30 years of near-continuous war had left the country in ruins. The victory brought both a shift from the *thời kỳ quá độ* ('transitional period') to *xây dựng chủ nghĩa xã hội* ('building socialism') and self-confidence from having defeated the 'American imperialists'. Vietnamese leaders thus saw 1975 as heralding a mature socialist and postcolonial period. Socialist designations that had been stashed away since the First Indochina War suddenly reappeared in 1976: the nation was reunified as the Socialist Republic of Vietnam, and the Fourth Party Congress renamed the Vietnamese Workers' Party the Communist Party of Vietnam. The same congress promulgated an ambitious Second Five-Year Plan that called for 13–14 per cent gross national income growth per annum, doubling within just five years. A key objective of this economic masterplan was the clearing of 1 million hectares of underutilised and war-ravaged land for cultivation.[38] During the war, the fighting in the countryside had driven massive numbers of refugees into the overcrowded cities. By putting the leaders of the fallen regime to work on the frontier as part of their reeducation and encouraging graduates to go to new economic zones in other parts of the frontier, the reeducation camps performed the critical task of redistributing labour from the crowded cities to the labour-scarce frontiers. A study of the broader historical context of the reeducation camps, therefore, reveals how the political reeducation system was critical for both the security and the economic aspects of Vietnam's state-building project.

Reeducation as practice

To fully understand reeducation as a social phenomenon existing beyond the typefaces of books and directives, we need to reconstruct and break down the component parts of the experience, which is no easy task. Many of the accounts on which this chapter is based are written in a very bitter, ideologically charged tone, which is entirely understandable in view of the severe hardships the authors claim to have undergone. While they give us valuable insight into the attitude the reeducation process inculcated in its graduates, the political agenda behind these works also compromises to

---

38 'Báo cáo của Ban Chấp hành Trung ương Đảng tại Đại hội đại biểu toàn quốc lần thứ IV do đồng chí Phạm Văn Đồng trình bày [Report of the Party Central Committee at the 4th National Congress of Deputies Presented by Comrade Phạm Văn Đồng]', in Communist Party of Vietnam, *Complete Document Series of the Party*, Vol.37, 610–701.

a certain extent their factual accuracy. In addition, many of the accounts were written long after the events and contain inevitable factual errors. For example, Ngọc Ngạn Nguyễn claims that in one of his lessons in June 1975, Hồ Chí Minh was hailed as 'the father of the new Socialist Republic of Vietnam', even though the two halves of the country were not reunified under that name until 2 July 1976.[39] There was also bound to be some variance in treatment between different camps and students. There is an inevitable process of self-selection at work among those who emigrated and published memoirs that can skew the data towards the harsher end of the reeducation experience. However, the fact they survived while others did not can skew the data the other way. To mitigate these problems, I focus on mining these accounts for facts rather than opinions. I also employ extensive cross-referencing as my main filter, such that each description of reeducation camps I examine has been testified to by three or more memoirs, making them more likely to be accurate and representative.

Within weeks or months of the fall/liberation of Saigon, officers of the fallen regime received orders via the public announcement system to present themselves according to rank at gathering points. They were told to prepare enough money and/or food for a reeducation course to last between 10 and 30 days—once again, depending on rank—on Secretariat Directive 218-CT/TW's recommendation that cadres, 'depending on the local political conditions, use suitable methods so that those who are still hiding are not too afraid, so that they dare to present themselves'.[40] Those who failed to come in good time received warnings, but most of those summoned willingly gave themselves up, believing the government's promise that reeducation would be only brief.[41] According to official figures, 443,360 people voluntarily turned themselves in to the authorities for reeducation, compared with only 4,162 people arrested by force.[42] This was largely because most believed in the official rhetoric of reconciliation and that they would undergo only a few weeks of relatively pleasant reeducation. Later, students would be continually reminded they

---

39 Ngọc Ngạn Nguyễn, *The Will of Heaven: A Story of One Vietnamese and the End of His World* (New York, NY: Dutton, 1982), 100–101.
40 Communist Party of Vietnam, *Complete Document Series of the Party*, Vol.37, 121–25.
41 Lê, *Prisoner of the Word*, 13–23.
42 Huy Đức, *The Winning Side*, 27.

7. RECYCLING VIOLENCE

had signed up for reeducation willingly. The emphasis on voluntarism and efforts to secure it through deception are proof of the lingering influence of Chinese reeducation theory.

This deception around the date of release would be maintained throughout the reeducation process. Students were told the length of their reeducation was entirely dependent on their progress, and thus release became the ultimate incentive for hard work and obedience.[43] There is the case of a man who saved his camp's entire rice supply during what was most likely a Khmer Rouge attack and who was released a few weeks later, but this seemed to be a rare occurrence.[44] At times, personal political connections, bribery or foreign intervention could also affect the length of a sentence, but this, too, was rare.[45] The indeterminate length of reeducation was reminiscent of the communist guerillas' own marathon struggle during the Vietnam wars, when their hopes for victory were dashed repeatedly in 1968 and 1972.

At first, students were required merely to submit their documents and answer questions, but later they would be asked to write a detailed *kiểm điểm* ('self-reflection').[46] This included their military service history, especially any war crimes they had committed. There was an expectation that soldiers who had served in certain theatres and won certain decorations had committed serious crimes against the revolution, and some prisoners were pressured to fabricate their confessions to match these expectations.[47] They also had to provide detailed biographies of their extended families, which would be used to classify their class background and access to opportunities in the new society after reeducation.[48] The level of detail was astounding: some students were reported to have filled 100-page notebooks and still asked for more paper.[49]

The seemingly bizarre thing about the entire exercise was the government already possessed much of the relevant biographical information: the archives and official papers of the Republic of Vietnam were captured

---

43   Nguyễn, *The Will of Heaven*, 128.
44   ibid., 166–67, 194–96.
45   Vo, *The Bamboo Gulag*, 114–15.
46   Metzner, *Re-education in Postwar Vietnam*, 7–8.
47   Tri Vu Tran, *Lost Years: My 1,632 Days in Vietnamese Re-education Camps*, Indochina Research Monograph 3 (Berkeley, CA: Institute of East Asian Studies, University of California, 1988), 21–22.
48   ibid., 20.
49   Huy Hùng Nguyễn, *Hồi Ức Tù Cải Tạo Việt Nam* [*Memories of Vietnam's Reeducation Prisoners*] (Los Angeles, CA, 2004), 257–59.

almost intact and the communist wartime intelligence network was very efficient.[50] The self-reflections served first and foremost, therefore, as confessions in lieu of a trial, reflecting what Žižek identified as Enlightenment influence on communist philosophy that distinguished it from Nazi philosophy: that there exists an onus on the state to prove a person guilty before condemning them to incarceration.[51] Following Katherine Verdery's landmark research on the secret police archives in Romania, I argue that the writing of *kiểm điểm* should also be understood as an ethnographic exercise.[52] By providing a thick description of their own and their extended family's backgrounds, written in the socialist language of 'crimes against the people and the revolution', the student produces a socialist-style ethnographic self-study by which they would be classified for further reeducation.

The writing of *kiểm điểm* did not end with classification into camps, but became a daily fixture in the life of a student, with some camps requiring students to write up to three times a day.[53] Since writing *kiểm điểm* was not confined to reeducation, and is an act still performed regularly today by all members of Vietnamese society from the time they are schoolchildren, it should be understood also as preliminary training for Southerners to use the formulaic, politically loaded language of official communist documents. According to Alexei Yurchak and Ann Anagnost, this performative use of language is central to communist pedagogy as it shapes the boundaries of 'progressive' or 'civilised' discussion.[54] Far from just an administrative form to be filled out, the writing of *kiểm điểm* was a core component of the quest to make new socialist men and women.

Students were then divided and transported in covered trucks to remote camps. It was common for a student to be cycled through several camps during the process of reeducation. The camps were spread throughout the country from north to south, often housed in abandoned ARVN military bases, French-era cash-crop plantations and former prison camps that had been used by the French and Americans to incarcerate communist

---

50   Tran, *Lost Years*, 19.
51   See Žižek, 'The Two Totalitarianisms'.
52   Katherine Verdery, *Secrets and Truths: Ethnography in the Archive of Romania's Secret Police*, Natalie Zemon Davis Annual Lecture Series (Budapest: Central European University Press, 2014), 155–212.
53   Vo, *The Bamboo Gulag*, 68–70.
54   Alexei Yurchak, *Everything Was Forever, until It Was No More: The Last Soviet Generation*, In-Formation Series (Princeton, NJ: Princeton University Press, 2006), 84–108; Ann Anagnost, *National Past-Times: Narrative, Representation, and Power in Modern China* (Durham, NC: Duke University Press, 1997), 17–44, doi.org/10.1215/9780822378402.

revolutionaries.⁵⁵ There, they were subject to a dual regime of manual labour in the day and political classes in the evenings. Topics for the classes included Marxist philosophy, the imperialist designs of Washington, the puppet regime of the South, the communist government's policy towards those who served the fallen regime and their responsibilities to the new society—all taught in a highly doctrinaire and wholly uncontradictable manner.⁵⁶ They were also taught revolutionary songs and asked to put together variety shows for honoured guests and traditional festivals.⁵⁷ Living conditions were tough: there was very little food and medicine, and communications with families were censored, although this was relaxed somewhat over time, allowing for family visits and even for husbands to spend some nights with their wives.⁵⁸ In many ways, this pattern of social and intellectual life reflects that of the common communist foot-soldier, drafted into the army and sent far from his native North to fight for decades in extremely difficult conditions.

Manual work in the countryside ranged from relatively pleasant vegetable growing and housebuilding to hard labour such as logging and rice farming. While the targets given were not unreasonable for healthy young men, the work was especially onerous for old or disease-stricken city folk who were never given adequate training, tools or food rations to perform their jobs effectively. The clearing of minefields so the land could be made agriculturally productive was the one task feared above all others and accounted for many injuries and fatalities. The teachers were very explicit about the purpose of such labour: it was hoped that by undertaking the same tasks the revolutionaries had performed with their own hands during the war, the former ARVN officers would come to understand and appreciate the work of the men across the barbed wire.⁵⁹

In addition to the presence of armed guards, psychological and organisational tactics played a major role in camp security. In one case, 20 'students' who had reported a concealed weapons storehouse, an anti-government network and even an older brother who did not report for reeducation were 'released'. This turned out merely to be

---

55   Nguyễn, *The Will of Heaven*, 119.
56   Lê, *Prisoner of the Word*, 36–37.
57   Nguyễn, *The Will of Heaven*, 144–53.
58   Tran, *Lost Years*, 35–36; Lê, *Prisoner of the Word*, 75–76.
59   Van Thanh Lu, *The Inviting Call of Wandering Souls: Memoir of an ARVN Liaison Officer to United States Forces in Vietnam Who Was Imprisoned in Communist Re-Education Camps and Then Escaped* (Jefferson, NC: McFarland, 1997), 54–55, 62–64.

a ruse to encourage students to do the self-reflections truthfully and thoroughly.[60] In another instance, a list of students soon to be released was intentionally left in a bathroom to raise students' hopes.[61] And, in an especially elaborate case, students' loyalties were tested by spreading false news of an American invasion and an anticommunist insurrection in the countryside, and having students dig trenches to prepare for the defence of the camp.[62] In concert with deception, the degree of reliance the regime placed on self-discipline was a classic manifestation of Foucaultian governmentality. Rewards were given to certain students derisively called 'antennas' or 'moles' to give information about what their comrades were up to.[63] At certain camps, students took turns to keep watch at night and had responsibility for maintaining discipline.[64] The total control of information and surveillance, including self-surveillance, in reeducation camps not only thwarted opposition, but also replicated the party's total control over information in the society beyond the camps' fences, and served to acclimatise students to life under such a system. These security measures, however, also had the undesired effect of undermining the spirit of comradeship among students and encouraging a strong individualistic ethos.[65]

The combined effect of these psychological tactics was that, even though some of the camps had lax perimeter security and their labours would often take students far from the fenced perimeter, few students tried to escape. The army's total control over the countryside meant all accounts of escape attempts ended in recapture.[66] Punishments were harsh, especially in the beginning when summary executions made examples of deserters.[67] Later, a noncooperative student might find themselves isolated in a CONEX box, confined to a tiger cage, tied to a pole and left in the elements, locked in a wooden cangue and/or having their rations reduced.[68] The locations of the camps and the methods of punishment employed were almost

---

60 Lê, *Prisoner of the Word*, 37–39.
61 Lu, *The Inviting Call of Wandering Souls*, 80.
62 Lê, *Prisoner of the Word*, 96–119.
63 Nguyễn, *The Will of Heaven*, 191–92.
64 Tran, *Lost Years*, 166.
65 Lu, *The Inviting Call of Wandering Souls*, 102–3.
66 ibid., 114; Viết Điền Dương, *Trại Ái Tử và Bình Điền: Hồi Ký Cải Tạo* [*The Ai Tu and Binh Dien Camps: Memoirs of Reeducation*] (San Jose, CA: Thằng Mõ, 1993), 201–7.
67 Nguyễn, *The Will of Heaven*, 117–18.
68 Tran, *Lost Years*, 159–60; Nguyễn, *The Will of Heaven*, 257.

identical to those used by the previous anticommunist regimes, such that they served, whether intentionally or not, to reconstruct even that aspect of the revolutionary experience.

The brutality of the punishment and surveillance regime coupled with the sheer workload and poor living conditions made any direct opposition nearly impossible. But resistance did eventually arise in the form of *stiob*—a concept explained by Dominic Boyer and Alexei Yurchak as 'such a degree of overidentification with the object, person, or idea at which [it] was directed that it was often impossible to tell whether it was a form of sincere support, subtle ridicule, or a peculiar mixture of the two'.[69] A captured deserter, instead of trying to defend themselves, would make an enthusiastic public speech condemning their own actions using all the flowery communist vocabulary they had been taught, for which they could be congratulated by their fellow students with impunity.[70] In another instance, a class received a lecturer's every pronouncement with such loud clapping and ironic repetitions of slogans that order had to be called for.[71] The similarly repressive environments of Vietnam's reeducation camps and the Soviet media had given rise to the same late-socialist aesthetics of resistance.

No anthropological account of the reeducation camps is complete without also paying attention to the other participants in the process: the guards and the students' families. The guards are often portrayed as very young and inexperienced, with those from the North more rigidly indoctrinated and thus less compassionate than those from the South.[72] They ostensibly shared the same diet as the students, but stories about the discovery of milk and chicken in their quarters dispelled this myth.[73] There are also many accounts of corruption and even sexual predation from poor and restless soldiers placed so far from their families, which gravely damaged the image of communist discipline they had carefully cultivated during

---

69   Dominic Boyer and Alexei Yurchak, 'American Stiob: Or, What Late-Socialist Aesthetics of Parody Reveal about Contemporary Political Culture in the West', *Cultural Anthropology* 25(2) (2010): 179–221, doi.org/10.1111/j.1548-1360.2010.01056.x.
70   Nguyễn, *The Will of Heaven*, 258–59.
71   Tran, *Lost Years*, 57–58.
72   ibid., 162.
73   Nguyễn, *The Will of Heaven*, 168.

the war.⁷⁴ In a sense, the guards and even the People's Army of Vietnam were the unmourned victims of the moral degeneration that occurred in the reeducation camp system.

Part of the reason Vietnamese reeducation camps never became permanent communities after closure like the Soviet gulags was because most of those in the Vietnamese camps were men, so no long-term community could be sustained from the original population.⁷⁵ The impact on women has often been ignored. While their husbands were undergoing reeducation, women had to lead the household and find employment—sometimes for the first time. As the communists saw women as having been victims of the old regime, they were encouraged to the forefront of state-building. Most were pressured to join the Association of Liberated Women, whose nightly activities took up enormous time, especially as they were expected to volunteer for public duties. Some women played the black market and the new regime well, using sex and connections as their tools for advancement.⁷⁶ Thus, women were able to play a much more prominent role in the new society as an indirect consequence of their husbands being sent to reeducation, but it is far from clear whether they uniformly appreciated this form of liberation. It is perhaps more accurate to describe their navigation of the new political space after the revolution as an exercise in the politics of disappointment.⁷⁷

Conclusion

In this chapter, I have examined three aspects of political reeducation in Vietnam: theory, policy and practice. In the theory section, I explored the pedagogical impetus behind reeducation and the Soviet and Chinese influences. In the policy section, I explained the security and economic motives behind the setting up of reeducation camps, and how the Second Indochina War shaped local conditions that were substantially different

---

74 Lu, *The Inviting Call of Wandering Souls*, 112–13; Nguyễn, *The Will of Heaven*, 256–71.
75 Anne Applebaum, *Gulag: A History of the Soviet Camps* (Oxford, UK: Penguin Books, 2012); Paul R. Gregory and Valery Lazarev, *The Economics of Forced Labor: The Soviet Gulag* (Stanford, CA: Hoover Institution Press, 2013); Aleksandr Isayevich Solzhenitsyn, *The GULAG Archipelago, 1918–1956: An Experiment in Literary Investigation* (New York, NY: Harper & Row, 1974); Gerhard Toews and Pierre-Louis Vezina, *Enemies of the people*, NES Working Papers No.w0279 (Moscow: New Economic School, December 2020), available from: ideas.repec.org/p/abo/neswpt/w0279.html.
76 Huỳnh Sanh Thông, *To Be Made Over*, 43–77.
77 Jessica Greenberg, *After the Revolution: Youth, Democracy, and the Politics of Disappointment in Serbia* (Stanford, CA: Stanford University Press, 2014), 23–50.

from those in the Soviet Union and China, leading to adaptation of reform-minded theory into punishment-oriented policy. In the practice section, I showed how the process of reeducation closely mirrored the experience of communist cadres during the Vietnam War. Reeducation, therefore, should be understood as another grand socialist experiment in social engineering, but with multiple and evolving objectives. It was to be a magic bullet for many of postwar Vietnam's problems.

Regardless of its objective, political reeducation in Vietnam has largely failed. If its purpose was revenge, reeducation became a massive waste of manpower and resources that also degraded the moral character and discipline of the cadres who took part in the project. If reeducation was meant to facilitate reunification and reconstruction, it was wasteful and unnecessary, because the communists already had total control of the country by 1975, and reeducation merely diminished the nation's pool of skilled labour and delayed the process of national reconciliation. Whereas some former prisoners of Siberian gulags moved back to the cities of Eastern Europe or emigrated, many remained in the areas around the old camps and, with their skills and education, improved the standards of living of these remote areas.[78] By contrast, no Vietnamese reeducation camps became significant settlements after their closure. If reeducation was meant to create new socialist men and women, it failed abjectly: most of its graduates never integrated into the new society even in the depoliticised capacity originally envisioned. Many chose the option of emigration when it was presented to them in the early 1990s. Today, they form the core of overseas dissident groups agitating against the government, driven in part by the suffering and indignity they endured during the reeducation process.[79]

Political reeducation in Vietnam was a grand project that was meant to alleviate the security dilemma of pacifying South Vietnam after the Vietnam War, contribute to reconstruction of the country by employing forced labour to expand agricultural activity and fundamentally remake the men who had served in the Saigon regime as new socialist citizens with limited political rights. It was to do this by placing these men in secluded camps, where they were exposed to an imperfectly reconstructed version of the wartime experience of the average communist revolutionary, from the forced conscription, remote location and shortage of food and

---

78 See Toews and Vezina, *Enemies of the people*.
79 See Hoang, 'From Re-education Camps to Little Saigons'.

medicine to the daily political study, hard labour and similar forms of punishment. Ultimately, political reeducation failed to achieve any of its lofty goals, wasting a great amount of skilled labour, resources and goodwill in the process.

But perhaps reeducation's greatest failure was its inability to break the cycle of political violence that had persisted since the colonial era, as overzealous cadres exercised on their prisoners the same inhumane methods that had been visited on the communists by the French and South Vietnamese regimes. This finding echoes the work of scholars who have found in both international and local contexts that the character of many colonial-era institutions has a longevity far beyond the collapse of formal empires.[80] The high-minded theories of the communist founding fathers were translated into the gulags of Stalin's Soviet Union, carried over into the reeducation camps for the intellectuals of Mao's China and finally adapted to Vietnam's context of postconflict reconstruction and national reconciliation. The political violence of the Vietnamese reeducation camps cannot be understood outside this tragic historical context. The case of the reeducation camps highlights both the difficulty of breaking such cycles of political violence and the greatness of those few leaders in recent memory—Nelson Mandela, Óscar Arias, Ellen Johnson Sirleaf—who managed such difficult transitions successfully.

---

80   Frantz Fanon, *The Wretched of the Earth* (New York, NY: Grove Press, 2004); Daron Acemoglu and James A. Robinson, *Why Nations Fail: The Origins of Power, Prosperity and Poverty* (New York, NY: Crown Publishers, 2012); Peter Zinoman, *The Colonial Bastille: A History of Imprisonment in Vietnam, 1862–1940* (Berkeley, CA: University of California Press, 2001).

8

Return to armed revolution: The Pathet Lao and the Chinese Communist Party on paths to national liberation

Nicholas R. Zeller

The Lao revolution's place in the broader historiography of the Cold War is minor. In globally oriented Cold War histories, Laos is often mentioned only in passing during larger discussions of conflicts in Vietnam or as the setting for the Kennedy administration's diplomatic defeat during the 1961–62 Geneva Conference.[1] The relative absence of Laos from histories of this scale is understandable. Even within Southeast Asia or Indochina–focused histories of Asian communist movements, Laos remains 'in the shadow of Vietnam', with the Lao People's Liberation Army (Pathet Lao) as little more than 'apprentice revolutionaries' serving under the Vietnamese Workers' Party (VWP).[2] More recent studies based on new archival evidence uphold this image of the Pathet Lao and the communist

---

1 See Odd Arne Westad, *The Global Cold War: Third World Interventions and the Making of Our Times* (Cambridge, UK: Cambridge University Press, 2007), 128, 291–92; Paul Thomas Chamberlin, *The Cold War's Killing Fields: Rethinking the Long Peace* (New York, NY: HarperCollins, 2018), 196; and Xiaobing Li, *The Cold War in East Asia* (New York, NY: Routledge, 2018), 103, 105, 133, 136. One exception is Gregg Brazinsky's treatment of CCP involvement in Laos in the mid-1960s: Gregg A. Brazinsky, *Winning the Third World: Sino-American Rivalry during the Cold War* (Chapel Hill, NC: University of North Carolina Press, 2017), 247–51.

2 W.D. Ehrhart, *In the Shadow of Vietnam: Essays, 1977–1991* (Jefferson, NC: McFarland & Co., 1991); MacAlister Brown and Joseph J. Zasloff, *Apprentice Revolutionaries: The Communist Movement in Laos, 1930–1985* (Stanford, CA: Hoover Institution Press, 1986).

party behind it, the Lao People's Party (LPP), as considerably subordinate to the VWP.[3] Based on Vietnamese-language sources, Christopher Goscha has demonstrated that VWP cadres and troops constituted the bulk of communist organisational and military forces in Laos through the 1950s and early 1960s.[4] Using similar sources, Shu Quanzhi has shown the VWP's level of influence came as a shock even to close allies like the Chinese Communist Party (CCP).[5] Chinese-language archival sources and memoirs offer almost nothing to counter the apprentice revolutionary narrative.[6] By the CCP's reckoning, LPP adherence to VWP dictates was an indisputable fact of the Lao revolution and the reason for the CCP to slowly back away from Laos when Hanoi turned to Moscow for aid in 1965.[7]

What, then, can the Lao revolution reveal about trends within Asian communism that cannot be learned simply from the VWP or CCP? In this chapter, I examine Sino-Lao relations between the 1954 and 1961–62 Geneva conferences to argue two points. First, during this period, Laos was an important laboratory for what was an international communist experiment with a political transition to socialism. This experiment required the People's Republic of China (PRC) to conduct a contradictory international relations campaign aimed at supporting the Pathet Lao while wooing the Royal Lao Government (RLG) and its prime minister, Souvanna Phouma, into a position of sustained neutrality. However, neutrality in this context should not be understood as political stasis. Instead, for the CCP, VWP and LPP, neutrality was a precondition for political revolution. Whether this experiment was doomed from the start cannot be known. Its practical failure, however, can be attributed to US intervention in Lao politics in 1958 forcing Souvanna's resignation. Second, this intervention and its fallout coincided roughly with the

---

3   The name was changed to the Lao People's Revolutionary Party in January 1972. Martin Stuart-Fox, *Historical Dictionary of Laos* (Lanham, MD: Scarecrow Press, 2008), 185.
4   Christopher E. Goscha, 'Vietnam and the World Outside: The Case of Vietnamese Communist Advisers in Laos (1948–62)', *South East Asia Research* 12(2) (2004): 141–85, doi.org/10.5367/0000000041524743.
5   Shu Quanzhi, 'From Armed Revolution to Neutralism: China and the Indochinese Revolution, 1950–1954', *Sojourn: Journal of Social Issues in Southeast Asia* 36(1) (2021): 124–56, doi.org/10.2307/26996176.
6   Xiaoming Zhang, 'China's Involvement in Laos during the Vietnam War, 1963–1975', *The Journal of Military History* 66(4) (2002): 1141–66, doi.org/10.2307/3093267; Nicholas R. Zeller, 'A world safe for revolution: China, Laos, and the possibility of revolutionary nationalism' (PhD diss., University of Wisconsin, Madison, 2021).
7   For a summary of the CCP's views on the LPP in late 1965, see Zeller, 'A world safe for revolution', 191–95.

radicalisation of domestic and international politics in the PRC (the Great Leap Forward and the Second Taiwan Strait Crisis) and the Democratic Republic of Vietnam (DRV) (the return to revolutionary violence in South Vietnam through Resolution 15). In this context, the return to armed revolution in Laos in the years before the 1961–62 Geneva Conference should be seen as a symptom of the broader radicalisation of Asian communist politics as well as one of its causes.

The Chinese-language sources I use to reconstruct Sino-Lao relations during this period do not challenge the generally accepted notion that the Pathet Lao was largely subordinate to the VWP. They do, however, provide a new window into how political revolution was intended to work in practice and the mutual reactions from Chinese, Vietnamese and Lao parties when the experiment failed. The result is a case for the importance of the Lao revolution within the history of Asian communism more broadly without taking on the difficult and dubious task of arguing for increased Pathet Lao and LPP agency in creating their own policies and analysis at the highest levels of party organisation. Most previous work on Sino-Lao and CCP–Pathet Lao relations during this period has been limited to analysis of PRC state publications like the *People's Daily* and *Peking Review*.[8] While these can be useful sources for understanding the CCP's presentation of its own positions, they offer little on how those positions were formed. More recent work by scholars like Zhai Qiang and Shu Quanzhi have done much to explain Sino-Vietnamese relations and their impact on Laos. However, even within these more detailed accounts, there is little effort to measure these relations against anything other than an assumed universal framework of national self-interest and national security.[9] While concerns for self-interest and security were certainly real, I argue the CCP's involvement in the Lao revolution should be understood as an attempt by the former to create the necessary conditions for the possibility of the latter. This approach is rooted in a specifically socialist political theory of international relations, which, while sometimes mentioned in mainstream histories, often garners little

---

8   Chae-Jin Lee, 'Communist China and the Geneva Conference on Laos: A Reappraisal', *Asian Survey* 9(7) (1969): 522–39; Chae-Jin Lee, *Communist China's Policy toward Laos: A Case Study, 1954–67* (Lawrence, KS: Center for East Asian Studies, University of Kansas, 1970); Paul F. Langer, *The Soviet Union, China, and the Pathet Lao: Analysis and Chronology* (Santa Monica, CA: RAND Corporation, 1972).
9   Qiang Zhai, *China and the Vietnam Wars, 1950–1975* (Chapel Hill, NC: University of North Carolina Press, 2000); Shu, 'From Armed Revolution to Neutralism'.

serious consideration. Thus, to understand the full international context of the return to armed revolution in Laos, it is necessary to reconstruct this theory.

Internationalism and intervention in Lenin, Marx and Mao

In 1916, Lenin offered what I argue is a first principle for understanding CCP thought on the Lao crisis during the late 1950s and early 1960s:

> Socialists must not only demand the unconditional and immediate liberation of the colonies without compensation—and this demand in its political expression signifies nothing else than the recognition of the right to self-determination; they must also render determined support to the more revolutionary elements in the bourgeois-democratic movements for national liberation in these countries and assist their uprising—or revolutionary war, in the event of one—against the imperialist powers that oppress them.[10]

According to Lenin, the task of socialist internationalists was twofold. First, they must demand an end to the political oppression of colonised people by demanding the right to self-determination. This demand was separate from the demand to end the economic oppression of the working classes by the capitalist class—an oppression that could occur with or without a system of liberal equality between states.[11] Second, although bourgeois-democratic movements should be supported in general, the more radical elements within these movements should be specifically sought out, lending socialist internationalism an interventionist quality. However, there were normative limits to intervention. Lenin quoted Friedrich Engels in an 1882 letter to Karl Kautsky: '[T]he victorious proletariat can force no blessings of any kind upon any foreign nation without undermining its own victory by doing so.'[12] The point was this: a socialist party or state must work to support movements for national

---

10   V.I. Lenin, 'The Socialist Revolution and the Right of Nations to Self-Determination', in *V.I. Lenin: Collected Works. Volume 22* (Moscow: Progress Publishers, 1964), 151–52.
11   V.I. Lenin, 'The Discussion on Self-Determination Summed Up', in *V.I. Lenin: Collected Works. Volume 22*, 326.
12   ibid., 352; Karl Marx and Friedrich Engels, *Karl Marx and Friedrich Engels: Selected Correspondence* (Moscow: Progress Publishers, 1955), 351.

liberation as part of a global revolution against capitalism but could not itself liberate a colonised nation. Instead, the goal was to create the conditions for the possibility of national liberation that would lead to class revolution.[13]

The history of socialist anticolonial leaders in Asia may make the connection between Marxism and the right to national self-determination appear to be straightforward. It is not. Marx's most famous line on revolution, nation and nationality comes from the 'Manifesto of the Communist Party': 'Workers have no nation of their own.'[14] This passage is traditionally understood as an expression of Marx's economism, in which the relations of capital were expected to destroy traditional forms of social organisation, pitting a global bourgeoisie against a global proletariat.[15] However, in the same passage, Marx added that once the proletariat had seized political control, it would 'constitute the nation itself' in a form that was 'still nationalistic, even if not in the bourgeois sense of the term'.[16] For the bourgeoisie, for whom 'nationality is already dead', the nation largely served as an ideological tool—a concept used to obscure exploitative class relations.[17] National liberation in the bourgeois sense would mean the freedom to continue these relations free of overt foreign political domination. Beyond this limited goal, Marx and later Lenin were clear that bourgeois nationalism was both exclusive and coercive.[18] On the other hand, because it would be an organic community free of class exploitation, the nation created through proletarian revolution would be inclusive and noncoercive. That this nation would differ from the bourgeois concept points to the ambiguity at the heart of nationalist politics.

---

13   That contemporary scholars of the PRC's international relations in the Mao era have missed the avowed interventionism of this tradition is evidenced in Julia Lovell's recent study of global Maoism in which the interventionism of Mao and other CCP leaders is presented as a revelation instead of an expected outcome. Julia Lovell, *Maoism: A Global History* (New York, NY: Knopf, 2019).
14   Karl Marx and Friedrich Engels, 'Manifesto of the Communist Party', in Karl Marx, *Marx: Later Political Writings*, Terrell Carver, ed. (Cambridge, UK: Cambridge University Press, 1996), 17.
15   Michael Löwy, 'Marxists and the National Question', *New Left Review* (96) (April 1976): 81–100.
16   Marx and Engels, 'Manifesto of the Communist Party', 17.
17   Karl Marx and Friedrich Engels, *The German Ideology* (New York, NY: International Publishers, 1966), 57.
18   Neil Harding, *Lenin's Political Thought: Theory and Practice in the Democratic and Socialist Revolutions. Volume 1* (Chicago, IL: Haymarket Books, 2009), 297–98; Paul Le Blanc, *Unfinished Leninism: The Rise and Return of a Revolutionary Doctrine* (Chicago, IL: Haymarket Books, 2014), 132.

Although Marx never developed systematic thoughts on proletarian nationalism and internationalism, his writing about Ireland leaves some clues. Marx and Engels advised Irish revolutionaries that national liberation was necessary for workers' emancipation, but it was not enough on its own. After all, not all exploitative landlords were British.[19] In addition to independence from Britain, Ireland needed an agrarian class revolution. However, Marx believed class revolution in Ireland was the task of the Irish alone, writing to Engels that, with the 'best intentions in the world the English cannot accomplish this for them'.[20] Instead, the role of the English worker in Irish national liberation was to demand Ireland's right to secede.

Lenin cited these ideas in his own writing on national self-determination to develop a prescriptive theory of socialist internationalism. He argued it was 'the Marxist's *bounden* duty' to demand radical democratisation of relations between all nations, even the right of oppressed nations to secede, as part of the development of conditions for socialist revolution.[21] The demand for the right to secede from the proletariat of oppressor nations was to be met by the demand of the working people of oppressed nations to reunite after liberation on equal terms—dialectically related political demands that Georg Lukács summarised as 'secede' and 'belonging together'.[22]

Nationalist sentiment—ambiguous in its politics—could therefore be harnessed and radicalised, but only under certain conditions. At the Second Congress of the Communist International (Comintern) in 1920, Lenin and Indian Marxist M.N. Roy argued there was a growing trend of colonised, reformist bourgeoisie both committed to national self-determination and willing to collaborate with imperialist powers—at least in quelling radical movements. Therefore, communists needed to be selective in their support for bourgeois-democratic liberation movements, endorsing them only 'when they are genuinely revolutionary, and when their exponents do not hinder our work of educating and organizing in

---

19   Kevin B. Anderson, *Marx at the Margins: On Nationalism, Ethnicity, and Non-Western Societies* (Chicago, IL: University of Chicago Press, 2010), 123.
20   Marx and Engels, *Karl Marx and Friedrich Engels*, 196–97.
21   Emphasis in original. V.I. Lenin, 'Critical Remarks on the National Question', in *V.I. Lenin: Collected Works. Volume 20* (Moscow: Progress Publishers, 1964), 34.
22   Georg Lukács, *History and Class Consciousness: Studies in Marxist Dialectics* (Cambridge, MA: MIT Press, 1971), 276.

a revolutionary spirit the peasantry and the masses of the exploited'.[23] In other words, nationalist movements would only be supported when they had the potential to turn the new or potential national state into what Marxist-Leninists would later refer to as a weakest link—a society in which integration into the global capitalist system through imperialism was not yet complete and in which the lack of bourgeois hegemony allowed the possibility of socialist revolution. As is shown below, the lack of bourgeois hegemony in Laos was a key element in CCP belief that Souvanna and the RLG could be swayed into friendly relations with the PRC and DRV. To be clear, this meant Souvanna was favoured not for his neutrality, but for a combination of his neutrality and his political weakness.

During the War of Resistance against Japan, Mao Zedong drew on this theory of internationalism to assess the global impact of the Chinese Revolution. He wrote that China's defeat of Japanese imperialism would help weaken a power that oppressed people throughout Asia. Participation in China's nationalist war was, therefore, 'applied internationalism'.[24] Following Lenin and Roy, Mao argued that foreign domination and a nationalist movement were not enough to turn China into a weakest link. National liberation required proletarian leadership, if not a thoroughly proletarian movement. To that end, Mao argued early in the revolution that CCP success was due to the strength of its organisations as well as the indirect nature of imperialism in China and conflict within right-wing factions, the existence of peasants and cadres with organising experience, the dynamism of the revolutionary situation and the existence of a standing Red Army.[25] Understanding Sino-Lao relations between the Geneva conferences requires appreciation of the interventionist element of socialist internationalism as well as the different forms this intervention could take. During the period of experimentation with political revolution, this intervention took the form of diplomatic overtures to the RLG—most notably, the defence of Lao neutrality, combined with CCP support for the LPP and Pathet Lao via Hanoi. Souvanna's ouster in 1958 was

---

23 John Riddell, ed., *Workers of the World and Oppressed Peoples, Unite! Proceedings and Documents of the Second Congress, 1920. Volume 1* (New York, NY: Pathfinder, 1991), 213.
24 Mao Zedong, 'The Role of the Chinese Communist Party in the National War', in *Selected Works of Mao Tse-Tung. Volume 2* (New York, NY: Pergamon Press, 1965), 196.
25 Wang Hui, 'Twentieth-Century China as an Object of Thought: An Introduction, Part 1, The Birth of the Century—The Chinese Revolution and the Logic of Politics', *Modern China* 46(1) (2020): 35–36, doi.org/10.1177/0097700419878849; Mao Zedong, 'Why Is It That Red Political Power Can Exist in China?', in *Selected Works of Mao Tse-Tung. Volume 1* (New York, NY: Pergamon Press, 1965), 65–67.

a significant setback for the political revolution strategy, but it was not until Kong Le's coup in 1960 and the response from Phoumi Nosavan and US-backed right-wing forces that Laos met conditions like those in China described by Mao above. These events—out of the hands of any communist force in Laos—encouraged and enabled the return to armed revolution. They made Laos a weakest link. They also coincided with a period of general radicalisation among Laos's communist neighbours and, therefore, gave changes in LPP strategy a larger international significance than is generally appreciated. In the leadup to the 1961–62 Geneva Conference, CCP policies towards Laos were still highly interventionist, seeking to create the conditions for the possibility of national liberation and class revolution. The form of that revolution had simply changed to a violent one.

The experiment with political revolution, 1954–58

Before the 1954 Geneva Conference, CCP leaders knew little about the Pathet Lao beyond a few observations made by members of a Chinese military advisory group stationed in northern Vietnam beginning in 1950.[26] Although Mao and Stalin agreed in 1949 that the CCP would assume leadership of the revolution in Asia, CCP work in Indochina before 1954 was overwhelmingly focused on northern Vietnam. The leader of the Chinese Military Advisory Group in Vietnam, Wei Guoqing, did not meet the public face of the Pathet Lao, the 'Red Prince' Souphanouvong, until March 1953—three years after the mission began.[27] Therefore, despite a long history of CCP–VWP interactions, CCP leaders entered the 1954 Geneva Conference with almost no knowledge of the situation in Laos. PRC Premier and Foreign Minister Zhou Enlai entered the conference in support of the VWP's call to partition Pathet Lao–controlled provinces from the rest of the country under the assumption that the Lao

---

26 For CCP–Pathet Lao interactions before 1954, see Lee, *Communist China's Policy toward Laos*, 14; Langer, *The Soviet Union, China, and the Pathet Lao*, 19; Xiaoming, 'China's Involvement in Laos during the Vietnam War', 1142; Shu, 'From Armed Revolution to Neutralism', 139.

27 Yu Huachen, 'Yuan Yue Kang Fa Douzheng Zhong de Wei Guoqing Tongzhi [Comrade Wei Guoqing during the Struggle to Aid Vietnam and Resist France]', in *Zhongguo Junshi Guwentuan Yuan Yue Kang Fa Shilu: Dangshi Ren de Huiyi [Record of Chinese Military Advisors in the War to Aid Vietnam and Resist France: Recollections of the People Involved]*, Benshu Bianxiezu, ed. (Beijing: Zhonggong dangshi chubanshe, 2002), 68.

resistance government was a substantial force.²⁸ In fact, the strength of the resistance government came mostly from the 17,600 Vietnamese troops and cadres operating in Laos.²⁹ Laos did not have its own communist party. Lao communists had been part of the Vietnamese-run Indochinese Communist Party, which began reorganisation into separate national parties in 1951. Although a Pathet Lao resistance government headed by Souphanouvong was founded in August 1950, four years later, it was still not powerful enough to earn its own delegation at Geneva. Instead, the DRV and French delegations agreed the former would act as the resistance government's representative.³⁰ The LPP was not established until March 1955.

Given this weak position, Zhou and the Chinese delegation decided in late May 1954 to soften their demands in Laos.³¹ The legitimacy of Souvanna and the RLG in the eyes of most Lao people, Zhou believed, meant the PRC and DRV delegations would have to recognise them as well.³² This took the partitioning of Laos off the table. The DRV delegation—most notably, Foreign Minister Phạm Văn Đồng—was slow to agree with this conclusion. However, as Pierre Asselin has shown, the VWP leadership eventually endorsed many of Zhou's positions.³³ At a meeting between the Soviet, PRC and DRV delegations in Geneva on 26 June, Phạm promoted partitioning liberated areas around the northern Lao cities of Sam Neua, Phongsaly and Muang Xay. He proposed these regions could be connected to liberated areas in central Laos, which would be linked to liberated areas inside Vietnam along Highway 12. However, he was also willing to relinquish control across southern and central Laos to safeguard claims in the north. Phạm argued that in the event of a coalition government, it probably would not be necessary to alter the existing administration of liberated areas. The Soviet delegation's K.V. Novikov protested that a coalition government would be a loss in Laos and pressed Phạm for further details, but Phạm claimed he required more time to form a better

---

28   Qiang, *China and the Vietnam Wars*, 56.
29   Goscha, 'Vietnam and the World Outside', 150.
30   'Shuangfang Silingbu Daibiaotuan Huiyi Jianbao Di Shi Yi Hao [Eleventh Brief on Meetings between Both Sides' Command Delegations]', 18 June 1954, 206-00047-11, People's Republic of China Foreign Ministry Archives [hereinafter PRCFMA].
31   Shu, 'From Armed Revolution to Neutralism', 144–45.
32   'Telegram, Zhou Enlai to Mao Zedong, Liu Shaoqi, and the CCP Central Committee [Excerpt]', 30 May 1954, Wilson Center Digital Archives, Washington, DC, [hereinafter WCDA], available from: digitalarchive.wilsoncenter.org/document/121150.
33   Pierre Asselin, 'Choosing Peace: Hanoi and the Geneva Agreement on Vietnam, 1954–1955', *Journal of Cold War Studies* 9(2) (Spring 2007): 95–126.

position. According to the PRC delegation's Li Kenong, Phạm expressed agreement with a proposal from Zhou that their efforts focus only on those areas closest to the PRC and DRV borders.[34] He had not, however, fully agreed with the political impossibility of partition.

At a now famous meeting with Hồ Chí Minh and Võ Nguyên Giáp in Liuzhou, China, in early July, Zhou elaborated the CCP's new position, explaining: 'The Indochina question has already been internationalised; this is its key characteristic. It has gone beyond the internationalising scope of the Korea question.'[35] Because the United States feared the expansion of Chinese influence into Vietnam, it would not abide the demands communist powers were currently making at Geneva. The best way to avoid an unwinnable global war was to isolate the United States through peaceful negotiations. Zhou argued that further war in Laos would push the RLG towards the United States and, therefore, a peaceful political path to socialism was necessary. This, however, did not mean abandonment of revolution in Laos. Under certain conditions, peaceful political methods were part of the 'internationalist mission of the international communist movement … Otherwise, it is not true internationalism.'[36] The Vietnamese were convinced.

In mid-July, Zhou organised a meeting with RLG Foreign Minister Phoui Sananikone and Secretary for Defence Kou Voravong to discuss their apprehension over the new plan to allow the Pathet Lao to consolidate itself in Houaphanh and Phongsaly provinces to await political integration into a new coalition government. Phoui and Kou were concerned this was effectively the same as partitioning Laos, but Zhou argued that focusing Pathet Lao forces in the north would reduce the possibility of local conflicts while the RLG and Pathet Lao worked out plans for a new government. He also assured them that the Five Principles of Peaceful Coexistence currently being promoted internationally by himself, Jawaharlal Nehru

---

34 'Su, Zhong, Yue San Fang Huiyi Neirong Jianbao [Brief on the Contents of Meetings between the Soviet Union, China and Vietnam]', 26 June 1954, 206-00046-34, PRCFMA.
35 Zhonggong Zhongyang Wenxian Yanjiushi [Chinese Communist Party Central Committee Documents Research Office], *Zhou Enlai Nianpu* [*Chronicles of Zhou Enlai*]. Volume 1 (Beijing: Zhongyang wenxian chubanshe, 1997), 394.
36 'Main Points, Zhou Enlai's Presentations at the Liuzhou Conference [Excerpt]', 3 July 1954, WCDA, available from: digitalarchive.wilsoncenter.org/document/121159.

8. RETURN TO ARMED REVOLUTION

and U Nu fully applied to China–Laos.[37] Agreements were signed on 20 July and 21 July that called for the formation of a coalition government through national elections, guaranteed the withdrawal of foreign military troops and established the International Commission for Supervision and Control (ICSC) to oversee elections and the Pathet Lao–RLG ceasefire.[38]

For Asian communist participants, the purpose of the agreements was to allow the Pathet Lao to consolidate its strength while planning a political transition to socialism via elections—a strategy the VWP adopted for itself in Vietnam.[39] While Zhai is correct to note the CCP represented a 'moderating element' in these negotiations, the essential point is that Lao neutrality was conceived of as a potentially new means for revolution.[40] Long-term RLG neutrality was never the goal. Instead, following Leninist principles of socialist internationalism, the Chinese, Lao and Vietnamese communist parties began working to create the best possible conditions for the Pathet Lao to launch a political revolution. To this end, despite withdrawal agreements, many advisers from the DRV stayed in Laos, integrating themselves into every level of Pathet Lao organisation.[41]

Beijing quickly implemented a 'dual policy' of covert party-to-party and overt state-to-state relations, sending aid to the Pathet Lao via Hanoi while facilitating agreements between the RLG and DRV at Bandung, Indonesia, in April 1955.[42] The PRC's role in Laos's political revolution quickly included attempts to get Souvanna to agree to aid. In August 1956, Souvanna led an official delegation to Beijing to discuss the possibility of aid agreements. Members of the delegation included Katay

---

37 'Minutes of Conversation between Zhou Enlai and Laotian Foreign Minister Phoui Sananikone [Summary]', 18 July 1954, WCDA, available from: digitalarchive.wilsoncenter.org/document/111067. The document in the WCDA names 'Ku Keolavong' as the RLG defence minister; this is a mistranslation.
38 Arthur J. Dommen, *Conflict in Laos: The Politics of Neutralization* (New York, NY: Praeger Publishers, 1971), 79.
39 Asselin, 'Choosing Peace'.
40 Qiang, *China and the Vietnam Wars*, 62.
41 'Zhu Laowo Sangnu Gongzuozu tong Yuenan Guwentuan Guanxi Wenti [Problems in Relations between the Sam Neua Working Group and the Vietnamese Advisors]', 24 January 1964 – 25 June 1965, 106-00902-02, PRCFMA.
42 I borrow this term from Carr's analysis of early Soviet foreign policy. Edward Hallett Carr, *The Bolshevik Revolution, 1917–1923. Volume 3* (New York, NY: W.W. Norton & Co., 1985), 70. For more on Bandung, see Zhonghua Renmin Gongheguo Waijiaobu Danganguan [People's Republic of China's Foreign Ministry Archive], ed., *Zhonghua Renmin Gongheguo Waijiao Dangan Xuanbian (Di Er Ji): Zhongguo Daibiaotuan Chuxi 1955 Nian Ya Fei Huiyi [Selections from the People's Republic of China's Foreign Affairs Archives (No. 2): The Chinese Delegation Attends the 1955 Afro-Asia Conference]* (Beijing: Shijie Zhishi Chubanshe, 2007), 117.

Don Sasorith, Boun Oum and others among Laos's right wing. Chinese sources do not mention Souphanouvong. Reporting on their departure from Laos, the PRC Foreign Ministry noted positively the absence of US representatives in Vientiane when the delegation left for Guangzhou. Despite his anticommunist position in Laos, Katay was the chief author of a joint statement from the Chinese and Lao governments promising close economic and cultural relations despite different 'political and social systems'.[43]

In China, Souvanna, whom Guangzhou officials found to be 'calm, seasoned, self-effacing, [and] amiable', stated he was seeking assistance in acquiring equipment for a planned sugar refinery and matchstick factory.[44] Discussions of Lao underdevelopment continued in Beijing, where the delegation told Zhou that Lao rice production had barely reached subsistence levels since the end of the war with France. CCP officials quickly set to work trying to ease their guests' minds about their socialist neighbour and encourage more aid requests. In Shenyang, Souvanna's delegation was shown an iron factory to demonstrate the potential economic development that could result from closer relations with the PRC. Economic concerns were not the only thing CCP officials believed they needed to overcome. While in Beijing, the delegation was also shown the decidedly nonrevolutionary film *The Butterfly Lovers*, based on a Tang Dynasty folktale, to demonstrate the preservation of pre-revolutionary culture, and, while touring the Forbidden City, they were introduced to a group of ethnic-minority visitors to assuage concerns about Han chauvinism.[45] The trip ended with a meeting with Mao at Zhongnanhai, where Mao and Zhou explained the PRC was not a threat to Laos. Mao congratulated Souvanna on the negotiations he had conducted with Souphanouvong thus far and promised the PRC would support the RLG in accordance with the Five Principles of Peaceful Coexistence. He also offered to allow the RLG to build a consulate in Kunming once formal relations were established.[46] As the delegation prepared to return home, Zhou stressed the PRC did not oppose Souvanna seeking aid from the

---

43 'Laowo Shouxiang Fuma Fang Hua Jianbao [Brief on the Lao Prime Minister Souvanna's Trip to China]', 16–31 August 1956, 204-00029-02, PRCFMA; 'Zhou Enlai Zongli he Laowo Shouxiang Fuma de Lianhe Shengming [Premier Zhou Enlai and Lao Prime Minister Souvanna's Joint Statement]', 16–31 August 1956, 204-00029-03, PRCFMA.
44 'Brief on the Lao Prime Minister Souvanna's Trip to China', PRCFMA.
45 ibid.
46 Chinese Communist Party Central Committee Documents Research Office, *Mao Zedong Nianpu* [*Chronicles of Mao Zedong*]. Volume 2 (Beijing: Zhongyang Wenxian Chubanshe, 2013), 604.

United States but also emphasised that any assistance from Beijing would come 'with no political conditions attached'.[47] PRC Foreign Ministry reports at the time reflected much satisfaction with the trip's results. Years later, however, officials recalled this visit left them with 'many doubts'; Souvanna was only willing to speak of Sino-Lao friendship in general terms and would 'not even dare to accept assistance'.[48]

In 1957, despite efforts to the contrary by US Ambassador to Laos J. Graham Parsons, Souphanouvong and Souvanna came to an agreement for the Pathet Lao's political party, the Neo Lao Hak Xat (NLHX, Lao Patriotic Front), to participate in national elections and to integrate the Pathet Lao's two remaining battalions into the Royal Lao Army.[49] To this point, the VWP had maintained substantial numbers of clandestine advisory personnel in Laos, many of whom were removed after negotiations secured the potential for a political struggle against the RLG.[50] Elections were held in May, and candidates from the NLHX and a left neutralist party, Santiphap Pen Kang, won 13 of 21 seats. In July, at Souvanna's request, the ICSC voted to end its work in Laos.[51] The results of the election and Souvanna's openness with his socialist neighbours sparked anger in Washington. The United States responded by revoking aid payments, resulting in Souvanna's ouster and replacement with the anticommunist Phoui Sananikone in the summer of 1958. Real power, however, was held by Defence Minister Phoumi Nosavan.

The details of these events are well known to Lao historians. What concerns us here is the international communist response. Before the Phoumi–Phoui coup, the plan between the LPP, VWP and CCP was to build Lao leftist forces to the point that Souvanna would have no choice but to maintain neutrality. Again, however, the point of neutrality was to prevent military alliances with capitalist powers, allowing for a political transition to socialism. Souvanna demonstrated his commitment to Lao neutrality through the 1957 agreements, exhibiting a long-established

---

47 Chinese Communist Party Central Committee Documents Research Office, *Chronicles of Zhou Enlai*, 612.
48 'Cable from the Chinese Foreign Ministry, "Regarding the Planned Discussion by Our Side during Souvanna Phouma's Upcoming Visit to China"', 12 April 1961, WCDA, available from: digitalarchive.wilsoncenter.org/document/120880.
49 Martin Stuart-Fox, *Buddhist Kingdom, Marxist State: The Making of Modern Laos* (Bangkok: White Lotus Press, 2002), 58.
50 Goscha, 'Vietnam and the World Outside', 175.
51 Seth Jacobs, *The Universe Unraveling: American Foreign Policy in Cold War Laos* (Ithaca, NY: Cornell University Press, 2012), 81; Stuart-Fox, *Historical Dictionary of Laos*, 139.

survival strategy by Lao elites to maintain contradictory relations with neighbouring states.[52] No external power or substantial faction in Laos was interested in such a solution. While the PRC conducted its own attempts to manipulate Lao politics through aid, its embassy in Hanoi described US financial manipulation as 'nothing more than a big racket'.[53] With the Pathet Lao too weak to begin an effective armed revolution, Beijing turned to diplomacy. China's domestic and foreign-language press made the case that the change in government had violated the Geneva agreements and requested the British and Soviet governments—co-chairs of the 1954 conference—reinstate the ICSC. The British, however, were satisfied with Phoui and claimed the remaining DRV troops in Laos were the real violation. In June 1959, members of the PRC, DRV and Polish embassies in Moscow met with Georgy Pushkin to learn that the British still believed restoring the ICSC against Phoui's wishes would constitute international interference.[54]

The possibility of political revolution continued to decline. Phoui's government began purging NLHX members and placed Souphanouvong and other Pathet Lao officials under house arrest. In Beijing, Deputy Foreign Minister Zhang Wentian told the Soviet ambassador that Kaysone Phomvihane and the LPP leadership had begun discussions with the VWP Central Committee on how to continue the revolution. Zhang predicted guerilla war but warned that the Pathet Lao was not ready—a position shared by the VWP's Working Committee on Laos.[55] The Pathet Lao's guiding principles were still to 'uphold the Geneva agreements, advocate for domestic unity, support the royal family, and take the road of peaceful neutrality and national independence'.[56] However, the CCP believed they must add opposition to US support for the Phoui government. In October 1959, Kaysone travelled to Beijing, where Mao assured him the right-wing takeover in Vientiane was evidence of the Pathet Lao's

---

52 C.J. Christie, 'Marxism and the History of the Nationalist Movements in Laos', *Journal of Southeast Asian Studies* 10(1) (1979): 146–58.
53 'Wo Zhu Yuenan Shiguan Guanyu Laowo Zhengju Qingkuang de Zhuanti Baogao [Our Embassy in Vietnam's Report on the Political Situation in Laos]', 15 August 1958 – 4 November 1958, 106-00416-04, PRCFMA.
54 'Rineiwa Waizhang Huiyi Qingkuang [Conditions at the Foreign Ministers' Meeting in Geneva]', 22 June 1959 – 6 August 1959, 110-00849-03, PRCFMA.
55 'Zhang Wentian Fuwaizhang Huijian Sulian zhu Hua Dashi Youjin Tan Laowo Jushi Deng Wenti [Deputy Foreign Minister Zhang Wentian Receives Soviet Ambassador to China Yudin to Discuss the Situation in Laos and Other Questions]', 25 May 1959, 109-00873-04, PRCFMA. For the VWP Central Committee's position, see Goscha, 'Vietnam and the World Outside', 177.
56 'Deputy Foreign Minister Zhang Wentian Receives Soviet Ambassador', PRCFMA.

strength; Phoui, Phoumi and the United States were acting out of fear of that strength. 'The final victory is yours,' Mao said, 'but you still have many difficulties in this stage.'[57] The following January, PRC Foreign Minister Chen Yi told Soviet ambassador Stepan Chervonenko that, while preparations were being made to protect the border, neither Beijing nor Hanoi intended to send military units into Laos (this did not include VWP advisers). Chen repeated an assessment he gave to Kaysone: 'The Lao struggle depends entirely on [the Lao people] … China and Vietnam can only aid them politically and sympathise spiritually; everything depends on their self-reliance in the struggle against the reactionaries.'[58] Following Engels' advice to Kautsky, the CCP could force no blessings on Laos. By this time, however, civil war had already begun.

The Kong Le coup: Laos becomes a weakest link

While conditions worsened for the Pathet Lao, politics in the PRC and DRV radicalised significantly. In late August 1958, Mao ordered the shelling of Jinmen Island, near Xiamen, where Guomindang troops were stationed. Designed to antagonise the United States and demonstrate the PRC's commitment to anti-imperialism internationally, the Second Taiwan Strait Crisis brought Sino-US relations to the brink of nuclear war.[59] Mao also launched his radical Great Leap Forward policies, which rapidly reorganised China's rural population into people's communes and resulted in the deaths of 15 to 25 million people.[60] As Lorenz Lüthi notes, the crisis was also created to mobilise the Chinese population for the implementation of Great Leap policies—all of which was a response to the deepening Sino-Soviet Split.[61] By the summer of 1959, the Great

---

57   Chinese Communist Party Central Committee Documents Research Office, *Mao Zedong Nianpu* [*Chronicles of Mao Zedong*]. *Volume 4* (Beijing: Zhongyang Wenxian Chubanshe, 2013), 201.
58   'Chen Yi Fuzongli Jiejian Sulian zhu Hua Dashi Qierwonianke de Tanhua Jilu [Record of Discussions between Vice-Premier Chen Yi and Soviet Ambassador to China Chervonenko]', 22 January 1960, 109-00934-01, PRCFMA.
59   Michael M. Sheng, 'Mao and China's Relations with the Superpowers in the 1950s: A New Look at the Taiwan Straits Crises and the Sino-Soviet Split', *Modern China* 34(4) (October 2008): 478, doi.org/10.1177/0097700408315991.
60   Felix Wemheuer, *A Social History of Maoist China: Conflict and Change, 1949–1976* (Cambridge, UK: Cambridge University Press, 2019), 151.
61   Lorenz M. Lüthi, *The Sino-Soviet Split: Cold War in the Communist World* (Princeton, NJ: Princeton University Press, 2008), 81.

Leap's failures were apparent. Mao received criticisms in a private letter from Defence Minister Peng Dehuai, prompting Mao to double down on his recent radicalism at the Lushan Conference in July and August.[62] Space does not allow for a full account of these events. The point is only to demonstrate that, as conditions worsened for the Pathet Lao (Souphanouvong was arrested in July 1959), the PRC was undergoing a process of radicalisation that would inform its interpretation of and recommendations for the revolutionary road ahead. This was also true of the DRV.

VWP leaders took the project of political revolution in Laos seriously. The Pathet Lao and RLG signed a ceasefire on 30 October 1957. Two weeks later, VWP officials agreed with the LPP Central Committee that it was time to begin removing political and military advisers from 'basic units'.[63] Plans to remove the key Vietnamese advisory group, the Group 100, were created in December and implemented in early 1958 while both parties prepared for the integration of the Pathet Lao into the Royal Lao Army and the next phase of the planned political struggle.[64] Although the VWP had more direct incentive to intervene in Lao affairs than the CCP, part of this intervention was the fruit of radicalisation vis-a-vis South Vietnam. In January 1959, the VWP Central Committee held its fifth plenum to discuss the course of the revolution in the south. At the plenum, Lê Duẩn made the case that growing US support for Saigon's military forces and recent communist defeats meant more aggressive action was necessary. Ngô Đình Diệm's Army of the Republic of Vietnam had become an 'alarming and immediate threat'.[65] In response, the VWP Central Committee passed Resolution 15—a policy statement Asselin describes as the most pivotal since the autumn of 1954.[66] In essence, Resolution 15 called for consolidating power in the DRV while supporting a renewed policy of armed revolution in the South. On 16 July 1959, the VWP created the Working Committee on Laos, headed by Võ Nguyên Giáp—a new group in charge of aiding and advising the Pathet Lao.

---

62   For a full discussion of the Lushan Conference, see ibid., 126–35.
63   Goscha, 'Vietnam and the World Outside', 175.
64   ibid., 176.
65   Pierre Asselin, *Hanoi's Road to the Vietnam War, 1954–1965* (Berkeley, CA: University of California Press, 2013), 52.
66   ibid., 53.

8. RETURN TO ARMED REVOLUTION

The VWP set about preparing the Pathet Lao armed forces, training as many as 700 troops in Vietnam and outfitting them with Soviet weapons by the end of that year.[67]

Neither the diplomatic campaign nor the preparations for armed struggle, however, did much to change the stalemate in Lao politics. Already overdetermined, the return to armed revolution was finally made possible by Kong Le's coup in August 1960 and Phoumi's countercoup the following December. The origins of Kong Le's coup remain uncertain. There is a tendency, however, to attribute Kong Le's motivations to Western interference.[68] Available Chinese sources offer a 1964 interview with Kong Le's lieutenant (and later Patriotic Neutralist) Deuane Sounnarath in Guangxi. Deuane recounted only that officers in Kong Le's US-backed forces developed serious criticisms of their regular orders to conduct 'operations to suppress the people'.[69] No solutions emerged, however, until a meeting was held in Attapeu, where a unanimous decision was made to break from US control. While Deuane's account of the planning lacks detail, it is worth noting he and Kong Le were on opposite sides of the Lao civil war by 1964. If Deuane had known of the Western origins of Kong Le's actions, it is likely he would have reported them to help undermine Kong Le's already weak position with the CCP.

Whatever the motivations, once in control of Vientiane, Kong Le demanded an end to 'Lao fighting Lao' and a return to genuine neutrality. Souvanna was put back in charge of the government.[70] In the *People's Daily*, Souphanouvong and the NLHX immediately credited their own work for awakening the national spirit among all classes of Lao society—'even officers and rank-and-file soldiers in the Royal Lao Army'.[71] In internal documents, the LPP praised the coup as a 'great victory for creating the conditions to expand the anti-US national united front and developing

---

67 Goscha, 'Vietnam and the World Outside', 177, 179.
68 For a review of differing theories on his motives, see Jacobs, *The Universe Unraveling*, 156.
69 'Dun Shangxiao Jieshao Laowo Qingkuang Jianbao [Brief on Colonel Deuane's Presentation of Conditions in Laos]', 2 February 1964, X1-35-116, 127–139, Guangxi Zhuang Autonomous Region Archives.
70 Martin Stuart-Fox, *A History of Laos* (Cambridge, UK: Cambridge University Press, 1997), 112.
71 'Laowo Aiguo Zhanxian Dang Shengming Zhichi Geming Weiyuanhui Zhuyao Zhengce [The Lao Patriotic Front Declares Support for the Revolutionary Committee's Main Policies]', *Renmin Ribao* [*The People's Daily*], 13 August 1960.

Lao revolutionary forces'.[72] Souvanna announced he would continue his previous policy of neutrality and begin negotiations with the Pathet Lao to create another coalition government. Souphanouvong responded that the NLHX was ready to begin at any time.[73]

Discussions between the LPP, VWP and CCP officials in Hanoi concluded the coup was of 'the national-democratic type' despite the fact it was 'launched by middle and lower officers in the Royal Lao Army and pro-French forces also took part'.[74] Their optimism, however, did not extend to Souvanna, who quickly travelled to Savannakhet to convince Phoumi to rejoin the government. The two agreed that Souvanna's government was unconstitutional and that Kong Le would be judged in parliament for his actions. Further, Souvanna and Phoumi both blamed the Pathet Lao for the current civil war. As for Kong Le, he rapidly grew close to the Pathet Lao, providing their armed forces with weapons and allowing a battalion of 500 troops to be stationed outside Vientiane. This alignment lasted only until the end of the 1961–62 Geneva Conference. Although the CCP, VWP and Pathet Lao saw Kong Le's passionate call for Lao neutrality and independence as a chance to revitalise a united front for national liberation, none supported him enough to extend military aid. Instead, aid to Kong Le's forces came from the Soviet Union and stopped flowing after the signing of the Geneva agreements. For the Pathet Lao, the next step was to pressure Souvanna into formalising relations with the socialist world.

Ironically, the biggest factor pushing Souvanna towards the socialist camp came from Thai dictator Sarit Thanarat, Phoumi's cousin. Sarit instituted a blockade of Vientiane along the Mekong River and the situation rapidly deteriorated. During a meeting between Souvanna and the king in mid-September in Luang Prabang, thousands rallied in Vientiane to demand Souvanna establish formal relations with socialist countries.[75] Officials at

---

72 Zhonggong Zhongyang Duiwai Lianluobu Yazhou Erzu [Chinese Communist Party Central Committee's Foreign Liaison Department, Second Asia Group], *Laowo Renmin Geming Dang Lijie Zhongyang Quanhui Wenjian Huibian* [*Documents from All Previous Plenary Sessions of the Lao People's Revolutionary Party Central Committee*] (Beijing: Zhonggong Zhongyang Duiwai Lianluobu Yazhou Erzu, 1975), 72.
73 'Laowo Aiguo Zhanxian Dang Zhuxi Sufanufeng Qinwang Fabiao Shengming [Statement from Lao Patriotic Front Chairman Prince Souphanouvong]', 25 August 1960, *The People's Daily*.
74 '1960 Nian Xiabannian Laowo Qingkuang Tongbao (Juemi) [Bulletin on the Situation in Laos in the Second Half of 1960 (Top Secret)]', August 1960, 106-00558-02[F], PRCFMA.
75 '1960 Nian Xiabannian Laowo Qingkuang Tongbao (Juemi) [Bulletin on the Situation in Laos in the Second Half of 1960 (Top Secret)]', September 1960, 106-00558-02[F], PRCFMA.

the Burmese Embassy in Phnom Penh reported to Chinese diplomats that their counterparts in Vientiane were pressuring Souvanna to formalise relations with the Soviet Union, the PRC and the DRV, but Souvanna felt the existence of Republic of China (Taiwan) and South Vietnamese embassies in the capital was an obstacle to relations with Laos's socialist neighbours. The Soviet Union was the only available option. Although the question of aid remained unresolved, the PRC Foreign Ministry's Chen Shuliang assured Soviet diplomat I.I. Safronov the Lao people had made 'great advances' compared with 1959. The PRC was willing to help, but, as Chen Yi told Pathet Lao leaders one year earlier, everything depended on the Lao people conducting their own revolution. 'Through struggle,' Chen said, 'the Lao people will actualise their strength.'[76]

The LPP Central Committee's evaluation of the revolutionary situation identified three distinct powers. First, the 'people's forces' consisted of the NLHX, Kong Le's coup committee and Santiphap Pen Kang, led by left neutralist Quinim Pholsena.[77] The Central Committee believed this alliance could be used to reach every stratum of Lao society, including the Buddhist *sangha* (monastic order) and military personnel. Although this new united front had increased the Pathet Lao's military strength, the Central Committee noted several weaknesses in their own operations. The mass movement remained shallow, with loose organisational discipline. The number of cadres was lacking, and those who were available were neither firm in their political positions nor experienced. The development of Pathet Lao armed forces had far outpaced the development of their 'political qualities', and party organisations within the military struggled for control. The Central Committee feared 'the party's organisational and leadership capacity cannot meet the demands of developments in the people's movement'.[78] In other words, the emergence of a broad nationalist movement was certain, but, as in earlier Marxist-Leninist thought, its political direction was ambiguous and malleable. From the LPP's perspective, the danger was it lacked the capacity to transform this movement into a socialist revolution. Nationalist sentiment could, at any point, be harnessed by the second power in Laos.

---

76 'Wo Waijiaobu Chen Shuliang Sizhang yu Sulian zhu Hua Shiguan Canzan Safulong Guanyu Laowo Wenti de Tanhua Jilu [Record of Discussions between Our Foreign Ministry Bureau Chief Chen Shuliang and Soviet Embassy Attaché Safronov on Problems in Laos]', 28 September 1960, 106-00557-01, PRCFMA.
77 Chinese Communist Party Central Committee's Foreign Liaison Department, Second Asia Group, *Documents from All Previous Plenary Sessions of the Lao People's Revolutionary Party Central Committee*, 74.
78 ibid., 74.

This second power was the 'capitalist and feudalist classes', including high-level civil servants and pro-French intellectuals with some nationalist consciousness.[79] The most significant figure in this group was Souvanna himself, but also several smaller neutralist factions whose politics were 'wavering and indeterminate'.[80] This was the reformist bourgeoisie Lenin and Roy delineated in opposition to revolutionary nationalist movements. The CCP had long warned that these elites were only reliable in a national liberation movement when foreign domination jeopardised their own political power.[81] What was not acknowledged in LPP reflections on Souvanna's vacillations was that the United States and the communist parties involved were actively preventing the possibility of nonalignment.[82]

Kaysone and other Central Committee members saw Souvanna as ultimately inclined towards Western powers but vacillating between France and the United States. His goal in negotiations with the Pathet Lao was to obstruct their movement and, abetted by the United States, use peaceful methods to eliminate them. Souvanna, despite his conflicts with Phoumi, was always more likely to align with pro-US forces than with the Pathet Lao. On the matter of Souvanna's 'essential duplicity', the LPP, VWP and CCP were in total agreement.[83] Given the LPP's assessment of its own weaknesses, Kaysone and his allies agreed the best hope was to combine nationalist pleas with military strength to compete with the West for Souvanna's ultimately ephemeral loyalty, forcing him into alignment with the socialist bloc; elements of the political revolutionary strategy were still in play. The final power was the pro-US feudal forces and comprador bourgeoisie led by Phoumi and Boun Oum, a former prince of the Champasak royal house in southern Laos and former French

---

79   ibid., 75.
80   ibid.
81   Liu Shaoqi, *Internationalism and Nationalism* (Beijing: Foreign Languages Press, 1952), available from: www.marxists.org/reference/archive/liu-shaoqi/1952/internationalism_nationalism/index.htm.
82   Bruce Lockhart argues the high level of US intervention in Lao politics, coupled with Souvanna's inability to build enough personal political support, was a key element in preventing the possibility of nonalignment. The CCP, VWP and LPP were equally involved in actively blocking such a possibility. Bruce Lockhart, 'The Fate of Neutralism in Cambodia and Laos', in *Cold War Southeast Asia*, Malcolm R. Murfett, ed. (Singapore: Marshall Cavendish Editions, 2012), 206, 210.
83   'Bulletin on the Situation in Laos in the Second Half of 1960', November 1960, 106-00558-02[F], PRCFMA.

8. RETURN TO ARMED REVOLUTION

collaborator.[84] The Pathet Lao succeeded in pushing Phoumi's military out of Sam Neua in September 1960 and believed (wrongly) he had become isolated in Savannakhet despite US and Thai support.

In October, efforts to control Souvanna seemed to have worked. Former US ambassador to Laos J. Graham Parsons returned to Vientiane to demand Souvanna end negotiations with the Pathet Lao, cancel plans to formalise relations with the Soviet Union and enter an immediate ceasefire with Savannakhet. Souvanna refused, and the CCP was quick to credit the Pathet Lao and Kong Le with forcing him away from the United States. Soon, however, Washington decided it had no choice but to restore aid to the government in Vientiane. As the LPP predicted, Souvanna became emboldened by US support. When the Soviet ambassador to Laos arrived in Vientiane, Kong Le held what Souvanna believed to be an overly lavish reception for which he placed Kong Le under house arrest. Souvanna then sent conservative neutralist Ouan Rattikun to Luang Prabang to establish new Royal Lao Army units with US funds. From Hanoi, the PRC Embassy reported Souvanna's attitude towards the Pathet Lao had become 'unyielding'.[85] It would not last.

The winds changed once more in November. Dissatisfied with Souvanna, Parsons outlined a plan to have him replaced once more with Phoui, whom the British and French were more likely to support than Phoumi. Before US offices in Vientiane could begin planning, however, a Royal Lao Army battalion in Luang Prabang revolted. Away from Vientiane, Ouan Rattikun had defected to Phoumi's side and, on 11 November, the Third Infantry Battalion in Luang Prabang launched a mutiny against the Souvanna government. Souvanna responded by denouncing US aid to Phoumi as illegal and planning friendship delegations to Beijing and Hanoi. His government in Vientiane would not last long enough for these trips to occur. The Eisenhower administration removed all restraints on US Central Intelligence Agency (CIA) payments to Phoumi's forces and, on 23 November, Phoumi began marching towards Vientiane.[86]

---

84 For Boun Oum's relations with the French, see Stuart-Fox, *A History of Laos*, 60. Ian Baird recasts Boun Oum's opposition to Souvanna in terms of grievances between once competing royal houses. Ian G. Baird, 'Elite Family Politics in Laos before 1975', *Critical Asian Studies* 53(1) (2021): 22–44, doi.org/10.1080/14672715.2020.1869573.
85 'Bulletin on the Situation in Laos in the Second Half of 1960', October 1960, 106-00558-02[F], PRCFMA.
86 Dommen, *Conflict in Laos*, 161–62; Jacobs, *The Universe Unraveling*, 166–67.

On 8 December, Colonel Kouprasith Abhay, head of the Chinaimo military base, announced he had switched allegiance to Phoumi by launching a coup in Vientiane that lasted less than 24 hours. Kong Le's troops were able to repel Kouprasith's troops back to Chinaimo, but the situation had become dangerous. Souvanna and much of his cabinet flew to Phnom Penh the following day. A smaller group fled to Rangoon (Yangon) while Quinim Pholsena stayed behind to run what was left of the RLG. Phoumi's forces entered Vientiane on 13 December, beginning a bloody two-day battle with Kong Le. During the fighting, the Lao king dissolved Souvanna's government, claiming he had allowed communists to usurp power, and placed Phoumi's organisation in charge, with Boun Oum as the new premier.[87] Overpowered, Kong Le's forces retreated to the Plain of Jars, where they regrouped with the Pathet Lao.

Although the Battle of Vientiane did little to change the military balance of power in Laos, the new alignments it created within the revolution are important. It temporarily forced many 'wavering and indeterminate' neutralists into an alliance with the Pathet Lao by creating two competing governments—one headed by Phoumi and Boun Oum in Vientiane, the other by Souvanna in Khang Khay, Xiangkhouang Province. These governments found patrons in the capitalist and socialist blocs, respectively. By the reckoning of the LPP Central Committee, it was a major service to their cause in a revolution still conducted 'under the slogan of peaceful neutrality, independent democracy, and respect for the constitution and king' because it allowed them to claim an even larger united front with no middle ground.[88] For the moment, nationalists among the Lao governing elite could side with the Pathet Lao or lose power completely. Phoumi's coup forced Quinim Pholsena, for example, to permanently align with the Pathet Lao and champion the PRC's aid in Laos until his assassination in 1963. Further, Kaysone and other LPP leaders also understood the Battle of Vientiane to signal a transition from political to armed struggle. The immediate tasks for the party were to combine direct attacks with the guerilla tactics already in use, strengthen party discipline within the military and expand base areas, all while 'tightly seizing' the national united front.[89]

---

87   Jacobs, *The Universe Unraveling*, 168–69.
88   Chinese Communist Party Central Committee's Foreign Liaison Department, Second Asia Group, *Documents from All Previous Plenary Sessions of the Lao People's Revolutionary Party Central Committee*, 90.
89   ibid., 95.

Martin Stuart-Fox argues that the coups in the last half of 1960 'marked no significant turning point' for Laos; they only worsened the chances of avoiding civil war.[90] The latter point is true; however, looking at this history from the socialist political theory of international relations outlined above, creating the possibility for civil war is precisely what made the coups significant. In the spring of 1960, the Sino-Soviet Split went public when Mao commissioned a series of polemical essays on Lenin's thought, arguing for armed resistance to capitalist imperialism and criticising Soviet capitulation to the West.[91] The radicalism of 1958–59 had now become an open rift in the socialist bloc. Alignment with the VWP and CCP placed the LPP on the side of this rift that favoured armed revolution, but conditions in Laos offered no clear means for beginning this revolution until the coups of 1960. Laos was now a rough approximation of the weakest link Mao described during the Chinese Revolution.[92] US rule was indirect and depended to some extent on the collaboration of less bellicose Western powers. Contradictions among Western powers and the United States' methods of sponsoring a strongman instead of direct intervention meant nonsocialist powers in Laos had repeated conflicts among themselves, grappling for international patrons. Meanwhile, the Pathet Lao and its military had been gaining experience in a constantly changing revolutionary situation for 10 years. What was missing from Mao's equation was disciplined party organisation, but that would have to wait until a veneer of neutrality had been restored.

The 1961–62 Geneva Conference and the return to armed revolution

In January 1961, two neutralist members of Souvanna's government, Pheng Phongsavan and Khamsouk Keola, travelled through Kunming on their way from Rangoon to Sam Neua. There they met with Chen Yi and General Luo Ruiqing. In the weeks prior, the existence of two internationally recognised governments in Laos and the alignment of Souvanna and Kong Le with the Pathet Lao at Khang Khay allowed the PRC to send overt military aid to the Pathet Lao without upsetting Souvanna,

---

90 Stuart-Fox, *A History of Laos*, 118.
91 Jeremy Friedman, *Shadow Cold War: The Sino-Soviet Competition for the Third World* (Chapel Hill, NC: University of North Carolina Press, 2015), 51.
92 Mao, 'Why Is It That Red Political Power Can Exist in China?'.

claiming it was unconditional aid to the rightful Lao government. Chen promised Pheng that a 'large arsenal of weapons, ammunition, provisions, and medicines' was still sitting in Vietnam waiting to be delivered and the PRC was prepared to continue aid indefinitely.[93] Chen assured his Lao guests they were part of a larger Afro-Asian movement against imperialism that required military conflict. 'International negotiations could be held,' Chen said, 'but not for the purpose of coming to any final resolution … Victory on the front lines is the main determining factor in Laos.'[94] General Luo drove the point home, emphasising the limits of diplomatic struggle against the United States. The Souvanna government could try to 'call on the international community' to end US military support for Phoumi, but Luo said: 'If you are defeated, relying on world-wide condemnation alone won't cause the Americans to retreat.'[95]

This attitude, shared by the LPP, CCP and VWP, was markedly different from that used by Zhou Enlai in response to Cambodian Prince Norodom Sihanouk's proposal of an enlarged meeting of the 1954 Geneva participants to negotiate an end to the Lao civil war. Sihanouk wrote to Zhou on 1 January with the proposal, and two weeks later the Chinese premier, who had been in Burma discussing the Lao crisis with Prime Minister U Nu, replied in full support. As international support for the conference grew, Zhou wrote to Sihanouk again, saying the PRC Government would support a conference of Geneva participants based on the principle of non-interference in Lao internal governance and respect for Lao unity and territorial integrity.[96]

Meanwhile, in mid-February, Chen Yi made clear to Soviet Ambassador Chervonenko that the Pathet Lao, the VWP and the CCP would not enter any conference with real hope of a political solution. Chen revealed that officials on the VWP and CCP central committees agreed that 'hope should be placed in a victory on the front lines'.[97] In addition to the public

---

93 'Transcript of Talks during Receipt of Representatives from Laos by Chen Yi and Vice Premier Luo Ruiqing', 16 January 1961, WCDA, available from: digitalarchive.wilsoncenter.org/document/120873.
94 ibid.; emphasis added.
95 ibid.
96 Chinese Communist Party Central Committee Documents Research Office, *Zhou Enlai Nianpu* [*Chronicles of Zhou Enlai*]. *Volume 2* (Beijing: Zhongyang Wenxian Chubanshe, 1997), 384, 390.
97 'Chen Yi Fu Zongli jiu Laowo Wenti Jiejian Sulian Zhu Hua Dashi Qierwonianke de Tanhua Jilu yiji Su Dashi Mianjiao Zhong Fang de Beiwanglu [Record of Discussions from an Interview Vice-Premier Chen Yi Granted to Soviet Ambassador to China Chervonenko and the Memorandum the Soviet Ambassador Delivered to the Chinese Side]', 13 February 1961, 109-03754-03, PRCFMA.

8. RETURN TO ARMED REVOLUTION

conditions for negotiation Zhou had elaborated to Sihanouk, the Pathet Lao needed to win enough military victories to place Phoumi's forces in a clear defensive position. Although a reconvening of the 1954 Geneva participants was inevitable, calling a ceasefire before the Pathet Lao had achieved a favourable military position would create serious problems during negotiations. Chen explained that, although the thoughts of some among the Pathet Lao and Kong Le's forces remained unclear, the CCP was pushing for the rapid development of military capacity before the conference. The CCP's views, however, were not intended to have any impact on the socialist camp's continued public campaign to negotiate. In Chen's words: 'Political struggle and armed struggle should be coordinated. As armed struggle better develops, the more the benefit to political struggle.'[98] It was too risky for the Pathet Lao to enter negotiations from a weak position.

Strengthening the Pathet Lao's position presented a challenge. In early February, the DRV sent troops across the border to replace Pathet Lao forces fighting to defend the Plain of Jars and was preparing to send two companies to Sam Neua with another battalion waiting for orders in Hanoi.[99] The CCP strongly disagreed. Chen feared the increased presence of DRV troops in violation of the 1954 Geneva agreements, if discovered, could cost the socialist camp several key allies (particularly Souvanna and Sihanouk) and expand the conflict beyond Lao borders. It also provided a pretext for direct invasion from US and Southeast Asia Treaty Organization forces. On the other hand, Chen was emphatic that fighting the Lao people's fight for them was of little use. As always, they could be aided, and the PRC had already sent enough ammunition, clothing and medical supplies to outfit 10,000 fighters. However, the CCP believed the Lao revolution only mattered if the Lao people conducted it themselves. While there were surely national security concerns behind this position, it was also in keeping with the normative commitment dating back to Marx that a society must conduct its own revolution. By Chen's estimation, there were already enough People's Liberation Army (PLA) troops in Guangxi and Yunnan to occupy Laos in less than a month.[100] Yet, doing this

---

98   ibid.
99   Dommen reports that DRV troops entered Laos in early January at Kong Le's request. Arthur J. Dommen, *The Indochinese Experience of the French and the Americans: Nationalism and Communism in Cambodia, Laos, and Vietnam* (Bloomington, IN: Indiana University Press, 2001), 431.
100 'Record of Discussions from an Interview Vice-Premier Chen Yi Granted to Soviet Ambassador to China Chervonenko', PRCFMA.

263

would risk nuclear war for actions inconsistent with principles of socialist internationalism. On 10 February, Chen expressed the same position to a Lao delegation to Beijing headed by Sisana Sisane, director of Radio Pathet Lao. The issues around upholding the 1954 Geneva agreements or determining Lao neutrality through a new conference were 'just quarrels' that could 'only be places in a subordinate position' to armed struggle.[101]

From Phnom Penh, Souvanna spent the early months of 1961 promoting Sihanouk's idea for a conference on Lao neutrality with letters to the Kennedy administration in Washington. As Phoumi suffered repeated losses and Boun Oum's government showed weakness outside Vientiane, US officials began to listen.[102] One official in the Kennedy administration went as far as calling a US-controlled Laos 'an incredible fantasy'.[103] In April, Souvanna began a tour of socialist and neutral countries to promote the conference. Souphanouvong stopped in Beijing on his way to meet Souvanna in Moscow, where he told Zhou that Souvanna's opinion towards the Pathet Lao and its international allies had changed because of aid provided to Khang Khay. However, he remained suspicious of the Pathet Lao growing too powerful. Souvanna attempted to place the Pathet Lao under Kong Le's command, but Souphanouvong convinced him they were already fighting on the same side. Souvanna then tried to turn to Khamouane Boupha, a neutralist commander in Phongsaly, to create a separate military force, but the onset of the rainy season prevented a meeting. It is unclear whether this move would have worked. In 1963, against Kaysone's advice that Khamouane was a worse ally than Souvanna, the CCP themselves began offering aid to Khamouane, ultimately bringing him into the Pathet Lao's united front.[104] In any case, Souphanouvong informed his contacts in Beijing that Souvanna favoured military nonalignment and domestic anticommunism. He was unlikely to ever see the United States as the 'supreme enemy'.[105]

---

101 'Transcript of the Reception between Vice Premier Chen Yi and the Delegation from Laos', 10 February 1961, WCDA, available from: digitalarchive.wilsoncenter.org/document/120875.
102 Dommen, *The Indochinese Experience of the French and the Americans*, 437.
103 Jacobs, *The Universe Unraveling*, 237.
104 'Liao Fang dui Kham Wen Kanfa [The Lao Side's Views on Khamouane]', 9 October 1963 – 2 December 1963, 106-01094-02, PRCFMA.
105 'Transcript of Talks during Zhou Enlai's Reception of Prince Souphanouvong', 17 April 1961, WCDA, available from: digitalarchive.wilsoncenter.org/document/120881.

8. RETURN TO ARMED REVOLUTION

The Lao princes returned to the PRC together on 22 April to meet with Zhou, Chen Yi and Mao in Hangzhou.[106] True to Souphanouvong's estimation, Souvanna expressed more fear of a Thai invasion of Laos than of US machinations. He expressed to Mao his hope that 'reason and the patriotism of the Lao people' could still convince Phoumi and Boun Oum to end the civil war.[107] Mao pointed out these people had already been part of a failed coalition government in 1958; they would only be willing to compromise as long as they were weak. The trip ended with the PRC committing to construction of a road connecting Xishuangbanna to Phongsaly and a joint statement establishing formal relations.[108]

The Geneva conference began on 16 May 1961. Chen Yi served as the PRC's head delegate and successfully demanded the NLHX be given its own representative, unlike at the 1954 conference. Debates quickly broke out about the nature of Lao neutrality. US Secretary of State Dean Rusk began by demanding that neutrality in Laos go beyond nonalignment to include assurances against threats within and beyond Laos. Chen responded that the US ruling class always understood people's movements as aggression organised by foreign powers and Rusk's real aim was to prevent the possibility of revolution within a neutral Laos.[109] The demand for 'permanent neutrality' was, therefore, clear interference in Lao domestic affairs. Outside formal conference sessions, Chen and Sihanouk worked with the French and Indian delegations to orchestrate negotiations between Souvanna, Souphanouvong and Boun Oum in Zurich. On 22 June, several weeks after presidents Kennedy and Khrushchev mutually agreed in Vienna to back away from Laos, the three princes agreed to a framework for a tripartite coalition government.[110]

Through the end of 1961, negotiations were consistently in favour of the Pathet Lao and CCP positions. In July 1961, although it maintained that party discipline lagged behind the military buildup, the LPP Central Committee counted among its united-front allies 'government members,

---

106 Chinese Communist Party Central Committee Documents Research Office, *Chronicles of Zhou Enlai*, Vol.2, p.407.
107 'Mao Zedong Zhuxi, Zhou Enlai Zongli deng Tong Lai Fang de Laowo Lingdaoren Tanhua Jilu [Record of Discussions between Chairman Mao Zedong, Premier Zhou Enlai and Visiting Lao Leaders]', 22 April 1961 – 6 May 1961, 204-01438-01, PRCFMA.
108 'Record of Conversation between Prime Minister Souvanna Phouma and Crown Prince Souphanouvong', 23 April 1961, WCDA, available from: digitalarchive.wilsoncenter.org/document/120882.
109 Lee, 'Communist China and the Geneva Conference on Laos', 529.
110 Qiang, *China and the Vietnam Wars*, 103.

265

the military, the youth, the *Sangha*, the gentry, and well known figures like Souvanna Phouma and Pheng Phongsavan'.[111] They believed the breadth of the united front was particular to the Lao revolution and could only aid in fanning dissent among Phoumi's ranks. However, within this front, there was still a pressing need to settle questions regarding the composition of the coalition government and elections. In short, the Pathet Lao had gone to great lengths to create broad nationalist sentiment but feared it could not ride the wave to a strictly socialist victory: 'We must cleverly make the Party Central Committee's line become the line of the united front.'[112] In the autumn, a PRC consulate was built in Phongsaly while He Wei, former ambassador to the DRV, and Liu Chun, PLA officer and future ambassador to Laos, established an economic and cultural mission near Souvanna's government headquarters in Khang Khay.[113]

In December, conference participants produced the 'Draft Declaration on the Neutrality of Laos', requiring all foreign troops and personnel to leave Laos within 30 days and banning all military aid except when contributing to the RLG's national defence. As negotiations appeared to be winding down, Boun Oum suddenly revoked his support for the Zurich agreements and demanded positions for Phoumi loyalists within the new cabinet. Phoumi himself still hoped for direct military intervention from the United States. In January, he began reinforcing a garrison in the northern town of Nam Tha near territory occupied by Pathet Lao and DRV forces. The US State Department, hoping to be rid of the Lao issue, decided that if Nam Tha was overrun by opposing forces, the responsibility would be Phoumi's. US officials even enlisted Sarit Thanarat to convince Phoumi to back down, but Phoumi refused. After weeks of mortar shelling, the Pathet Lao occupied Nam Tha on 6 May. The United States, which had accepted a Souvanna-headed government as the only viable exit, sent no aid.[114] Phoumi was forced back to the negotiating table. In June, Souphanouvong, Souvanna and

---

111 Chinese Communist Party Central Committee's Foreign Liaison Department, Second Asia Group, *Documents from All Previous Plenary Sessions of the Lao People's Revolutionary Party Central Committee*, 113.
112 ibid., 115.
113 'Zhongguo Renming He Wei he Liu Chun Wei Zhu Laowo Jingji Wenhua Daibiaotuanzhang Futuanzhang [China Appoints He Wei and Liu Chun as Head and Deputy Head of the Economic and Cultural Delegation]', 28 June 1961 – 18 October 1961', 117-00898-03, PRCFMA.
114 Dommen, *The Indochinese Experience of the French and the Americans*, 447–51.

Boun Oum, this time joined by Phoumi, met in Khang Khay to work out an agreement for a coalition government. The Geneva agreements on Lao neutrality were finally signed on 23 July 1962.

Speaking to an Albanian group, Deng Xiaoping offered the CCP's assessment of the results. Moving forward, it would be much more difficult for the United States to intervene in Lao affairs. 'The most important thing,' Deng said, 'is to gain time for the Pathet Lao to strengthen its work with the masses.'[115] The coalition itself would likely fail, but its success had never been the point. From the perspective of the Asian communist parties, the coalition existed only to buy time. As Kaysone recalled in a speech to the LPP Central Committee in 1965, the immediate task after Geneva was to defend the coalition government to 'promote a situation of short-term stability to create favourable conditions for comprehensively building revolutionary strength'.[116] In the final days of the Geneva conference, Chen Yi gave a victory speech claiming no power could now suppress the Lao people's desire for national liberation. Lao neutrality might mean tensions would arise elsewhere in Southeast Asia, but, he believed, the conference had 'broken through a link in the chain of tensions … and we should enlarge this breakthrough'.[117]

Conclusion

The return to armed revolution in Laos was an overdetermined event. It was caused by the failure of the experiment with political revolution in Laos; fragmentation between Lao neutralists and the right wing, allowing the Pathet Lao to continue consolidating its own strength; the radicalisation of politics in Vietnam and China; and broader calls for support for violent resistance to imperialism in the Sino-Soviet Split. Chinese-language sources neither increase nor diminish the agency the LPP or broader Pathet Lao had in deciding on this transition, leaving 'apprentice revolutionaries' an apt phrase. However, reevaluation of Lao

---

115 'Fifth Official Meeting between the Delegation of the Albanian Labor Party and the Delegation of the Chinese Communist Party', 19 June 1962, WCDA, available from: digitalarchive.wilsoncenter.org/document/110806.
116 'Liao Fang Zhongyang Wenjian: Kaishan zai Zhongyang Changwei Guangda Huiyi Shang de Baogao Deng [The Lao Side's Central Committee Documents: Kaysone's Report at the Central Committee's Expanded Standing Committee Meeting]', 1 April 1965 – 30 July 1965, 106-00896-02, PRCFMA.
117 'Chen Yi's Speech at Geneva', *Peking Review*, 27 July 1962, 6.

revolutionaries' agency is not necessary to understand events in Laos as both a symptom and a cause (one among many) of larger transformations in the aims of Asian socialist internationalism in the late 1950s and early 1960s.

Throughout this period, Sino-Lao relations, from the CCP's perspective, were built on Leninist concepts aimed at creating the conditions for the possibility of a Lao revolution. Although national security concerns about conflicts along its borders were serious, the CCP's behaviour from the mid-1950s to the end of the 1961–62 Geneva Conference was broadly consistent with internationalist commitments dating back to Marx. Although the means of revolution changed, the continuous line from the CCP was its normative commitment to 'forcing no blessings' on the Pathet Lao. The revolution was theirs to make; the CCP could only remove certain obstacles (namely, US intervention) and provide military and economic aid.

For the LPP—by their own estimation, organisationally weak throughout this period—the goal was to create and lead the broadest united front possible. Lukács, reflecting on debates before the Russian Revolution, insisted that for Lenin's ideas on national liberation to be effective, movements in oppressed and oppressor nations needed to work in opposite directions. As the proletariat in oppressor nations must demand the right of oppressed nations to secede, the revolutionary elements of oppressed nations must operate under the slogan 'belonging together'. The intended result was a transitional phase of equal association between proletarian nations. The existence of socialist states changed this equation. Thus, while the CCP attempted to win over nonsocialist nationalists through international aid and public support for neutrality (secession), the Pathet Lao demanded the formalisation of relations with the socialist bloc (belonging together). To this end, it is significant to note that the roots of the rift between Beijing and Hanoi that emerged in the late 1960s can already been seen in the CCP's disapproval of the VWP's over-involvement in Laos in early 1961. The VWP broke with this framework by sending troops into Laos in February 1961 against CCP warnings that the LPP needed to operate on its own. Lê Duẩn worried in July 1961 that his party's overbearing involvement had made the LPP incapable of organising on its own, but the two parties' closeness continued throughout the civil war.[118]

CCP–LPP relations eventually soured in 1968 over the Pathet Lao's refusal to follow CCP recommendations on land reform and peasant mobilisation and its turn, along with the VWP, to the Soviet Union for aid. After the signing of the Geneva agreements in 1962, however, CCP and LPP leaders felt they had gained a significant win. Celebrating the PRC's National Day at the mission in Khang Khay in October that year, Nouhak Phoumsavan, a member of the NLHX and LPP central committees and close associate of Kaysone, made a toast: 'Today, our two countries' diplomatic relations are ever closer. This is our victory.'[119]

---

118 Goscha, 'Vietnam and the World Outside', 183.
119 'Zhuwai Shiguan Guoqing 13 Zhounian Zhaodaihui: Jianpuzhai, Laowo, Xuliya, A'erjiliya, Jiana, Yilake, Jineiya, Mali, Tangannika [Receptions for the 13th Anniversary of National Day at Embassies Abroad: Cambodia, Laos, Syria, Algeria, Ghana, Iraq, Guinea, Mali, Tanganyika]', 1 October 1962 – 23 November 1962, 117-01052-03, PRCFMA.

9

'Victory of the aggregate strength of the era': Lê Duẩn, Vietnam and the three revolutionary tidal waves

Khuê Diệu Đỗ[1]

> Our might is the might of the two flags—national independence and socialism—that combines with the three revolutionary tidal waves of the era.
>
> — Lê Duẩn

The longest-serving general secretary of the Central Committee of the Vietnamese Communist Party (VCP)[2] and an 'excellent student of Hồ Chí Minh', Lê Duẩn (1907–86) and his contribution to the Vietnamese revolutionary cause, especially his strong leadership during the country's *kháng chiến chống Mỹ cứu nước* ('war of national salvation and resistance against America'), have been the focus of much scholarship.[3] Vietnamese historian Phạm Quốc Sử praises Duẩn as 'one of the few figures who

---

1 The author is grateful to her late father, Đỗ Tiến Thắng, for helping her understand Lê Duẩn's thinking and writing. A student at the Đại học Tổng hợp Hà Nội (University of Hanoi) between 1973 and 1977, he was taught and even took exams in *ba dòng thác cách mạng* (the 'three revolutionary tidal waves')—an experience he vividly remembered until recently. His narration both inspired and encouraged the author to continue her research.
2 Lê Duẩn assumed office in September 1960 and remained general secretary until his death in July 1986, serving for a total of 25 years and 303 days.
3 The National Library of Vietnam's online catalogue shows that, as of December 2021, there were as many as 54 books and 32 scholarly articles that included 'Lê Duẩn' in their titles. See: opac.nlv. vn/pages/opac/wpid-home.html.

had stature and influence over the country's development' during its modern history.⁴ Like Hồ, he clung to the nationalist ideal of a united, independent Vietnam, but demonstrated himself to be a more 'practical' personality who 'made history the final judge of his deeds'. Duẩn also belonged to the minority of Vietnamese leaders who did not write a memoir or autobiography.⁵

Fourth president of Vietnam, General Lê Đức Anh holds that Lê Duẩn was the one who not only steered Vietnam's 'revolutionary ship', but also gave way to the landmark *Đổi Mới* ('Economic Renovation') reforms at the VCP's Sixth Congress in December 1986. Lê Duẩn had already been deeply critical of the planned economy and bureaucracy at the March 1982 Fifth Party Congress, and had looked for steps to eliminate the system. Duẩn was thus responsible for 'the mindset of economic renovation and national reform that appeared at the door of the Fifth Congress'.⁶

Although his true identity and early life remain secret,⁷ it is widely known that Lê Duẩn was born as Lê Văn Nhuận on 7 April 1907 into a lower-class family in Quảng Trị Province, Annam, French Indochina. The son of a railway clerk, he developed a commitment to revolutionary politics as a young man. Through his own job as a clerk for French railways in Hanoi during the 1920s, Duẩn first came in contact with revolutionary thoughts and several communist activists.⁸ He joined Hồ Chí Minh's Canton-based Hội Việt Nam Cách mệnh Thanh niên (Vietnamese Revolutionary Youth League) in 1929 after leaving the Tân-Việt Kách-mệnh Đảng (Tân Việt Revolutionary Party), and co-founded the Indochinese Communist Party (ICP) the next year.⁹ Over the next five decades, he became one of the most powerful leaders in Vietnam while maintaining a much lower profile than Hồ.

---

4   Phạm Quốc Sử, 'Lê Duẩn: Nhân vật lớn của lịch sử Việt Nam [Le Duan: A Prominent Figure of Vietnam's History]', 13 April 2017, available from: nghiencuuquocte.org/2017/04/13/le-duan-nhan-vat-lon-cua-lich-su-viet-nam/#more-21084.
5   ibid.
6   'Đại tướng Lê Đức Anh viết về nguyên Tổng bí thư Lê Duẩn [General Lê Đức Anh Writes about Former General Secretary Lê Duẩn]', *Vietnamnet*, [Hanoi], 8 July 2016, available from: vietnamnet.vn/vn/tuanvietnam/dai-tuong-le-duc-anh-viet-ve-nguoi-anh-le-duan-314397.html.
7   Some historians suspect he came from a middle-class family, as he had received a good education in French-speaking schools. British historian P.J. Honey even held that Duẩn was part-Chinese. 'Le Duan', *Encyclopedia of World Biography. Volume 9*, 2nd edn (Gale eBooks, 2004), 278–79.
8   'Le Duan', *Vietnam War Reference Library. Volume 2: Biographies* (Gale eBooks, 2001), 211.
9   'Chương trình viết tiểu sử các đồng chí lãnh đạo của Đảng và Nhà nước [Party-State Leaders' Biographic Writing Program]', *Lê Duẩn Tiểu sử* [*Lê Duẩn Biography*] (Hà Nội: Chính trị Quốc gia, 2007), Chs1–2. Though part of a state-run project published by an official publishing house and essentially a hagiography, this seems to be the most complete biography of Lê Duẩn in any language.

This chapter examines the evolution of Lê Duẩn's thought across 40 years by focusing on his perceptions of the revolutions that were carried out in Vietnam and globally. It argues that Duẩn was the principal ideologue of the Vietnamese revolution and an architect of Vietnam's foreign policy for two decades, beginning with his rise to power in the 1960s until his death in 1986, through his invention of the 'three revolutionary tidal waves' theory. In examining his political writings closely, the chapter approaches his contributions via a discourse analysis with consideration of important historical events during his political career. By examining a variety of Vietnamese primary sources and by tracking his political career, this chapter highlights how Lê Duẩn's development of the 'three revolutionary tidal waves' exemplified his commitment to world revolution, particularly through his designs to export the Vietnamese revolutionary experience beyond Vietnam after its reunification.

Appraising Lê Duẩn: Scholarly interpretations

Outside Vietnam, Lê Duẩn draws scholars' attention due to his mysterious profile, especially during 1930–69, when the country was still under Hồ Chí Minh's leadership. Scholars generally agree Duẩn was a consistent advocate for the *tiến công* ('offensive') to send the People's Army of Vietnam (North Vietnamese Army) as support to South Vietnam and for stronger support for the Hanoi-backed Việt Cộng guerillas following the escalation of US involvement in Vietnam.[10] He earned a reputation for opposing Chinese advice to de-escalate the war and as a headstrong leader who believed that only through conventional offensive warfare, as practised against the French, could Vietnam expel the 'foreign invaders'. Some scholars have also speculated about his personality in alleging that Lê Duẩn, the party's leading extremist, was fiercely prowar because of his somewhat 'undesirable' background. As an ardent opponent of French colonial rule, Lê Duẩn was imprisoned twice (1931–36 and 1940–45) on charges of political subversion.[11]

---

10   Spencer C. Tucker, ed., *Encyclopedia of Insurgency and Counterinsurgency: A New Era of Modern Warfare* (Santa Barbara, CA: ABC-CLIO, 2013), 314.
11   ibid.

One approach to appraising Lê Duẩn's contributions is from Cheng Guan Ang, who accounts for the extant controversial assessments of Duẩn by academics and his contemporaries. Between 1956 and 1963, Duẩn was widely known as 'pro-Chinese', but was later relabelled 'pro-Soviet' in the debate over the pace of Vietnam's war efforts.[12] Lien-Hang Nguyen, by contrast, lionises Lê Duẩn as 'the architect, main strategist, and commander-in-chief of Communist Vietnam's war effort',[13] the one who, in reality, 'called the shots in Hanoi',[14] particularly during 1967. Sophie Quinn-Judge focuses her attention on the 'Anti-Party Affair' during which Duẩn presided over a purge of senior party and military figures, including several of General Võ Nguyên Giáp's closest supporters.[15]

Appraisals that are more critical, but nevertheless favourable come from Zachary Shore, who highlights Lê Duẩn's strategic empathy for the United States, his ability to grasp 'the enemy's sensibility to casualties' and his acumen in understanding the US Government's 'vulnerability'. Shore contends that Duẩn 'succeeded in knowing his enemy well'.[16] Pierre Asselin, meanwhile, notes Lê Duẩn's importance was primarily in state-building.[17] Several authors point to the group of hardliners led by Duẩn, who were responsible for Vietnam suffering a brain drain and economic flight; severe hardships, including starvation; and international isolation for a decade (1975–85).[18] But David Coffey acknowledges the difficulties the general secretary faced after 1975 and his contributions:

> As the leader of a united Vietnam, Le Duan faced the mammoth task of rebuilding a country ravaged by 35 years of almost continuous war. Reconciling opposing ideologies, restoring the

---

12 Ang Cheng Guan, *The Vietnam War from the Other Side* (Abingdon, UK: Routledge Curzon, 2002), 10.
13 Lien-Hang T. Nguyen, *Hanoi's War: An International History of the War for Peace in Vietnam* (Chapel Hill, NC: University of North Carolina Press, 2012), 2.
14 Lien-Hang Nguyen, 'Who Called the Shots in Hanoi?', *The New York Times*, 14 February 2017, available from: www.nytimes.com/2017/02/14/opinion/who-called-the-shots-in-hanoi.html.
15 Sophie Quinn-Judge, 'The Ideological Debate in the DRV and the Significance of the Anti-Party Affair, 1967–68', *Cold War History* 5(4) (2005): 479–500, doi.org/10.1080/14682740500284838.
16 Zachary Shore, 'Provoking America: Le Duan and the Origins of the Vietnam War', *Journal of Cold War Studies* 17(4) (Fall 2015): 86–108, doi.org/10.1162/JCWS_a_00598.
17 Pierre Asselin, 'Le Duan, the American War, and the Creation of an Independent Vietnamese State', *Journal of American–East Asian Relations* 10(1–2) (Spring–Summer 2001): 1–27, doi.org/10.1163/187656101793645605.
18 Nhan Tri Vo, *Vietnam's Economic Policy Since 1975* (Singapore: ASEAN Economic Research Unit, Institute of Southeast Asian Studies, 1990), Chs2–3; Frederick Z. Brown, 'Vietnam Since the War (1975–1995)', *The Wilson Quarterly* 19(1) (1995): 64–87; Shelton Woods, 'Việt Nam in the Twenty-first Century', *Education About Asia* 23(3) (2018): 40–47.

economy, and feeding the people of Vietnam all posed major obstacles, and he dealt with these to varying degrees of success. A devoted Marxist, he maintained close ties with the Soviet Union, a relationship that he solidified with the signing of the Friendship Treaty in 1978.[19]

Last, and most importantly for our purposes, Tuong Vu was the first scholar to look deeply into Lê Duẩn's ideological contributions to the Vietnamese revolution. Vu wisely translated into English Duẩn's signature concept of the *ba dòng thác cách mạng* as the 'three revolutionary tidal waves',[20] rather than the 'three revolutionary currents', as political scientist Carlyle Thayer had termed it in 1984.[21] However, Vu and all the above scholars have hitherto failed to trace both the origin and the purpose of the concept.[22] As a result, he and those who preceded him somewhat overlook the impact of this notion on the overall ideological development of the Vietnamese communists through the three Indochina wars.

An inseparable organ of world revolution

After his release from prison in the wake of the 1945 August Revolution, Lê Duẩn became a trusted associate of ICP leader Hồ Chí Minh. The First Indochina War broke out shortly afterwards. To resist the French—the first Euro-American enemy in Vietnam's long history of wars of patriotic resistance against foreign invasion (particularly against ruling dynasties in today's China)—Vietnam's revolutionaries needed popular support at home and abroad.

---

19 Coffey, in *Encyclopedia of Insurgency and Counterinsurgency*, 315.
20 Tuong Vu, *Vietnam's Communist Revolution: The Power and Limits of Ideology* (New York, NY: Cambridge University Press, 2017), Ch.7; Tuong Vu, 'In the Service of World Revolution: Vietnamese Communists' Radical Ambitions through the Three Indochina Wars', *Journal of Cold War Studies* 21(4) (Fall 2019): 4–30, doi.org/10.1162/jcws_a_00905.
21 Carlyle Thayer, 'Vietnamese Perspectives on International Security: Three Revolutionary Currents', in *Asian Perspectives on International Security*, Donald McMillen, ed. (London: Macmillan, 1984), 57–76.
22 Vu ('In the Service of World Revolution') claims 'the 1960s' is when North Vietnamese leaders first mentioned the concept (p.11), while he specifies 1965 as the starting point in *Vietnam's Communist Revolution* (p.201). He does not cite any sources. Moreover, Lê Duẩn is not clearly or directly acknowledged as the author of this concept in either publication. Meanwhile, Thayer ('Vietnamese Perspectives on International Security', p.65) mentions several times that Duẩn's advocacy for this political theory began in 1970. As shown in this chapter, the 'three revolutionary tidal waves' appeared for the first time in a July 1967 letter from Duẩn to his comrades in South Vietnam.

Under Democratic Republic of Vietnam (DRV) President Hồ's leadership, the logic of Indochinese revolution in general and Vietnamese revolution in particular had two foundational principles. First, *độc lập dân tộc gắn liền với chủ nghĩa xã hội* ('the struggle for national independence must go hand-in-glove with the socialist development'). Second, through the creative adaptation and application of Marxism-Leninism to the Indochinese context, Vietnamese revolutionaries must use the *nhân tố quốc tế* ('international factor')—that is, foreign support. In his signature friendly, rural tone, Hồ once famously said: 'Whoever in the world wishes to conduct a revolution is a comrade of the Annam people.'[23] He also explained the importance of organic coherence between all revolutions and the need for cooperation between all revolutions globally:

> If Annam's nationalist revolution succeeds, French capitalism will be weakened. If the French capitalism is weakened, French workers and peasants will easily conduct their class revolution. And if the French workers and peasants succeed, Annam will then be free. Therefore, Annam revolution and French revolution must contact each other[24] ... If Annam wants to conduct a successful revolution, without question, it must rely on the Third International.[25]

As someone who was deeply influenced by Hồ's ideas, Lê Duẩn upheld both these principles from the very beginning of his long political career. Duẩn particularly emphasised these two tasks once he was chosen by Hồ to lead Hanoi's prosecution of the war of resistance against US forces. During the 1940s, he directed Việt Minh efforts in French Cochinchina (South Vietnam) while he continued to work in the VCP's headquarters.

Lê Duẩn continued to emphasise the importance of national and international situations in achieving true freedom for Vietnam. In a 1949 speech, he asserted that among extant socioeconomic classes in Vietnam, only the proletarians equipped with a true *lập trường dân tộc* ('national outlook') and a correct *lập trường quốc tế* ('international outlook') could bring about genuine independence.[26] Although the national outlook was

---

23 'Quốc tế Cứu tế đỏ [International Red Aid]', excerpts from 'Đường Cách mệnh [Revolutionary Path]', [1927], in Hồ Chí Minh, *Hồ Chí Minh Toàn tập* [*Complete Works of Hồ Chí Minh. Volume 2*] (Hà Nội: Chính trị Quốc gia, 2011), 329.
24 'Cách mệnh [Revolution]', in ibid., 287.
25 'Quốc tế [Communist International]', in Minh, *Complete Works of Hồ Chí Minh*, 312.
26 'Đảng Cộng sản Đông Dương và cách mạng Việt Nam [Indochinese Communist Party and Vietnamese Revolution]', in Lê Duẩn, *Một vài đặc điểm của cách mạng Việt Nam* [*Some Characteristics of Vietnamese Revolution*] (Hà Nội: Sự thật, 1959), 29–38. This collection includes the important speeches by Lê Duẩn throughout 1949.

vital to resisting the French and all other imperialists, the international outlook helped to unite every possible force in the world—the most heartfelt allies—to vanquish imperialism. These two outlooks then formed the *nhiệm vụ dân tộc* ('national duty') and *nhiệm vụ quốc tế* ('international duty') of the ICP.[27]

In another speech that same year, Duẩn further specified how these characteristics of the Vietnamese revolution were linked intrinsically and inextricably:

> The national and international characteristics of Vietnamese revolution are self-explanatory. Without a clear international outlook, Vietnam's national revolution could not succeed. Meanwhile, without a nationalist feature and a firm, genuine patriotic standpoint, success is also out of the hands of the Vietnamese revolutionaries.
>
> That which is similarly obvious is the correlation between these two characteristics. Vietnam's revolution for national liberation must assume all the difficulties caused by the international and domestic contexts. At the same time, it ought to take full advantage of its domestic, internal situation and the revolutionary movement all over the world.[28]

Evidently, Lê Duẩn was firm in his conviction about the importance and distinctness of the Vietnamese revolution. He also recognised that the Vietnamese revolution played no small role in the general development of global revolution, which indeed preoccupied his mind as soon as the First Indochina War broke out. In October 1950, for instance, he stated unequivocally that the Vietnamese revolution had not materialised purely as an outcome of the democratic movement against fascism that was rampant elsewhere during and after World War II. He also criticised the notion that a global 'détente moment' was soon to come.[29]

---

27 ibid.
28 ibid., 26.
29 'Thế tiến công của cách mạng vô sản sau chiến tranh thế giới thứ hai [The Offensive Posture of Proletarian Revolution after World War Two]', Trích bài Ý kiến về bản dự thảo 'kiểm điểm chính sách chung' viết tháng Mười 1950 [Excerpt from the 'Commentary on "General Policy Review"' written in October 1950], in Lê Duẩn, *Về những vấn đề quốc tế* [*On International Issues*] (Hà Nội: Sự thật, 1965), 7–9.

To Lê Duẩn, the reason for the ICP's stalling and errors in policy was its leadership simply could not provide a correct assessment of the global situation after World War II—not unlike some communist parties elsewhere. He surmised that, unlike during the post–World War I period, democratic and independent movements were rising all over the globe while the capitalist world was weakening. This was all due to the significant growth of the Soviet Union after 1945 under Joseph Stalin's leadership. In this context, Duẩn pleaded, the proletarian revolution ought to make use of its own preponderance to attack capitalism. As a result, the 'temporary détente' of the previous period had ended and now was the time for Vietnam's revolution to ride the forward momentum to independence.[30] Indeed, to Duẩn, Vietnam's revolutionary war represented part of this 'first wave' of the rising tide of world revolution, rather than simply an outcome of far-flung international events. In fact, Vietnam's revolution belonged to the 'proletarian movement that is constantly attacking and wiping out capitalism', he maintained.[31] As such, Duẩn rejected the 'passive attitude' and tactics of the Vietnamese revolution that were markers of this period in the ICP's leadership of the independence movement, and instead advocated for a more 'proactive' attitude. This strong stance was strengthened in the 1960s, as this section discusses further.

Once Lê Duẩn was elected to membership of the Đảng Lao động Việt Nam (Vietnamese Workers' Party, VWP) Politburo in 1951—though his deputy Lê Đức Thọ replaced him so he could move to the North—his writings established him as a major contributor to VWP strategy. After the 1954 Geneva Conference accords divided Vietnam along the *vĩ tuyến 17* ('seventeenth parallel'), Duẩn returned to South Vietnam, where he again served as secretary of the Xứ Ủy Nam Bộ (Central Committee for the Southern Region). In August 1956 in Saigon, he finished writing *Đề cương cách mạng miền Nam* ('*Tenets of the Revolution in the South*'), which argued it was time to complement the political struggle in South Vietnam with direct military action from the North. His treatise, which the VWP Politburo adopted in late 1959, later informed the guidelines of Resolution 15 that allowed Vietnamese in the South to resist repression by the Ngô Đình Diệm government. In this 'credo for a new struggle' in the

---

30 ibid.
31 ibid.

South, fighters no longer took 'political struggle' as their line of action, but instead adopted more violent tactics. Duẩn's position within the party was thus significantly enhanced thanks in no small part to this writing.

At the Third VWP Congress in September 1960, when Duẩn officially became first secretary, the structure of the Vietnamese *chiến tranh nhân dân* ('people's war') for national reunification was officially formulated as having two fronts. The congress was also important for Duẩn regarding his position within the party: he succeeded Hồ as the VWP's de facto leader even though the latter remained chairman (his deteriorating health led to the expansion of Duẩn's role in the decision-making process in Hanoi). After the third congress, Vietnam's North and South were deep in the throes of a violent anti-imperialist war in which the North served as the *hậu phương lớn* ('great rear') and the South as the *tiền tuyến lớn* ('great front').[32] Although socialist revolution continued in the North, the South was host to the *cách mạng dân tộc-dân chủ* ('national-democratic revolution'). A highly practical person, Duẩn strongly believed that without vigorous and prompt attacks on the battlefields, the advantage would fall into the hands of the enemy.

In December of that year, Lê Duẩn declared that, strategically speaking, the revolutionary forces were clearly on the offensive, while the reactionary forces of imperialism were on the defensive. However, as the decline and collapse of capitalism would not come smoothly, the 'forces of peace, national independence, democracy, and socialism' must embrace a special kind of fighting tactic: a *đấu tranh từng bước, từng phần* ('step-by-step, part-by-part approach)'.[33] Vietnamese revolutionaries ought to point the spearhead of their struggle directly at the American imperialists—the *đầu xỏ* ('ring leaders') of global imperialism.[34] As first secretary, Duẩn believed in a watershed moment of world revolution just as much as he envisioned a fierce struggle against US imperialist adventurism in Vietnam. Lê Duẩn knew the United States was the major force behind the government of

---

32 Although the two notions became very popular in Vietnam throughout the war and afterwards, it was the first time they were introduced to the Vietnamese population.
33 'Tăng cường đoàn kết nhất trí tiến tới những thắng lợi mới [Strengthening Solidarity and Unity of Views and Advancing towards Further Successes]', Trích báo cáo tại Hội nghị lần thứ 3 của Ban chấp hành trung ương Đảng Lao động Việt Nam, tháng 12 năm 1960, về Hội nghị đại biểu các đảng cộng sản và đảng công nhân tháng 11 năm 1960 ở Mát-scơ-va [Excerpt from the 'Report of the Meeting of Representatives of the Communist and Workers' Parties in November 1960 in Moscow' to the Third Session of the VWP Central Committee in December 1960], in Duẩn, *On International Issues*, 27.
34 ibid.

South Vietnam, and that Washington was sponsoring the Army of the Republic of Vietnam (ARVN) and commanding internal and external affairs. As such, Duẩn insisted that the Vietnamese communists' top priority was to reunify the country by frustrating American efforts in Vietnam. He therefore decided to invest heavily in VWP strategy in the South—the main battlefront. Over the course of the next three years, and largely under Duẩn's direction, the Mặt trận Dân tộc Giải phóng Miền Nam Việt Nam (National Liberation Front of South Vietnam, or Việt Cộng; established in 1960) initiated a sweeping program of assassinations, urban terrorism and accelerated forms of conventional warfare.

Importantly, whereas in the 1950s Lê Duẩn had stressed the link between Vietnamese revolution and the larger global struggle, he now sought to theorise this connection by recognising the effects of imperialism elsewhere in the Global South. The national liberation movement and the global struggle for socialism, as promulgated by Duẩn in 1960, were closely interrelated and interacting. In fact, the former was an 'inseparable organ' of the international proletarian revolution. As he averred, at the time when socialism was turning the tide against imperialism in many countries, the national-democratic revolution was a *tiền đề* ('precondition') of socialist revolution.[35] The fact he placed primacy on national liberation rather than socialist construction indicates Duẩn had some inkling that Vietnam's violent struggle against the Americans would be a prolonged one. In December 1963, he reaffirmed and expanded on his thinking in this regard:

> The characteristic of the national-liberation movement in the present era is that the national struggle against imperialism cannot be separated from the class struggle within the nation, that is to say, the struggle for full national independence is linked organically to the struggle for democracy and against the feudal and comprador bourgeois forces, against the reactionary forces in the service of imperialism, and to the struggle between the two paths—capitalist development and non-capitalist development.[36]

---

35 ibid., 39. The term 'precondition', however, was officially translated into English as 'premise' in Duẩn, 'Strengthening Solidarity and Unity of Views and Advancing towards Further Successes', 40.

36 'Một vài vấn đề trong nhiệm vụ quốc tế của Đảng ta [Some Problems Concerning the International Tasks of Our Party]', Bài phát biểu tại Hội nghị Trung ương Đảng lần thứ 9 họp vào tháng chạp 1963 [Speech delivered at the 9th session of the VWP Central Committee held in December 1963], in Lê Duẩn, *Một vài vấn đề trong nhiệm vụ quốc tế của Đảng ta* [*Some Problems Concerning the International Tasks of Our Party*] (Hà Nội: Sự thật, 1964), 30.

He also emphasised the significance and value of *khu vực Á-Phi-Mỹ La-tinh* ('Asia, Africa and Latin America') on the world political map after World War II. In his view, these regions were where the revolutionary movement was most active. Only in Asia, Africa and Latin America were people witnessing all the following: 1) severe conflicts between imperialism and suppressed/colonised nations, 2) tense competition among imperialists and 3) fierce confrontation between the imperialist camp and the socialist bloc.[37] As the tide of anti-imperial revolution was on the rise, reactionary authorities were relatively weak in these areas, which represented fecund ground for enhanced revolutionary activity.

Indeed, in Duẩn's assessment, the ruling bourgeoisie in many Asian, African and Latin American countries differed from their Western European and North American counterparts in that they lacked a developed economy, a strong politico-cultural base and a capable organisation. This so-called Third World region was the 'weakest link in the chain of imperialism-capitalism', he continued.[38] For this reason, he averred, the development of revolution in these areas could quickly change the balance of power in favour of the forces of peace, independence, democracy and socialism. Importantly, Duẩn admitted his assessment was not an underestimation of the most fundamental conflict of the era—that between capitalism and socialism. But apart from the socialist camp, he observed, the most profound revolutionary changes of the time were taking place nowhere but in Asia, Africa and Latin America. He thus concluded that the national-democratic revolutionary movement in these areas had brought about 'the most momentous upheavals' in the world.[39]

The three revolutionary tidal waves

After the 2 August 1964 Gulf of Tonkin incident, US combat troops began to dispatch to South Vietnam and, from 1965, US Marines and air forces deployed in North Vietnam. The Indochina War had now expanded to the whole country. The rapid sequence of events and subsequent US response drew international attention to Vietnam, and support for Hanoi against US imperialism flowed from the Soviet Bloc,

---

37 ibid., 26.
38 ibid., 34.
39 ibid.

many Third World nations and even some US allies. After successfully binding the Vietnamese revolution to its international body in the 1950s, it was now high time for Lê Duẩn to fully develop the concept of the 'three revolutionary tidal waves' and take advantage of international attention and support. Duẩn introduced the concept in a July 1967 letter to the Khu Ủy Sài Gòn–Gia Định (Saigon–Gia Định Communist Party Regional Committee):[40]

> Today's era is the era of the proletarian revolution that reached its climax after World War II, the era of the *three revolutionary tidal waves on their offensive against imperialism*, driving it back step by step, overthrowing it bit by bit, and eventually inflicting a total defeat on it so as to realise the transition [*quá đô*] from capitalism to socialism on a global scale.[41]

But it was not until late 1967 that Duẩn clearly listed these 'tidal waves' in an article written on the fiftieth anniversary of the October Revolution. They included the following three components: 1) the *global socialist revolutionary movement*; 2) the *workers' movement in capitalist countries*; and 3) *national liberation movements in colonised countries*, with Vietnam as the vanguard. Although these 'waves' may play out somewhat differently across the diverse range of countries and historical situations, together, they comprised the three 'marvellous waves' of socialist revolution of the era. The goal was to rescue humankind from the 'capitalist orbit' and to return humanity to the path to socialism.[42]

In previous decades, the focus of communists worldwide had been squarely on the first 'wave': the construction of socialism and communism globally. But the emergence of second and third 'waves' after World War II, Duẩn contended, determined the historical trajectory of the present era. According to his analysis, if the national liberation movement in colonised countries caused damage to the rearguard—specifically, the

---

40   Located in Bến Tre Province, the regional committee was coded as 'T4' and 'Y4' bases, serving as the nerve-centre commanding the resistance activities of the vast Saigon–Gia Định area from July 1969 to October 1970.

41   'Gửi Khu Ủy Sài Gòn-Gia Định, ngày 1/7/1967 [Letter to Saigon–Gia Định Regional Committee, 1 July 1967]', in Lê Duẩn, *Thư vào Nam* [*Letters to the South*] (Hà Nội: Sự thật, 1985), 159. Emphasis added.

42   'Hăng hái tiến lên dưới ngọn cờ vĩ đại của cách mạng tháng Mười [Advance Fervently under the Great Flag of the October Revolution]', Bài viết nhân dịp kỷ niệm lần thứ 50 cuộc Cách mạng xã hội chủ nghĩa tháng Mười vĩ đại, tháng 11 năm 1967 [Article written on the 50th anniversary of great socialist October revolution in November 1967], in Lê Duẩn, *Hăng hái tiến lên dưới ngọn cờ vĩ đại của cách mạng tháng Mười* [*Advance Fervently under the Great Flag of the October Revolution*] (Hà Nội: Sự thật, 1969), 25–26.

storage depot of imperialist capitalism—the workers' movement could strike at the core of capitalism: *chính quốc* ('the metropolis').[43] Duẩn went further, arguing that where the national liberation movement had united the 'three waves', revolutionary tendencies would crystallise, the defensive line of capitalism would be most vulnerable and the revolutionary forces could take the offensive.[44]

Accordingly, the significance of the third 'wave' to the global socialist revolution became even more important once US troops had landed on Vietnamese soil, and its development coincided with major intraparty decisions. In one of Lê Duẩn's letters to the Trung ương Cục miền Nam (Central Office for South Vietnam, COSVN)—the North Vietnamese political and military headquarters in South Vietnam—he intimated that Vietnam was the epicentre, where all three waves coalesced:

> It is only in Vietnam that the three revolutionary waves fully converged. Here in our country, the three tides do not run apart but flow into a common fall. As a result, it is by no chance that the American imperialists chose Vietnam as the major target of its global efforts to demolish the [Vietnamese] movement of national liberation.[45]

Lê Duẩn sought to achieve several goals when he sent this letter to VWP comrades in the South. First, he underlined the importance and loftiness of the Vietnamese people's struggle against the Americans. Second, he asked his comrades in South Vietnam to be patient and encouraged them to endure a protracted war against this powerful enemy. Third, and most importantly, he consolidated the belief among his comrades in South Vietnam that Vietnam had a distinct, unparalleled might that would help it win the war and reunify the country. He sought to strengthen belief and confidence among his fellow Vietnamese in maintaining their prolonged and arduous struggle against the US military.

As for major decisions within the VWP, 1967 was a challenging time for the party leadership, including Duẩn, but also a watershed in the Vietnam War. In the summer of that year, Duẩn disagreed with General

---

43   ibid.
44   Trần Nhâm, *Lê Duẩn–Trường Chinh: Hai nhà lí luận xuất sắc của cách mạng Việt Nam* [*Lê Duan–Trường Chinh: Two Excellent Ideologues of Vietnamese Revolution*] (Hà Nội: Chính trị Quốc gia, 2002), 56. Trần Nhâm was a secretary of Trường Chinh (Lê Duẩn's successor in 1986) and later became a Marxist political scientist known for his works on the two former party secretaries.
45   ibid.

Võ Nguyên Giáp and other VWP leaders over the plan for the 1968 Tết Offensive. He successfully stamped out internal tensions by eliminating several senior party and military figures. On Hồ's death in September 1969, Lê Duẩn became the undisputed leader of the party and the North Vietnamese Government and, in February 1970, the party secretary published one of his most celebrated works.

Compulsory reading for a generation of North Vietnamese college students,[46] Lê Duẩn's 1970 *Dưới lá cờ vẻ vang của Đảng vì độc lập, tự do, vì chủ nghĩa xã hội, tiến lên giành những thắng lợi mới* ('*Under the Glorious Flag of the Party for Independence, Freedom and Socialism, Let Us Advance and Achieve New Victories*') summarised the international situation since the end of World War II in three main parts. First, Duẩn wrote that socialism extended well beyond a country's bounds as it was an international, not solely a national, system. With each victorious resistance against capitalism, socialist countries proved socialism was a 'decisive factor in the development of the human society', the 'bastion of revolution' and the 'pillar preserving world peace'.[47] Second, he stressed the unprecedented, powerful struggle of tens of millions of the working masses and labouring people constituted a mighty force against capitalism that had hit hard the 'reactionary rule of the state-monopolising capitalists [*tư bản lũng đoạn nhà nước*] and their warlike policy' right in its *sào huyệt* ('den').[48] Third, under the influence of socialism, the national liberation movement had 'developed monumentally not only in terms of quantity, but also in terms of quality'.[49] The powerful revolt of the national liberation movements in Asian, African and Latin American countries had resulted in the disintegration of most colonial systems of enslavement. The movement was now continuing its struggle to break the chains of imperialism, old and new, striking decisively at its rearguard. In Duẩn's view, these three big currents converged into a socialist revolutionary high tide that would draw all humanity into the 'orbit of socialism' and he encouraged people in different countries to unite and advance to complete the transition to socialism.[50]

---

46 During the first half of the 1970s, the main contents and key assessments of this work dominated the exam questions of college students in North Vietnam, especially the qualifying exams for graduation.
47 'Tăng cường đoàn kết, đẩy mạnh đấu tranh vì hoà bình, độc lập dân tộc, dân chủ và chủ nghĩa xã hội [Strengthening Solidarity, Boosting the Struggle for Peace, National Independence, Democracy and Socialism]', in Lê Duẩn, *Dưới lá cờ vẻ vang của Đảng vì độc lập, tự do, vì chủ nghĩa xã hội, tiến lên giành những thắng lợi mới* [*Under the Glorious Flag of the Party for Independence, Freedom and Socialism, Let Us Advance and Achieve New Victories*] (Hà Nội: Sự thật, 1970), 155.
48 ibid.
49 ibid.
50 ibid., 157.

Lê Duẩn also regarded American intervention in Vietnam as an important part of its global imperialist strategy. The American initiation of war after the conclusion of the French–Việt Minh war (1946–54) demonstrated that the US Government and policymakers held evil ambitions for Vietnam, not the least of which was to repulse socialism. In using Vietnam as a laboratory in which to test its anti-socialist strategies, invasive war tactics and new weapons, Washington also intended to 'suppress the revolutionary movement and prepare for a global war'.[51] The Vietnamese people's war of resistance was therefore a pinnacle of the global struggle against US imperialism. It played a crucial role as the host site in which to resolve the world's 'principal contradictions' of the times, and contribute to the protection of socialism, national independence and peace. Duẩn also concluded that Vietnam provided encouragement to the struggle for freedom, justice, human dignity and people's rights to life worldwide.[52]

As a result, the Vietnamese people were truly proud to be the *chiến sĩ xung kích* ('strike force soldiers') at the forefront of the global revolutionary struggle against American imperialists—humanity's most dangerous enemy. Duẩn stated fervently that Vietnamese committed to strain every nerve to defeat the invasion of US imperialists and their lackeys and to bring the war to final victory in fulfilment of their 'sacred national duty as well as lofty international duty'.[53] Apart from the strategy's original goal of spurring on the Vietnamese communists in the mid-1960s, Lê Duẩn also sought to justify the 'offensiveness' (that is, aggressiveness) of Hanoi's war effort when he decided to fully develop and publicise the 'three waves' strategy to the country in the early 1970s. From this point, the keyword 'offensive' accompanied the concept in each of Duẩn's attempts to promulgate his 'three tidal waves' strategy.

Two months later, in an essay written on the one-hundredth anniversary of the birth of V.I. Lenin, Lê Duẩn reaffirmed these 'three tidal waves' (as 'three new elements') would 'determine the development of the whole human society'.[54] It was on this occasion that he developed the notion of *sức mạnh tổng hợp* ('aggregate strength'), which he and the VWP promoted later as one of his signature theories and strategies to swing the

---

51   ibid., 159
52   ibid., 160.
53   ibid.
54   Lê Duẩn, *Chủ nghĩa Lênin soi sáng mục tiêu Cách mạng của thời đại* [*Leninism Sheds Lights on the Revolutionary Goals of the Era*] (Hà Nội: Sự thật, 1970), 19–21.

war in Vietnam's favour.⁵⁵ According to Duẩn, the three waves converged to create an 'aggregate strength' of the era's proletarian revolution.⁵⁶ These converged waves combined with the peaceful movement so a new balance of power could form globally and signal the revolutionary forces were winning against the warmongers.⁵⁷ He concluded that the strategic offensive posture of the revolutionary and peaceful forces of the time had been premised on this strong foundation.⁵⁸

Victory of the aggregate strength of the era

On the signing of the January 1973 Paris Peace Accords that stipulated the US withdrawal from South Vietnam and ended American bombings of the North, Hanoi announced the Vietnamese communists' victory in the protracted diplomatic struggle against Washington. Because the Vietnamese communists considered diplomacy a key front alongside the political and military ones, they proudly declared their fulfilment of the first strategic goal of *đánh cho Mỹ cút* ('expelling the American invaders'). The peace agreement paved the way for the revolutionary forces to overpower their enemies on the battlefield, which in turn facilitated their accomplishment of the final goal of *đánh cho Ngụy nhào* ('overthrowing the puppet regime'). The 'three revolutionary tidal waves' were thus especially prominent in Lê Duẩn's speeches at various events and meetings, as he referenced them to glorify the Vietnamese people's triumph over the mighty imperialist American forces.

---

55 In his remarks at the forty-fifth anniversary of the VCP's establishment on 3 February 1975, Duẩn said: 'Our aggregate strength … [included] combining armed struggle with the political one; incorporating uprisings and offensives; launching attacks on *three* directions [*ba mũi giáp công*] of military, politics and agitprop; on *three* fronts [*ba mặt trận*] of politics, military and diplomacy; on all *three* strategic areas [*ba vùng chiến lược*] of mountainous, rural and urban.' 'Diễn văn tại lễ kỷ niệm lần thứ 45 ngày thành lập Đảng (3-2-1945 – 3-2-1975) [Remarks at the 45th Anniversary of the Party Establishment (3 February 1945 – 3 February 1975)]', in Lê Duẩn, *Lê Duẩn Tuyển tập* [*Complete Works of Lê Duẩn. Volume 2*] (Hà Nội: Chính trị Quốc gia, 2008), 1283. Emphasis added. He repeated this rhetoric for the rest of his political career whenever he mentioned Vietnam's 'recipe for victory'. 'Aggregate strength' has been discussed in most of the studies of Lê Duẩn's leadership by Vietnamese academics. Some also note Duẩn's unusual fondness for the number 'three' when constructing his thoughts; as the third of four children in the family, he was informally called *Ba* ('three' in Vietnamese) throughout his life, even by his comrades.
56 Lê Duẩn, *Leninism Sheds Lights on the Revolutionary Goals of the Era*, 25.
57 ibid.
58 ibid.

9. 'VICTORY OF THE AGGREGATE STRENGTH OF THE ERA'

In his February 1974 address to the Labour Union of Vietnam, Lê Duẩn reaffirmed the Vietnamese revolution remained the 'integral component' of world revolution through its close association with 'all three proletarian revolutionary tidal waves of the present time'.[59] By taking advantage of the general offensive posture of world revolution, and in exploiting the aggregate strength of the era's revolutionary high tides, the Vietnamese resistance gained the upper hand in the fight against the American imperialists. In turn, Duẩn reasoned, the Vietnamese people's victory contributed further to the three waves of revolution because: 1) it further consolidated socialism's position globally, 2) it strongly supported the anti-imperialist struggle of Third World nations and 3) it contributed to the enhancement of the working class and labouring people's revolutionary struggle within capitalist countries.[60] Together with these waves, the initial victory of the Vietnamese resistance 'further deepened the crisis within the imperialist system'.[61] US-led global imperialism had thus suffered a 'severe decline', whereas the global revolutionary forces' offensive was trending upward and gaining strength.[62]

Lê Duẩn also delivered an important speech in front of senior VWP cadres in which he raised philosophical questions about the 'three waves' strategy and proposed some novel solutions. As Duẩn now pointed out, Hanoi's diplomatic achievements in Paris had signalled the transformation of the international stage of the 'three waves':

1. U.S. imperialist, the world 'gendarme' [*sen đầm*] had fallen into a sharp decline and its position on the international arena had decreased drastically;
2. Never before had the imperialist camp encountered such a severe conflict with effects felt across the U.S. and its allies in Japan and Western Europe;
3. Never before were the *three revolutionary tidal waves* more fierce and powerful.[63]

---

59 'Giai đoạn mới của cách mạng và nhiệm vụ công đoàn [A New Phase of Revolution and Tasks of the Union]', Bài nói tại Đại hội Công đoàn Việt Nam lần thứ III, ngày 11/2/1974 [Speech at the Third Congress of the Labour Union, 11 February 1974], in Lê Duẩn, *Cách mạng xã hội chủ nghĩa ở Việt Nam* [*Socialist Revolution in Vietnam*] (Hà Nội: Sự thật, 1976), 539.
60 ibid., 539–40.
61 ibid., 540.
62 ibid.
63 'Bài nói tại Hội nghị phổ biến nghị quyết của Quân Ủy Trung ương cho cán bộ cao cấp, ngày 25/4/1974 [Speech at the Conference Disseminating the Resolutions of the Party Central Committee's Military Commission for Senior Cadres, 25 April 1974]', in Duẩn, *Complete Works of Lê Duẩn*, 1182–83. Emphasis added.

Now facing unfavourable changes in the balance of power, especially after its withdrawal from Vietnam, Washington, Duẩn asserted, was seeking a 'temporary détente' with Beijing and Moscow to concentrate its attacks on small revolutionary states. He highlighted such a détente as the fruit of the offensive strategy taken by the world revolutionary forces, rather than the outcome of some 'clever schemes'.[64] Strategically speaking, the world revolution, in his assessment, 'is still on the offensive; and it should hold the offensive by all three revolutionary tidal waves, instead of employing a peaceful offensive or détente strategy'.[65]

In the latter half of his speech, Lê Duẩn stressed the equal importance of each wave of revolution, beginning with the 'extremely significant' role played by the socialist system. Despite the 1960 Sino-Soviet Split, the socialist camp persisted and even held the kind of power 'that frightened the imperialists'.[66] Absent the socialist system, Lê Duẩn argued, a small and weak country such as socialist Cuba could not exist and stand firm against its more powerful neighbour, the United States. But this was just one leg of a tripod. The revolutionary movement of the working masses in developed countries, he asserted, would decide the 'future collapse of capitalism'.[67] He asked, if the socialist camp could not export revolution, who other than the workers of capitalist countries would overthrow capitalism? Equally important was the revolutionary movement in Third World nations, which Duẩn reasoned would be the 'immediate factor' in deciding whether the colonial system—the reserve source of imperialism—would collapse completely.[68] He concluded that each 'wave' played its own decisive part, and all three waves 'were deciding the main content, essential methods, and the prime characteristics of the development of world history'.[69]

In late 1974, when the VWP planned its final assaults from Hanoi, Party Secretary Duẩn encouraged his comrades in the South to prepare themselves psychologically. He sent a letter to COSVN Commander Phạm Hùng[70] in which he stressed that comrades in the South must clearly understand the Vietnamese forces' great capabilities and mobilisational capacity that

---

64   ibid., 1185.
65   ibid.
66   ibid., 1186.
67   ibid., 1187.
68   ibid.
69   ibid.
70   Code name Bảy Cường, the commissar to the command of the Hồ Chí Minh Campaign that ended the Vietnam War.

were necessary to develop the 'aggregate strength' to win the war against the Americans.[71] He emphasised, first, Hanoi's 'decisive' importance and contribution to the last stretches of the war. Duẩn now reasoned that although the people's national-democratic revolution in the South and the socialist revolution in the North joined as one, the most decisive strength indeed came from the North (the rearguard). In his appraisal, when the war ended, the pivotal, decisive role played by the rearguard in the North would be even more pronounced. Not only would the Vietnamese communists mobilise political and military forces in the South, they also would commit elite forces, strategic reserves and abundant resources from Hanoi to win this decisive battle. He then assessed that Vietnam's might came from the combination of the 'two flags' of national independence and socialism and the three revolutionary tidal waves of the era.[72] As a result, the Vietnamese people's war of resistance received great support from fraternal socialist countries and progressives across the globe. This, Duẩn concluded, was ultimately one of the firm guarantees for Vietnam's ultimate victory.

On the long-awaited fall of Saigon, Lê Duẩn's confidence in his now-successful signature strategy was confirmed and he fixed his eyes on the horizon. In his remarks at the 15 May 1975 victory ceremony in Hanoi, the party secretary stated proudly that Vietnam was where the most severe clash in history had occurred. The combatants in this war, as everyone knew by then, were the warlike, stubborn imperialist invaders and their strong economic and military forces and the people's forces of national independence, democracy and socialism, with Vietnam as the *đội xung kích* ('strike team').[73] The Vietnamese victory represented a monumental international moment and was therefore symbolic of the era. As Duẩn described, 'it demonstrates that the three revolutionary tidal waves of our time are on the offensive'.[74] For the first time, too, Duẩn initiated what became one of his most common formulae for the Vietnamese forces'

---

71 'Thư gửi đồng chí Bảy Cường về kết luận của Hội nghị Bộ Chính trị, ngày 10/10/1974 [Letter to Comrade Bảy Cường about the Conclusion of the Politburo Conference, 10 October 1974]', in Duẩn, *Letters to the South*, 366.
72 ibid.
73 Lê Duẩn, 'Dân tộc ta có đủ tinh thần và nghị lực, sức mạnh và tài năng, biến nước ta thành một nước văn minh, giàu mạnh [Our Nation Has Adequate Moral Fortitude, Power and Talent in Making Vietnam a Civilised, Prosperous Country]', Diễn văn trong buổi lễ mừng chiến thắng, ngày 15/5/1975 [Speech at the victory ceremony, 15 May 1975], in Đảng Cộng sản Việt Nam [Vietnamese Communist Party (hereinafter VCP)], *Văn kiện Đảng toàn tập* [*Complete Collection of Party Documents*]. Volume 36: 1975 (Hà Nội: Chính trị Quốc gia, 2004), 212.
74 ibid.

historic victory: the combination of *sức mạnh dân tộc* ('national strength') and the *sức mạnh thời đại* ('strength of the era')—that is, 'combining internal forces with international forces to cultivate a marvellous aggregate strength to fight against America and triumph'.[75]

In December 1976, the renamed Đảng Cộng sản Việt Nam (Vietnamese Communist Party, VCP) held the Fourth Party Congress—its first after 16 years of war and civil strife. At this landmark meeting, the 'three revolutionary tidal waves' officially became a *nhận thức tập thể* ('collective understanding') of the organisation and the country. From this moment, the strategy became the VCP's official guideline and represented its view of *sự vận động của thế giới* ('global dynamics') since World War II and continuing after 1975. As the congress's resolution proclaimed:

> The strength of our era is the aggregate strength of the three revolutionary tidal waves … Based on such power of the three waves and a constant, sound deployment of the offensive strategy, the working masses from all countries will advance the revolutionary high tide to a new development, achieving greater victories in the struggle for the lofty objectives of the era.[76]

Now the general secretary of the newly established Socialist Republic of Vietnam (SRV), Lê Duẩn read the VCP Central Committee's political report. He stated: 'In the collective offensive of the three revolutionary tidal waves in the world, four objectives of the era—peace, national independence, democracy and socialism—closely intertwined.'[77] Earlier in August, the Vietnamese Ministry of Foreign Affairs had given its assessment of the global situation: 'The three revolutionary tidal waves developed profoundly and took full advantage of the strategic offensive … Vietnam has become a strong force with [a] remarkable international

---

75 ibid., 213. *Kết hợp sức mạnh dân tộc với sức mạnh thời đại* ('combining national strength with the strength of the era') appeared in all the reports of the party congresses from the fourth in December 1976 until the thirteenth in January 2021. The formula indeed became a guideline for the VCP in dealing with any complex situation, from the 1986 *Đổi Mới* policy to the collapse of the Soviet Union, two financial crises, globalisation and, most recently, the Fourth Industrial Revolution.

76 'Nghị quyết của Đại hội đại biểu toàn quốc lần thứ IV của Đảng, ngày 20/12/1976 [Resolution of the Fourth Party Congress, 20 December 1976]', in VCP, *Complete Collection of Party Documents. Volume 37: 1976*, 1039–40.

77 'Báo cáo chính trị của Ban chấp hành Trung ương Đảng tại Đại hội đại biểu toàn quốc lần thứ IV do đồng chí Lê Duẩn trình bày, ngày 14/12/1976 [Political Report of the Party Central Committee Presented by Comrade Lê Duẩn at the Fourth Party Congress, 14 December 1976]', in VCP, *Complete Collection of Party Documents. Volume 37*, 471, 485, 489.

position and role, particularly in the Southeast Asian region.'[78] This meant the 'three waves' strategy had also become the VCP's official foreign policy, which each Vietnamese diplomat ought to learn and apply in service to the SRV.

Although Lê Duẩn's original goal for the strategy was to add global significance and value to Vietnam's war of resistance against the United States, the communist takeover in 1975 had boosted the VCP leadership's confidence in its strategy to the point that the party opted to 'export' the 'three revolutionary tidal waves' to the world. Neighbouring communist parties in Laos and Cambodia, unsurprisingly, were the first 'export' sites on Hanoi's list. Deputy Prime Minister and Foreign Minister Nguyễn Duy Trinh announced in June 1975 to the National Assembly that by 'contributing further' to a 'new offensive posture' of the three waves, Hanoi was 'committed to make every effort to fulfill its duties with [the] Lao and Cambodian revolutions'.[79] The strategy then appeared frequently in VCP Politburo resolutions regarding Laos and Cambodia and in joint statements between Hanoi, Vientiane and Communist Party of Kampuchea (CPK) representatives in Phnom Penh.[80]

The Soviet Union came next. At an October 1975 mass rally organised by workers on a factory production line in Moscow, Lê Duẩn declared that by launching their invasion of Vietnam, the US imperialists had 'attacked the two biggest revolutionary currents of our times: national

---

78   'Báo cáo tình hình công tác sáu tháng đầu năm 1976 của Bộ Ngoại giao [The Ministry of Foreign Affairs' Report on the Foreign Affairs of the First Six Months of 1976]', August 1976, Folder 9833, Phông Phủ Thủ tướng [Collection of the Prime Minister's Office], Trung tâm Lưu trữ Quốc gia III [National Archives III], 1.
79   'Kiên trì đường lối quốc tế của Đảng, phát huy thắng lợi vĩ đại của dân tộc, đẩy mạnh công tác ngoại giao nhằm phục vụ công cuộc xây dựng nước nhà và làm nghĩa vụ quốc tế [Preserving the International Line of the Party, Promoting the Great Victory of the Nation, Stepping up Diplomatic Work to Serve the Cause of State-Building and Fulfil International Obligations]', in *Báo cáo của Chính phủ do ông Nguyễn Duy Trinh, Phó Thủ tướng kiêm Bộ trưởng Bộ Ngoại giao trình bày tại kỳ họp thứ nhất, Quốc hội khoá V, ngày 4/6/1975 [Government's Report Presented by Deputy Prime Minister and Foreign Minister Nguyễn Duy Trinh at the First Session of the Fifth National Assembly, 4 June 1975]*, Folder 2252, Phông Quốc hội [Collection of the National Assembly], National Archives III.
80   One example is this document: 'Về tăng cường đoàn kết, giúp đỡ và hợp tác với cách mạng Lào trong giai đoạn mới [On Strengthening the Solidarity, Assistance and Cooperation with the Lao Revolution in the New Stage]', Nghị quyết của Bộ Chính trị Số 251-NQ/TW, ngày 30/4/1976 [Resolution No.251-NQ/TW of the Politburo, 30 April 1976], in VCP, *Complete Collection of Party Documents. Volume 37*, 102–7. The 'three revolutionary tidal waves' appeared three times in this relatively short text.

independence and socialism'.[81] At a February 1976 event to welcome the twenty-fifth congress of the Communist Party of the Soviet Union, Duẩn noted that a '[s]alient feature of today's world situation is the unstoppable growth of the three revolutionary tidal waves of the era ... [which have merged] into a vigorous revolutionary high tide that is on the offensive'.[82] Somewhat surprising, however, was the fact Vietnam sought international support for this concept at the Non-Aligned Movement (NAM), a forum of Third World nations whose leaders wished to remain neutral in the capitalist–socialist rivalry through nonalignment.

In considering their minor *individual* influence at the US-led United Nations General Assembly, participant nations in the NAM made it the preeminent diplomatic forum for Hanoi on the international stage throughout the Cold War. The NAM was also a favourable place for Hanoi at which it could popularise the 'three waves' strategy. The August 1976 Fifth Summit Conference of the NAM in Colombo, Sri Lanka, was the SRV's first appearance as a unified country, and its first opportunity to cast itself as champion of the heroic anti–American imperialist struggle. After this debut, an editorial in the VCP daily, Nhân Dân (*'People'*), declared the 'grand victory' of the organisation was inseparable from the national liberation movement and from 'all three revolutionary tidal waves of the era'.[83] The article also urged that 'only by uniting with each other and with the socialist countries and peaceful forces could [the] NAM find its source of strength'.[84]

Three years later, in an address to the Sixth Summit Conference of the NAM in Havana, Cuba, SRV Prime Minister Phạm Văn Đồng stated confidently: 'Our [the NAM's] struggle for national independence ... is the inevitable trend of the era when the three revolutionary tidal waves were rising up like violent storms, attacking imperialism and expansionism at different sides.'[85]

---

81 'Tình hữu nghị Việt–Xô đời đời bền vững như non sông đất nước chúng ta [Vietnam–Soviet Friendship is Ever Unshakeable Like Our Homelands]', Diễn văn tại cuộc mít tinh của công nhân Nhà máy sản xuất dây chuyền tự động ở Mát-xcơ-va tháng 10 năm 1975 [Speech at a mass rally organised by workers of factory production line in Moscow in October 1975], in Lê Duẩn, *Tiến lên dưới ngọn cờ cách mạng tháng Mười vĩ đại* [Advance Under the October Revolution Great Flag] (Hà Nội: Sự thật, 1977), 181.
82 'Lời chào mừng tại Đại hội lần thứ 25 của Đảng cộng sản Liên-xô (tháng 2 năm 1976) [Welcoming Remarks at the 25th Party Congress of the Communist Party of the Soviet Union (February 1976)]', in Duẩn, *Advance Under the October Revolution Great Flag*, 190.
83 'Hội nghị Cô-lôm-bô, thắng lợi rực rỡ của trào lưu chống đế quốc [The Colombo Conference: Splendid Victory of the Anti-Imperialist Movement]', *Nhân Dân* [People], [Editorial], 21 August 1976, 1.
84 ibid.
85 'Thủ tướng Phạm Văn Đồng phát biểu tại Hội nghị cấp cao các nước Không liên kết [Prime Minister Phạm Văn Đồng Spoke at the Summit Conference of the Non-Aligned Countries]', *Nhân Dân* [People], 7 September 1979, 3.

Astonishingly, while propagandising this concept to the NAM, Hanoi emphasised the importance of the third 'wave' and how tightly it was linked to the 'nature' of the organisation. To the Vietnamese communists, it was correct to say the origin of nonaligned policy was 'nothing else but the determination of certain countries to defend their independence and the legitimate right of their own peoples'.[86] Although hoping to obtain a 'neutral' stance between socialist and capitalist countries, they reasoned that the NAM's tendency towards the defence of national independence against imperialism would gradually grow over time. To conclude, they asserted that the national liberation movement (that is, the third wave) was the *bản chất* ('nature') of the NAM, and its continuous growth reflected 'the growth of one of the three revolutionary tidal waves of this era against imperialism', with the support of the remaining two.[87]

The next step was to put this concept into an official publication, which was undertaken by Hoàng Tùng, a member of the VCP Central Committee, chairman of the Vietnamese Journalists Association and *Nhân Dân*'s chief editor. In May 1978, Tùng published *Thế tiến công của ba dòng thác cách mạng* ('*The Offensive Posture of the Three Revolutionary Tidal Waves*'),[88] which cited and summarised the important elements of Lê Duẩn's strategy—most notably, its definition, background and contribution to the Vietnamese revolution and, vicariously, to world revolution. By underlining the 'offensiveness' of the three waves, Tùng reaffirmed the vitality of the strategy despite newly emerging contentions among Asian communists after Vietnam's 1975 reunification.

The first 'wave' in crisis

The late 1970s was host to a series of crises within the communist bloc worldwide—specifically, in the former Indochina. In the summer of 1977, CPK forces invaded Vietnamese villages in the south-western An Giang and Tây Ninh provinces and killed hundreds of civilians as part of the their plan to 'reclaim' Kampuchea Krom.[89] In September, CPK General

---

86 Socialist Republic of Vietnam, *Phong trào Không Liên kết* [*The Non-Aligned Movement*] (Hà Nội: Sự Thật, 1979), 28.
87 ibid., 36.
88 Hoàng Tùng, *Thế tiến công của ba dòng thác cách mạng* [*The Offensive Posture of the Three Revolutionary Tidal Waves*] (Hà Nội: Sự thật, 1978).
89 Matthew Galway, *The Emergence of Global Maoism: China's Red Evangelism and the Cambodian Communist Movement, 1949–1979* (Ithaca, NY: Cornell University Press, 2022), 198, 267n.132.

Secretary Pol Pot arrived in Beijing for one of the last of several trips to Beijing (he had visited in 1965–66 and 1975).[90] In the Chinese capital, he denounced 'the Soviet Union, Vietnam and Cuba [who] are cooperating to fight us in the border areas'.[91] In turn, China promised to support Democratic Kampuchea's efforts 'in the struggle against imperialism and hegemonism'.[92] The Vietnamese responded with a large-scale military operation in December, after which the CPK in Phnom Penh suspended diplomatic relations with Hanoi.

The deterioration of China–SRV relations represented a significant obstacle for Lê Duẩn, the VCP and the 'three revolutionary tidal waves'. Before the December 1977 counteroffensive, Duẩn led a high-level SRV delegation on a visit to China for what became the last friendly direct communication between the two sides.[93] After 1975, Chinese and Vietnamese forces engaged in periodic skirmishes along the disputed border between the two countries on land and at sea. In June 1978, after Beijing severed its aid agreement with Hanoi and the subsequent economic fallout in Vietnam, Hanoi dropped its earlier resistance to moving from observer status to full membership of the Soviet-sponsored Council for Mutual Economic Assistance (Comecon). Beijing retaliated by shuttering Vietnamese consulates and closing its border to Vietnamese in July. By November, Duẩn and Phạm Văn Đồng boarded a Soviet jet to Moscow for a historic event: the signing of the 25-year Treaty of Friendship and Cooperation between Vietnam and the Soviet Union. Hanoi would hence receive 'consultation and assistance' in the event China attacked Vietnam.[94]

With the normalisation of US–China diplomatic relations on 15 December 1978, the CPK moved 19 of its divisions to the Vietnamese border, and its backers in Beijing militarised China's southern border with Vietnam.

---

90   ibid., 64–70; and Matthew Galway, 'From Revolutionary Culture to Original Culture and Back: On New Democracy and the Kampucheanization of Marxism-Leninism, 1940–1965', *Cross-Currents: East Asian History and Culture Review* (24) (September 2017): 132–58.
91   'Hua Guofeng and Pol Pot, September 29, 1977', in *Seventy-Seven Conversations between Chinese and Foreign Leaders on the Wars of Indochina, 1964–1977*, Odd Arne Westad, Chen Jian, Stein Tønnesson, Nguyen Vu Tung and James G. Hershberg, eds (Washington, DC: Woodrow Wilson Center Cold War International History Project, 1998), 193.
92   Nayan Chanda, *Brother Enemy: The War after the War* (San Diego, CA: Harcourt Brace Jovanovich, 1986), 101.
93   Stephen J. Morris, *Why Vietnam Invaded Cambodia: Political Culture and the Causes of War* (Stanford, CA: Stanford University Press, 1999), 184–85.
94   Chang Pao-Min, *Kampuchea between China and Vietnam* (Singapore: NUS Press, 1985), 189–93.

The VCP leadership recognised it could not wait any longer and turned the counteroffensive of 1977 to repel CPK forces from Vietnam into an invasion of Democratic Kampuchea (CPK-ruled Cambodia) on 25 December 1978. VCP forces occupied and then captured Phnom Penh on 7 January 1979, which effectively ended CPK rule over Cambodia.[95] The Vietnamese occupation of Phnom Penh and total defeat of a Beijing ally placed a great deal of pressure, especially from Washington, on Beijing to act. The Chinese Communist Party did just that by deploying 170,000 soldiers to its southern border with Vietnam on 17 February. Moscow then quickly militarised its border with China and, by the end of the year, Soviet troops had invaded Afghanistan—a move that prompted US President Jimmy Carter to support Beijing's ally in the CPK and to denounce the Vietnamese occupation of Phnom Penh.[96] To make matters worse for the Vietnamese, the longstanding friendship between Vietnam and the Democratic People's Republic of Korea (North Korea) also fell into aversion and hostility around this time.[97]

This sequence of events, especially for those within the Asian communist bloc, undoubtedly weakened the first 'wave' that was the foundation of Lê Duẩn's 'three revolutionary tidal waves' strategy. In coping with this new hindrance, the Vietnamese communists moved to construct new interpretations of Duẩn's strategy, with Nguyễn Duy Trinh taking the first step towards this rebranding effort. In his December 1977 report on the global situation to the National Assembly, Nguyễn Duy Trinh repeated the VCP's standpoint of the time:

> The post–Vietnam War era marked a new milestone in the world history after World War II up to now: the three revolutionary tidal waves have developed with a new impetus and strength on a global scale … The balance of power is now leaning towards the revolutionary side and compared to thirty years ago the offensive posture of revolution now generates changes in terms of quality.[98]

---

95 Grant Evans and Kelvin Rowley, *Red Brotherhood at War: Vietnam, Cambodia and Laos since 1975* (New York, NY: Verso, 1990), 104–11.
96 Kenton Clymer, 'Jimmy Carter, Human Rights, and Cambodia', *Diplomatic History* 27(2) (April 2003): 245–78, doi.org/10.1111/1467-7709.00349.
97 Khue Dieu Do, 'Comrades at Enmity: Pyongyang–Hanoi Split after the Fall of Saigon', *Cold War History* (2021), doi.org/10.1080/14682745.2021.1923698.
98 'Những nét lớn của tình hình thế giới và hoạt động đối ngoại của ta năm 1977 [Main Features of the World Situation and Our Diplomatic Activities in 1977]', Báo cáo của đồng chí Nguyễn Duy Trinh tại kỳ họp thứ 3 Quốc hội khoá 6 tháng 12 năm 1977 [Report by Comrade Nguyễn Duy Trinh at the Third Session of the Sixth National Assembly in December 1977], Folder 2332, Collection of the National Assembly, National Archives III.

Then, merely a day after Vietnamese troops occupied Phnom Penh and 10 days before Chinese troops overran Vietnam's northern provinces, a commentary in the People's Army of Vietnam daily, *Quân đội Nhân dân* ('*National Army*'), provided equally puzzling positive assessments of the global revolutionary situation. It said the revolutionary movement had found its way forward with 'ceaselessly vigorous growth of the three revolutionary tidal waves' while standing at the 'centre of the storm'.[99] In total ignorance—wilful or unwitting—of the deterioration of relations between Hanoi and some of its nearby ideological allies in 1978, the *Quân đội Nhân dân* nevertheless reckoned world revolution had advanced its offensive posture with new victories 'that frightened the capitalists'.[100]

After Vietnam, the article continued, the American imperialists faced 'unprecedented failure' and were 'on the verge of decline'.[101] As 'reactionary forces' were ill equipped to challenge the three waves' power and halt the revolutionary offensive, the United States had implemented an 'evil, cunning plot' through which it sought to: 1) disunite, sabotage and tarnish the prestige and decisive role of the socialist system in the development of world revolution; and 2) undermine the convergence of the three waves by placing a buffer between them.[102] The imperialists were beginning to find ways to assemble new forces and gain an efficient ally—the elements of *bành trướng và bá quyền nước lớn* ('great-power–type expansionism and hegemony')—within the Beijing leadership.[103] Sino-American relations and the Sino-Japanese Peace and Friendship Treaty, argued *Quân đội Nhân dân*, went beyond normal relations between countries because 'Beijing considered anti-expansionism and anti-Soviet [policy] as its diplomatic prerequisites'.[104] This demonstrated the alliance between the imperialist forces and their 'reactionary friends' in a scheme to launch an all-out offensive against world revolution. The commentary insisted the Soviet Union and socialist countries were the most marvellous results of the world revolution that had built a reliable base and brought new hope for the world's revolutionary and progressive forces. In the current era, each national revolutionary victory was a product not of that nation alone, but

---

99 'Thế tiến công của cách mạng thế giới phát triển không ngừng [The Offensive Posture of World Revolution Develops Ceaselessly]', *Quân đội Nhân dân* [*National Army*], [Commentary], 8 January 1979, 4.
100 ibid.
101 ibid.
102 ibid.
103 ibid.
104 ibid.

'of the whole era'.¹⁰⁵ A complete revolution of national liberation, *Quân đội Nhân dân* maintained, could not be successful if it lacked the support and assistance of the Soviet Union and socialist countries.

In the article's concluding paragraph, *Quân đội Nhân dân* asserted that the convergence of the three revolutionary tidal waves had become a 'subjective reality'. It was a 'natural alliance' of the forces fighting for peace, independence, democracy and socialism against imperialist and reactionary forces. The article charged that to separate oneself from this synergy and think one could 'become great' without any support from the revolutionary waves was a 'naive illusion', a 'sophism' that would cause one to 'fall into the hands of imperialist and reactionary forces in reality'.¹⁰⁶ Undoubtedly, these strident criticisms and warnings were directed by *Quân đội Nhân dân* at Beijing.

The next month, chairman Hoàng Quốc Việt read his political report at the Fourth Meeting of the Fatherland Front Central Committee, in which he declared that in '[g]oing against the three revolutionary tidal waves of the era, the Beijing reactionary expansionists would not escape failure'.¹⁰⁷ In short, troubled by wars and hostility—this time with their one-time Asian communist comrades-in-arms—the Hanoi leaders could not but reaffirm to their people that the first 'wave' was standing firm. At the same time, they blamed China for resisting the 'inevitable' three tides of revolution and undermining their union by colluding with the Americans. These claims arose during Vietnam's so-called anti-Chinese decade (1979–89), which receded after the fall of communism in Eastern Europe, and Hanoi was reconciled with Beijing in 1991.

Conclusion

On 10 July 1986, Lê Duẩn died in Hanoi. Throughout his 40-year political career, the party secretary had viewed his home country's struggles against Euro-American imperialism as the driving force of world

---

105 ibid.
106 ibid.
107 'Khai mạc hội nghị lần thứ Tư Ủy ban Trung ương MTTQ Việt Nam, Đồng chí Hoàng Quốc Việt: Bọn phản động bành trướng Bắc Kinh đi ngược ba dòng thác cách mạng của thời đại, nhất định không tránh khỏi thất bại [Opening the Fourth Meeting of the Fatherland Front Central Committee, Comrade Hoàng Quốc Việt: Going Against the Three Revolutionary Tidal Waves of the Era, the Beijing Reactionary Expansionists Are Destined for Defeat]', *Hà Nội Mới* [*New Hanoi*], 27 February 1979, 4.

revolution. As such, there was no reason for Vietnamese communists to yield any ground, even ideologically. Lê Duẩn's development of the 'three revolutionary tidal waves' strategy was thus not purely for propaganda purposes, but always with a view towards the bigger picture of global socialist revolution.

From its inception, Lê Duẩn's strategy served as a timely encouragement and spiritual inspiration for the Vietnamese people to confidently pursue war on all fronts against America. As the vanguard of the third 'wave', which contained the greatest revolutionary potential, Vietnam's war for national liberation would prove *chính nghĩa* ('righteous'). Accordingly, the 'strike team' that led the offensive against imperialism on behalf of the world's people was supported nationally and internationally no matter how aggressive their efforts might turn. Hanoi's offensive campaigns at the end of the war were therefore rational and legitimate in the eyes of audiences both at home and abroad. If Hồ Chí Minh pioneered the VWP/VCP use of the 'international factor', Lê Duẩn deserves credit for exploiting this potential source of support skilfully and creatively. From the late 1970s, the situation in Asia and the world further weakened the role of the first 'wave', yet highlighted the third wave's magnitude—a reality about which the party secretary was already optimistic when devising the 'three revolutionary tidal waves' strategy.

Since its establishment, Vietnamese socialism has deliberately avoided one-person rule through institutionalised collective leadership. Scholars of Vietnamese politics and history find it difficult to identify and assess the role of and give due credit to certain individuals in the decision-making processes of the Vietnamese party-state. Nevertheless, as this chapter has shown, Lê Duẩn presents a noteworthy case study for his development of the 'three revolutionary tidal waves' strategy; his efforts to theorise and popularise the strategy were made with domestic and international audiences in mind, and with a view towards export abroad. Under Duẩn's leadership, the 'three revolutionary tidal waves' indeed became the cause, political line, legitimating factor and ambition of the Vietnamese communists for more than two decades. As this chapter has sought to show, the 'three revolutionary tidal waves' prove Lê Duẩn was much more than simply a capable war strategist and tactician, as the extant literature has often contended. Indeed, the party secretary proved himself to be a devoted proletarian-internationalist ideologue and theorist, and his 'three revolutionary tidal waves' strategy remains one of his most prominent legacies.

10

Becoming Marxist: Ethnic Hmong in the Communist Party of Thailand

Ian G. Baird[1]

Thousands of ethnic Hmong people joined the Communist Party of Thailand (CPT) in the 1960s and lived in CPT base areas between the late 1960s and the early 1980s. However, the extent to which Hmong in the CPT came to understand and internalise Marxism and Maoism is a topic that has so far escaped academic inquiry. Between the 1960s and the 1980s, ethnic Hmong started to study politics with the CPT and later joined the armed struggle, particularly with the People's Liberation Army of Thailand (PLAT). The Hmong became one of the key ethnic groups—along with the Lua[2]—in the mountainous areas of northern Thailand controlled by the CPT.

Beginning in 1968–69, several key CPT strongholds were established in the mountains where Hmong had previously lived. Most were along Thailand's borders with Laos and Burma, including in Chiang Rai, Phayao, Nan, Phitsanulok, Phetchabun, Loei and Tak provinces. There is little doubt the Hmong were key combatants for the PLAT; however,

---

1   Thanks to all the Hmong and Thai people whom I interviewed for this chapter. Thanks also to Marc Opper and Katsu Takahashi for useful comments on an earlier version of this chapter.
2   The CPT museum at Phu Phayak in Nan Province near the border with Laos demonstrates this. There are specific exhibitions devoted to the way the houses of two upland ethnic groups looked; one was the Lua (sometimes incorrectly referred to as being ethnic T'in) and the other was the Hmong.

what was their contribution to the political doctrine of the CPT? The Hmong were certainly 'communists' by the time they took advantage of a government amnesty and left the forest and the CPT, but to what extent did they really understand and internalise the Marxist political philosophy the CPT espoused?

I have been researching Hmong involvement in the CPT since 2013 and have conducted more than 200 interviews, mainly with Hmong previously with the CPT/PLAT, but also with some ethnic Thais and Chinese Thais.[3] In addition, I have interviewed Hmong and people from other ethnic groups who sided with the government and fought against the CPT, and members of the military who fought against the CPT. However, in this chapter, I focus only on CPT/PLAT Hmong. Virtually all interviews were conducted in central Thai language—a dialect typically known well by former CPT Hmong. Apart from the interviews, I also gathered documents related to the CPT and particularly Hmong involvement with the party, in both Thai and English. These materials include newspaper clippings, internal party documents, orders and reports that relate in whatever way to Hmong involvement in the CPT. I have also reviewed the relevant published academic literature in Thai and English. I make use of historical and ethnic studies methods to discern the political development of Hmong in the CPT, Hmong political leadership and broader understandings of Marxism among Hmong CPT.

I contend that all Hmong in the CPT understood little about communist political philosophy when they first joined. In extreme cases, some had never heard of communism when they entered the CPT. What I have heard from them is consistent with other communist revolutions in Asia during the twentieth century.[4] At best, new Hmong recruits in northern Thailand knew very little about political theory. Rather, even before the Hmong began to join the CPT in larger numbers, the Thai military accused many of them of being communists, forcing them to flee into the forests after their houses were burnt to the ground (the first such incident occurred in Huai Chompu Village in Thoeng District, Chiang

---

3   For ease of understanding, I will mainly refer to the PLAT as the CPT.
4   Jeffrey Race, *War Comes to Long An: Revolutionary Conflict in a Vietnamese Province* (Berkeley, CA: University of California Press, 2010 [1972]); David W.P. Elliott, *The Vietnamese War: Revolution and Social Change in the Mekong Delta, 1930–1975*, 2 vols (Armonk, NY: M.E. Sharpe, 2003); Lucian W. Pye, *Guerrilla Communism in Malaya: Its Social and Political Meaning* (Princeton, NJ: Princeton University Press, 1956).

Rai Province).[5] This follows the logic laid out by Stathis Kalyvas and Matthew Kocher[6] in their influential article showing that violence against populations can result in increased insurgent recruitment.

While no Hmong were ever appointed to the CPT's Central Committee or Politburo, many eventually became party members, which certainly indicates they had strong political knowledge, for only trustworthy and knowledgeable people were invited to join the party. Some Hmong became base area/stronghold military leaders and a few men (and only men) eventually rose to become *samachik kammakan khet* or *khana khet* ('zone party committee members'), which advised *sapha tambon* ('district congresses') where they existed. These *sapha tambon* were able to adopt somewhat different rules from place to place based on local conditions.[7] The highest level of membership for Hmong was as *samachik kammakan changwat* or *khana changwat* ('provincial party committee members').

In addition, some young Hmong were assigned to work closely with CPT Thai-Chinese political leaders, including Politburo members, and these associations allowed some to learn a considerable amount about Marxist political philosophy through reading and political guidance. However, this knowledge was quite unevenly distributed across the Hmong population within the CPT strongholds. Hmong who lived in the villages in the strongholds generally had much lower levels of formal education than many of the Chinese Thais and Thais from other parts of the country who joined them, so they often knew less about political philosophy.

In the next section of this chapter, I explain my research methods. I then briefly outline the history of the CPT before considering how the Hmong became involved with the party. I then consider the circumstances that led many Hmong to join and stay with the party until its members largely accepted offers of amnesty from the Thai Government, at which

---

5   Thomas A. Marks, 'The Meo Hill Tribe Problem in North Thailand', *Asian Survey* 13(10) (1973): 929–44, doi.org/10.2307/2643003; Jeffrey Race, 'The War in Northern Thailand', *Modern Asian Studies* 8(1) (1974): 85–112, doi.org/10.1017/S0026749X00004765; Ian G. Baird, 'The Hmong and the Communist Party of Thailand: A Transnational, Transcultural and Gender Relations-Transforming Experience', *TRaNS: Trans-Regional and -National Studies of Southeast Asia* 9(2) (2021): 167–84, doi.org/10.1017/trn.2020.11.
6   Stathis Kalyvas and Matthew A. Kocher, 'How "Free" is Free Riding in Civil Wars? Violence, Insurgency, and the Collective Action Problem', *World Politics* 59(2) (2007): 177–216, doi.org/10.1353/wp.2007.0023.
7   Sahai Khon (Wisut Sae Jiang), Pers. comm., Huai Loi Village, Boklua District, Thailand, May 2021.

point the CPT rapidly disintegrated.⁸ I then consider Hmong political positions within the CPT and their engagement with Marxist political philosophy throughout the CPT period, before considering present-day understandings of Marxist political philosophy among former CPT Hmong in northern Thailand.

The Communist Party of Thailand

The CPT was officially founded on 1 December 1942, after previously being known as the Communist Party of Siam. Communist organising apparently began in Siam (Thailand) as early as 1927, but initially most of those involved with the party were Chinese Thais living in urban areas, particularly the capital city of Bangkok. No Hmong were involved. However, in the late 1950s, after Mao Zedong led the communist takeover and establishment of the People's Republic of China (PRC), the CPT decided to adopt a new approach, emphasising the building up of the party in rural areas.⁹ This shifted the CPT's geographical focus, and recruiters started coming into contact with the Hmong.

There has been a considerable amount written about the history of the CPT, with Kasian Tejapira, Somsak Jeamteerasakul and Eiji Murashima[10] focusing on its early days, before it shifted focus from urban to rural areas in the late 1950s.

However, the armed conflict between the CPT and the Thai Government, which began in north-eastern Thailand in 1965, has been the main focus. Another has been on the periods when university students went to the forests in large numbers to join the CPT (in 1973 and 1976). CPT history, however, has been written by people with quite different

---

8   Thomas A. Marks, *Making Revolution: The Insurgency of the Communist Party of Thailand in Structural Perspective*, Studies in Contemporary Thailand No.3 (Bangkok: White Lotus Press, 1994).
9   Patrice de Beer, 'History and Policy of the Communist Party of Thailand', *Journal of Contemporary Asia* 8(1) (1978): 143–58, doi.org/10.1080/00472337885390071; Kasian Tejapira, *Commodifying Marxism: The Formation of Modern Thai Radical Culture, 1927–1958* (Kyoto: Kyoto University Press, 2001); Somsak Jeamteerasakul, 'CPT History of the CPT: Part 1', [in Thai], *Fa Dieo Kan* 1(1) (2003): 154–200; Somsak Jeamteerasakul, 'CPT History of the CPT: Part 2', [in Thai], *Fa Dieo Kan* 1(2) (2003): 164–200; Chris Baker, 'An Internal History of the Communist Party of Thailand', *Journal of Contemporary Asia* 33(4) (2003): 510–41, doi.org/10.1080/00472330380000311.
10   Kasian, *Commodifying Marxism*; Somsak, 'CPT History of the CPT: Part 1' and 'CPT History of the CPT: Part 2'; Eiji Murashima, *Kamnoet phak khommununit sayam* [*The Origins of the Siam Communist Party*], [translated from Japanese] (Bangkok: Sinpawattanatham, 2012).

perspectives, including members of the CPT itself,[11] Thai academics,[12] Thai politicians and military figures,[13] foreign academics interested in communist movements in Asia,[14] other foreign academics[15] and lowland urban Thai students who spent a few years in the forests with the CPT. Most of these students were motivated to join the CPT after the political crises in Bangkok that began on 14 October 1973 and 6 October 1976.[16]

---

11 Jinta Tuangjinda, *Khabuan karn khommunit haeng pratet Thai* [*The Communist Movement in Thailand*] (Bangkok: Bhannakij Trading Company, 1974 [2517]); Communist Party of Thailand [hereinafter CPT], *The Road to Victory. Documents from the Communist Party of Thailand* (Chicago, IL: Liberator Press, 1978); Baker, 'An Internal History of the Communist Party of Thailand'; Khunphol, ed., *Phu wae phu phayak: Damnan dao phrao phrai* [*Wae Mountain, Phayak Mountain: The Story of the Stars in the Forest. Volume 1*] (Bangkok: Art Age Graphics, 2005 [2548]); Khunphol, ed., *Phu wae phu phayak: Damnan dao phrao phrai* [*Wae Mountain, Phayak Mountain: The Story of the Stars in the Forest. Volume 2*] (Bangkok: Art Age Graphics, 2009 [2552]); Khunphol, ed., *Phu wae phu phayak: Damnan dao phrao phrai* [*Wae Mountain, Phayak Mountain: The Story of the Stars in the Forest. Volume 3*] (Bangkok: Art Age Graphics, 2014 [2557]).

12 Thawatt Mokarapong, *History of the Thai Revolution: A Study in Political Behavior* (Bangkok: Chalermnit, 1972); Somsak, 'CPT History of the CPT: Part 1' and 'Part 2'; Kanok Wongtrangran, 'Communist revolutionary process: A study of the Communist Party of Thailand' (PhD diss., Johns Hopkins University, Baltimore, MD, 1982); Kanok Wongtrangan, 'The Revolutionary Strategy of the Communist Party of Thailand: Change and Persistence', in *Armed Communist Movements in Southeast Asia*, Lim Joo-Jock and Vani S., eds (New York, NY: St Martin's Press, 1984), 133–82; Kanokrat Lertchoosakul, *The Rise of the Octobrists in Contemporary Thailand* (New Haven, CT: Yale Southeast Asia Studies, 2016).

13 Saiyud Kerdphol, *The Struggle for Thailand: Counterinsurgency 1965–1986* (Bangkok: S. Research Company Co., 1986); Saiyud Kerdphol, *Ph.Kh.Th Hai Pai Nai?* [*Form Over Substance: The Communist Party of Thailand*] (Bangkok, 2001 [2554]); Thannit Kraiwichian, *Latti lae withikarn khong khommunit* [*The Ideology and Method of Communism*], 3rd edn (Bangkok: Ministry of Education, 1977 [2520]); Jutcheep Chinwanno, *Chanuan songkhwam: Thai chin and indochin* [*The Reasons for War: Chinese Thais and Indochina*] (Bangkok: Samakhee Sasn Company, 1986 [2529]).

14 Stephen I. Alpern, 'Insurgency in Northeast Thailand: A New Cause for Alarm', *Asian Survey* 15(8) (1975): 684–92, doi.org/10.2307/2643385; Marks, 'The Meo Hill Tribe Problem in North Thailand'; Marks, *Making Revolution*; Glenn Ettinger, 'Thailand's Defeat of its Communist Party', *International Journal of Intelligence and CounterIntelligence* 20(4) (2007): 661–77, doi.org/10.1080/08850600701472996.

15 Katherine Bowie, *Rituals of National Loyalty: An Anthropology of the State and the Village Scout Movement in Thailand* (New York, NY: Columbia University Press, 1997); de Beer, 'History and Policy of the Communist Party of Thailand'; Race, 'The War in Northern Thailand'; David Morell and Chai-anan Samudavanija, 'Thailand's Revolutionary Insurgency: Changes in Leadership Potential', *Asian Survey* 19(4) (1979 [1950]): 315–32, doi.org/10.2307/2643854.

16 Gawin Chutima, *The rise and fall of the Communist Party of Thailand (1973–1987)*, Occasional Paper No.12 (Canterbury, UK: Centre of South-East Asian Studies, University of Kent, 1990); Janthana Fongthale, *Jak doi yao theung phu pha ji: Bantheuk prawatsat kan dern thang khong num sao haeng deuan tula* [*From Yao Mountain to Pha Ji Mountain: Recording the History of a Journey of the Octoberists*] (Bangkok: Phreo Samnak Phim, 2013 [2556]); Thonthan Looklanthai, *La korn hin rong kla: Leuang neung khong khwam Song Jam Jak karn to soo khong Prachachon* [*Goodbye Hin Rong Kla*], 3rd edn (Bangkok: Phimdee Ltd, 2011 [2554]); Khongchet Phromnamphon, *Bantheuk phnom dong rak* [*The Phnom Dong Rak Mountains*] (Bangkok: Samosorn 19, 1999 [2542]); Mai Lee, *Phayu fon: Bon phu pha ji—pha chang* [*Storm and Rain: On the Pha Ji Mountain*] (Bangkok: Rangsit University Press, 2016 [2559]); Phanthiwa, *Nak samoraphum leuat: Phu sia sala pheua phaen din* [*The Blood Warrior: A Person's Sacrifice for the Land*] (Bangkok: Animate Group, 2005 [2557]); Meuan Fon, *Su samoraphum neo na: Lang mik dao daeng phak 2* [*Frontline Battlefield: Behind the Mike of the Red Star, Part 2*] (Bangkok: 6 Tula Ramleuk, 2008 [2551]); Thongchai Winichakul, *Moments of Silence: The Unforgetting of the October 6, 1976, Massacre in Bangkok* (Honolulu: University of Hawai'i Press, 2020), doi.org/10.1515/9780824882853.

Until quite recently, however, the literature has barely provided any point of view of the ethnic minorities who joined or struggled against the CPT in the 1960s and 1970s.[17] Moreover, no-one has tried to assess the political importance of ethnic minority involvement in the CPT or the extent of minorities' political engagement with Marxist and Maoist theory—something I do here, particularly in relation to the Hmong, who were one of the main ethnic groups to ally with the CPT.

The Communist Party of Thailand and the Hmong

Jong Teng Vang (*sahai* or comrade Kham) was probably the first ethnic Hmong to join the CPT. He was born in the rural mountains of eastern Chiang Rai Province, and his father died when he was young. As he was a member of the Vang clan, his mother urged him to travel to Laos to meet with the well-known right-wing Hmong head of Lao Military Region 2 in north-eastern Laos, General Vang Pao, in the hope the general might take pity on the fatherless boy from his own clan. In 1960, Jong Teng ventured out, but he had no idea how to find the general. Instead, he ended up in neighbouring Xayaboury Province, in north-western Laos, with Hmong communists led by Shoua Nou Xiong and Wakoua Yang, who were not aligned with the communist Lao People's Liberation Army (Pathet Lao). Jong Teng was staying in a Hmong communist village in Laos when some Thai communists came down from China and heard there was a young Hmong Thai in the village.[18]

These early recruiters were associated with a faction of those who supported Pridi Banomyong after he fled to China following the November 1947 coup d'état organised by Lieutenant-General Phin Choonhavan and Colonel Kat Katsongkhram in support of the return to power of Plaek Phibunsongkhram. Pridi apparently rejected overtures from Mao to become the political leader of the CPT, instead opting to retire to France. However, members of a more radical faction of those who fled to China with Pridi in 1947 took up China's offer to support the building up of the CPT, following a new Maoist rural-based approach more in tune with

---

17 For recent exceptions, see: Baird, 'The Hmong and the Communist Party of Thailand'; Ian G. Baird and Urai Yangcheepsutjarit, 'Hmong Women's Rights and the Communist Party of Thailand', *Journal of Southeast Asian Studies* (forthcoming).
18 Baird, 'The Hmong and the Communist Party of Thailand'.

Mao's own revolution in China.[19] Some of these early agents were the first to encounter Jong Teng, meeting him in Laos before they arrived in Thailand, travelling overland from China.[20] They claimed Pridi had sent them, due to his name recognition, but it was probably Prayom Chulanont (Sahai Khamtan) who was behind the plan.[21]

Since Jong Teng Vang did not yet speak Thai, his first discussions with the Thai CPT recruiters had to be translated; they offered Jong Teng the opportunity to 'study'. Initially, like others who would come after him, he did not understand what communism was, but he was interested in any opportunity 'to study', without really understanding what that meant. He thus became the first Hmong to study with the CPT, walking to a place along the Laos–China border called A-30.[22] Some say it was in Louang Namtha Province; others believe it was in Oudomxay Province. In any case, it was a temporary camp and school in the forest where new CPT recruits from northern Thailand, including the Hmong, received basic political and military training generally lasting for three months.

Jong Teng was a student, but all the instruction was in the central Thai language. There were no Hmong–Thai translators at that time, so he had to plunge in and try to learn Thai as he studied. After three months of perseverance, he could speak basic Thai. Other young Hmong men arrived in A-30 from Thailand, and they, too, did not yet speak Thai. Jong Teng therefore became their translator, although translation must have been quite rough.[23] Crucially for this chapter, those Hmong who came for basic political and military training knew little about Marxism or Maoism or what they were getting into. Rather, they wanted 'to study', as even though they had little contact with the lowlands at the time, children were beginning to understand there were schools in lowland cities, and studying was beginning to become an important ambition for many young Hmong, although it was initially out of reach for most. However, for the few who could access formal education, it was only for Hmong boys, not girls.

---

19 Christopher John Baker and Pasuk Phongpaichit, *A History of Thailand* (Cambridge, UK: Cambridge University Press, 2005).
20 Baird, 'The Hmong and the Communist Party of Thailand'.
21 Lo Meng Sae Fa (Sahai Surat, Phu Kong Surat), Pers. comm., Thung Sai Village, Chiang Khong District, Thailand, September 2016.
22 Baird, 'The Hmong and the Communist Party of Thailand'.
23 ibid.

Jong Teng was later sent to China for additional political training, including in Marxism and Maoism. After a few years there, he returned to Thailand in 1963 to help recruit more Hmong to join the CPT at A-30 and beyond.[24] The main message Jong Teng conveyed to other Hmong was that the CPT intended to end lowlander discrimination against them and make the Hmong equal to lowlanders in terms of wealth, status and power. This was a message that fitted well with the grievances Hmong already had. Thus, Jong Teng started teaching small groups in the forests surrounding their villages. He was mobile and moved from village to village on foot, from Chiang Rai in the north, where he was born, down the mountain range to upland areas in Phitsanulok Province. Initially, Jong Teng operated covertly. When asked why he was travelling from village to village, he often claimed he was looking for a wife, as this kind of travel by young men was often linked to such an activity. This allowed him to maintain his cover.

Initially, the CPT did not want to provoke violence, for fear it would attract attention to the political work it was doing at the grassroots level. The party wanted to continue the small political meetings that were being organised in villages or in the surrounding forest without attracting the attention of government officials or security forces. Jong Teng and others who followed him, both Hmong and non-Hmong, gradually increased the number of villages in which they covertly operated.

Fighting between Hmong and the authorities first occurred by accident, because of a conflict between Hmong villagers, lowland Thai Government officials and a unit of the Border Patrol Police (BPP). The conflict started when lowland government officials tried to fine four Hmong families in Huai Chompu Village, Thoeng District, Chiang Rai Province, for undertaking swidden agriculture in a restricted area. The officials and some BPP came to collect the fine on 8 May 1967, but the villagers had been alerted they were on their way and fled into the forest. The officials and BPP could not find anyone and started searching the bamboo houses. One Hmong woman who had fled to the forest realised she had left her valuable silver necklace in her house. She was afraid the officials would find it, so she returned to retrieve it. Some BPP saw her and followed her back to the forest, where they started shooting at the villagers. The Hmong fired back with their flint rifles. Jong Teng had already been providing some political lessons in the village before this incident, and the BPP

---

24 ibid.

may have heard rumours before they arrived. A Hmong man was injured, but a BPP soldier was killed. The BPP retreated. The Hmong were angry when they realised their houses had been looted, so they detained the lowland Thai subdistrict chief and declared they would not release him until their stolen goods had been returned.

The BPP, enraged the Hmong had killed one of their own and taken a local government official hostage, returned to Huai Chompu Village a few days later in much greater numbers. The Hmong heard a large contingent approaching, so they released their unharmed hostage just before the BPP arrived and fled into the forest. The BPP fired their guns in the village, killing some domestic animals. They then burned down all the houses, except for the one where the hostage had been kept. The Hmong whose houses were destroyed had nowhere to go, so they joined the CPT, who were waiting for them in the forest and were willing to support them to rise up against the injustices of the Thai state.[25]

In late 1967, fighting spread further south to Nan Province.[26] However, one event involving ethnic Lua and Hmong clashing with Thai Government officials in Boklua District in early 1968 was particularly important for escalating the conflict. In Tak Province, to the west, near the border with Burma, Hmong reportedly began fighting Thai Government security services in November 1967 when they attacked a police station. The next month, they attacked a border patrol station, killing 10 officers and capturing a quantity of rice sent to Tak by the Thai Government.[27]

The BPP unexpectedly flew a helicopter to Doi Pha Daeng Village, which was about 10 kilometres from Huai Chompu, and arrested Nhia Ja Sae Fa, the village's Hmong headman. They accused him of being linked to communists, but no-one in the village had been in contact with any communists. Indeed, they hardly knew what communism was. The villagers thought Nhia Ja had been killed; he was imprisoned for years, without anyone in the village knowing he was still alive. Anger about his abduction contributed to his nephew, Lo Meng Sae Fa, joining the CPT to avenge the death of his uncle.[28] Other Hmong joined the CPT

---

25   ibid. See other versions of this story by Marks, 'The Meo Hill Tribe Problem in North Thailand'; and Race, 'The War in Northern Thailand'.
26   Peking NCNA International Service, 'Thais Will Oust US–Thanom Clique Hit by Hit', *Foreign Broadcasting Information Service*, [Washington, DC], 28 January 1968.
27   ibid.
28   Lo Meng Sae Fa, Pers. comm., September 2016.

for less dramatic reasons, but even they knew little about its political philosophy. However, the CPT was able to link Hmong concerns with its anti-government politics. Once they had joined the CPT, those who were with the military or held other full-time positions with the CPT put considerable effort into learning Marxist political philosophy, even though they started from very low levels of formal and political education, which limited the advancement of many.

In November 1968, the fighting spread further south to Nakorn Thai District, Phitsanulok Province, where Hmong CPT attacked village defence volunteers in Huai Sai Neua Village. This led to most of the Hmong population in Phitsanulok, Phetchabun and Loei provinces—*khet ngan 3 changwat* ('the three-province region')—fleeing to the forest to join the CPT.[29]

The Thai military moved aggressively to suppress the threat of communism in various Hmong areas in northern Thailand, but these operations were more likely to encourage Hmong to join the communists than discourage them, as the military was not adept at determining which Hmong were procommunist and which were not. The Hmong were subjected to simplistic ethnic stereotyping, which assumed they were against Thais—something some members of the military tried to discourage.[30] Soon, much of the Hmong population living on the Thai side of the border with Laos had joined the CPT and, by early 1969, a significant portion of the Hmong living in northern Thailand, except for those in Chiang Mai and Phrae provinces,[31] were working with the CPT in the forest, although only some became party members. By this time, the CPT's radio station in Kunming, China, was openly urging Hmong in northern Thailand to take up arms against the Thai military.[32] This is not surprising, since they were an important ethnic group in the CPT in northern Thailand.

The main concerns of those who fled to the forest were:

1. Predatory and unfair taxation by lowlanders.
2. Racialisation of Hmong by lowlanders.

---

29 Baird, 'The Hmong and the Communist Party of Thailand'.
30 See Saiyud, *The Struggle for Thailand*.
31 See Nicolas Tapp, *Sovereignty and Rebellion: The White Hmong of Northern Thailand*, 2nd edn (Bangkok: White Lotus Press, 2005).
32 Voice of the People of Thailand, 'Meo Tribesmen Urged to Fight Government (In White Hmong)', *Foreign Broadcasting Information Service*, [Washington, DC], 30 August 1969.

3. Unwanted sexual advances on Hmong women and sometimes the abuse of young and married Hmong women.
4. The killing of pigs and chickens by security forces for food without asking permission or providing compensation.
5. Concerns about a lack of development and education services in their communities.
6. A sense that they were not eligible for citizenship in Thailand and were therefore not welcome in the country.
7. Particularly in the three-provinces region, extremely unpopular government plans to resettle Hmong villagers from the Khao Kho/Khao Ya area.[33]

The CPT was able to connect its politics with the issues about which Hmong were already dissatisfied in relation to the government.

CPT strongholds in the mountains of northern Thailand

As a direct result of the mountainous terrain of northern Thailand, and its close proximity to Laos and Burma, by the 1970s, the CPT was able to establish 15 *than thi man* ('base areas' or 'strongholds') there. They were places where the CPT was able to impose *amnat rat* ('state power') within its territory. They were *than thi man, khet daeng* ('red areas')—places where the CPT was in full control. Of the 15 strongholds, Hmong dominated 10—two in Chiang Rai, two in Phayao Province, two in Nan Province, three in Phitsanulok, Phetchabun and Loei provinces, and one in Tak Province. Only four strongholds in Nan Province and one in Tak Province were not numerically dominated by Hmong; the four in Nan Province were dominated by ethnic Lua (T'in).[34] Crucially, these fully 'red areas', outside the control of the government, only existed thanks to the high mountain topography, which was easy to defend. In other parts of the country, such as north-eastern and southern Thailand, there were only *khet jarayut* ('pink areas'), which were not as secure as 'red areas'.

The highest-level Hmong in the CPT were provincial party committee members. Each *changwat* ('province') had one or more *khet* ('zones'). In Chiang Rai Province, Lao Wit (Joowit Sae Yang) and Lao Phak

---

33 Baird, 'The Hmong and the Communist Party of Thailand'.
34 ibid.

(Waseu Sae Yang), both from Saeng Maeng Village, were provincial party committee members.[35] In the three-province region, there were three other Hmong provincial party committees: Somwit (Lao Jai Sae Vang, Phu Hin Rong Kla Village), Sai Kham (Jong Teng Vang, Huai Sai Neua Village) and Yang Seng Sae Xiong (Tapboek Village).[36]

In 1974, the CPT's Kunming-based radio station, the Voice of the People of Thailand, openly broadcast that they had 'liberated areas' (strongholds) in the mountains of northern Thailand, and encouraged people to come to live there. They were organised as zones and the zones were grouped into provinces. The Hmong were the main group living in the part of Chiang Rai Province adjacent to Xayaboury Province in northern Laos, known by the CPT as Khet 8 (Thoeng and Wiang Kaen districts), and also in the small base area of Khet 52 (Chiang Khong, Chiang Saen and Phan districts). Further south, in what is now Phayao Province, the Hmong also dominated Khet 7 (Pong District)[37] and Khet 9 (Chiang Kham District). Phayao was part of Chiang Rai Province until it was later established as a separate province. Once separated, Khet 8 was in Chiang Rai Province and Khet 7 and 9 were in the CPT's Phayao Province.[38] Further south, in Nan Province, there were six strongholds in the mountain range that constituted the border between Laos and Thailand. The Hmong dominated two of these, Khet 1 in the far north of Thung Chang District[39] and Khet 6 in the far south of Mae Jarim District.[40] Khet 2, 3, 4 and 5 were geographically in between, and were dominated by ethnic Lua and upland Thai Muang, rather than Hmong.[41] Khet 1 and 6 were both in Nan Province.[42] However, the Hmong also dominated

---

35 Both came from Rat Phak Dee (Saeng Maeng) Village, Thoeng District. Lo Meng Sae Fa, Pers. comm., Chiang Khong District, Thailand, April 2021.
36 Sahai Ek, Pers. comm., Huai Nam Khao Village, Phitsanulok, Thailand, May 2021; Blia Sae Xiong (Sahai Nomjai), Pers. comm., Toop Kaw, Dansai District, Thailand, May 2021.
37 Mai, *Storm and Rain*; Janthana, *From Yao Mountain to Pha Ji Mountain*; Khunphol, *Wae Mountain, Phayak Mountain*, Vol.2.
38 Technically, Khet 9 was in Nan Province, but it was under the management of the CPT in Phayao Province. It was a place for passing between provinces. Savengsak Suriyaphadoongchai (Ja Fua Sae Xiong, Phu Kong Pheung), Pers. comm., Telephone call to Santisuk Village, Pong District, Thailand, May 2021.
39 Khunphol, *Wae Mountain, Phayak Mountain*, Vols 1, 3.
40 Ian G. Baird, 'Different Hmong Political Orientations and Perspectives on the Thailand–Laos Border', *Georgetown Journal of Asian Affairs* 4(1) (2018): 29–36.
41 Meuan Fon, *Frontline Battlefield*; Phanthiwa, *The Blood Warrior*.
42 Chiang Rai, Phayao and Nan provinces were the same CPT province until 1973, when they were separated into three provinces. Lo Meng Sae Fa, Pers. comm., 2021. There were no Hmong or Lua on the Nan Province party committee. Daeng Noi Sae Lee, Pers. comm., Telephone call to Wiang Kaen District, Thailand, April 2021.

Khet 10 and 15 in Phitsanulok, Loei and Phetchabun provinces to the south,[43] and the Phu Khat (Khet 30, 561 or no number) stronghold as well. They were also in the three-provinces region.[44] Finally, the CPT set up another two strongholds in north-western Thailand adjacent to the border with Burma, known as Khet Tai ('South Zone') and Khet Neua ('North Zone').[45] Khet Tai was dominated by ethnic Karen people, while Khet Neua was dominated by Hmong, with a smaller number of Karen; both were in Tak Province.[46] Several Hmong were elevated to become *samachik sapha tambon* ('district committee members'). Although districts were not created in all strongholds, they were established in many and were equivalent to '*amphoe*' in Thai. For example, although there were no *tambon* in Tak strongholds, Khet 8 had four *tambon*[47] and there were *tambon* in Khet 10, 15,[48] 1, 4, 5, 6 and 7.[49]

Walong Sae Lee (older brother of Wa Meng Sae Lee) was the head of the *sapha tambon* for Khet 15, which was generally responsible for organising the community and maintaining adherence to the rules.[50] *Tambon* were only established in places where it was believed the civilian population was ready to govern. In contrast, in Khet 9 and 52, there were just single villages, so *tambon* were not established in either zone.[51] Zone party committees generally had seven, nine or 11 members, depending on size.[52]

---

43 Baker, 'An Internal History of the Communist Party of Thailand'.
44 There were three *khet* there.
45 There was initially just one *khet* in Tak, but later it was expanded to two.
46 Her Po Sae Xiong (Sahai Prasong), Pers. comm., Nam Juang Village, Chattakarn District, Thailand, July 2017; Sahai Lek and Sahai Narong, Pers. comm., Bangkok, April 2021.
47 One was centred on Lao Oo Village (Lor Yia Blia Sae Hang was village head), one on Phraya Phiphak Village (Sahai Pracha or Za Jia Sae Lee was head) and one on Saeng Maeng Village (Jooan Tsong Sae Yang was head). There were nine Hmong villages, and two to three villages per district congress, each of which had five members. There was also a *sapha tambon nitibanyat* ('legal district congress') based in Huai Han village and led by Lo Nhia Por Sae Lee, with Lor Nor Her Sae Yang (Jim Sieu Village) as his deputy. Lo Meng Sae Fa, Pers. comm., April 2021; Mo Daeng (Nor Daeng Sae Lee), Pers. comm., Telephone call to Huai Han Village, Thailand, April 2021. All three district committee members in Saeng Maeng Village in Khet 8—Jooan Tsong Sae Yang, Blia Yia Sae Hang and Pracha Sae Lee—were Hmong. The district congress often worked to solve local village problems or would investigate when soldiers were accused of bad behaviour.
48 In 1971, the Phu Hin Rong Kla stronghold (Khet 15) established three districts within it: Phu Hin Rong Kla (District 1), Phu Khi Thao/Pa Wai (District 2) and Khao Kho/Khao Ya (District 3).
49 There may have been district congresses in Khet 2 and 3. Sahai Lek and Sahai Narong, Pers. comm.
50 Sahai Phet, Pers. comm., Thonburi, Thailand, April 2021.
51 Savengsak Suriyaphadoongchai, Pers. comm., May 2021.
52 Sahai Khon, Pers. comm.

Sapha tambon generally had one representative per village. In individual villages, there were also *kammakan moo ban* ('village committees'), which generally had five or seven members. In Nan Province, for example, there were six *kong roi* ('companies'), 301, 302, 303, 304, 306 and 309—one for each zone. Company 244, which was a rapid mobilisation unit, was also located there.[53] These forces together made up the provincial Kong Thap Rot Ek Prachachon Haeng Prathet Thai (Thai People's National Army) of the CPT in Nan Province. The leadership consisted of a political *phu kong* ('zone commander'), a military *phu kong* and a *phalithikan* or *phala* ('logistical leader'). Company 708,[54] which was separate, was especially responsible for protecting the CPT headquarters at Phu Phayak (Khet 4).[55]

The 'pink areas', which were not as secure as fully communist-controlled 'red areas' (see Figure 10.1), were never strongholds. For example, Nam Juang (also referred to as *thap* 4 or /4) never had a provincial party committee.[56] The same is true for Khet Kiti, south of Tak, part of Fang District, in Chiang Mai Province.[57] Another small zone was Khet 9, between Phayao and Nan provinces. There were just 30 soldiers assigned to each of these zones.[58] Still another was Khet 16 in Santisuk District, Nan Province.[59] These areas were considered expansion areas,[60] over which the CPT was trying to gain more control.[61]

---

53 ibid.
54 It was initially 307 and then changed to 708.
55 Sahai Lek and Sahai Narong, Pers. comm.
56 Her Po Sae Xiong, Pers. comm.
57 Sahai Lek and Sahai Narong, Pers. comm.
58 Savengsak Suriyaphadoongchai, Pers. comm., May 2021.
59 Sahai Chao (Soo Malee Sae Thao), Pers. comm., Tha Vang Pha District, Thailand, May 2021.
60 There was no zone commander based there, only a *phu muat* ('platoon commander')—a Hmong man from Pha Mon who was responsible for 30 soldiers. There were also three doctors there, two of whom were Hmong who had studied in China, Sahai Taowan and Sahai Daw Deung. Lo Meng Sae Fa, Pers. comm., April 2021; Anonymous, Pers. comm., Thung Phatthana Village, Chiang Khong District, Thailand, April 2021.
61 Lo Meng Sae Fa, Pers. comm., April 2021.

Map 10.1 CPT strongholds from the late 1960s to the early 1980s.

Note: Full strongholds were found only in northern Thailand, due to the mountainous topography there, which provided greater security.

Source: Author's map.

The leadership of the CPT

This section is designed to provide some information about the leadership of the CPT, to demonstrate who they were and that they were not Hmong.

Charoen Wan-Ngam (Sahai Mit Samanan), who was half-Thai, half-Vietnamese, from Ubon Ratchathani, was the third CPT secretary[62] during the period when Hmong were especially involved with the party, from the late 1960s to the early 1980s. He was apparently chosen because the party wanted more of a Thai (rather than a Chinese) face to the movement.[63] Few Hmong I have interviewed ever met Mit Samanan, although many knew of his revolutionary or forest name. He was sometimes in northeastern Thailand at Phu Phan in Nakorn Phanom Province, and he spent some time in Nan Province. He also spent a significant amount of time in China.

The leader of the CPT in northern Thailand, someone whom many Hmong did meet, was a Chinese-Thai man named Song Noppakun (known mainly as Sahai Ba). He was based in northern Thailand for many years, including at Office 708 at Phu Phayak in Khet 4 in the mountains of eastern Nan Province, near the border with Laos. This office was responsible for logistics for the CPT and PLAT. Many Hmong worked closely with him.

Another key CPT leader in northern Thailand was Damri Ruangsutham (Sahai Dang),[64] a Chinese-Thai communist labour organiser from an elite background and a member of the CPT Politburo from 1953, who was responsible for Khet 10, 15 and Phu Khat in the three-provinces area. Sahai Dang was reportedly the chief of staff for PLAT at one point, although Phayom Chulanont (Sahai Khamtan), who fled Bangkok after the 1947 coup d'état (see above) and had a strong military background,[65]

---

62   Lee Keung and Song Noppakun were secretaries general of the CPT before Charoen Wan-Ngam. Thong Sae Xiong, Pers. comm., Nam Tuang Village, Mae Jarim District, Thailand, July 2017; Yingkiat Liu, Pers. comm., Bangkok, April 2021.
63   Sahai Lek and Sahai Narong, Pers. comm.
64   His aliases included Pradit Ruangsutham, Boo, Wong, Wang U, Som, Kist and Sanoh Charoenphanit.
65   Phayom Chulanont (Sahai Khamtan) was the father of General Surayud Chulanont (prime minister of Thailand after the 2006 coup d'état) and a member of the CPT's Politburo. He was a lieutenant-colonel in the Thai Army before the 1947 coup d'état. He fled to China after the coup d'état that removed Pridi Banomyong as prime minister of Thailand.

replaced him in 1971.⁶⁶ Both worked closely with Hmong. The head of PLAT in the three-province area, which included three zones (Khet 10, 15 and Phu Khat) was Sahai Phichai, the son of Khong Chandawong, an early CPT leader in north-eastern Thailand who was assassinated by the Thai military. Phichai was also a member of the zone party committee (Khet 15) for the three-provinces area.⁶⁷

The other CPT Politburo members were apparently Wirat Akhalatthawan (Sahai Than), Thong Jamsri (Sahai Din), Lee Keung (an early CPT leader responsible for foreign affairs and mainly based in China), Udom Srisuwan (who looked after allied groups based near A-30 in northern Laos), Sin Dermlin (Sahai Prawat, who was responsible for southern Thailand) and Sahai Khap. Other leaders were Pluang Wannasi, Prasit Kapiangthong and Asanee Poljantra (Nai Phi). Some of these were on the Central Committee and some were also in the Politburo. The exact positions people held were never discussed publicly,⁶⁸ resulting in some guesswork being required, even for mid-level political and military figures in the CPT.

Wirat Akhalatthwan was apparently a theorist who knew more about Marxist political theory than others in the Politburo and travelled and worked closely with Mit Samanan. However, he reportedly did not speak Thai clearly.⁶⁹ He and many other leaders were Chinese Thais. None was from a Thai ethnic minority and all were men. I expected that this paradox of Hmong joining the CPT due to grievances with Thais and then finding the party was led mainly by Chinese Thais would have given them a negative impression. However, most Hmong did not seem to be concerned—something that still puzzles me a bit but is the opinion of the vast majority of the people I interviewed. They felt they had the opportunity to be promoted if they knew enough to justify promotion. In any case, I will return to the role of the Hmong in relation to Chinese-Thai and other Thai leaders later in the chapter.

---

66 Daeng Noi Sae Lee, Pers. comm., Huai Khu Village, Wiang Kaen District, Thailand, June 2018.
67 Sahai Lek and Sahai Narong, Pers. comm.
68 ibid.; Thong Sae Xiong, Pers. comm.
69 Sahai Lek and Sahai Narong, Pers. comm.; Thong Sae Xiong, Pers. comm.

The rise and fall of the CPT

In October 1976, progressive students were massacred at Thammasat University in Bangkok after they protested the return to Thailand of exiled military leader Field Marshal Thanom Kittikachorn.[70] The military took control of the government and many students and other progressives fled to the forests and CPT strongholds in the mountains of northern Thailand, where many lived with the CPT.[71] By 1977–78, the CPT was militarily and politically stronger than it had ever been, and there was hope it might be able to take power in the country if things continued to advance as planned.

However, several events in the late 1970s eventually led to the rapid decline of the CPT. First, there was a deep rift in the communist world between the Soviet Union and the PRC, and this greatly affected relations between China and Vietnam, which deteriorated badly in 1978–79. This related to escalating border tensions between Vietnam and Cambodia's Khmer Rouge, with China coming down clearly on the side of its close ally the Khmer Rouge.[72] Finally, in late 1978, the Vietnamese entered Cambodia and successfully removed the Khmer Rouge from power. What was left of the Khmer Rouge fled to the Thai border, which enraged the Chinese. Tensions also escalated due to the Vietnamese treating ethnic Chinese in the country poorly.[73] Finally, a short but bloody war erupted along the China–Vietnam border, with Chinese troops entering Vietnam to teach the smaller country a lesson. However, the month-long campaign resulted in heavy losses on both sides, before the Chinese withdrew. The confrontation led to regional conflict that became known as the Third Indochina War.[74]

Given the CPT was politically aligned and materially dependent on China, it should be no surprise it eventually came down on the side of its most important patron. On the other hand, the Lao Government sided with Vietnam. This, in turn, led to a serious rift between the CPT

---

70 Thongchai, *Moments of Silence*; Baker and Phongpaichit, *A History of Thailand*.
71 Thonthan, *Goodbye Hin Rong Kla*.
72 C.Y. Chang, 'The Sino-Vietnam Rift: Political Impact on China's Relations with Southeast Asia', *Contemporary Southeast Asia* 4(4) (1983): 538–64; Ian G. Baird, *Rise of the Brao: Ethnic Minorities in Northeastern Cambodia during Vietnamese Occupation* (Madison, WI: University of Wisconsin Press, 2020), doi.org/10.2307/j.ctvz0h8kw.
73 Baird, *Rise of the Brao*.
74 Nayan Chanda, *Brother Enemy: The War after the War* (San Diego, CA: Harcourt Brace Jovanovich, 1986).

and Laos and, in January 1979, Laos ordered the CPT/PLAT to leave its territory within a month. This was a serious blow for the CPT in various ways. First, the CPT lost its safe areas and bases inside Laos. Second, the CPT received supplies from China through Laos, but this was no longer permitted. This had a huge negative material and moral impact, as the Chinese had been providing a lot of ideological and material support. Moreover, the disagreement between China and Vietnam seeped into the CPT, with most members sympathising with China and a smaller number thinking it was a terrible mistake to side with China against Laos and Vietnam.[75] Some tensions also emerged between former students in the CPT and the older guard.[76]

To make matters worse, despite the CPT siding with China, China was chiefly concerned with supporting the Khmer Rouge, who were fighting the Vietnamese in Cambodia and, to do that effectively, they needed the cooperation of the Thai Government to transfer arms and other supplies through Thailand. However, the Thais would not cooperate unless China agreed to stop materially supporting the CPT. The Chinese agreed. On 10 July 1979, it was announced that the Voice of the People of Thailand would cease transmitting, with the last broadcast the following day. Moreover, supplies stopped flowing from China to the CPT.[77]

In 1980, the Thai Government released Resolution 66/2523(1980), which amounted to an amnesty for those who had worked for the CPT or the PLAT. Although some took advantage of the amnesty during that year,[78] many in the CPT did not initially trust that the Thai military was serious about the amnesty. However, after the announcement of the second amnesty, Resolution 66/2525(1982), which essentially repeated the amnesty offer of 1980, large numbers of CPT fighters and dependents surrendered. Many were demoralised due to the lack of material support from China, Laos and Vietnam, and because of internal ideological disagreements and general fatigue.

---

75 Martin Stuart-Fox, 'Factors Influencing Relations between the Communist Parties of Thailand and Laos', *Asian Survey* 19(4) (1979): 333–52, doi.org/10.2307/2643855; Gawin, *The rise and fall of the Communist Party of Thailand*.
76 Gawin, *The rise and fall of the Communist Party of Thailand*.
77 William R. Heaton, 'China and Southeast Asian Communist Movements: The Decline of Dual Track Diplomacy', *Asian Survey* 22(8) (1982): 779–800, doi.org/10.2307/2643647; Robert Garson, 'China policy to Thailand 1958–1984' (Master's thesis, Carleton University, Ottawa, 1984); Baker, 'An Internal History of the Communist Party of Thailand'.
78 Siam Nakorn, 'CPT Defector Interviewed on Communist Strategy, Problems', *Foreign Broadcasting Information Service*, [Washington, DC], 1 November 1980.

In late 1980, as the Thai military took Khao Kho and Khao Ya, Damri Ruangsutham (Sahai Dang), the leading CPT politician in the three-provinces area, arranged with Thai authorities for more than 1,000 CPT insurgents to surrender.[79] Damri did not surrender himself and instead tried to move to Surathani in southern Thailand, to where the CPT headquarters had been moved in late 1980 from Nan Province.[80] He did not make it and, in April 1981, he was captured by the Thai military en route.[81] According to the *Bangkok Post*,[82] Damri claimed 'he was on a mission to see former political activist Sang Patthanothai [a leading public figure in Thailand] to act as a middleman in truce talks between the CPT and the government in an effort to form a united front against the Vietnamese'.[83] At the time, there was concern that Vietnamese forces based in Laos might invade Thailand.[84]

As the strongholds lost people, the movement lost momentum and those who remained became increasingly demoralised, the Thai military gained the opportunity to attack some of the strongholds and, while they had not had much success previously, the balance began to turn in their favour. By the end of 1982, all the strongholds had fallen apart—most as a result of the military campaigns,[85] but also because of a lack of spirit among the CPT and because most inhabitants had taken advantage of the amnesty bills and surrendered to the government.[86] However, some holdouts continued to operate along the border with Laos, including at Phu Soi Dao, until the mid-1980s (holdouts from the three provinces),[87] and in Khet 6 in Nan Province until 1990.[88]

---

79 Ettinger, 'Thailand's Defeat of its Communist Party'.
80 Baker, 'An Internal History of the Communist Party of Thailand'.
81 'Army Captures Senior Communist Party Member', *Nation Review*, [Melbourne], 19 May 1981.
82 'Critical Time for Thai Communists', *Bangkok Post*, 22 November 1981, 6.
83 Sang Phathanothai was accused of being a communist when Sarit Thanarat was in power. He went to China and had a daughter named Daeng, who was said to be like an adopted child to Chinese leader Zhou Enlai. Apparently Sang liked Sudsai Hatsadin, to whom he was introduced by his first son, Dr Man. Amnuaysart (Jang) Hatsadin, Pers. comm., Bangkok, August 2015.
84 Saiyud, *The Struggle for Thailand*.
85 Bangkok Domestic Service, 'Statement on Return', *Foreign Broadcasting Information Service*, [Washington, DC], 21 November 1982.
86 Bangkok Domestic Service, 'Supreme Command Reports on Anti-CPT Operations', *Foreign Broadcasting Information Service*, [Washington, DC], 8 August 1982; Bangkok Post, '800 Communist Insurgents Surrender in Tak', *Foreign Broadcasting Information Service*, [Washington, DC], 28 December 1982; Yuangrat Wedel, 'Current Thai Radical Ideology: The Returnees from the Jungle', *Contemporary Southeast Asia* 4(1) (1982): 1–18, doi.org/10.1355/CS4-1A.
87 The leaders at Phu Soi Dao were Phu Kong Seum and Sahai Pritchai. Sahai Prawit was responsible for soldiers. Her Po Sae Xiong, Pers. comm., Nam Juang Village, Chattakarn District, Thailand, July 2017; Prawit Sae Lee (Jooa Seng Sae Lee), Pers. comm., Khek Noi Village, Khao Kho District, Thailand, May 2021.
88 Baird, 'Different Hmong Political Orientations and Perspectives on the Thailand–Laos Border'.

Some CPT members escaped to southern Thailand, where they continued their struggle for some years. The last holdouts ended up living in Phetburi (Khet Tai) and Prachuap Khiri Khan (Khet Neua) provinces in western Thailand, near the border with Burma, where they were able to operate with support from the Burmese Communist Party and Bo Mya, the leader of the Karen National Union. There were more than 100 CPT fighters in the two provinces at the beginning of the 1990s, of whom about 20 were Hmong.[89] Finally, in 1993–94, the last CPT members in the forest gradually left and secretly integrated into Thai society without surrendering. The CPT had essentially ceased to exist. Even before then, many CPT operatives in the cities found the party stopped contacting them, without providing a reason. Notably, however, a small number of Hmong were committed enough to the CPT that they were among the last to give up the fight. They had spent more than 25 years in the forest with the CPT and their commitment to continue, even as many others gave up, indicates their commitment to Marxist politics.

Hmong knowledge of the politics of the CPT

I have interviewed dozens of Hmong men and women who went to study at A-30 between the early 1960s and the late 1970s, and all reported knowing very little about communist theory or political philosophy before making the trip to the Laos–China border.[90] After basic training, which generally lasted three months, some were selected for further study in either China or Vietnam. Some received military training in northern Vietnam, while those studying politics, medicine and other subjects went to China, either Yunnan Province or the capital, Beijing. However, almost everyone reported deciding to join the CPT for reasons other than political theory. In those times, the general idea of 'studying' carried great weight, signifying the path to modernity and advancement. Most joined because they wanted 'to study' since formal education was limited or nonexistent in many Hmong villages, and the CPT offered them the chance to gain knowledge, without telling them explicitly what they would learn. For most, they only started to understand the political philosophy of the CPT once they began training at A-30, although sometimes they learned

---

89   Thong Sae Xiong, Pers. comm.
90   Baird, 'The Hmong and the Communist Party of Thailand'; Baird and Yangcheepsujarit, 'Hmong Women's Rights and the Communist Party of Thailand'.

some general information about the party being against discrimination and for equality before this. Sometimes students joined the CPT without their parents' permission, while in other cases parents or other relatives encouraged their children to take the opportunity to learn from the CPT. Experiences varied, but the point is that the children almost never chose to study 'communism' per se; they chose 'to study' more generally. This broadly coincides with the experiences of ethnic minorities in Laos who went to 'study' in Vietnam via the Pathet Lao communists in the 1950s and 1960s.[91]

After studying with the CPT, many Hmong continued to receive political training while doing different kinds of work. For example, one young woman studied at A-30 for three months and was then sent back to one of the strongholds in northern Thailand, where she was assigned to do propaganda work with civilians. This was known as *muanchon* or 'public work'. After a year working in Hmong villages for the CPT, she was given the opportunity to study to be a doctor in Yunnan Province in south-western China. Once she completed her studies, she returned to one of the northern Thai strongholds to work as a doctor. She continued working there until the stronghold was taken over by the Royal Thai Army.[92]

This, however, is not the end of the story. Even though the Hmong knew very little about communist political philosophy when they first joined the CPT, over time, many did learn a considerable amount about Marxist and Maoist thought. It is not easy to estimate the exact level of political knowledge each person gained and some were more focused on practice than texts. However, the number of Hmong who joined the party and gained higher political positions is a good indicator of the trust put in them politically and the knowledge some of them gained. In the CPT, as with other communist parties around the world, one could not simply ask to join, as is the case for political parties in multiparty democratic systems. Instead, only those deemed to have the qualities necessary to make them 'party material' were invited to join—first, as an alternative party member and, later, as a full party member once they had proven their worthiness to other members. Some became party members through political work;

---

91 See: Vatthana Pholsena, 'Highlanders on the Ho Chi Minh Trail', *Critical Asian Studies* 40(3) (2008): 445–71, doi.org/10.1080/14672710802274151; Vatthana Pholsena, 'War Generation: Youth Mobilization and Socialization in Revolutionary Laos', in *Changing Lives in Laos: Culture, Politics, and Culture in a Post-Socialist State*, Vanina Boute and Vatthana Pholsena, eds (Singapore: University of Singapore Press, 2017), 109–34; Baird, 'The Hmong and the Communist Party of Thailand'.
92 Baird, 'The Hmong and the Communist Party of Thailand'.

10. BECOMING MARXIST

others entered the party through medical service, as doctors and nurses; and still others joined the party through military service with the PLAT—something that was especially common for the Hmong, since many had lower levels of formal education than their Thai colleagues from other parts of the country.

Party membership was secret and, even now, some are sensitive about discussing who were party members and who were not, although many people knew who other members were. More than 100 Hmong—mainly men but also some women—in Thailand became full CPT members, and the number might have been significantly higher. There was an even larger number of Hmong soldiers and officials who never became party members, and of villagers who joined the mass organisation set up by the CPT. Because of the secrecy associated with party membership, it may never be possible to know the true number.

There were training schools created in most large districts in northern Thailand, including two at Khet 8 in Chiang Rai.[93] A Hmong man, Lo Meng Sae Fa, was the military zone commander at one of the schools. At Khet 15, there was a basic training school for new recruits, where a Hmong man named Phu Kong Rak[94] was responsible for the military training, while a Chinese-Thai man named Lao Ya oversaw political training.[95] The school was moved after its location was revealed to the enemy and bombed; a new school was established near Nong Mae Na on the Khek River.[96] There were apparently schools for new recruits in most zones in northern Thailand.[97] Lo Meng Sae Fa was clearly considered someone who understood politics well before then, as he was a teacher for two years at the CPT's basic political training school, the 'October 6 School', which was located on the Lao border, about 5 kilometres inside Laos near Phu Chee Fa, in Thoeng District. Most of the students, and all new recruits, had to complete a three-month course before being allowed to operate.[98] This ensured everyone working with the party in stronghold

---

93 ibid.
94 He was known as Phu Kong Rak, but he was not a *phu kong*. Sahai Fong, Pers. comm., Bangkok, June 2021.
95 ibid.
96 ibid.
97 Pornsuang Phothong, Pers. comm., Bangkok, April 2021.
98 The first school established in the area was called the October 14 School, and was about 1 kilometre inside Laos. After 6 October 1976, many more students started arriving and a second school was built to accommodate them. Wanchai Chaloonsakonwong (Jooan Tsong Sae Yang), Pers. comm., Rat Phak Dee (Saeng Maeng) Village, Thoeng District, Thailand, June 2015.

areas had at least basic political and military training. Lo Meng Sae Fa provided the military training, while another teacher was responsible for teaching politics.[99] There were basic training schools in other strongholds as well—for example, in Phayao Province (Khet 7) and at Phu Hin Rong Kla (Khet 15). At the latter centre, one of the first trainers was a Hmong man named Sor Lor. Later, another Hmong man, named Thongsuk Sae Lor, became a trainer.[100] The Hmong trained others, including ethnic Thai recruits.

Nor Her Sae Yang, a Hmong man, was the president of the Khana Sapha ('Assembly Committee'),[101] which included 30–40 people.[102] In Khet 7, Joo Sua Sae Xiong, who had studied politics in China, was the president of the Assembly Committee.[103]

A smaller number of Hmong were elevated to zone party committee membership,[104] the level above district committee. Provincial party committee membership was the highest political position held by Hmong. No Hmong were ever elevated to the CPT's 23-member Central Committee[105] or the seven-member Politburo. According to Wiang Sae Xiong, who stayed at Khet 1: 'There were no Hmong in the Central Committee. They did not have high enough knowledge.'[106] This idea of 'knowledge' related to a certain type of formal theoretical knowledge or even formal education.

Several Hmong obtained positions on zone party committees, although for some this occurred not long before they surrendered to the government in the early 1980s. The first Hmong zone party committee member in Khet 15 was Jong Teng Vang (Sahai Sai Kham), as already discussed. He was followed by You May Sae Lee (Sahai Narong).[107] Eventually, in Khet 15, there were four Hmong zone party committee members, Sahai Somwit (Lao Jai Sae Vang), Sahai Sai Kham (Jong Teng Sae Vang),

---

99 Lo Meng Sae Fa, Pers. comm., September 2016.
100 Nor Jai Sae Lor, Pers. comm., Khek Noi Village, Khao Khor District, Thailand, August 2015.
101 Wanchai Chaloonsakonwong, Pers. comm.
102 Kriangsak Anusawaleedoi (Wakua Sae Lee), Pers. comm., Huai Khu Village, Wiang Kaen District, Thailand, June 2015.
103 Savengsak Suriyaphadoongchai (Ja Fua Sae Xiong, Phu Kong Pheung), Pers. comm., Santisuk Village, Pong District, Thailand, October 2016.
104 The zone party committee's head office was called *samnak khet*.
105 Baker, 'An Internal History of the Communist Party of Thailand'.
106 Wiang Sae Xiong, Pers. comm., Pak Klang Village, Pua District, Thailand, October 2016.
107 You May Sae Lee (Sahai Narong), Pers. comm., Nam Juang Village, Chattakarn District, Thailand, July 2017.

10. BECOMING MARXIST

Sahai Narong (You May Sae Lee) and Sahai Lao Sai. Sahai Charoen (*sapha tambon/amnat rat* ['district assembly/government power']) also had an important position.[108]

In Khet 10, six of the 15 members of the provincial party committee were Hmong: Wa Meng Sae Lee (Phu Kong Chot), Chue Jong Hua Sae Lee (Sahai Charoen),[109] Ya Seng Sae Xiong (Tabboek Village), Phu Kong Somwit (Phu Hin Rong Kla Village), Phu Kong Seum and Phu Kong Bouaphanh (political side). Most of the other members of this committee were Chinese Thais from central, southern and north-eastern Thailand.[110] Lao Saeng (Sahai Ia), from Phu Miang Village, was a zone party committee member at Phu Khat/Nam Juang.[111] Khet 10 had the strongest PLAT contingent and was politically the strongest. They fought more than PLAT units elsewhere, so they especially needed to come together as a coercive unit.[112]

In Khet 8, one of the most secure strongholds, six of the nine zone party committee members were Hmong: Lao Wit and Lao Phak (both also provincial party committee members), Wa Ger Sae Yang (Phu Kong Lao Yee, Pho Luang Kert Phanakamneut), Lo Meng Sae Fa (Phu Kong Surat), Cha Sae Lee (Sahai Cha) and Khammouan Sae Yang.[113] Jia Kua Sae Vang, who had studied politics in China, also played a significant role here at one point.[114] Phu Kong Lao Ji, a Hmong from Phraya Phiphak Village, was the zone commander responsible for soldiers in Khet 8 until he was killed in battle.[115]

In Khet 7, a little to the south in Phayao Province, there were at least four Hmong men who became zone party committee members, including Jua Leng Sae Vang (Sahai Suphot, Santisuk Village), Long Jue Sae Vang (Sahai Santi) and Lao Ying Sae Hang (Sahai Saeng).[116] The fourth, Nu Shua Sae Xiong (Sahai Xiong Sang), still lives in Khun Kamlang Village, Pong District. Although the CPT valued literacy and formal education, Xiong

---

108 Sahai Ek, Pers. comm., May 2021.
109 Thong Sae Xiong, Pers. comm.
110 Wa Po Sae Yang (Sahai Saweng), Pers. comm., Nam Juang Village, Chattakarn District, Thailand, July 2017.
111 Her Po Sae Xiong, Pers. comm.
112 Sahai Fong, Pers. comm.
113 Lo Meng Sae Fa, Pers. comm., April 2021; Mo Daeng, Pers. comm.
114 Savengsak Suriyaphadoongchai, Pers. comm., October 2016.
115 Sahai Boon, Pers. comm., Chiang Mai, Thailand, June 2021.
116 Savengsak Suriyaphadoongchai, Pers. comm., October 2016.

Sang admitted to being illiterate. Yet, the CPT leadership clearly felt he had sufficient political knowledge to become a zone party committee member. He told me he was often called on to resolve conflicts between villagers over party theory and rules.[117]

In Khet 9, which was closely connected with Khet 7, there was one Hmong zone party committee member, Lak Sao Sae Xiong, whose older brother was Phu Kong Pheung, the military commander of the rapid mobile company in the area.[118]

In Khet 1, in the north-east of Thung Chang District, Nan Province, there were at least two Hmong zone party committee members: Shoua Sae Thao (Sahai Laola), a soldier, and Sahai Lao Yia Chiang from Many Pheuk Village, even though he could not speak Thai well.[119]

A Hmong man named Nu Cha Sae Lee (Sahai Cha), and possibly other Hmong, was a provincial party committee member in Tak Province.

Some Hmong only gained these higher political positions in the early 1980s after the CPT was critically weakened by internal strife, including between the old guard and student leaders, and by the loss of Chinese, Lao and Vietnamese support. Those in the CPT knew this time as the *wikritsathan* or 'crisis period'. For example, Lo Meng Sae Fa became a zone party committee member in Khet 8, but only after *wikritsathan* when they were becoming weaker. He did not serve for long before he was forced to flee to Burma as the stronghold fell to the Thai Army.[120]

The Hmong especially excelled in the military, probably because they were used to hunting and moving around in the mountains and forests. As an indication of how well they did in the military, at least 13 Hmong men were elevated to the level of zone commander, in six different strongholds: Phu Kong Prayat/Soo (Nhia Ja Sae Xiong) and Daeng Noi Sae Lee, Company 306, Khet 6; Phu Kong Pheung (Savengsak Suriyaphadoongchai, Ja Fua Sae Xiong), Khet 7; Phu Kong Somwit (Lao Jai Sae Vang), Phu Kong Cheep (Sae Vang) and Phu Kong Saveng, Khet 15, Nam Juang Village; Phu Kong Chot (Wa Meng Sae Lee), Company 515; Phu Kong Seum,

---

117 Nu Shua Sae Xiong (Sahai Xiong Sang), Pers. comm, Khun Kamlang Village, Pong District, Thailand, June 2018.
118 Savengsak Suriyaphadoongchai, Pers. comm., May 2021.
119 Suthipong Thiwannan (Sahai Man), Pers. comm., Pang Kae Village, Thung Chang District, Thailand, October 2016.
120 Daeng Noi Sae Lee, Pers. comm., June 2018.

Phu Kong Leu and Phu Kong Kriang (both at Nam Juang), Company 520, Khet 10; and Phu Kong Lao Yee (Wa Ger Sae Yang), Phu Kong Surat (Lo Meng Sae Fa) and Lao Vue Sae Fa (Kamnan Boonchert, logistical leader), Company 85, Khet 8). Phu Kong Somwit and Phu Kong Seum were responsible for *thahan thong thin* ('village militias') in Khet 10 and 15. Somwit had only studied for three months in Vietnam, so had limited formal knowledge. Another Hmong man, Phu Muat Dao Thong, spent longer studying in Vietnam, but was killed in a battle in Phetchabun Province not long after returning to Thailand. He stood up to launch a rocket-propelled grenade and was shot; he had commanded a *nuai book* ('offensive unit').[121]

The Hmong who learned about politics with the leaders

Some Hmong gained political knowledge through specific training and study, while others learned political philosophy simply through spending considerable time with CPT Politburo leaders. These Hmong included Thong Sae Xiong, Daeng Noi Sae Lee, Lao Zong Sae Vang, Ya Seng Sae Vue (Siriphat Vonviriyachat, Sahai Than) and Jua Saeng Sae Lee (Sahai Prawit).

Thong Sae Xiong (Ja Her Sae Xiong) learned a lot from spending time with CPT leaders and was the *thahan phithak* or *ong kharak* ('personal guard') for Politburo member and party secretary Thong Jamsri for six years when the latter was based in southern Thailand in the late 1980s. Later, Thong Sae Xiong lived in Phetburi Province in western Thailand until 1994, when he secretly left the forest and slipped back into society without the authorities knowing. Thong Sae Xiong said he studied three of Marx's theories when he was with the secretary general of the CPT: *wiwattanakarn sangkhom* ('evolution of society'), *pratya wattooniyom wiphat* ('philosophy of dialectical materialism') and *wa duay thun pheua attibai sangkhom niyom wittayasat* ('capital and the explanation of scientific socialism'). He was aware of the political differences that existed between Chinese and Soviet communism at the time but said both sides agreed Thailand should be characterised through the *paen kan chon chan kamacheep* ('plan of the proletariat class'). However, according

---

121 Sahai Phet, Pers. comm.; Lo Meng Sae Fa, Pers. comm., April 2021; Prawit Sae Lee, Pers. comm.

to Thong: 'The Soviets wanted to put all classes together, while China did not.' The conflict between Stalin and Mao took place at the Third Congress of the Communist International. Hồ Chí Minh was the Asian representative of the Soviet Union. Thong told me: 'Stalin, Lenin and Mao had different theories. China wanted to get peasants to revolt but the Soviets wanted to support the proletariat workers.'[122]

Daeng Noi Sae Lee learned a considerable amount about politics from spending time with CPT leaders. He was the personal guard for Song Noppakhun (Sahai Ba),[123] the CPT's chairman for northern Thailand[124] as well as a Politburo and Central Committee member[125] in the 1970s.[126] In 1980, he was made the zone political commander for Company 306 in Khet 6, with Nhia Ja Sae Xiong (Sahai Prayat/Soo) as the zone military commander. However, he held the position for only three to four months in 1980. He was later sent to do political work with the people in CPT areas. Daeng Noi became the second secretary of the CPT in Phetburi and Tak provinces in the 1980s, where he was close to Politburo member Udom Srisuwan.[127] According to Sahai Prayat/Soo, 'Daeng Noi knows most Marxism and Maoism, as he was with leaders all the time, and he reads a lot'.[128] Daeng Noi was the only Hmong observer at the CPT's Fourth Party Congress in Surathani Province in southern Thailand in 1982, at which only members of the Central Committee were officially allowed to participate.[129] However, other Hmong were involved in preparatory provincial-level meetings, including provincial party committee members Jong Teng Vang (Sahai Sai Kham), who joined the discussions for Phetchabun, Phitsanulok and Loei provinces, and Nou Cha Sae Lee (Sahai Cha), who participated in discussions in Tak Province.

Lao Zong Sae Vang, a Hmong man, spent considerable time with the CPT's political leaders while serving as the personal guard for Politburo member Damri Ruangsutham (Sahai Dang), who was responsible for the three-provinces area.[130]

---

122 Thong Sae Xiong, Pers. comm.
123 He also had the aliases Phairat, Mu, Prasong Wongwiwat, Dang, Som and Ba.
124 Daeng Noi Sae Lee, Pers. comm., June 2018.
125 ibid.
126 Her Po Sae Xiong, Pers. comm.
127 Thong Sae Xiong, Pers. comm.
128 Nhia Ja Sae Xiong (Phu Kong Prayat/Soo), Pers. comm., Nam Tuang Village, Mae Jarim District, Thailand, February 2017.
129 Daeng Noi Sae Lee, Pers. comm., June 2018.
130 Her Po Sae Xiong, Pers. comm.

Ya Seng Sae Vue (Sahai Than) also worked closely with CPT leaders. Between 1975 and 1981, he was the personal guard for Damri, based at Office 708 at Phu Phayak, Nan Province, until Damri left northern Thailand to try to reach the south of the country but was arrested. Ya Seng Sae Vue had carried messages for him. He was under orders to destroy the messages if captured and be prepared to die to keep the information secret, but fortunately, although he was willing to kill himself for the party, he was never captured. He travelled with Sahai Dang on trips and served as his food taster to ensure his food was not poisoned.[131] Sahai Than was certainly committed to the party.

Sahai Prawit was another Hmong man who worked as the personal guard for a Politburo member, Prayom Chulanont (Sahai Khamtan).[132] He ended up leading those CPT members who refused to give up after the three-provinces region fell to the Thai military in 1980–81 around Phu Soi Dao.[133] There were also other Hmong who worked closely with political leaders for many years and learned political theory through them.

Other Hmong also learned a considerable amount about political theory. According to Sahai Prayat/Soo, Mo Daeng (Nor Daeng Sae Lee) knew a lot about politics;[134] he studied to be a doctor and acupuncturist in China, and later worked as a doctor in Khet 8.

However, Wa Meng Sae Lee (Phu Kong Chot), who was himself a provincial party committee member, told me there were no Hmong political intellectuals with the CPT. He felt Daeng Noi Sae Lee was not higher than others, as Phu Kong Prayat/Soo had said. As he put it: 'All party members knew the same. They had to be fair people and have leadership skills.'[135]

One indicator of the extent to which Hmong people internalised CPT political theory is how they view those ideas today. In the houses of former CPT Hmong, it is not unusual to find photos of Mao Zedong on the interior walls, CPT flags, or the communist hammer and sickle symbol. There are also frequently old photos on display of the men from their

---

131 Siriphat Vonviriyachat (Ya Seng Sae Vue, Sahai Than), Pers. comm., Jaeng Phatthana Village (Phu Khat), Chattakarn District, Thailand, July 2017.
132 Urai Yangcheepsutjarit, Pers. comm., Chiang Mai, Thailand, July 2013.
133 Lee Long Fue, Pers. comm., Khek Noi Village, Khao Khor District, Thailand, July 2013.
134 Nhia Ja Sae Xiong, Pers. comm.
135 Wa Meng Sae Lee (Phu Kong Chot), Pers. comm., Village 16, Phop Phra District, Thailand, May 2017.

time with the CPT. There are also sometimes CPT-produced communist books and magazines lying about. Moreover, since it became legal to commemorate the CPT some years ago, former CPT Hmong often wear their CPT/PLAT uniforms for community and group ceremonies, including official functions, and when protesting in Bangkok for land rights. They now refer to themselves as *phu ruam phatthana chart thai* ('people who are helping to develop the nation')—a term the government also uses. They are clearly not ashamed of having been in the CPT; in fact, they are proud of it. Many have organised to receive monetary compensation from the government that was promised but never given after the government amnesties for CPT members in 1980 and 1982. Some have refused such compensation and instead have lobbied to be allowed to return to areas where they lived before the CPT period, many of which are now national parks, wildlife sanctuaries and other types of protected areas, making it difficult for them to achieve their objectives.[136]

Finally, memorials associated with the CPT period have been established, such as one for dead CPT soldiers near Santisuk Village in Pong District, Phayao Province; a major museum at Phu Phayak Mountain in Nan Province; and another monument, in Thoeng District, Chiang Rai Province. Thus, the politics of representation has become important for Hmong former CPT members.

The new party

Two crucial indicators of the extent to which Hmong with the CPT internalised Marxist politics are their present-day political beliefs and associated political activities. In fact, those previously with the CPT, whether Hmong or from other ethnic groups, have become involved in a wide range of political organisations. For example, some sided with the royalist Yellow Shirts, while others sided with their political rivals, the Red Shirts, in recent protests.

Crucially for this chapter, however, many former CPT leaders, including several Hmong, remain highly engaged in leftist politics. Thong Jamsri, the last secretary general of the CPT, who died in 2019 at the

---

136 Yuttapong Suebsakwong and Ian G. Baird, 'Ban Khee Thao, a Site of Political History, and a Symbolic Space of Resistance and Land Politics of the Hmong in Thailand', *Thammasat Review Journal* 23(2) (July–December 2020): 73–105.

age of 98,[137] reportedly organised a secret group of former CPT members in 2009–10, which included some who had been in the Politburo and Central Committee, and some Marxist theorists. They changed the name of the party to Phak Prachathipatai Prachachon Haeng Prathet Thai ('People's Democracy Party of Thailand'), but people generally refer to it as the Phak Mai ('New Party'). Many Hmong previously with the CPT, including some of my informants, are involved in this group.

All the positions in the New Party were filled with representatives from all regions in the country, and a central committee with 35 members and a politburo with nine or 11 members were established. The New Party considers Thailand to be a *sakdina* ('feudalistic') country: *thoon niyom mee amnat neua rat* ('feudalist capitalist country that has powers above the government'). They secretly organised a party congress in 2013 and approved four political documents. There are apparently secret underground units in each region of Thailand and rules for admitting new members. There are also new rules for those joining and they have a new flag that is red and white with a red star in the centre. People in the New Party use the terms *phrai* ('serfs') and *amnat* ('the powerful') and consider themselves to be *neo ruam* ('allies') of the Red Shirts, many of whom were allied with former prime minister Thaksin Shinawatra, who was removed from office during a military coup in 2006. Crucially for this chapter, many Hmong previously in leadership positions in the CPT have joined the New Party,[138] although it is safer for them not to mention their names here. The involvement of several Hmong in this new clandestine political party clearly indicates their continued belief in CPT-inspired Marxist politics.

Conclusion

In this chapter, I have considered the various ways Hmong people engaged politically and gained Marxist knowledge through involvement with the CPT between the 1960s and the 1990s. There is no doubt that few if any Hmong initially joined the CPT because of a deep understanding

---

137 Teeranai Charuvasta, 'Thong Jamsri, Thailand's Last Communist Leader, Dies at 98', *Khaosod [The Fresh News]*, [Bangkok], 10 July 2019.
138 Prayuth Chumnasiew, Pers. comm., Ubon Ratchathani, Thailand, November 2016.

of Marxist political philosophy. Rather, some joined simply for the opportunity 'to study', some joined after being attacked by the military or BPP, and many had not even heard of communism when they joined.

However, it would be a mistake to assume that because the Hmong knew little about Marxism when they joined the CPT, they never learned much. Many Hmong learned a lot, studying politics at various levels, in the forests and CPT political schools and the bases of CPT leaders, but no Hmong ever made it to the Politburo or Central Committee. A number did reach middle-level positions, such as district leaders, zone commanders or committee members, and provincial committee members. Most Hmong political leaders in the CPT shared similar sentiments to those of Jong Teng Vang, who said: 'I am not disappointed that Hmong were not in the Central Committee.'[139] Their argument was this was because Hmong had less political knowledge than others, and they would not have been prevented from serving in higher political positions, including on the Central Committee and Politburo. Phu Kong Lao Yee said: 'The CPT leadership didn't look down on the Hmong; they just wanted people who were capable.'[140] To my surprise, many others made similar comments. It appears the CPT made this clear over time.

There were, however, other views. According to Phu Kong Pheung, there should have been Hmong on the central committee. In fact, Pheung explained that because membership of the Politburo was kept secret, he and others initially assumed there were Hmong in the Politburo given the party's politics of equality. When they later realised there were no Hmong members, they were a little disappointed, but still believed the CPT had good policies. As Pheung put it: 'Maybe the leaders in the CPT were prejudiced against the Hmong.'[141] A small number of others echoed that view. For example, Daeng Noi Sae Lee said: 'It took me a while to realise it, but the Hmong were not always appreciated by Chinese Thais in the central committee.'[142] He meant the Chinese Thais did not always value the practical knowledge of the Hmong compared with their own theoretical knowledge.

---

139 Jong Teng Sae Vang, Pers. comm., Huai Sai Neua Village, Thailand, June 2014.
140 Pho Luang Kert, Pers. comm., Khun Klang Village, Thailand, May 2014.
141 Nu Shua Sae Xiong, Pers. comm.
142 Daeng Noi Sae Lee, Pers. comm., June 2018.

Although the CPT disintegrated in the early 1980s, and the last vestiges of the armed struggle ended in the 1990s, it is noteworthy that many Hmong formerly with the CPT remain nostalgic about their time in the strongholds. Moreover, many continue to display photos of Mao and wear their CPT uniforms for both celebratory events and protests. Some even joined a new underground political party inspired by former CPT leaders. While they knew little about Marxist or Maoist politics when they first encountered the CPT, there is no doubt many were profoundly affected by the party's politics and they continue to believe in many of the core political ideas associated with it.

Index

Numbers in bold type represent images.

AAKC, *see* Khmer–Chinese Friendship Association
Aceh 58, 170
Acehnese 37
AEK, *see* Khmer Students Association
AFPFL, *see* Anti-Fascist People's Freedom League
Aguinaldo, Emilio 154, 157
Aidit, D.N. 160, 161
Alimin 60, 166, 167, 169, 173n.23, 175, 179, 184, 193, 194
America, *see* United States
Amoy (Xiamen) 169, 177, 180, 181, 186, 195
Amsterdam 15, 41
Angkar or Angkar Paṭivatt (the Organisation, or Revolutionary Organisation) 71, 103
Anti-Fascist People's Freedom League (AFPFL) 129, 132, 134
Army of the Republic of Vietnam (ARVN) 220, 221, 228, 232, 233, 254, 280
Association d'Amitié Khmero–Chinoise, *see* Khmer–Chinese Friendship Association
Association des Étudiants Khmers, *see* Khmer Students Association
Atatürk, Mustafa Kemal 50, 61, 66

Bandung 39, 40, 249
Batavia (Jakarta) 39, 40, 52, 53, 165, 180, 183, 184, 188, 190, 191, 192, 195
Batuah, Haji Datuk 53, 58, 64
Beijing 81, 83, 85, **97**, 98, 250, 252, 259, 264, 294, 319
Bhoās, *see* Hu Nim
Bolshevism 7, 41–2, 43, 47, 48
Bonifacio, Andres 154, 157
Boo, Chih Fu 217, 218
Borneo 168, 180, 181, 186
Boun Oum 250, 258, 259n.84, 260, 264, 265, 266–7
Britain 62, 116, 135, 244
British 108, 148n.38, 188n.29, 195
and Laos 252, 259
and Malayan Communist Party 201, 203, 206, 207, 208, 209–12, 216, 217
anticommunist cooperation with Dutch 166, 179, 183, 192, 193, 195
anticommunist measures 169, 179, 185, 191–2, 195
Asian colonialism xiv, 187, 195
as imperialist enemy 174, 210
in Burma 108, 114, 124
in Singapore 174, 178, 179, 185
resistance to 178, 191, 192, 205, 206, 208, 211–12, 217

333

British Borneo 180, 186
British India xiv, 195
British Malaya 166, 182, 184, 185, 193, 200, 201, 203, 208
  see also Malaya, Singapore, Straits Settlements
Burma (Myanmar) xiv, 8, 25, 26–7, 107–36, 257, 262, 299, 307, 309, 311, 319, 324

Cambodia xiv, 8, 9, 25, 26, 70, 74, 82, 83n.47, 93, **97**, 102, 103, 264, 295
  and Vietnamese Communist Party 291
  anticolonialism 77, 78, 80, 84
  Chinese friendship associations 26, 72, 83, 95
  French rule 76, 78, 90
  independence 79, 80
  indigenisation of Maoism 23, 26, 69–70, 72–4, 84, 105
  influence of China 18, 22, 69–70, 74, 75, 81, 82–3, 84, 97–9, 257, 295, 316, 317
  Maoism in 22, 25, 26, 71, 72–4, 81, 82, 84, 92, 93, 97–9, 105
  Paris group of communists 71, 74, 77, 79–80, 104, 105
  political repression in 74, 81
  politics 22, 72, 79, 80, 95, 100
  revolution 72, 93, 104, 105, 291
  social problems 72, 85–93, 95–6, 105
  Vietnamese invasion of 228, 295, 316, 317
  see also Communist Party of Kampuchea, Democratic Kampuchea, Khmer Rouge, Phnom Penh
Canton 15, 193, 272
Carter, Jimmy 295
CCP, *see* Chinese Communist Party
Chand, Prithvi 184, 191

Chen, Yi 253, 257, 261, 262, 265, 267
Chervonenko, Stepan 253, 262
Chiang Kai-shek 138, 171
Chin Peng 205, 206ns10–11, 208, 209–10, 213, 215
China, *see* People's Republic of China
Chinese
  bourgeoisie 211
  in Cambodia 82
  in Philippines 162–3
  Malayans 15, 22, 178, 186, 200–1, 208
  Nationalists 216
  Thais 160, 300, 301, 302, 315, 323, 330
  see also People's Republic of China, Sino
Chinese Bureau (Philippines) 162
Chinese Communist Party (CCP) 82, 88, 89, 93, 138, 162, 200, 211, 242, 245, 256, 258, 262
  and Chinese Revolution 200, 245
  and Lao People's Party 245, 256, 258, 261, 268, 269
  and Malayans 15, 200
  and Pathet Lao 29, 241, 245, 246, 256, 259, 267, 268
  and United States 248, 252, 262, 268
  and Vietnamese Workers' Party 240, 246, 251, 256, 258, 268
  at Geneva conferences 246, 249, 269
  Comintern support for 17–18
  conflict with Guomindang 200, 216
  ideology 18, 29, 139, 140, 141, 216, 240
  in Laos 240–2, 245, 246, 248, 249, 250, 251, 252, 253, 254, 255, 256, 262–9
  leadership of 18, 95, 140, 243n.13

on role of revolution 29, 240, 241, 242, 246, 249, 263, 268
see also People's Republic of China
Chong Chor 210, 213
Cold War 1, 2, 3, 4, 5, 18, 108, 124, 195, 239, 292
    hegemonic powers of 115, 122, 127, 130, 133, 136
Comintern (Communist International) 6, 14, 16, 43, 167, 193, 244
    doctrine 41n.29, 57, 175
    in China 17, 171
    in Indonesia 60, 167, 169, 170, 171, 174
    in Malaya 15, 200, 202, 217
    Indonesian break from 24, 27, 35, 171, 172, 173, 175, 194
Communist Party of Indonesia (Partai Komunis Indonesia, PKI) 34, 35, 37, 42, 160
    anticolonial resistance 34, 39, 49, 50n.61, 56, 59, 165–6, 167, 168, 179, 181, 182, 185, 186
    ideology 4, 34, 161, 162
    imprisonment of members 59, 194
    influence on nationalists 49–50, 52, 67
    leadership 53, 166, 167, 175
    Lembaga Kebudajaan Rakjat (People's Cultural Institute) 161, 162
    Maoist turn 160–1, 163
    members in exile 166, 167, 176, 178, 179, 181, 184, 185, 188, 189, 190, 194
    membership 60, 160, 166, 175
    networks 178, 182
    reincarnation of 166, 168–75, 194
    Sarekat Rakyat (People's Associations) 49, 50n.61, 56
    split 28, 166–7, 176, 194
    suppression of 35, 41, 43n.40, 50n.61, 56, 165–6, 169, 170, 176, 179, 185, 194
Communist Party of Kampuchea (CPK) 7, 96, 103, 104, 105, 291, 295
    and Maoism 22, 25, 70–1, 74, 81, 104, 105
    capture of Phnom Penh 104, 105, 294
    Central Committee 71, 73, 102
    ideology 4, 9, 18, 69–71, 81, 85
    influence of Hu Nim 103, 104, 105
    leadership 70, 71, 79n.28, 101–2, 104
    membership 23, 73, 75, 77, 93n.82
    Paris group 71, 74, 77, 79–80, 104, 105
    relations with Vietnam 293, 294, 295
Communist Party of Thailand (CPT) 24, 30, 160, 299–331
Communist Party of the Philippines (CPP) 27, 137, 142, 143–5, 154n.62, 164
    see also Partido Komunista ng Pilipinas-1930
Confucian 20, 141, 150n.43
CPK, *see* Communist Party of Kampuchea
CPP, *see* Communist Party of the Philippines
CPT, *see* Communist Party of Thailand
Cultural Revolution 27, 83, 96, 97, 99, 100, 138, 139, 141, 158

Daeng Noi Sae Lee 324, 325, 326, 327, 330
Daja bin Joesoef 185, 188, 192
Damri Ruangsutham (Sahai Dang) 314, 318, 326

Darsono 53, 166, 167
Democratic Kampuchea (DK) 4, 7,
    90–1, 103, 105
  and Maoism 22, 70, 71, 81
  Chinese support for 294, 295
  'Kampucheanisation' of Maoism
    23, 26, 69–70, 72–4, 84, 105
  Vietnamese invasion of 30, 295
  see also Cambodia, Kampuchea
    Krom, Khmer Rouge,
    National United Front
    of Kampuchea, Royal
    Government of the National
    Union of Kampuchea
Democratic People's Republic of
    Korea, see North Korea
Democratic Republic of Vietnam
    (DRV) 233, 235, 278, 286
  and Laos 245, 247, 249, 252,
    257, 263, 266
  anti-imperialist war 279, 289
  at Geneva conferences 247–8
  censorship 224
  involvement in Pathet Lao 239,
    249, 263
  leadership 276, 284
  Maoism in 159, 160, 162
  politics 241, 253, 254
  socialist model 85, 88, 104, 284,
    295–8
  see also Hanoi, Vietnam
Deng, Xiaoping 267
Dickinson, Arthur Harold 191,
    192n.76, 195
Diniyyah 37, 38, 44, 55n.78
Djalaluddin Thaib 59, 190
Dương Văn Minh 220
Dutch 16, 40, 46, 169, 184
  and Islam 37, 46, 47, 48, 56, 57
  and Javanese royalty 51, 53,
    56ns84–5
  archives 169, 172
  colonialism xiv, 17, 37, 53, 55

education system 38, 48, 51, 53,
    54–6
'Ethici/Ethical Policy' 37
Marxism 16, 45, 60, 166
planter community 39n.19, 46, 51
resistance to rule 17, 27, 36n.5,
    41, 46, 48–9, 56, 167, 170,
    176, 181, 193, 194
response to unrest 47, 48, 165
security apparatus 39, 41, 51, 170
Dutch East Indies (DEI) 16, 25,
    36, 60n.94, 171, 178, 181n.44,
    189n.72
  adaptation of Marxism 25, 57, 62,
    171–2
  and British anticommunist
    cooperation 166, 179, 183,
    192, 193, 195
  and PARI operations 167, 182,
    183–4, 192, 193, 194
  communist dormancy in 27, 194
  'Ethici/Ethical Policy' 37n.9
  Government 166, 169, 176, 177,
    179, 183–4, 185, 192, 193,
    194
  governor-general 40
  nationalist movement 24, 36n.5,
    41, 46, 48, 49, 50
  penal code 35
  political representation in 39n.19,
    52n.67
  polity 38
  resistance to rule 17, 27, 36n.5,
    41, 46, 48–9, 56, 167, 170,
    176, 181, 193, 194
  social unrest 47, 48, 165
  suppression of Communist Party
    of Indonesia 35, 41, 43n.40,
    50n.61, 56, 165–6, 169, 170,
    176, 179, 185, 194
  Volksraad 37, 39, 58
  see also Batavia, Indonesia
Dutch East Indies Railway Company
    (NIS) 182

Dutch Republic 39n.19, 48, 50, 60n.94, 166
  see also Holland, Netherlands

Effendi, Rustam 39n.19, 60
Engels, Friedrich 54n.75, 65, 80, 204n.8, 242, 244, 253
Euro-American
  cultural hegemony 27, 134, 275, 297
  modernisation model 109, 115, 127, 130, 136

'Filipinisation' of Maoism 23, 27, 137, 142, 144–6, 152, 153, 155, 157, 158, 162–3, 164
First Indochina War 229, 275, 277
Five Principles of Peaceful Coexistence 99, 248, 250
Foucault, Michel 18, 19, 226, 234
France 77–8, 79, 84, 105, 78, 250, 304
  see also Paris
French
  and Cambodia 76, 78, 90
  and Laos 247, 250, 256, 258–9, 265
  anticommunist measures 195, 232–3
  colonialism xiv, 17, 75–7, 90
  influence on Souvanna Phouma 258, 265
  Lai Teck as spy for 202, 216
  Marxist circles 74, 79
  Revolution 11, 76
  Sûreté Générale 168, 202
  Vietnamese connections in 194
  Vietnamese resistance to 159n.74, 168, 273, 275, 276–7, 285
French Cochinchina (South Vietnam) 276
French Communist Party (Parti Communiste Français, PCF) 79, 80, 81

French Indochina xiv, 1, 201, 202, 272
  see also Indochina
Front uni national du Kampuchéa, *see* National United Front of Kampuchea

Galo, Adam 189–90, 191
Geertz, Clifford 12, 13, 20
Germany 63, 148n.38, 171
Global South 17, 280
  see also Third World
Gouvernement royal d'union nationale du Kampuchéa, *see* Royal Government of the National Union of Kampuchea
Great Leap Forward 139, 140, 241, 253
gulag 222, 223, 236, 237, 238
Guomindang (GMD) 138, 178–9, 200, 253
Guzmán, Abimael 216

Hadji Abbas 187, 188
Haji Abdul Majid 58, 187, 188
Hanoi 15, 16, 94, 256, 259, 263, 272, 288, 289, 297
  Chinese Embassy in 252, 259
  Hu Nim in 95, 103
Hatta, Mohammad 35, 37n.10, 38, 39–41, 44–5, 49, 53, 59, 60, 65, 67, 191
Hmong 24, 30, 299–331
  see also Thailand
Hồ Chí Minh xiii, 15, 95, 248, 271, 325
  communist movement 193, 272, 275
  in Hong Kong 195, 202
  leadership 230, 273, 298
  'Thought' 159n.74
Hồ Chí Minh Campaign 220, 288n.70

Holland 44, 166
　see also Dutch, Netherlands
Hong Kong 15, 186, 193, 195, 202
Hou Yuon 71, 73n.15, 75n.15, 78, 79, 80, 86, 89, 93, 98, 99, 101, 102, 103, 104
Hu, Nim (Bhoãs) 71–105, **73**, **102**
　engagement with Maoism 22, 25, 71–5, 81, 83–6, 93–4, 104, 105
　in Hanoi 95, 103
　in Paris 72, 74, 75–84, 93, 105
　in Phnom Penh 71, 72, 76, 77, 81, 94, 95
　in Sihanouk's government 78n.23, 81, 85, 86, 92, 93
　influence on Communist Party of Kampuchea 103, 104, 105
　Paris cohort of 93, 98, 101, 102, 104, 105
　split with Sihanouk 74, 93, 95, 97, 98–101
　support for China 81, 83, 85, 88, 93, 94–5, 97, 101, 104
　Vietnamese Communist Party contacts 94–95
Hundred Flowers Campaign 224, 225

Ibrahim, Djamaluddin 178, 179, 180, 186
ICP, see Indochinese Communist Party
Ieng Sary 77, 79, 80, 103
India xiv, 16, 51, 66, 118, 135, 195, 205, 244, 265
　see also British India
Indies, see Dutch East Indies
Indochina xiv, 239, 246, 248, 293
　see also French Indochina
Indochina Federation 80
Indochina War
　First 229, 275, 277
　Second 79, 223, 226, 236, 275, 281

Third 220, 275, 316
Indochinese Communist Party (ICP) 202, 247, 272, 275, 277, 278
Indonesia 8, 9, 27, 33–67, 165–95, 249
　and China 65, 168, 169, 181, 182, 186
　and Maoism 24, 158, 160–3
　and Soviet Union 35, 41, 43, 49, 63, 175, 194
　anticolonialism 17, 33, 35, 50, 56, 61, 66–7, 193
　break with Comintern 24, 27, 35, 171, 172, 173, 175, 194
　Comintern in 60, 167, 169, 170, 171, 174
　indigenisation of Marxism 22, 24, 25, 33–4, 35, 43, 46, 57–67
　nationalist movement 24, 25, 28, 33, 37, 49, 51–2, 59–60, 167, 172–7, 181, 189–90, 193–4
　politics 27, 66, 67, 166, 167, 193, 194
　see also Dutch East Indies
Indonesia Party (Partai Indonesia, Partindo) 39–40, 45, 59
Indonesian Association (Perhimpunan Indonesia) 38, 41n.29, 60
Indonesian Muslim Union (Persatuan Muslim Indonesia, Permi) 35, 37, 40, 44, 57–65, 66, 67
Indonesian National Party (Partai Nasional Indonesia, PNI) 34, 38–9, 52, 56, 176, 178, 180, 183
Indonesian Republican Party (Partai Republik Indonesia, PARI) 24, 43n.40, 165–95
internationalism 29, 51, 61, 94, 144, 148, 157, 172, 215, 242–6, 248, 249, 264, 268, 298
Islamic Association Party of Indonesia (Partai Sarekat Islam Indonesia, PSII) 37, 45, 58, 59, 190, 191

Jakarta 16, 94
  see also Batavia
Japan 216
Japanese
  Chinese War of Resistance to 138, 216, 245
  imperialism 16, 114, 148n.38, 245, 287
  in Malaya 204, 206, 207, 208, 216
  invasion of Burma 113, 114
  invasion of China 61, 138
  Malayan People's Anti-Japanese Army (MPAJA) 204n.7, 205, 207, 208, 210
  'Nine-Point Anti-Japanese Program' 204, 205
  occupation of Dutch East Indies 36, 192
  Sino-Japanese Peace and Friendship Treaty 296
  Vietnamese campaign against 159n.74, 287
Java 38, 40, 59, 168, 176, 182, 183, 184, 186, 189, 192
Javanese 40, 49, 51, 53, 54, 56, 170
Jong Teng Vang 304–6, 310, 322, 326, 330

Kabataang Makabayan (Nationalist Youth) 143, 144
Kampuchea, *see* Democratic Kampuchea
Kampuchea Krom 96, 293
  see also Democratic Kampuchea
Kampuchean People's Revolutionary Party (KPRP) 80, 100
'Kampucheanisation' of Maoism 23, 26, 69–70, 72–4, 84, 105
Kandur 178, 179, 180, 186, 190, 192n.79
Karen 125, 311
Karen National Union 319
Katay, Don Sasorith 249–50

Kautsky, Karl 60, 65, 242, 253
Kaysone, Phomvihane 252, 253, 258, 260, 264, 267, 269
Kennedy administration 239, 264, 265
Khang Khay 260, 261, 264, 266, 267, 269
Khieu Samphan 71, **73**, 75, 79, 80, 86, 89, 98, 99, 101, 102–3
Khmer–Chinese Friendship Association (Association d'Amitié Khmero–Chinoise, AAKC) 26, 72, 73n.11, 83, 85, 94, 95, 97, 98
Khmer Rouge 231, 316, 317
Khmer Students Association (Association des Étudiants Khmers, AEK) 79, 81
Khmer Students Union (Union des Etudiants Khmers, UEK) 79, 81
Khrushchev, Nikita 223, 224, 265
Kong Le 29, 246, 253–61, 263, 264
Kuala Lumpur 186, 187

Labour Union of Vietnam 287
Lai Teck 201–9, 210, 211, 213, 214, 216, 217–18
Lao Patriotic Front (Neo Lao Hak Xat, NLHX) 251, 252, 255, 256, 257, 265, 269
Lao People's Liberation Army, *see* Pathet Lao
Lao People's Party (LPP) 240, 247, 255–6
  and Chinese Communist Party 245, 269
  Central Committee 254, 257, 260, 265, 267, 269
  leadership 252, 260, 269
  revolutionary policy 257, 258, 259, 261, 267–8
  strategy 246, 251, 262
  subordinate to Vietnamese Workers' Party 240, 241, 268–9

Laos xiv, 6, 8, 25, 29, 30, 239–69, 291, 299, 304–5, 308, 309, 310, 314, 315, 316–21, 324
  and British 252, 259
  and China 29, 240–1, 245, 247–53, 257, 259, 260–3, 265, 266, 268, 269
  and Democratic Republic of Vietnam 245, 247, 249, 252, 257, 263, 266
  and Mao Zedong 250, 252–3, 261, 265
  and Soviet Union 247, 252, 253, 255, 256, 257, 259, 262, 269
  and United States 99, 240, 246, 248, 250–5, 258, 259, 261–8
  and Vietnam 239, 245, 247, 253, 291, 316–17, 318, 252, 257, 263
  and Vietnamese Workers' Party 247, 251, 252–6, 258, 262, 268
  border with China 30, 305, 319
  Chinese Communist Party in 240–2, 245, 246, 248, 249, 250, 251, 252, 253, 254, 255, 256, 262–9
  'Laoisation' of Maoism 23
  Vietnamese advisers in 251, 253, 254
  see also Pathet Lao, Royal Lao Army, Royal Lao Government, Vientiane

Latin America 151, 281, 284
Lê Duẩn 24, 29, 30, 254, 268, 271–98
Lee An Tung 211, 218
Lin, Biao 138, 140, 141
Little Leap 88, 93
Liu, Shaoqi 81, 83, 140, 141
Lo Meng Sae Fa 307, 321, 322, 323, 324, 325
Lon Nol 96, 103, 104
LPP, *see* Lao People's Party

Mabini, Apolinario 154, 157
Malay States 185, 187, 189
Malaya 14, 15, 179n.35, 203, 208, 209
  and Chinese Communist Party 15, 200
  anticommunist measures 184, 193, 195
  bourgeoisie 202, 214
  China's involvement in 14, 18, 200–1, 204n.7, 205, 208, 211, 212
  Comintern in 15, 200, 202, 217
  Djamaluddin Tamin in 187, 188, 189
  Government 201, 218
  independence movement 187
  Indonesian communists in 166, 168, 182, 183, 184, 185
  Japanese in 204, 206, 207, 208, 216
  Minangkabau tradition 185, 187
  policing in 184, 202
  proletariat 215, 218
  see also Singapore, Straits Settlements

Malayan Chinese 15, 22, 178, 186, 200–1, 208
Malayan Communist Party (MCP) 14, 15, 18, 200, 203
  admission of errors 214–15
  and mass mobilisation 23, 199, 200, 202–3, 212–13, 216, 217
  approach to revolution 22, 199–200, 201, 202, 214, 215, 216, 218
  armed forces of 205, 207, 208
  citizen support for 204, 212, 215, 217
  development program 203, 206
  ethnic composition of 201, 215
  ideology 18, 28, 199, 200, 201–3, 217–18

inclusion of bourgeoisie 202–3, 211, 214
labour agitation 202, 208, 211
lack of support for 22, 199, 211, 212, 213, 216
Lai Teck as leader 201, 202, 203, 206, 210–11, 214, 217–18
leadership 199, 200, 201, 206, 207, 213, 215, 216, 218
membership 207, 208, 210, 212
postwar policies 203–4, 208, 209–10, 212–15, 217
relations with British authorities 201, 203, 206, 207, 208, 209–12, 216, 217
scholarly attention to 8, 9, 14, 201, 217
support for democracy 203, 205
support for independence 204–5, 206, 210
united-front strategy 199, 200, 202, 206, 208–15, 212
use of violence 28, 200, 211–14, 216, 217
Malayan Emergency 28, 201, 211, 212, 216, 217
Malayan National Liberation Army (MNLA) 205, 212
Malayan People's Anti-Japanese Army (MPAJA) 204n.7, 205, 207, 208, 210
'Malayanisation' of Marxism-Leninism 23, 28
Malays, ethnic 205, 215
Manila 15, 16, 177
Mannheim, Karl 10, 18, 19, 65
Mao, Zedong xiii, 7, 22, 92, 99, 140, 159, 216, 253, 254, 261
and Chinese revolution 302, 305
and Joseph Stalin 246, 326
and Laos 250, 252–3, 261, 265
and Nikita Khrushchev 224
and Sinification of Marxism 21, 23n.58, 164

and Thailand 304
as Communist Party leader 18, 83, 139, 140
class analysis 91–2
Cultural Revolution 27, 83, 96, 97, 99, 100, 138, 139, 141, 158
Five Golden Rays (*FGR*) 27, 138, 142–58, 163, 164
'Five Old Articles' 27, 137–8, 139, 141, 142, 143, 144, 158, 159, 160, 161, 162, 163, 164
Great Leap Forward 139, 140, 241, 253
Hundred Flowers Campaign 224, 225
internationalism 148n.38, 245
Little Red Book 27, 98, 137, 140, 144, 145
'On New Democracy' 80, 92
on peasants 86, 87, 92
personality cult 141, 331
'Quotations' 98, 137, 144, 145, 146
revolutionary thinking 245–6, 253
Selected Works 80, 137, 143n.20
Soviets as revisionist 97, 261
'Thought' xiv, 23, 83, 86, 94, 138–40, 145, 159n.74, 161, 162, 214, 320
'Three Old Articles' 138, 139, 140, 142
translation of works 20, 21, 23, 25, 94, 98, 137, 142, 152n.54, 157, 158, 160, 162
'vulgarisation' of work 141, 142, 163
Maoism 3, 7, 8, 22, 82, 83, 89
and Cambodia 22, 25, 26, 71, 72–4, 81, 82, 84, 92, 93, 97–9, 105
and Communist Party of Kampuchea 22, 25, 70–1, 74, 81, 104, 105

341

and Khmer–Chinese Friendship
   Association 72, 85
and Malayan Communist Party
   213, 214
canon 9, 22
'Filipinisation' of 23, 27, 137,
   142, 144–6, 152, 153, 155,
   157, 158, 162–3, 164
global 164, 243n.13
Hu Nim's engagement with 22,
   25, 71–5, 81, 83–6, 93–4,
   104, 105
in China 27, 138, 142, 143,
   146–7, 158, 159n.74
in Democratic Kampuchea 22,
   70, 71, 81
in Indonesia 24, 158, 160–3
in Philippines 27, 137–38,
   142–64
in Thailand 24, 30, 160, 299,
   304–6, 320, 326, 327, 331
in Vietnam 159, 160, 162
indigenisation of 10, 13, 22–5, 71
'Kampucheanisation' of 22, 23,
   71, 72–4
'Laoisation' of 23
'Malayanisation' of 23
Maoist China 22, 70, 74, 81, 83n.43,
   88, 224, 238
Mardjono 169, 180, 181–2, 183, 184
Marxist Circle 79–80, 84
Masyumi Party 34, 45
McLane, Charles B. 5, 6, 8
MCP, *see* Malayan Communist Party
Minangkabau 15, 38, 182–93
Misbach, Haji 53, 54
Mit Samanan, Sahai 314, 315
Moscow 14, 15, 166, 169, 202, 252,
   264, 291, 294
MPAJA, *see* Malayan People's Anti-
   Japanese Army
Muchtar Lutfi 59, 60
Muhammadiyah 38, 58

Musso 60, 166, 167, 169n.11,
   173n.23, 175, 179, 184, 193, 194
Myanmar, *see* Burma

Nagani Book Club 26, 113, 116,
   117, 119
National Liberation Front of South
   Vietnam, *see* Việt Cộng
National United Front of Kampuchea
   (Front uni national du
   Kampuchéa, FUNK) 72, 102
Negeri Sembilan 185, 187, 188, 207
Neo Lao Hak Xat, *see* Lao Patriotic
   Front
Netherlands 38, 39, 47n.54, 166,
   189n.72, 191
see also Dutch, Holland
Netherlands East Indies, *see* Dutch
   East Indies
Ngô Đình Diệm 254, 278
Nguyễn Duy Trinh 291, 295
Nixon, Richard 1, 3
Non-Aligned Movement (NAM) 30,
   292, 293
North America 281
see also United States
North Korea 85, 88, 93, 95, 104, 295
North Vietnam, *see* Democratic
   Republic of Vietnam
North Vietnamese Army, *see* People's
   Army of Vietnam
Nosavan, Phoumi 6, 246, 251, 253,
   255, 256, 258–60, 262, 263, 264,
   265, 266–7

Pak Said 184, 190
PARI, *see* Indonesian Republican
   Party
Paris 72, 84, 105
   Cambodian communists in 71,
      74, 77, 79–80, 104, 105
   Hu Nim in 72, 74, 75–84, 93, 105
   Hu Nim's cohort from 93, 98,
      101, 102, 104, 105

radicals in 15, 17, 26, 79, 98
    see also France, French
Paris Peace Accords 286, 287
Parsons, J. Graham 251, 259
Partai Indonesia, *see* Indonesia Party
Partai Komunis Indonesia, *see*
    Communist Party of Indonesia
Partai Nasional Indonesia, *see*
    Indonesian National Party
Partai Republik Indonesia, *see*
    Indonesian Republican Party
Partai Sarekat Islam Indonesia, *see*
    Islamic Association Party of
    Indonesia
Parti Communiste Français, *see*
    French Communist Party
Partido Komunista ng Pilipinas-1930
    (PKP-1930) 143, 162
Partindo, *see* Indonesia Party
Pathet Lao (Lao People's Liberation
    Army) 23, 29, 239–69, 304, 320
    and Chinese Communist Party
        29, 241, 245, 246, 256, 259,
        267, 268
    and Vietnamese Workers' Party
        239, 241, 246, 251, 255
    Vietnamese involvement in 239,
        249, 263
    Vietnamese training of 245, 249,
        255, 262, 320
Peking Review 83, 143, 241
People's Army of Vietnam (North
    Vietnamese Army) 219, 236, 273
People's Daily 141, 241, 255
People's Democracy Party of Thailand
    329
People's Liberation Army (PLA)
    (China) 138, 140, 141, 263, 266
People's Liberation Army of Thailand
    (PLAT) 299, 300, 314, 315, 317,
    321, 323, 328
    see also Communist Party of
        Thailand

People's Republic of China (PRC) 10,
    22, 29, 91, 153, 154n.63, 168,
    296–7
    and Indonesia 65, 168, 169, 181,
        182, 186
    and Japan 61, 245, 296
    and Laos 29, 240–1, 245,
        247–53, 257, 259, 260–3,
        265, 266, 268, 269
    and Maoist thought 27, 138, 142,
        143, 146–7, 158, 159n.74
    and Thailand 300, 301, 302,
        304–5, 306, 308, 314,
        315–17, 320–4, 330
    and Vietnam 159, 193, 241, 248
    and Vietnam War 273, 274
    border with Laos 30, 305, 319
    Comintern policy on 171
    conflict with Soviet Union 295,
        316
    conflict with Vietnam 30, 228,
        268, 275, 294, 295, 296, 297,
        316, 317
    founding of 138, 139, 302
    Hu Nim's support for 81, 83, 85,
        88, 93, 94–5, 97, 101, 104
    ideology 17n.42, 23, 141, 297,
        325–6
    in Malaya 14, 18, 200–1, 204n.7,
        205, 208, 211, 212
    influence on Cambodia 18, 22,
        69–70, 74, 75, 81–4, 97–9,
        257, 295, 316, 317
    influence on Vietnamese
        reeducation 28, 221, 223,
        224–5, 226, 231, 236–8
    Khmer/Cambodian friendship
        associations 26, 72, 83, 95
    land reform 199, 200, 253
    leftists' visits to 14, 83, 85, 95, 98,
        171, 180, 306, 314, 319
    Little Leap 88, 93
    media 83n.43, 241, 252

Military Advisory Group in
  Vietnam 246
modernisation model 81, 83, 85,
  88, 104, 139, 141
Pol Pot in 294
politics 241, 253, 254, 267, 296
relations with United States 30,
  248, 253, 268, 288, 294, 295,
  296, 297
Revolution 138, 148, 178, 245,
  246, 261, 305
revolutionary influence 14, 21,
  35, 50, 139, 143
scholarly attention to 1, 4, 5, 7,
  243n.13
Second Taiwan Strait Crisis 241,
  253
Sinification of Marxism 21,
  23n.57, 164
support for Kampuchea 294, 316,
  317
  see also Chinese, Chinese
    Communist Party, Cultural
    Revolution, Great Leap
    Forward, People's Liberation
    Army, Sino
Perhimpunan Indonesia, *see*
  Indonesian Association
Permi, *see* Indonesian Muslim Union
Persatuan Muslim Indonesia, *see*
  Indonesian Muslim Union
Phạm Văn Đồng 247, 292, 294
Pheng, Phongsavan 261, 262, 266
Philippines 137–64, 162–3, 168, 177
  'Filipinisation' of Maoism 23, 27,
    137, 142, 144–6, 152, 153,
    155, 157, 158, 162–3, 164
  Maoism in 27, 137–38, 142–64
  see also Communist Party of the
    Philippines
Phnom Penh 26, 80,83, 84, 98, 99,
  101, 257, 260, 264, 291
  Communist Party of Kampuchea
    capture of 104, 105, 294

Hu Nim in 71, 72, 76, 77, 81,
  94, 95,
Vietnamese capture of 295, 296
see also Cambodia
Phoui, Sananikone 248, 251, 252–3,
  259
Phu Kong Pheung 324, 330
PKI, *see* Communist Party of
  Indonesia
PNI, *see* Indonesian National Party
Pol Pot 70, 71, 75, 79, 80, 93n.82,
  100, 103, 105, 294
Prambanan Decision 169, 173n.23,
  175
Prayom Chulanont (Sahai Khamtan)
  305, 327
Pridi, Banomyong 304, 305, 314n.65
PSII, *see* Islamic Association Party of
  Indonesia

Quinim Pholsena 257, 260

Rangoon (Yangon) 16, 107, 195,
  260, 261
Republic of China (Taiwan) 241,
  253, 257
Republic of Vietnam (RVN) 6, 28,
  222, 227, 231–2, 233, 237, 254,
  257, 279
  communist resistance in 278–9,
    283, 288–9
  communist takeover of 24, 219,
    220
  penal system 227, 238
  reeducation in 24, 28, 219–38
  revolution 254, 279, 289
  revolutionary violence in 241, 273
  US support for 254, 279–80
  US withdrawal from 286, 288
  see also Saigon, Vietnam
Rizal, José 61, 66, 154, 157, 164
Roy, Manabendra Nath 15, 244, 245,
  258

Royal Government of the National Union of Kampuchea (Gouvernement royal d'union nationale du Kampuchéa, GRUNK) 72–3, 102
Royal Lao Army 251, 254, 255, 256, 259
Royal Lao Government (RLG) 240, 245, 247, 248–9, 250, 251, 254, 260, 266
Royal Thai Army 320, 324
Rusk, Dean 265

Saigon 15, 93n.82, 202, 278, 282
  fall/liberation of 219, 227, 230, 289
Sakdalistas 149, 150
Saṅgam Rāstr Niyam (Popular Socialist Community, Saṅgam) 72, 93, 94, 96, 99, 100, 101
Sarit Thanarat 256, 266, 318n.83
Sarosan 180, 181–2, 183
Second Indochina War 79, 223, 226, 236, 275, 281
Second Taiwan Strait Crisis 241, 253
Semarang 38, 53, 181, 182
Semaun 53, 166, 167
Setiawan, Hersri 160, 161
Siam xiv, 168, 169, 183, 302
  see also Thailand
Sihanouk, Norodom **73**, 84, 94, 96, **97**, **102**, 262–3, 264, 265
  antidemocratic moves 80–1, 85
  disbanding of Khmer–Chinese Friendship Association 85, 98
  disbanding of Khmer Students Association 81
  Hu Nim in government with 78n.23, 81, 85, 86, 92, 93
  National Assembly 71, 100, 101
  opposition to 80, 96, 101, 103, 104
  Saṅgam government 72, 93
  split with Hu Nim 74, 93, 95, 97, 98–101
  suspicion of leftists 93, 99, 100
  unhappiness with China 81, 97–9, 100
Singapore 8, 15, 166, 168, 169, 174, 178–81, 183–93, 195, 208, 211
  see also Malaya, Straits Settlements
Sino-Japanese Peace and Friendship Treaty 296
Sino-Khmer Daily 82, 83n.43
Sino-Khmers 74, 75
Sino-Soviet border 202
Sino-Soviet Split 5, 84, 228, 253, 261, 267, 288, 316
Sino-US relations 30, 248, 253, 268, 288, 294, 295, 296, 297
Sino-, *see also* Chinese, People's Republic of China
Siregar, Arief 180, 188, 192
Siregar, M. Ali Tholib 64
Sison, Jose Maria 142, 143–5, 155
Sjech Ahmad Wahab 168, 169, 186, 187
Sjech Taher 168, 169
Socialist Republic of Vietnam (SRV) 229, 230, 290, 291, 292, 294
Solo (Surakarta) 40, 52, 53, 54
Souphanouvong ('Red Prince') 246, 247, 250, 251, 252, 254, 255, 256, 264, 265, 266
South Vietnam, *see* Republic of Vietnam
Souvanna Phouma 240, 245–6, 247, 249–51, 255–65, 266
Soviet Bloc 5, 281
Soviet Union 18, 47, 171, 202, 204n.7, 235, 278, 296
  and Indonesia 35, 41, 43, 49, 63, 175, 194
  and Laos 247, 252, 253, 255, 256, 257, 259, 262, 269
  and Marxism-Leninism xiv, 23, 89

and Malayan Communist Party 14, 18
and Philippines 143
and Vietnam 202, 228, 274, 275, 281, 288, 291–2, 297
collapse of 290n.75
cooperation treaty with Vietnam 275, 294
criticism of 294, 134, 261
de-Stalinisation 97, 223
dictates of 1, 7, 41, 43, 65, 167
Geneva delegation 247, 252
gulags 223, 236, 238
ideology 6, 18, 35, 43, 292, 325, 326
influence on Vietnamese reeducation 28, 221, 223, 226, 235, 236–7, 238
invasion of Afghanistan 295
leftists' visits to 14, 95, 202
modernisation model 109, 127, 130, 136
non-aggression pact with Turkey 61
resistance to 130, 171, 175
revisionism 84, 94, 97
scholarly attention to 1, 4, 5
support to revolutionaries 14, 42, 191–2, 193, 240
see also Sino-Soviet Split
Stalin, Joseph 20, 63, 171, 172, 213, 246, 278, 326
criticism of 84, 223
gulags 223, 238
Stalinism 84, 169
de-Stalinisation 97, 223
Straits Settlements 178, 184, 185
see also Malaya, Singapore
Sukarno 34, 38, 60, 176, 177, 180, 190n.74
arrest 183
imprisonment 39, 189n.72
nationalist organisations 34, 38, 39–40, 59, 65, 176, 180

release from prison 40, 189
writings 44–5, 46, 54
Sumatra Thawalib 38, 43, 55n.78, 58, 59, 168, 187n.64, 189, 191
Sun Yat-sen 50, 66
Surabaya 38, 39, 178
Surakarta, *see* Solo

Taiwan, *see* Republic of China (Taiwan)
Taman Siswa 38, 55n.78
Tamin, Djamaluddin 168–9, 173n.23, 176–8, 179, 180, 181, 182–92, 194–5
Tan Malaka 15, 16, 17, 27, 34, 43, 46, 54, 65, 166–7, 168, 169–83, 185–6, 189, 193–5
Tapanuli 58, 188
Thaib, Aziz 62
Thaib, Darwis 44, 50
Thailand xiv, 8, 25, 30, 168, 299–330
and China 300, 301, 302, 304–5, 306, 308, 314, 315–17, 320, 321, 323, 324, 330
and Laos 256, 259, 265, 299
and Vietnam 317, 318, 319, 324, 325
border with Burma 125n.43, 299, 311
border with Laos 299, 308, 310
Chinese Thais 160, 300, 301, 302, 315, 323, 330
Government 301, 302, 306, 307, 317, 318
Maoism in 24, 30, 160, 299, 304–6, 320, 326, 327, 331
military 30, 300, 308, 315, 316, 317, 318, 327
People's Democracy Party 329
People's National Army 312
Royal Thai Army 320, 324
Vietnamese revolutionaries in 168, 193

see also Communist Party of Thailand, Hmong, People's Liberation Army of Thailand, Siam
Thai People's National Army 312
Thakin Nu, *see* U Nu
Third Indochina War 220, 275, 316
Third International, *see* Comintern
Third World 113, 281, 287, 288, 292
  see also Global South
Thong Jamsri (Sahai Din) 315, 325, 328
'three revolutionary tidal waves' theory 24, 29, 30, 271, 273, 275, 281–98
Trotsky, Leon 170, 172
Trotskyism 169, 173, 175

Udom Srisuwan 315, 326
UEK, *see* Khmer Students Union
Umar Giri 180, 190
Union des Etudiants Khmers, *see* Khmer Students Union
Union of Soviet Socialist Republics, *see* Soviet Union
United Kingdom 135, 216
  see also Britain, British
United States (US) 1, 62, 96, 99, 135, 146, 148n.38, 221, 255, 288, 292
  and Cambodia 264, 295
  and Chinese Communist Party 248, 252, 262, 268
  and Laos 99, 240, 246, 248, 250–5, 258, 259, 261–8
  and Philippines 154n.63
  and Vietnam 220, 221, 232, 234, 248, 254, 273, 274, 276, 279–83, 285–9, 291, 296
  anticommunism 5, 195
  as colonial power xiv, 154n.63, 195
  as imperialist 83, 229, 233, 279, 281, 283, 285, 286, 287, 291, 292, 296
  Congress 220
  Government 5, 274, 285
  relations with China 30, 248, 253, 268, 288, 294, 295, 296, 297
  see also Euro-American
U Nu (Thakin Nu) 24, 26–7, 107–36, 249, 262
USSR, *see* Soviet Union

Vientiane 250, 256, 259, 260
  Battle of 260
  Kong Le's control of 255, 256, 260
Việt Cộng (National Liberation Front of South Vietnam) 94, 273, 280
Việt Minh 159, 276, 285
Vietnam 29, 221, 227, 232, 289
  advisers in Laos 251, 253, 254
  and Indochinese Communist Party 247, 248
  and Laos 239, 245, 247, 253, 316–17, 318, 252, 257, 263, 291
  and North Korea 295
  and Sino-Soviet Split 228
  and Soviet Union 202, 228, 274, 275, 281, 291–2, 296–7
  and Thailand 168, 193, 317, 318, 319, 324, 325
  and United States 220, 221, 232, 234, 248, 254, 273–4, 276, 279–83, 285–9, 291, 296
  anticolonialism 66, 229
  campaign against Japanese 159n.74, 287
  Chinese influence on reeducation 28, 221, 223, 224–5, 226, 231, 236–8
  Chinese Military Advisory Group in 246

colonial legacy 28, 222
communist ideology 4, 25, 29, 275
Communist Party of Kampuchea invasion 293–4
conflict with China 30, 228, 268, 275, 294, 295, 296, 297, 316–17
conflict with United States 276, 280, 281, 283, 285–6, 288–9, 291, 298
conflicts in 239, 274, 275
cooperation treaty with Soviet Union 275, 294
development policy 229
division of 278
foreign policy 220, 273
in French Indochina xiv, 78
independence 272, 276, 277, 278, 283, 285, 289, 292
Indochina Federation proposal 80
internationalism 248, 275, 276, 277
invasion of Democratic Kampuchea 30, 295, 316, 317
leaders 272–5
leadership of Kampuchean People's Revolutionary Party 80, 100
occupation of Cambodia 228, 295, 296
post-reunification policy 222, 273
radicalisation 15, 267
reconciliation 238, 274–5
relations with China 159, 193, 241, 248, 294, 297
relations with Communist Party of Kampuchea 293–4, 295, 316
resistance to French 159n.74, 168, 273, 275, 276–7, 285
reunification 29, 279, 280, 283, 289, 293
revolution 241, 271, 272, 273, 275–9, 282, 293

Soviet influence on reeducation 28, 221, 223, 226, 235, 236–7, 238
training of Pathet Lao 245, 249, 255, 262, 320
US involvement in 273, 279–80, 283
victory over United States 286, 287
see also Democratic Republic of Vietnam, Hanoi, Republic of Vietnam, Saigon, Socialist Republic of Vietnam
Vietnam News Agency 103
Vietnam War 29, 231, 237, 283
and China 273, 274
Vietnamese Communist Party (VCP) 201–2, 229, 276, 286n.55, 290n.75, 294
and global revolution 29, 30, 277, 280, 282, 285, 287, 289–90, 295–8
and Non-Aligned Movement 30, 292–3
Central Committee 278, 290, 293
congresses 272, 290
foreign policy 291, 295
Hu Nim's contacts with 94–95
ideology 4, 158–9, 272, 290, 295, 298
Politburo 291
reeducation system 24, 28, 219–38
revolutionary networks 168, 193
socialist model 5, 28, 69, 85, 88, 104, 284, 295–8
study of ideology 8, 9, 168, 220, 298
'three revolutionary tidal waves' theory 24, 29–30, 271, 273, 275, 281–98
Vietnamese Revolutionary Youth League 272

Vietnamese Workers' Party (VWP)
229, 249, 269, 278
   advisers in Laos 251, 253, 254
   and Chinese Communist Party
      240, 246, 261, 268
   and Lao People's Party 240, 254,
      261
   and Laos 247, 251, 252–6, 258,
      262, 268
   and neutrality principle 240, 256
   and Pathet Lao 239, 241, 246,
      251, 255
   Central Committee 252, 254,
      262, 279n.33
   leadership 247, 254, 279, 283–4
   policy 249, 254, 278, 279, 280,
      284, 285, 287, 288, 298
   Politburo 278
   turn to Soviet Union 240, 269,
      281
Võ Nguyên Giáp 248, 254, 274, 284
Volksraad 37, 39, 58
Vu, Tuong 2, 4, 5, 275

Wa Meng Sae Lee (Phu Kong Chot)
   323, 324, 327

Xiamen 169, 253
   see also Amoy

Yangon, *see* Rangoon
Yogyakarta 40, 50, 160

Zhou, Enlai 83, **97**, 99, 211n.28,
   248, 250, 264, 265, 318n.83
   at Geneva conferences 246, 247,
      248, 262–3
   visit to Cambodia 83n.47

www.ingramcontent.com/pod-product-compliance
Lightning Source LLC
Chambersburg PA
CBHW041438300426
44114CB00026B/2926